BIG MED

BIG MED

MEGAPROVIDERS AND THE HIGH COST
OF HEALTH CARE IN AMERICA

DAVID DRANOVE AND LAWTON R. BURNS

The University of Chicago Press   CHICAGO AND LONDON

The University of Chicago Press, Chicago 60637
The University of Chicago Press, Ltd., London
© 2021 by The University of Chicago
Published 2021
Paperback edition 2022
Printed in the United States of America

31 30 29 28 27 26 25 24 23 22   1 2 3 4 5

ISBN-13: 978-0-226-66807-9 (cloth)
ISBN-13: 978-0-226-82392-8 (paper)
ISBN-13: 978-0-226-75684-4 (e-book)
DOI: https://doi.org/10.7208/chicago/9780226756844.001.0001

Library of Congress Cataloging-in-Publication Data

Names: Dranove, David, author. | Burns, Lawton R., author.
Title: Big med : megaproviders and the high cost of health care in America /
David Dranove and Lawton R. Burns.
Other titles: Megaproviders and the high cost of health care in America
Description: Chicago ; London : The University of Chicago Press, 2021. |
Includes bibliographical references and index.
Identifiers: LCCN 2020051202 | ISBN 9780226668079 (cloth) |
ISBN 9780226756844 (ebook)
Subjects: LCSH: Health facilities—United States—Business management. |
Medical economics—United States.
Classification: LCC RA971.3 .D73 2021 | DDC 362.110680973—dc23
LC record available at https://lccn.loc.gov/2020051202

♾ This paper meets the requirements of ANSI/NISO Z39.48-1992
(Permanence of Paper).

CONTENTS

Preface vii

Introduction 1

Chapter 1: The Evolution of the Modern Hospital 11

Chapter 2: From Hospital to Health System 31

Chapter 3: Why Integration Failed 53

Chapter 4: The Fall and Rise of the Antitrust Agencies 81

Chapter 5: History Repeating: The Second Wave of Integration 106

Chapter 6: Integration Is Still Failing 125

Chapter 7: New Antitrust Challenges 152

Chapter 8: Countervailing Power 179

Chapter 9: Will Disruptors Save the Health Economy? 198

Chapter 10: Recommendations for Competition Policy 226

Chapter 11: Recommendations for Management Policy 250

Epilogue 277

Acknowledgments 279

Notes 281

Index 319

PREFACE

Economists and sociologists rarely see eye to eye. It is even rarer for them to team up and write a book. But it was clear from the beginning of this venture that the story of health care integration was too big to be viewed through a single disciplinary lens. Despite our different training and approaches to research, our partnership seemed inevitable.

We have known each other for nearly forty years, since we were junior faculty at the University of Chicago. By the time we received tenure in the early 1990s, we had moved on to our permanent homes at Northwestern University and the University of Pennsylvania. It was during this decade that we witnessed the first great wave of health care consolidation, with the emergence of integrated delivery systems. We independently conducted research on systems, bringing different perspectives to our work. Dranove the economist demonstrated the limited benefits of scale and scope and the potential dangers of rising market concentration, while Burns the sociologist documented the difficulties of managing large health care organizations and the special problem of integrating physicians. We shared our skeptical findings with students, alumni, practitioners, and the media, but our voices were drowned out by the chorus of supporters of integration.

Events would soon bear us out. By the early 2000s, integration had failed to reduce spending or improve quality, but did enhance market power and lead to higher prices. Spending rapidly increased through the decade. Concerned about these trends, we did what academics always do: we engaged in more research. We continued to find evidence that systems were harming the health economy, and shared our conclusions with our academic colleagues. Nowadays many academics are studying the same issues, and in many ways their work supersedes our efforts, even while reaching the same conclusions.

We are beginning to have some real-world impact. Media outlets increasingly report on the high and rising prices charged by medical providers, and the two of us have been among a handful of academics to testify in hospital antitrust cases, where courts have blocked several problematic horizontal and vertical mergers. Yet systems continue to grow, and the current political debate about our health care system seems to avoid any discussion of them.

This is a huge mistake. Large, integrated hospital-based systems— we call them megaproviders—bear the greatest responsibility for the cost and quality of medical care: more than drug companies, more than insurers, more than the government. Through a combined seven decades of research, we have learned that we cannot hope to meaningfully reform our health care system—"bend the cost curve" in the parlance of health policy gurus—without reforming the megaproviders.

Our research shows that megaproviders are harming the health care system in two distinct ways. First, they possess and use market power, raising prices and avoiding the difficult steps required to be more efficient. Second, they have failed to successfully integrate with their physicians, whose decisions are crucial to the performance of the entire health economy. As a result, physicians are demoralized and seem unable or unwilling to work with hospitals to drive health system change. The result is health system stagnation.

The current health policy debate seems obsessed with Medicare for All, insurer profits, and drug prices. Even the most radical changes along these dimensions will not repair our health care system unless we address the problems created by our megaproviders, who collectively account for anywhere from one-half to two-thirds of all health care spending. We have written this book to spread this message beyond our "base" of academia and the courtroom. We want everyone to recognize that megaproviders are harming the health care system and begin discussing what we can do about it.

INTRODUCTION

"Dangers lurk in all systems. Systems incorporate the unexamined beliefs of their creators. Adopt a system, accept its beliefs, and you help strengthen the resistance to change."

FRANK HERBERT, *GOD EMPEROR OF DUNE*

In the spring of 2018, Northwestern Medicine opened its new hospital campus in the leafy Chicago suburb of Lake Forest. The $400 million dollar complex is the latest addition to Northwestern Memorial HealthCare's impressive system. The sprawling main campus, which sits immediately east of luxury shopping on Chicago's famed Michigan Avenue, includes the recently constructed $280 million Prentice Women's Hospital and $600 million Lurie Children's Hospital. The nearby flagship Northwestern Memorial Hospital has undergone more than $1 billion in expansions and renovations. Northwestern's four thousand physicians, including fifteen hundred who are employed by the system, practice at more than two hundred facilities throughout Chicagoland, delivering the whole gamut of patient services, from basic primary care to the most technologically advanced diagnostic and surgical procedures. Northwestern also seems to have converted any number of defunct Borders, Office Depots, and Linens and Things into freestanding medical office buildings.

This enormous medical care provider is also a big business. Northwestern is Chicago's sixteenth largest employer and, with annual reve-

Table I.1. The nation's largest megaproviders, as of 2017

System	Location	Revenue	Comparable
UPMC	Western Pennsylvania	$16b	Whole Foods
Partners	Eastern Massachusetts	$13.4b	Gucci
Sutter	Northern California	$12b	Tesla
Northwell Health	Long Island	$9.0b	Adobe Systems
Cleveland Clinic	Northeast Ohio	$8.4b	National Basketball Association
Intermountain	Mountain states	$7.6b	Jet Blue
Advocate Health	Northern Illinois	$6.2b	Spotify
NY Presbyterian	New York City	$5.6b	Regeneron
Sentara Health	Southeast Virginia	$5.3b	Yahoo
Baylor, Scott, and White	Dallas, Texas	$4.8b	Chipotle
Total		$88.8b	Boeing
			Hyundai Motor
			IBM
			Johnson & Johnson

nues of around $5 billion, it brings in as much money as many well-known global businesses, such as Goldman Sachs and Tiffany, and about the same as Fox News, CNN, and MSNBC combined![1] Northwestern is not even the largest health system in the Chicago metro area. That honor belongs to Advocate Health, whose annual revenues exceed $6 billion. Northshore University Health, the University of Chicago, and Loyola Medicine are not that far behind. As big as they currently are, they continuously plow their revenues into further growth, spreading their tentacles further and further across the Chicago metropolitan area.

Chicago is far from unique. Nearly every metropolitan area has its own giant health care systems; we call them megaproviders. Table I.1 gives annual revenues for some of the top *local* megaproviders, and identifies *national* and *global* companies in other industries that have similar revenues. Baylor, Scott, and White, which dominates the Dallas health care landscape, does as much business as Chipotle worldwide. Northwell, which dominates Long Island, is as big as Adobe Systems. The University of Pittsburgh Medical Center, which has a near stranglehold on Pittsburgh and much of the rest of western Pennsylvania, is as big as Whole Foods. These megaproviders are so large because the overall health care industry is enormous. With total US health care spending approaching $4 trillion, equivalent to roughly 18 percent of gross domestic product, even a locally based health care organization can be as big as giants in other industries.

These are just the tip of the iceberg. Other megaproviders include Fairview Health Services (eleven hospitals in the Twin Cities), Emory Healthcare (ten hospitals in the Atlanta metro area), BJC Healthcare (nine hospitals in and around St. Louis) and Jefferson-Einstein (eighteen hospitals in the Philadelphia area).[2] Some systems span several local markets, with dominant positions in some places if not everywhere. Adventist-Providence St. Joseph operates nine hospitals across northern California; ProMedica has thirteen hospitals in Ohio and Michigan; Greenville-Palmetto owns thirteen hospitals across South Carolina; Wellmount-Mountain States operates twenty-one hospitals in Tennessee and Virginia; and Atrium Health runs forty-eight hospitals in the Carolinas and Georgia. All megaprovider systems own several hospitals, employ or ally with thousands of physicians, and have countless freestanding outpatient facilities and long-term care beds. A few offer their own health insurance products.[3]

With mega-sized revenues comes mega-sized executive compensation. In 2017, at least fifty executives at nonprofit systems earned more than $4 million.[4] At the top end, seven executives earned more than $8 million, with Inova's CEO bringing home $14 million, topped only by the $16 million that Kaiser paid to its CEO. These figures may seem excessive, but they are in line with how other big businesses pay their executives. If we equate size with success, then health system CEOs have earned every penny. If we instead demand that our CEOs contain costs, then some would be lucky to make the minimum wage.

Teflon Coated Providers

As health spending spirals out of control, putting health care beyond the reach of many Americans and eating into the savings of many more, it is no wonder that a large majority of Americans believe that the US health care system is broken.[5] According to a recent Leavitt survey, 70 percent of respondents believe that the system requires fundamental changes or even a complete rebuild.[6] Most Americans blame insurers, drug makers, and the government for the current predicament, and it is no surprise that drug makers compete with health insurers for most frequently being described as "rapacious."[7] Very few Americans—no more than 5 percent in the Leavitt survey—blame hospitals or doctors. Likewise, politicians are quick to blame insurers and drug makers—some prominent Democrats refuse to accept contributions from them—but they rarely blame hospitals and physicians, and eagerly accept their big dollar contributions. The blame is misplaced. Neither insurers nor the government order tests, write prescriptions, or perform surgeries. While many drugs are expensive to the point of seeming exorbitant, prescription drug spending accounts for less than 11 percent of total health spending.[8] You could eliminate all administrative costs, wipe out insurance and drug industry profits, and slash their executives' salaries, and health care would still be incredibly expensive.

As much as we complain about insurers, drug companies, and government bureaucrats, it is our health care providers who are largely responsible for the cost and quality of care. About 52 percent of every dollar spent on health care goes directly to hospitals and doctors. Even this understates their importance. Doctors make decisions that affect roughly 80 to 85 percent of every dollar spent.[9] The most expensive medical technology is not drugs or magnetic resonance imaging (MRI); it is the physician's pen.[10]

Megaproviders like those listed in table I.1 assume the biggest responsibility for the state of our health system. They generate the lion's share of expenses, and their executives are handsomely rewarded. Yet Americans are unwilling to take them to task. This might be understandable if megaproviders were slowing the pace of spending growth, but the facts that we will lay out suggest just the opposite. A recently published study by Zack Cooper and colleagues offers one compelling piece of evidence.[11] The title of the paper hints at the findings: "The Price Ain't Right? Hospital Prices and Health Spending on the Privately Insured." Cooper et al. explain why health spending varies so much from one place to another, even after controlling for local differences in the medical needs of patients. They find that fully half of the variation stems from variation in provider prices.[12] Prices are higher where hospitals have more market power, and prices increase when hospitals merge, especially when those hospitals are nearby and are likely to have been close competitors. This latter finding bears on an important theme of this book: health care is local, and megaproviders have a great deal of power in their local markets.

"The Price Ain't Right" is just one of many studies documenting how megaproviders accumulate market power and use that power to drive up prices without creating offsetting efficiencies. Other studies find no improvements in patient outcomes; if anything, megaproviders contribute to lower-quality care. This means that wherever megaproviders dominate local markets, health care spending is higher, often much higher, and health care quality is no better, and sometimes lower. This is a big win for megaproviders, and a big loss for everyone else. If this is not bad enough, rather than engaging physicians in the process of reforming healthcare, megaproviders have caused them to become increasingly disaffected, disgruntled, and distrusting, making it harder to effect meaningful improvements in costs and outcomes. While the executives who put the megaproviders together may not have intended to cause such damage, they have failed to turn their size to our advantage. It is time that we recognize the megaproviders for the megaproblems they are.

If They Are So Successful, How Can They Be So Bad?

Many economists, including Nobel Prize winners Kenneth Arrow and George Stigler, have offered a quasi-Darwinian view of markets. Firms dominate their industries by offering superior value to consumers.[13] Some, like Walmart and Amazon, might have lower costs. Others, like Microsoft and Facebook, offer products and services that consumers covet. Whatever the means for value creation, the firms that create the most value survive and grow. Big firms are not perfect, of course—no organization is—but their strengths more than offset their weaknesses. In other words, we should not make knee-jerk objections to large, financially successful firms, because most big firms got that way by building better mousetraps.

This view rests on two big assumptions. The first is that all organizations face the cauldron of competition from current rivals and future entrants. The second is that at least some firms know how to create value for their customers. When both of these are true, competition can work its magic. Those organizations that best create value will usually outcompete their rivals, and a few may even dominate their markets. Thus, firms like Hyundai and Boeing are big because they know how to meet the needs of their customers. Hyundai makes really good small cars and, for the most part, Boeing makes the best large airframes for commercial air travel (although the 737 Max debacle shows how even the mighty can fall). There is nothing wrong when firms grow large because they deliver more value than their rivals.[14]

After a combined seven decades of research, we have a difficult time embracing the quasi-Darwinian view in health care markets. As things now stand, too many megaproviders face too little competition, and too many of their executives seemingly do not know how to manage the complex process of organizing and delivering health care. What is especially troubling is that the two problems are intertwined. As we will detail, megaproviders came together out of the misguided belief that integration would generate scale economies and other efficiencies. It hasn't happened. Instead, megaproviders have concentrated health care markets and have avoided the pitfalls of competition. Instead of effective managers facing the cauldron of competition, we have ineffective managers avoiding competition. So much for Darwin.

While many forces have indeed transformed the US health care system over the past century, they have not meaningfully transformed large hospitals.[15] The organization, lines of authority, and workflows of the modern hospital are not all that much different from what they were decades ago, and the same inefficiencies persist. Hospitals have instead transformed their financial relationships with each other, and with other stakeholders. By merging to become megaproviders, hospitals have learned how to exercise local market power, charge higher prices, and exclude competitors. Some health insurers, especially Blue

Cross Blue Shield, have accumulated power of their own, leaving the two sides battling over the division of the health care pie rather than diligently working to reduce the size of the pie. While the antitrust agencies do what they can to limit the accumulation of market power, and have enjoyed some notable recent successes, they are limited by a combination of factors that we will discuss. Competition policy alone will not rescue our health care system; and if it is poorly implemented, it will do more harm than good.

We believe that most health care executives sincerely want to reduce costs and improve quality. Unfortunately, many of them remain convinced that scale and scope are the answer. At the same time, even the most sincere executives cannot resist exploiting market power, bringing in more revenue, and investing in further growth. Like the cat chasing its tail, they may never realize the efficiencies and higher quality they seek, for the simple reason that size is no guarantee of performance. The result is higher health spending without commensurate higher quality. Is it any wonder that the American health care system is ailing?

Things are so bad that everyone seems to be seeking a cure; not just politicians. Corporate bigwigs like Warren Buffett, Jeff Bezos, and Jamie Dimon are trying to fix the health care system through innovative business practices drawn from outside health care. No matter how you look at the present situation, megaproviders, which have relied far too long on market power rather than effective performance, seem ripe for disruption. Given that the promise of disruption in health care served up by Clay Christensen two decades ago has yet to materialize, we question whether the answers will come from the outside.[16] The health care industry must heal itself.

As with any illness, finding the right cure requires an accurate diagnosis. The first step is taking a medical history, which can provide many clues about the disease. The ills of the American health care system have been incubating for a long time, so our history begins a century ago. We will examine how health care providers brought us miracles of modern medicine, but also fought to defend their turf. Exercising political influence while wielding market power, sometimes illegally, the medical establishment kept at bay outsiders who had new ideas for reducing costs and improving access, ideas that would have eroded the power of organized medicine. Hospitals worked especially hard to retain their dominance of local markets; and as hospitals grew bigger and more powerful, health care spending began a long ascent that shows no sign of abating.

The illness metastasized in the 1990s, when hospitals sought further protection by creating integrated delivery systems. These systems combined academic medical centers and community hospitals with physician groups, outpatient care centers, and health insurance offerings. Thus began the takeover of health care delivery in entire metropolitan areas. As a strategy for reducing health spending, integration was a complete failure. Much of the blame fell squarely on health care executives, who bought into the ideas of scale and scope economies without any evidence that these economies existed, and without any notion of how to make the organizational whole greater than the sum of its member parts. This was made most apparent by examining the fate of physicians, who gave up their private practices to become hospital employees, turning what was a professional calling into an unsatisfying job. Integration may not have served the interests of health care consumers or physicians, but there was a silver lining for the systems, which used their newfound market clout to fight off the cost-containment efforts of employer-sponsored insurance plans.

In the second part of this book, we examine the current state of American health care. Emboldened by ineffective antitrust enforcement, integrated systems continued to grow, becoming today's mega-providers. The takeover was complete. Despite their lofty compensation, health care executives have not figured out how to make systems work for patients or physicians. They have figured out how to wield their ever-increasing market power.

In the third part, we offer our diagnosis and recommend treatment. The diagnosis: Megaproviders need better management, but remain dominant by exercising market power. The treatment: Combining our experiences in the fields of economics and sociology, we will offer guidance to managers on how to create value in complex health care organizations. We will also offer ideas for reforming competition policy, so that all participants in health care markets, from solo practitioners to megaproviders, including newcomers like Buffett et al., have a fair opportunity to prove themselves in the cauldron of competition. Time will tell whether megaproviders emerge from the cauldron in better shape than when they went in. We suspect not.

The Elephant in the Room

As we write this book, Americans are engaged in a strenuous debate about whether to replace our market-based health system with top-down control. We will not wade into the policy debate about the relative merits of "Medicare for all," "repeal and replace," or something in between. Nor will we presume that we know with any certainty whether our current market-based health system will remain largely intact. Although Democrats prevailed in the 2020 election, that may not spell the end of private health insurance, and it will almost certainly leave megaproviders intact.

Private health insurers currently play a large role in Medicare and Medicaid. More than one third of Medicare beneficiaries, and most patients on Medicaid, have private health insurance that operates under government rules. If private health insurance survives a government takeover, the ongoing battle for market power between insurers and providers will continue unabated. If there is no private insurance option, Medicare may still promote integration. Consider that the most significant catalysts in the recent growth of megaproviders—accountable care organizations—are a Medicare initiative tied to the Affordable Care Act. If Medicare makes further cuts to provider prices, hospitals and physicians may circle their wagons even tighter, leading to yet another wave of integration. The total elimination of commercial insurance may spell the end of antitrust action against providers, if only to transfer the exercise of market power to the political arena. Even with Democrats taking power in the 2020 election, megaproviders will still dominate the health care landscape, and we will remain worse off for it, unless we figure out how to either eliminate them or make them work for us. That is what this book is about.

1

THE EVOLUTION OF THE MODERN HOSPITAL

"History never really says goodbye. History says 'See you later.'"

EDUARDO GALEANO[1]

The story of the megaprovider begins in the nineteenth century. Massachusetts General Hospital, the jewel of the Partners system, dates to 1811. The University of Pittsburgh Medical Center's flagship Presbyterian hospital was founded in 1883, and New York Presbyterian opened in 1868. The nineteenth-century hospital was mostly a place where society cordoned off the sick, not to heal them but to stop the spread of whatever ailed them. Over the course of the next few decades, medical breakthroughs transformed hospitals from places of dying to places of healing. By the second half of the twentieth century, hospitals were firmly entrenched as the center of their local communities' health care world. They spent the next several decades defending their turf while expanding their geographical and service boundaries. They made sure the spigot of health care spending opened wider and wider, and that hospitals would continue to receive the lion's share of the dollars. In the process, they discovered a formula that continues to serve them well: make outsized claims on the public purse, ignore efficiencies, and maintain local dominance.

To their credit, today's megaproviders can work miracles, saving and extending lives, albeit at enormous cost. In the nineteenth century, there was little that hospitals could do except contain infectious diseases and amputate limbs. And then the era of modern medicine began. A host of innovations, including X-rays, blood typing, and anti-septics, greatly boosted the odds of surviving surgery. Researchers dis-covered insulin and aspirin; learned how to transfuse blood; devel-oped vaccines against cholera, rabies, and the plague; and introduced treatments for rickets and malaria. If you wanted to benefit from the latest advances, you had to go to a hospital.

All these new technologies came at a cost, and only the wealthy could access all that the hospital had to offer. To make matters worse, many physicians lacked the training to administer all the newly avail-able treatments. The Flexner Report of 1910 led to reforms in medi-cal education that further drove up costs by raising the standards and length of training, as well as the required medical school infrastruc-ture. In 1928 a group of leading academics formed the Committee on the Cost of Medicare Care (CCMC) to study the problems plaguing the US health system and to recommend how to fix it. Their report, *Health Care for the American People*, condemned the system for high and often wasteful spending that made health care inaccessible for most Americans.[2] They called for changes that still resonate: health in-surance for all Americans, integration of medical providers, payment reform, and an emphasis on prevention.

National health insurance was not a new idea. Germany started theirs in the late nineteenth century. Opposition from the American Medical Association (AMA), and hostility during World War I toward anything German, helped quash a similar program in the United States; and by the time of the CCMC report, few Americans had any kind of health insurance beyond compensation for workplace injuries. As the Great Depression took hold, things started to change. Average Ameri-cans struggled to pay their medical bills and, as a result, hospitals and doctors struggled to turn a profit. In 1929, the year of the stock market crash, Baylor Hospital in Dallas offered prepaid hospital insurance to local teachers. Soon thereafter, hospitals in New Jersey and Ohio were doing the same. The idea quickly caught on and by 1940, fifty-six groups of hospitals were offering insurance plans to six million enrollees. These became known as Blue Cross plans, named after a poster for the Minnesota plan that used a blue cross, a variant on the familiar red Geneva cross used to identify medical facilities in wartime. Hospitals created an umbrella organization, the Blue Cross Association, which coordinated the activities of the individual plans. Medical societies soon followed suit, offering Blue Shield plans covering physician services. The non-profit Blue Cross and Blue Shield plans offered nearly unlimited access to all hospitals and doctors, paid full charges, required minimal cost sharing, and left medical decision making to providers.

Following World War II, a combination of economic growth and new medical technologies developed to treat wartime injuries catalyzed further growth in the demand for medical care. As spending accelerated, the need for health insurance intensified. While several European nations introduced national health insurance after the war, the United States continued to rely on private insurers. When the federal government made health insurance benefits tax deductible, employer-sponsored health insurance took off. Enrollments in Blue plans steadily increased, and investor-owned commercial insurers entered the market to compete with them. By the mid-1950s, the majority of Americans had health insurance.

These were heady times for hospitals. By 1950, more than five thousand community hospitals received the largest share of all US health expenditures.[3] The federal Kerr-Mills program funded construction of new hospitals and the expansion of existing hospitals. Private insurers—the biggest of which were sponsored by hospitals—and the government gave hospitals blank checks to spend whatever they deemed necessary to treat their patients. Unsurprisingly, inflation-adjusted health spending increased by 2.6 percent per year between 1950 and 1980. But there is a time-honored business principle that if someone is making money, someone else will either want a piece of the action or will look to the government to rein them in. Hospitals were not immune to this principle. There is another principle worth noting. When firms are threatened, either by competition or by regulation, there are two very different strategies for survival. The first is to create more value for consumers: find a way to become more efficient, improve the product, or both. The second is to use whatever power they have to subvert the competition and capture the regulators. Faced with competitive and regulatory threats in the mid-twentieth century, hospitals chose the latter strategy, with considerable success.

The Challenge from HMOs

In the 1950s there were two anchors to the health care system of nearly every big city: large hospitals, some affiliated with medical schools, and Blue Cross Blue Shield insurance plans. Most of the Blue plans were sponsored by providers. Nevertheless, they remained independent community "social welfare organizations" under federal law, which meant that they were supposed to benefit the community as a whole, and not just their sponsors.[4] In trying to meet this obligation, they must have been sorely conflicted. Hospital executives served on the boards of Blue plans and had enormous influence over their strategic direction. Indeed, the American Hospital Association and the national Blue Cross Association were located in the same building, at 840 North Lake Shore Drive in Chicago. Dominating both the provision and financing of medical care, hospitals and physicians had a near stranglehold on the health economy.

The "social welfare organization" label notwithstanding, the Blues structured their insurance policies to benefit providers. They did not question medical bills. They did not close networks. By requiring only minimal cost sharing, they assured that patients would have no financial reason to question their providers' decisions.[5] If you were a provider, life in a Blue-dominated world was good.

If you were a patient, life was pretty good too. Doctors and hospitals saved lives, and insurers paid the medical bills. But not everything was rosy. Someone had to pay all these bills, and patients who lacked insurance might have to draw down their life's savings or go bankrupt. This was just one way in which the goals of the CCMC remained unmet. Care was still fragmented. Fee-for-service payments promoted overspending, and prevention remained an afterthought. Although not well documented at the time, the quality of care was variable and often substandard.

In a few places around the nation, a different way of organizing and paying for medical care was emerging. Health maintenance organizations (HMOs) seemed to be just what the CCMC had ordered.[6] HMOs eliminated fee-for-service incentives and featured teams of physicians working together in groups, and their very name spoke of prevention. By the 1940s, HMOs enjoyed limited success in a few regional pockets, mostly on the West Coast: Ross-Loos Medical Group in Los Angeles, Kaiser in California, the Group Health Cooperative (GHC) of Puget Sound, and the Health Insurance Plan of Greater New York. In some places, HMO enrollments rivaled that of commercial insurers.

The CCMC's proposals and their embodiment in the form of HMOs represented a major threat to hospitals and doctors. After all, what the CCMC called wasteful spending was income to providers, and what the CCMC called integration was the end of autonomy. Two prominent features of HMOs—group practice of physicians and prepayment—ran counter to principles published by the AMA in the 1930s.[7] Organized medicine needed to respond. Hospitals and doctors might have worked to curtail spending and improve care coordination, but that would have required rethinking how medical care would be delivered, and might have eaten into provider incomes. Instead, the providers turned to the government for protection.

Providers lobbied state governments for a range of regulations restricting HMO growth, including forcing HMOs to have open physician panels, prohibiting HMO advertising, and requiring that physicians constitute all or most of HMO boards.[8] Hospitals and doctors were among the biggest political donors and had sterling reputations among voters, so legislators were more than happy to oblige. In case regulation proved insufficient at deterring HMOs, providers took further steps of an even less salubrious nature. Local medical societies organized boycotts, which denied membership to physicians who participated in HMOs. Hospitals limited admitting privileges to only those physicians who were in good standing with their medical societies. Providers also spread false information about the nature of HMO operations, calling into question, without any evidence, the quality of care that would be provided under "socialism," which was a curious way to describe employment in the private sector.[9]

Finding it difficult to recruit physicians, HMOs turned to the courts for redress. The Washington-based Group Health Association (GHA)

HMO provided an important test case.[10] GHA was organized in 1937 by employees of the Federal Home Loan Bank. Employees paid monthly subscription fees to the GHA health plan, which hired physicians who worked for an elected board. GHA represented everything that was anathema to organized medicine: prepaid coverage, salaried physicians, and independent lay control. The AMA and the Medical Society of the District of Columbia asked regulators to ban GHA. When that failed, they prevailed on physicians to refuse referrals from GHA physicians, and convinced hospitals to stop granting them admitting privileges. The battle between GHA and organized medicine received national media attention, and Congress threatened a full-blown investigation. In 1938, the US Department of Justice (DOJ) filed an antitrust claim against GHA. A district court convicted the AMA and the Medical Society of the District of Columbia of violating the Sherman Act, and in 1943 the Supreme Court upheld the conviction.

Undeterred by this decision, many local medical societies continued to organize boycotts, and HMOs again sought remedy in the courts. In a 1951 case that should have been the last nail in the coffin of organized opposition to HMOs, the GHC of Puget Sound won a boycott claim against the King County Medical Society in Washington state.

Neither boycotts, false rumors, nor regulations proved totally effective on their own, but taken together they helped organized medicine achieve its goal. As late as the 1970s, HMOs operated in just ten states and enrolled just six million Americans. This represented slightly more than 3 percent of all insurance enrollments.[11] Organized medicine had contained the threat from HMOs. Although both authors of this book studied health care management in the 1970s, we learned next to nothing about HMOs, which our professors derisively referred to as a "West Coast thing."

Our professors did not serve us well. In the 1970s things were starting to change, and it would soon be impossible to ignore HMOs. President Nixon gave them a shot in the arm by supporting the HMO Act of 1973, which lent them legitimacy and overrode many state regulations.[12] As HMO enrollments slowly accelerated, organized medicine returned to boycotts. In 1976, the Federal Trade Commission (FTC) successfully challenged a Blue Shield plan that refused payments to

HMO physicians in Spokane, Washington.[13] In 1979 the Department of Justice successfully challenged the American Society of Anesthesiologists, which denied membership to physicians who accepted prepayment or salary.[14] In the same year, the FTC ordered Forbes Health System in Pennsylvania to grant privileges to HMO-affiliated physicians, regardless of their standing with medical societies.[15] Organized medicine finally got the message and ended the boycotts.

Organized medicine suffered another blow in the 1980s, when many Blue Cross plans established their own HMOs to compete with the growing roster of for-profit entrants, mostly concentrated on the coasts (like HealthNet and PacifiCare on the West Coast, and US Healthcare on the East Coast). Unlike Kaiser and GHC, these new HMOs were not a true fusion of insurer and provider. They were insurers first and foremost, and they did not own hospitals or employ physicians. Instead, they contracted with a wider panel of local providers and paid primary care physicians (PCPs) by capitation, which gave them modest incentives to hold down medical costs. Insurer-sponsored HMOs not only grew rapidly over the next decade, but consolidated, gaining bargaining leverage against providers.

HMOs were met by a furious patient backlash in the 1990s. Enrollees balked at access restrictions and questioned HMO quality, and organized medicine threw its weight behind hundreds of legislative proposals to weaken if not cripple HMOs, including any-willing-provider and freedom-of-choice requirements, which research has since tied to higher prices.[16] Organized medicine also sought to eliminate gag rules that prevented physicians from advocating for treatments that HMOs did not approve. It had nearly achieved all its goals in 1998 when President Clinton proposed a Patient Bill of Rights, which fell victim to the partisan politics of the time. Despite all of these efforts to stop them, HMOs survived. Their enrollments peaked in the 1990s, when less restrictive preferred provider organizations gained favor. Recently, HMO enrollments have fallen in percentage terms, but they have hardly disappeared. Today, more than ninety million Americans are enrolled in HMOs, aided in part by a steady increase in Medicare and Medicaid enrollments.[17]

Many of today's most successful HMOs have been around more

than fifty years. Kaiser, with more than twelve million members, is the gold standard not just for HMOs, but for all integrated health systems. On the West Coast, its closed panel of salaried physicians, Kaiser Permanente Medical Groups, practicing exclusively at Kaiser-owned hospitals and outpatient facilities, purportedly delivers medical care at a fraction of the cost of other health providers, with arguably comparable or superior quality. It is no wonder that advocates of integration point to Kaiser as proof of concept, even as other systems fail to perform up to Kaiser's standards. As we will discuss, Kaiser itself has not always performed up to its own standards, especially when it attempted to expand beyond its West Coast base.

For much of the twentieth century, organized medicine's reaction to HMOs was consistent and predictable. Unwilling to accept changes that threatened their dominance, doctors and hospitals used their market clout and political power to preserve the status quo. As new challenges emerged, doctors and hospitals found other ways to protect themselves that we detail in later chapters.

Regulatory Threats

Before 1960, government largely stayed out of health care markets. The most important policies that emerged after World War II—preferential tax treatment for employer-sponsored health insurance, and the 1948 Hill-Burton Program for hospital construction—pumped money into the health care system with few strings attached.[18] Whenever the federal government attempted to directly provide health insurance, organized medicine objected. When President Truman offered a plan for national health insurance, the AMA called White House staffers "followers of the Moscow party line."[19] Two decades later, the AMA would strongly oppose the creation of Medicare and Medicaid—among other things, paying for a recording titled "Ronald Reagan Speaks Out against Socialized Medicine."[20]

Medicare and Medicaid did survive as key parts of Lyndon Johnson's Great Society programs. By reducing the fraction of Americans without health insurance from nearly 25 percent to under 15 percent, these programs proved to be a boon to hospitals and physicians.

Supply rose to meet the dramatic increase in demand. Between 1965 and 1975, the number of hospital beds swelled by 27 percent.[21] Hospitals also added an arsenal of new and costly medical services, and increasingly linked up with university-based medical schools to form academic medical centers. By 1973, four hundred hospitals had CT scanners, while five hundred performed coronary-artery-graft-with-bypass procedures.[22] Subsequent technology enhancements included joint replacements, balloon catheterization, LASIK eye surgery, radiation therapy, and organ transplants. While large academic medical centers were expected to embrace new technologies, many other (community) hospitals got the technology bug and emulated them.

The United States would need more doctors to deliver all these services, and medical school enrollments swelled by 40 percent in the 1970s.[23] At the same time, the federal government and state medical societies lifted restrictions on immigration and postgraduate training of foreign medical graduates. When Medicaid and Medicare started in 1966, the United States had about 300,000 physicians. By 1980 there were over 460,000.[24] Nearly all of the increase was in specialists, with the ratio of specialists to generalists increasing from roughly 1:1 to nearly 2:1.[25] With more hospitals, more specialists, better technology, and more insurance to pay for it, total US health care spending rose from 6 percent of GDP in 1965 to 10 percent in 1982.

This placed enormous strains on government budgets. Medicare quickly became the largest purchaser of health care in the United States, and Medicaid was the first or second largest budget item in most states, after education. Looking to reduce health expenditures, governments took aim at hospitals, which were the biggest drivers of health spending, accounting for roughly 36 percent of national health expenditures in 1970. New York, which had a large Medicaid program, led the way by introducing a "prospective payment" program that paid per diem rates (i.e., a fixed payment per hospital day) dictated by the state. Seven other states soon followed suit, adding a few wrinkles to the payment rules. Medicare and private insurers in these states joined in, creating "all payer" programs. These proved modestly successful at containing costs, reducing annual hospital inflation by one or two percentage points.[26] They might have been even more effective had hospitals not figured out how to game the system. Hospitals in New York offset reduced per-diem payments by increasing the number of "diems" — that is, they increased the length of stays. In other states that used different payment rules, hospitals found different ways to adjust. It did not help when health management training programs began teaching students how to exploit loopholes in payment rules. By 1980, hospitals accounted for 39.4 percent of national health expenditures.

Hospital rate setting gave payers their first taste of the balloon principle: if you squeeze one part of the health care spending balloon, other parts expand. When payers squeezed the price they would pay for a hospital day, hospitals responded by increasing the number of days. Payers learned that they needed to squeeze the entire balloon and not just one end. Medicare's prospective payment system (PPS), introduced in 1983, featured a fixed fee per admission, with the fee adjusted for the patient's medical condition and treatment, classified into 470 "diagnosis-related groups" (DRGs). Many state Medicaid programs followed Medicare's lead, as did most private insurers. By the end of the 1980s, nearly all payers were squeezing the entire hospital stay, not just one day. This forced hospitals to analyze and then manage care patterns for each DRG, to avoid ruinous losses.

The move to the PPS had immediate results. Medicare spending per hospital admission fell by 10 percent in just two years, and hospital expenditures fell back to 34.7 percent of national health expenditures by 1990. Even so, there was no way to contain the entire health care balloon, as hospitals found creative ways to game the DRG system. Many hospitals exploited subjectivity in diagnostic coding, to move patients into more remunerative DRGs.[27] This "upcoding" was particularly pronounced in for-profit hospitals. Hospitals shifted some diagnostic work to outpatient facilities, and discharged patients early under the care of hospital-owned or affiliated home health agencies and skilled nursing facilities; the latter phenomenon was derisively referred to as discharging patients "quicker but sicker." Unbundling services in these ways enabled hospitals to receive outpatient and home care payments in addition to the fixed DRG payments. They also reduced their inpatient mortality rates, which were being publicly reported, without actually saving any lives. In the 2000s, hospitals moved chronically ill patients out of inpatient beds into their own long-term care facilities, which often were little more than repurposed inpatient wings. One study suggests that this tactic accounts for one-third or more of the recent growth in long-term care.[28]

It seems obvious that if you want to shrink the size of a balloon, you cannot squeeze it; you have to let the air out of it. For the health care balloon, that means you cannot just cap spending in just one or a handful of service areas; you have to reduce the total amount of dollars available for all care. At the risk of pushing the analogy too hard, you also have to make sure you do not let out too much air, or you will not have much of a balloon. This means not cutting spending too much, lest quality suffers.[29]

While government payers used rate setting to squeeze one part of the balloon, insurer-sponsored HMOs turned to capitation in an effort to squeeze the whole balloon at once. Under capitation, insurers paid providers a fixed fee per patient (or per "head"—hence the name). Providers could only profit by holding spending below the capitated amount, and could actually lose money if spending got out of hand. Ideally, HMOs would hold providers financially accountable for all health spending. This proved impractical for several reasons. For starters, HMOs could not figure out how to assign patients to specialists and hospitals, so they restricted capitation to primary care physicians. Many PCPs balked at taking on so much financial risk, especially if they were held responsible for all the expenses of catastrophically ill patients. Ultimately, HMOs restricted capitated payments to PCPs' own office expenses, medications, and office fees for some specialist referrals. Limited in this way, capitation also fell victim to the balloon principle, as it left specialists free to order expensive tests and procedures, and had no impact on hospital spending. Meanwhile, many patients wondered whether their PCPs were skimping on services covered by the capitated fee.

Capitation of PCPs has since morphed into global capitation, in which payers give health systems a single annual fee meant to cover all medical services, coupled with quality-of-care incentives meant to discourage skimping. In this way, payers incentivize the system to squeeze the entire balloon, but not squeeze too hard. This just passes the buck, as now it falls to the system to push incentives down to its member physicians. A few organizations, like Kaiser, seem to have figured out how to make this work (with a lot of help from a closed delivery system and an in-house insurance arm). Most have not, however, for reasons we will explore later in this book.

At the same time that states were experimenting with price controls, they were also attempting to limit supply. It is unclear whether the resulting regulations were intended to hold down spending or maintain the status quo. New York again led the way. The Metcalf-McCloskey Act of 1964 protected New York hospitals by requiring all proposed health care facilities to obtain a certificate of need (CON) from a politically appointed regional health planning board. The board was supposed to deny applications when supply exceeded "needs," as determined by epidemiological studies. The CON was heavily influenced by "Roemer's Law," named after epidemiologist Milt Roemer, whose research showed a correlation between the number of beds built and the number of beds filled.[30] If supply creates its own demand, as Roemer was suggesting, then one way to curb demand, and therefore curb health spending, would be to limit supply. At the same time, this would allow the handful of providers who did receive CONs to benefit from economies of scale. The theory was reasonable, and by 1972, nineteen states had CON laws. Two years later, Congress passed the National Health Planning and Resources Development Act, which required all states to follow the New York model.

To the surprise of many, hospitals and the Blue Cross plans they sponsored were among the biggest proponents of CON.[31] Fearful of rate setting and other regulatory controls, the medical establishment viewed the planning process as a way to legitimize the status quo. According to legal scholars Sallyanne Payton and Rhoda Powsner, the hospital and public health establishments shared a common ideology: the idea of a "regional health care system with a large teaching hospital at its center and with all other elements of the health care system as satellites."[32] This is a prescient description of today's megaproviders. CON would help pave the way.

Unfortunately, the CON process was not so much an exercise in health planning as it was a lesson in how local politics protected incumbents.[33] In order to win CON approval for a new hospital, applicants spent millions on lawyers and consultants to prepare lengthy CON applications. This favored deep-pocketed incumbents, and deterred many potential entrants. Entrants who could afford the legal fees and consulting studies faced an even bigger barrier: gaining board approval. On the designated day for the CON hearing, the applicant would present its proposal to the board. Incumbent hospitals lined up against them, presenting their own consulting studies purportedly showing that the community did not need a new hospital. Many incumbents hoarded unused bed licenses, which gave them authority from the state to expand without CON. These hospitals promised that they would use their licenses to meet growing demand, provided that the board reject the outsider's application. Some kept their promises. Others kept their licenses in reserve, in order to block future applications.

The deck was stacked against the applicants. A key principle we will repeat throughout this book is that health care is local. Hospitals held enormous sway in their local communities. They were often the most respected local institutions. They were among the largest employers. Business leaders vied for prestigious seats on local hospital boards. All of this gave local hospitals political clout. Planning board members gained nothing for their political handlers if they approved outsiders' proposals, and would gain the enthusiastic support of their clout-heavy constituents if they said "no." Board members never questioned whether their local hospitals offered high-quality care or operated efficiently. They always questioned the applicant. All of this is still true today.

Politics being what it is, the politicized health planning process sometimes went off the rails. Illinois has one of the most corrupt political cultures, and not even health planning could escape its long tentacles. In 2004, Edward Hospital in Naperville applied for a CON to build a satellite hospital in nearby Plainfield. The hearing was open to the public, and the audience witnessed quite a spectacle. After Edward Hospital made its case, the planning board began its deliberations.

After just a few minutes, one board member, banker Stuart Levine, walked around the table and appeared to whisper in the ears of several other members. Moments later, the board denied Edward's application. Edward Hospital's president, Pamela Davis, approached the board, told them things were going to change, and then stormed out of the room.

Few knew it at the time, but Davis was guarding a secret. Shortly before the hearing, she had met with a banking executive and a construction company president. They had told her that CON approval hinged on whether she used their firms. Anticipating such shenanigans, Davis had been in touch with the FBI and she had come to the meeting wearing a wire. This soon all came to light. The banker and construction company president pled guilty to various felonies, explaining that they paid millions of dollars to Levine for other CON-related contracts and expected similar demands from Levine if the board approved the Edward deal. Levine allegedly passed on some of this money to Illinois Governor Rod Blagojevich in exchange for placing Levine on the board. Levine pleaded guilty to multiple counts of corruption. He spent five and half years in federal prison, a term that might have been longer had Levine not testified against Blagojevich in the latter's criminal corruption trial. Trump commuted Blagojevich's sentence in February 2020.

The thought of politicians exercising so much power over one-fifth of the economy should send shivers down the spine of everyone—at least everyone who lives in Illinois. But it doesn't. Most state hospital associations and many local health care systems still support CON. Even so, CON is hardly the incumbent protector that it once was. In the deregulatory atmosphere of the 1980s, most states eased or eliminated CON rules. CON remains in effect in thirty-five states, but is thought to have teeth in only a handful.

Twenty years after the introduction of Medicaid and Medicare, hospitals were sitting pretty. They had navigated the potential pitfalls of rate setting; they were exempt from the cost-cutting incentives created when HMOs capitated PCPs; and, thanks to CON, they enjoyed protection from competition. Their success could be seen in the data.

In 1965 the average hospital had 129 beds. Over the next two decades, while CON was in full force, the average hospital grew to 175 beds. While many small rural and inner city hospitals closed, big hospitals thrived. If one were to compare a list of "largest hospitals" in 1965 against the same list in 1985, there would be a startling amount of overlap. Many could trace their roots to the nineteenth century. The same hospitals dominate today's landscape. One is hard pressed to identify any institutions, aside from hospitals, that have dominated their local markets for so long.

As the health care system evolved away from inpatient care, big hospitals were positioned to transform themselves into megaproviders. Before doing so, they would have to gain control of the emerging market for outpatient surgery.

The Threat from Outpatient Surgery

Throughout most of the last century, surgery required an extended stay in a hospital. In the early 1970s, a few hospitals repurposed existing wings as ambulatory surgery centers (ASCs), where they offered one-day care for some simple procedures such as hernia repairs and appendectomies. Patients could enter a separate hospital entrance (with separate parking) in the morning, have their surgery by noon, and be home for dinner. Like customers of auto paint shops that advertised at the time, you could "get in by nine, out by five."

In 1970, Wallace Reed and John Ford opened the SurgiCenter in Phoenix, the first independent, freestanding ASC. Patients had many reasons to love freestanding ASCs: they were less threatening, easier to get to, easier to get in and out of, and less expensive. Payers, both public and private, encouraged their growth as a lower-cost alternative to hospitalization. Many doctors enjoyed the freedom and financial success that came with owning an ASC; in addition to professional fees, they received a portion of the facility fees.

Before long, everyone, including hospitals, could see the potential for ASCs to disrupt the inpatient marketplace. In a famous *Harvard Business Review* article, prominent health policy analyst Jeff Goldsmith argued that the threat from ASCs was existential: "The hospital is the core institutional provider of health care. Yet ... as their costs increase, hospitals will be in an increasingly vulnerable position within the healthcare market."[34] Goldsmith seemed prescient. At the time the article appeared in 1980, there were about two hundred ASCs. By 1988 there were more than a thousand.[35] Ongoing innovations in anesthetics and surgical techniques now make it possible for ASCs to perform two-thirds of all surgeries.

What Goldsmith did not fully anticipate was that ASCs presented an opportunity for hospitals. A simple procedure such as a hernia repair can seem daunting to patients. Patients preferred providers with established reputations for quality, and didn't mind if the ASC adjoined a hospital, in case something went wrong. This gave a huge demand-side advantage to local hospitals over upstart ASCs. Once they got the cost accounting figured out, hospitals realized that their own ASCs were often more efficient as well. As a result, hospital-based ASCs proliferated. The percentage of community hospitals with organized outpatient departments tripled from 26 percent in 1975 to 77 percent in 1988, when same-day surgeries accounted for 15 percent of all hospital-based surgeries.[36]

Not satisfied with this competitive advantage, some hospitals threw their weight around, refusing to contract with insurers unless they were granted exclusivity over outpatient surgery. Insurers needed to offer attractive hospital networks to win market share, and that meant contracting with most if not all local hospitals, and especially with the largest and most sought-after health systems. Insurers acquiesced to the demands for exclusivity, which prompted many ASCs to take legal action, claiming that hospitals were using their power in local markets to exclude competition. In a series of decisions that anticipated the outcomes of hospital merger cases a decade later, courts repeatedly dismissed the cases. Courts agreed with the hospitals that competition was not local, appearances to the contrary. It seems that when it came to defining the extent of the market, hospital markets did not satisfy the duck test. These markets looked local, but the courts ruled otherwise. We will explain, but not defend, the courts' twisted logic in chapter 4. These rulings helped assure that dominant hospitals would remain that way, and they had a chilling effect on entry by start-up ASCs.

Several factors have helped level the playing field for independent ASCs. ASC management companies emerged in the 1980s and 1990s to give entrepreneurial physicians the requisite management expertise and financial capital to compete with hospitals. Patients became more accepting of freestanding ASCs; many prefer dealing with them to navigating the campus of a large hospital. Insurers have taken a harder line against exclusivity, and courts are more willing to find that hospitals possess market power. Unfortunately, in the last decade megaproviders have found ways to protect themselves from competition that seem less susceptible to antitrust claims. We will discuss these in chapter 7. At the same time, many medical groups have had financial trouble and have turned to hospitals to purchase their assets, including their ASCs. As a result, many of the surgeons who used to compete against hospitals have now joined them, choosing the security of employment over the risks of entrepreneurship.

Selective Contracting

As powerful as they were, hospitals and medical associations were not the largest health care organizations in their markets, as measured either in dollars or customers. Health insurers were larger, especially the Blues. In 1980, big academic medical centers like Massachusetts General Hospital and New York Presbyterian each had about $150 to 200 million in revenues and treated upwards of forty thousand inpatients.[37] By contrast, Blue Cross of Massachusetts and Empire Blue Cross of New York each had around $1 billion in revenues from nearly two million subscribers.[38] Despite their massive size advantage, insurers had virtually no leverage over providers. Whether for strategic reasons or state laws, insurers paid for all medical care given by all providers, no questions asked. Narrow networks were restricted to closed-panel HMOs. Patients had minimal out-of-pocket expenses and did not shy away from expensive providers. As a result, every provider, even small community hospitals and solo physicians, could price like a monopolist.[39] This was the rationale behind state rate setting. Some private insurers tried to rein in spending through fee schedules and prospective payment. These tactics were no more successful than government rate controls.

The power relationship between payers and providers changed with the arrival of selective contracting in the 1980s. The history of selective contracting has been told elsewhere, so we will only provide a thumbnail sketch.[40] During the 1980s, states dropped decades-old regulations that required insurers to reimburse all licensed providers. Insurers responded by creating preferred provider organizations (PPOs), whose central feature was a network of contracting providers. Patients paid substantial out-of-pocket costs if they ventured outside the network, which meant that out-of-network providers could lose enormous market share. Insurers used this threat to negotiate discounts off of providers' usual charges. Most providers preferred to be in-network at a discount, rather than out-of-network at full price, so most PPO networks ended up including most providers. Able to obtain lower-cost coverage without surrendering access, enrollees flocked to PPOs. Starting from essentially zero in 1983, the number of PPO enrollees rose to twenty-eight million in 1987 and to fifty million by 1995.

Large corporate employers were especially eager to build their health benefits packages around PPOs. Employers financed much of the rising cost of health care generated after the passage of Medicare, and some pundits quipped that the cost of employee insurance coverage exceeded the cost of steel used in Detroit automobiles.[41] The Employee Retirement and Income Security Act (ERISA) of 1974 provided further impetus for PPOs. ERISA meant that self-insured employers could avoid state insurance taxes and mandated benefits. Employers embraced the PPO model because it allowed them to directly receive provider discounts while avoiding costly regulations.

Some employers shopped around for a more stringent cost-containment solution, and found it in the HMOs that had already staked a place in their markets. Employers enlisted the help of their insurance carriers to develop new HMO plans, and either pushed or enticed employees to join them. Between 1984 and 1996, the share of employees in large firms enrolled in HMO plans jumped from 8 to 33 percent.[42] Thanks to both PPOs and HMOs, this was a period of near zero inflation-adjusted growth in private health care spending, something we have not achieved before or since. By the end of the 1990s, roughly 70 percent of employees with employer-based health insurance were enrolled in either an HMO or a PPO plan.

The growth in private-sector managed care began to spread to the public sector. State Medicaid programs nudged their enrollees into managed care plans (usually HMOs) in the early 1990s. Between 1983 and 1993, the percentage of Medicaid enrollees in managed care plans rose from 1 to 15 percent.[43] Medicare moved more slowly toward managed care, propelled by the Tax Equity and Fiscal Responsibility Act (1982) and the Balanced Budget Act of 1997. Today, one in three Medicare beneficiaries is in a private HMO or PPO.[44]

By the early 1990s, hospitals and physicians had lost their monopoly pricing power. If anything, insurers acted as if all providers were interchangeable, much like barrels of oil or bushels of wheat. Playing one provider off against another for network inclusion, insurers demanded and obtained discounts of 20 percent or more. While small hospitals were especially at risk, even the largest hospitals, some of which had dominated their markets for a century or longer, faced unprecedented competitive pressures. Hospitals were unlikely to find a friend in the government, where Medicare and Medicaid were exploiting economic incentives to hold down spending. Hospitals knew that if they were to continue to dominate the health economy, they had three options: become more efficient, find new sources of revenue, or regain pricing power. Seemingly overnight, a remedy emerged that encompassed all three: the integrated delivery network. Success would prove elusive, however.

Coda and Preview

In the rest of this book we describe how providers have created ever larger organizations in a quest to improve care delivery and meet the competitive challenge created by insurers, the companies they originally sponsored. While hospitals and insurers seemed to be at each other's throats, the two sides have a symbiotic relationship in which both have thrived. Success does not imply omniscience or beneficence, however. Even the most successful firms often make poor business decisions; and when challenged by competitive pressures, they tend to circle the wagons at the expense of consumers. Doctors and hospitals are not exempt from these truths, and we must resist placing them upon a pedestal. The facts, as we explain below, are not always kind to our medical providers.

2

FROM HOSPITAL TO HEALTH SYSTEM

"Successful enterprises are built from the ground up. You can't assemble them with a bunch of acquisitions."

LOUIS V. GERSTNER JR.[1]

Throughout much of the twentieth century, hospitals used their clout to fight off external pressures. By the 1990s, they seemed to have lost their influence as Medicare, Medicaid, and PPOs all squeezed payments. Hospitals needed a fresh approach, and they found it in an idea that some academics had been touting more than a decade. They called it vertical integration.

The first wave of vertical integration began in earnest in the early 1990s and took many forms. Hospitals integrated with physicians, hospitals and physicians integrated with health plans, and physicians integrated with equity-backed physician practice management firms. Adding to the complexity, in some cases the merging parties combined into a single firm, whereas at other times their relationships were purely contractual; the latter arrangement was called virtual integration. Other than Kaiser and a handful of other HMOs, these combinations were new to health care.

The vertical integration movement of the 1990s was a direct response to the trends of the 1980s. Medicare prospective payment placed new financial strains on hospitals. Independent outpatient surgery centers were luring away profitable patients. Employers eager to find low-cost insurance options embraced HMOs and PPOs, which successfully demanded discounts from all providers. Capitation became the rage as a new payment method that threatened the viability of some providers, while others saw it an opportunity to make vast profits if only they could figure out how to contain costs. These conditions provided a combustible mix to fuel vertical integration; the only thing lacking was a spark.

Managed Competition

To understand the vertical integration movement, we need to go back a bit earlier. Like every decade before and since, the 1970s saw rising health care costs and uneven access to care. In 1972, Senator Ted Kennedy proposed a single-payer health care system that would rely on coinsurance to constrain spending growth. With Richard Nixon in the White House, the proposal had no chance of becoming a reality. Even so, it forced Nixon to offer a counterproposal: the HMO Act of 1974, which breezed through Congress and catalyzed the growth of HMOs but fell short of reorganizing health care delivery or expanding insurance coverage.

In the 1980s and early 1990s, several academics, led by Stanford University's Alain Enthoven and Northwestern University's Stephen Shortell, offered market-based solutions to the cost and access problems.[2] Enthoven, a Stanford professor and an advisor to Kaiser, called his approach "managed competition," and the term stuck. Today, managed competition is embodied in health insurance exchanges set up under the Affordable Care Act. As Enthoven and Shortell described it, the idea was for local governments to promote organized delivery systems that would compete against each other in a well-regulated marketplace. The managed competition movement picked up momentum in the early 1990s when the concept was endorsed by an informal network of executives, physicians, academics (including Enthoven), and policy wonks known as the Jackson Hole Group, who met regularly in the Wyoming home of their leader, Paul Ellwood.[3] While these efforts further stimulated employer interest and employee enrollment in managed care plans, they spooked health care providers.

It did not help that all of the groups discussing reform deliberated in secret. Providers sensed that something portentous was coming their way, and began wondering how they should respond.

Propulsion from the Public Sector

Rapid political changes reinforced this perception. The 1991–92 recession brought several Democrats to prominence and, with them, calls for health care reform. In 1991 the former president of Bryn Mawr College, Harris Wófford, won election to the US Senate from Pennsylvania with a promise of health care reform. The following year, Senator Bob Kerrey of Nebraska built his presidential campaign around the promise of universal coverage. Another presidential candidate, former Senator Paul Tsongas of Massachusetts, began talking in New Hampshire meeting halls about restructuring the health care marketplace. The presidential sweepstakes got even more interesting when billionaire Ross Perot entered, exited, and then re-entered the race—and published his own health care reform—ultimately siphoning off enough votes to hand the 1992 election to Bill Clinton, who won with 43 percent of the popular vote.[4]

Clinton's election served as the tipping point. The efforts of the Jackson Hole group were now supplemented by a series of working groups with hundreds of members, formed by Hillary Clinton and her policy advisor, Ira Magaziner. Together, they developed a national health reform proposal in 1993 known as the Health Security Act, also known as the "Clinton Health Plan."[5] Loosely following the Enthoven and Shortell blueprint, the Clinton Plan called for a massive restructuring in the payment and delivery of health care, including (1) state-level "regional health alliances" that would purchase care on behalf of nearly all the non-Medicare population; (2) health plans organized by local providers and insurers; and (3) fee schedules set by the alliances, which would serve as price controls. The Clinton Plan bore some resemblance to voluntary arrangements passed in a few states (Washington, Florida, and Minnesota). It had no shortage of well-regarded academics working on Hillary Clinton's task forces, many of whom would go on to work on Obama's Affordable Care Act; and it enjoyed

the endorsement of five hundred economists who praised the legislation. To skeptics, it was eerily reminiscent of the "450 prophets of Baal"
who led people astray.[6]

The Clinton Plan dominated the headlines for nearly two years. This
long gestation period gave providers, and the consultants who advised
them, a lot of time to mull over its implications. What seemed clear to
everyone was that "transformation" of the payment system from fee-
for-service to capitation and managed care was at hand, with concomitant changes in the delivery system to follow shortly.[7] Self-proclaimed
health care futurist Russell Coile opined that this transformation
would be largely completed by the end of the decade.[8] While the Clinton Plan died on arrival in Congress in the spring of 1994, it nevertheless frightened providers into a variety of integration efforts. As Coile
explained in 1995, "American health care is being restructured, reengi-
neered, and reinvented in a new systems model — the integrated delivery network."[9]

The "Logics" of Health Care Market Evolution

Provider integration was not just a response to proposed health care
reforms. It was cast as an inevitable evolutionary progression toward
the promised land: progressive managed care as in states such as California and Minnesota. The California marketplace featured Kaiser, as
well as large primary-care dominated medical groups, aggressive purchasers (CalPERS, which managed benefits for retired state employees, and the Pacific Business Group on Health, which represented large
employers), widespread use of capitation, and relatively low health insurance premiums. According to one analyst, by 1995 there were fifteen medical groups in California reporting that 90 to 95 percent of
their revenues were capitated.[10] The Twin Cities marketplace included
another large employer coalition (Buyers Health Care Action Group),
large medical groups, one of the earliest community-based prepaid
plans (Group Health, established in 1957), and nascent integrated systems. It was often referred to on the speaker circuit as the "Mesopo-
tamia of managed care."

The natural presumption was that the rest of the nation would soon replicate what was happening in these vanguard states. As various observers put it, "California here you come," or "as California goes, so goes the nation." Capitated payments and integrated staff/group HMOs would dominate the landscape. Everyone would be like Kaiser. It did not matter that primary care physicians were the only ones who were heavily capitated in these states, while specialists and hospitals remained stuck in the fee-for-service world. Nor did it matter that Kaiser's regional market share had held steady at around 30 percent for decades. Instead, analysts assumed that large medical groups and HMOs had unlocked the mystery of value creation, and they focused on the strategies those organizations employed to manage capitated risk. Hospital executives started thinking, "If Kaiser can do it, why can't I?"

This evolutionary theme provided fodder for "frameworks," the lifeblood of many of the strategic management consultants who were advising hospitals. Drawing on the experience of California and Minneapolis, futurist Coile posited the "five stages of managed care," basically suggesting a huge domino effect.[11] Pressures from employers for premium reductions would motivate managed-care payers to consolidate and then use their market power to impose capitation and utilization review on providers, thus reducing the latter's volumes and payments. In response, providers would develop new delivery models and strategies, including horizontal and vertical integration, and would exert pressure on their upstream suppliers. It did not matter that there was no evidence for such a domino effect; no one in the health policy and management communities questioned it. Research published a decade later demonstrated that there was no causal impact of insurer consolidation on provider consolidation; in fact, there was scarcely any insurer consolidation. Rather, it was the "fear" among providers that managed care was coming that drove their integration efforts.[12]

Evolutionary models abounded. Starting in 1993, the University HealthSystem Consortium (UHC) codeveloped a model (with a consulting firm, APM) to classify the urban markets of its hospital members.[13] The model hypothesized the existence of four market stages: "unstructured," "loose framework," "consolidation," and "managed competition." The last was renamed "hypercompetitive" in 1996—

a curious term, for, as we will soon see, this stage involved a small number of big organizations, not exactly the recipe for "hypercompetition." These four stages were driven by intensifying managed care pressures and the emergence of capitated payment. Providers had to increasingly organize and integrate as markets "evolved" through these four stages. As one analysis described it:[14]

> In stage 1, there is very little managed care (0–10 percent penetration) ... Without pressure to reduce costs, there is little movement among hospitals or physicians to horizontally integrate.
>
> In stage 2 (HMO penetration of 11–30 percent), HMOs and other payers ... demand and obtain discounts. In response, hospitals begin to consolidate to augment their bargaining power with payers. A growing number of physicians (particularly primary care) also organize in groups. Overall, however, relationships among providers remain informal.
>
> In stage 3, there is further HMO penetration ... as well as consolidation among HMOs. HMOs increasingly drop certain physicians and hospitals from their panels to lower their contracting costs. In response, providers increasingly form horizontally integrated systems to improve their bargaining power and to increase scale economies and geographic coverage to attract payers. Payers also begin to shift the risk of care to providers through the use of withholds and capitated payments. In response, physicians organize to accept and manage risk. . . . In addition, physician groups and hospitals link together in vertically integrated networks.
>
> In stage 4, managed care and capitated payments dominate the market (50 percent or more HMO penetration). Providers and payers have consolidated, leaving few health care players ... There is also continued pressure to develop a full continuum of care outside the hospital's walls. Providers and insurers organize to serve covered lives in response to the incentives of capitated payments.

The model caught on with consultants, who classified urban markets into these four stages to let hospital executives know where they stood and where they were going. They claimed that most major markets were already stage 3 and stage 4 markets, so the pressure was really on.

This four-stage model had an enormous impact on the hospital industry. It was the subject of many presentations at various "symposia on integrated health care" held dozens of times across the nation. Hospital executives commonly referred to their geographies as "stage X markets." It was replicated in the publications of professional societies like the American College of Healthcare Executives, and consulting firms like the Advisory Board.[15] It was mimicked by hospital associations, one of which issued a report on the four phases of delivery system integration: from fee-for-service to managed payment to organized care and to accountable care.[16] The evolutionary frameworks appeared in peer-reviewed academic research, and in at least one major book.[17] Seemingly overnight, everyone knew where health care was heading: toward integration.

Case Studies as the New Evidence Base

According to these evolutionary logics, if a hospital was to survive it would have to employ massive numbers of PCPs, develop ambulatory care networks with outpatient surgery centers in every cranny of their community, coordinate care, manage specialty referrals and inpatient admissions, and, most importantly, assemble a large enough base of providers and covered lives to manage capitated risk. They might even have to become insurers in their own right. Only through these massive changes could a hospital transform into an integrated delivery network (IDN).

Consultants advised hospitals to emulate the early movers, mainly from the West Coast and Minnesota, whose experiences were formalized in compilations of case studies and distillations of case study "lessons," many authored by the consultant Dean Coddington and his associates.[18] Trade industry publications such as the *Integrated Healthcare Report* contained additional case studies on progress made along the way to stage 4. None of these cases expressed any criticism or skepticism. Like their counterparts at the Harvard Business School, case study writers received access to companies in exchange for describing their history, structure, accomplishments, and successes.[19] Case writers often buried all too brief discussions of "issues and challenges."

Case studies are a useful tool for teaching concepts to MBA students, but are less useful as an empirical foundation for committing vast resources to new business ventures. Whether in medicine or in business, case studies are the weakest form of evidence, offering a single data point about the poor health of a patient, or the great success of a business, while inviting the reader to choose among multiple possible explanations. Consider Kaiser. Is it successful because it is vertically integrated? Or is it because of the way it recruits and compensates physicians? Is its success "path dependent," so that Kaiser's history is a key contributor? Does it matter that Kaiser largely operates in tech-savvy and highly educated communities? There is just not enough information to determine which of these explanations, if any, are valid. One picks one's preferred answer and invests accordingly, at one's peril. This is far from the only problem with case studies. They are often biased due to the reluctance of struggling organizations to put themselves under the microscope. In the 1990s we learned about successful firms that integrated. The unsuccessful integrating firms, and there were many of them, kept their failures to themselves. (The one abject failure that we profile at length in the next chapter, AHERF, came to our attention through bankruptcy proceedings.) To make matters worse, predicting future performance based on prior case studies becomes more perilous the further out one projects. The Harvard case study library is filled with exemplars of excellence whose fortunes turned soon after publication. This problem was intensified in health care, where consultants and futurists were predicting events that would unfold in five, ten, or even twenty years' time in a remarkably complex sector of the economy where predicting one year ahead is fraught with difficulty. Eager to counter the threats from government regulations and private insurers, providers believed the predictions.

Cover from Academic Research

Joint research conducted by consultants and academics provided a veneer of credibility to the evolutionary frameworks and the march to integrated health care they forecast. Many of these investigations resembled the laudatory case studies mentioned above.[20] Others were based in academic theories of organizational sociology, such as the Health Systems Integration Study (HSIS), conducted by academic faculty at Northwestern University and consultants at Deloitte.[21] These researchers conducted a multiyear investigation of several "organized delivery systems." They conceptualized integration as a "house" with a foundation of functional integration, layered with physician-system integration, and capped off by clinical integration. Surveys of their hospitals served as the data for some of the first empirical, peer-reviewed studies of IDNs.

The powerful role of academia in spreading IDN fervor was on display at a 1991 meeting for hospital executives at the Kellogg School of Management, hosted by Stephen Shortell.[22] At the meeting, Shortell explained how the US health care system was fragmented into self-interested components: hospitals, physicians, therapists, home health agencies, pharmacies, insurers, and so forth. Each component tried to maximize its own success, without regard for patients' overall needs or total medical spending. This created an opportunity for organizations that could combine the disparate components and take full responsibility for costs and outcomes: what we today call "risk contracting" and "population health." The result would be a community of providers dedicated to keeping patients healthy and, when illness struck, coordinating care to achieve maximum outcomes at minimum cost.

In his research and writings, Shortell speculated that many different types of organizations could successfully coordinate care.[23] Both hospitals and physician groups could organize integrated systems. Providers could also achieve significant degrees of coordination through virtual integration, implying that it was not necessary to merge into a single corporate structure. At the meeting, Shortell cited the potential for hospital-led IDNs to revolutionize care delivery and stay at the forefront of market evolution. To the ears of the executives in attendance, this was nothing less than academic-certified IDN Kool-Aid. They went back to their hospitals convinced that integration was the future of health care. In no time at all, they were transforming the health care landscape. Shortell was not the only academic preaching the virtues of coordinated care, and there were countless other hospital executives who heard similar sermons and responded in similar fashion.

Academic enthusiasm for integration was accompanied, and perhaps fueled, by press coverage of integrated systems. The press had no shortage of pro-IDN opinions to draw on from academics, consultants, futurists, and various think tanks. Hospital executives who attended academic seminars and industry symposia, listened to the consultants, or simply read the trade magazines heard the same mantra so many times that they assumed it must be true: To succeed, you must integrate. Coverage in the leading trade magazine, *Modern Healthcare*, is a case in point. In 1991 the magazine published less than one article a month about IDNs.[24] Things started to change near the end of 1992, when the magazine noted the growing academic support for integration in an article titled "Seamless Delivery: Integrated Approach Gets Experts' Vote."[25] *Modern Healthcare* kept its pulse on the trend, and by 1994 articles on IDNs were appearing ten times a month, a tenfold increase in coverage. Executives following this lavish coverage surely felt they had to either hop on the IDN bandwagon or get hopelessly left behind. Shortell put it this way: "The danger of waiting . . . is that others may have beaten you to the punch, leaving you with a long, uphill struggle."[26]

Some academics refused to get on board. Some noted the lack of empirical proof of the IDN concept, Kaiser notwithstanding. Others cast doubt on the four-stage model, pointing out that markets were not evolving through these four stages during the early to mid-1990s.[27] Even with its air of self-fulfilling prophecy, the model did not predict trends in vertical integration, except at a coarse national level. By the mid-1990s, several analyses of vertical integration should have served as flashing yellow lights on the road to integration.[28] The best one could take away from these studies was that cost cutting would take time. The worst was that costs would actually increase. These studies were far from definitive; they were closer in spirit to case studies than they were to the kinds of systematic research that would emerge a decade later.

When examined through an economic or management lens—as by us in the next chapter—these mixed-to-negative findings were not surprising. Scale economies are always easier to discuss than to realize. Coordination and alignment of incentives are worthy goals, but integration assures neither. At the same time, large firms inevitably face problems of bureaucracy and motivating workers. In the 1980s these problems had plagued many corporate giants outside health care, which led in the 1990s to downsizing, unbundling, and virtual organizations. Those waving the flag for integration failed to ask a fundamental question: Why should health care be exempt from economic and organizational fundamentals that caused businesses elsewhere in the economy to trend in the other direction? Nor did anyone ask if consumers wanted "integrated care," let alone understand what it meant to them. Instead, the race to integrate was on. True believers drowned out the voices of skeptics. Integration had joined God, mother, and country as something whose virtue you could not question.

A Tidal Wave

Hospital executives wasted no time putting words into actions. Within just a few years, the entire health care industry radically transformed, with independent providers coalescing into IDNs. IDNs usually revolved around a flagship tertiary-care hospital, often an academic medical center like New York Presbyterian or Northwestern Memorial. These hospitals took referrals of the most difficult and often most profitable cases. The hospital's CEO often became the system's CEO, and all key management decisions and financial resources flowed from the flagship hospital. IDNs also included most, if not all, of the following components:

- horizontal mergers with other hospitals, especially community "feeder" institutions

- primary care and specialty physician practices

- freestanding outpatient and/or diagnostic facilities

- therapy and/or home health care services

- long-term care facilities

In addition, many IDNs offered their own insurance product, or contracted with insurers to cover lives on a full-risk basis. Such an array of components supposedly enabled the IDNs to offer "a seamless continuum of care" and hopefully capture the premium dollar across it. Seamless is the opposite of fragmented, and carried only the best possible connotations. A chart developed by the Advisory Board depicting this continuum may have been the most popular slide on the speaker circuit during the 1990s.

There are many different sources of data on the size and speed of the IDN tidal wave. All of them agree that it was big and happened quickly. For example, Deloitte and Touche estimated that the percentage of US hospitals belonging to IDNs increased from 16 percent in 1994 to 50 percent in 1998.[29] While the tentacles of IDNs reached into nearly every corner of health care delivery, several features stood out: horizontal integration into hospital systems, vertical integration with physicians, and forays into health plans and risk contracting. Various organizations collected data on each of these strategies, which we discuss in turn.

Horizontal Integration into Hospital Systems

The assemblage of previously independent hospitals into hospital systems, as well as the merger of smaller hospital systems into larger hospital systems, formed the bedrock of IDNs. Consolidation occurred quite quickly during the 1994–98 period, ignited by the Clinton Health Plan of 1993. For the entire period from 1980 to 1993, there were fewer than three hundred hospitals involved in horizontal mergers. In 1994 alone the number jumped to over six hundred, and remained above five hundred each year until 1998, when the merger wave finally

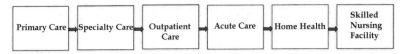

Figure 2.1. Continuum of care efforts: the Integrated Delivery Network. Adapted from the Advisory Board Company.

crested.[30] The numbers show all the symptoms of a contagion, in which one member of the population gets infected and rapidly spreads the infection to others. In this case, the hospitals' resistance was worn down by the futurists, consultants, and academics promoting integrated health care.

Vertical Integration with Physicians

Historically, physicians and hospitals had a unique partnership. They utterly relied on each other, yet operated as independent business entities. The closest thing to a formal relationship came through admitting privileges, which entitled physicians to bring their patients to the hospital and command the hospital's resources. Hospital executives had little say over how doctors practiced or how they were compensated. Doctors had little input into hospital service offerings, staffing, or pricing. Advocates of integration cited this separation of powers as a key source of inefficiency, which made it difficult for hospitals to cope with rising financial pressures that were due, many believed, to the ways in which physician used (or misused) their "pens."

Much of the cost-containment effort of the 1980s focused on hospital payment reform. Because DRGs capped payments for an entire hospitalization, hospital executives had to analyze and then manage care patterns and the intensity of resource use, or face potentially ruinous losses. At the same time, HMO contracts replaced open-ended hospital reimbursements with negotiated rates determined, in many cases, on a per-diem or even per-case basis. This was impossible to manage without the active support of the medical staff. Executives approached physicians for the first time for their help in operating within a budget constraint. Getting physicians to pay attention to costs proved to be a very stressful moment for both parties. Physicians were not quite ready for such conversations, and that inevitably bred distrust in their hospital "partners."

IDNs attempted to reduce this fragmentation by creating new financial arrangements between hospitals and physicians. Academics classified IDN models into a wide array of categories, each with its own three-letter acronym (TLA), based largely on the nature of the hospital-physician partnership.[31] The physician-hospital organization (PHO) was a joint venture in which physicians and hospitals partnered to accept capitated risk contracts. In an independent practice association (IPA), a loose network of physicians contracted with a hospital, again to accept risk contracts. The integrated salary model (ISM) drew the most attention. In the ISM, hospitals employed physicians, often hundreds, who gave up their autonomy in exchange for financial security. There were other TLAs—too many to mention them all. Many analysts believed that IDNs could not transform health care delivery without employing physicians, and hospitals rushed to buy up as many practices as possible. According to one study, by 1997 IDNs were employing seventeen thousand primary care physicians.[32] This proved to be a big mistake, as we will discuss in the next chapter.

Hospitals developed these vertically integrated models with physicians at the same time that they developed horizontally integrated systems by merging with other hospitals. Like horizontal integration, vertical integration between hospitals and physicians dramatically ramped up in 1994, and leveled off, though only slightly, after 1999.[33]

Health Plans and Risk Contracting

IDNs also got into the health insurance business, either as owners of in-house plans or by contracting for capitated lives. Consultants lectured hospitals that the HMOs in California markets were facing stiff competition from indemnity insurers. So California hospitals thought twice about starting their own HMOs. Elsewhere, however, HMOs or IDNs could underprice indemnity plans and earn profits by adopting California-style payment and delivery models. The question was: Who would manage the care and earn those profits? IDNs that combined all three Kaiser components (hospital, physician, and health plan) were known as integrated health care organizations. Today they are called provider sponsored plans, about which we will have much more to say later on.

Many hospitals entered the health plan business to try to "disintermediate" the new managed care payers ("We will be our own payer"). Some even thought that they could pay their own hospitals and physicians more than what the HMOs were paying them. Others entered to get direct experience with risk contracting and prepare themselves for the "inevitable" spread of capitation. Since Medicare represented roughly 40 percent of the hospital's business, and because Medicare had developed interest in moving its enrollees into private HMO plans (today known as Medicare Advantage), the Medicare market seemed to hold high potential for revenue upside. The timing of hospital entry into the health plan business coincided with other integration initiatives: a dramatic increase in 1994, followed by a slightly earlier slowdown after 1998. At the zenith in 1996 and 1997, about one hospital in four sponsored a private health insurance plan. Many of those plans had minimal impact, however, with enrollments mainly limited to the hospital's own employees—or, worse yet, patients.

In addition to developing in-house health plans, hospitals also integrated with their physicians to engage in risk contracting with external health plans. The spread of these IDN models was linked to the growing penetration of local markets by HMOs and other forms of managed care. Roughly one-third of IDNs studied in 1995 had at least one capitated contract with payers. These proved more popular than the IDNs' in-house plans. For those with capitated contracts, the mean number of contracts was roughly five, and the mean number of covered lives was thirty-eight thousand.[34]

New Managerial Strategies and Structures

Prior to the 1980s, hospital executives were schooled in dealing with largely protective regulatory environments. The 1990s brought a new set of business challenges. To meet them, hospital executives embraced the language and practice of traditional business management.[35] This transformation in the executive's mindset is reflected in this 2001 statement from the American College of Healthcare Executives Career Resource Center:

> In the past, most students chose the traditional route of a master's degree in health administration or public health. Today, however, students are investigating other options, including graduate degrees in business . . . with course concentration in health services management.[36]

With an emphasis on traditional business management came traditional business approaches. Hospitals pursued scale economies through more centralized management, systems building, and group purchasing—positioning them to directly profit from the resulting savings. Providers developed complex corporate structures, such as holding companies, that oversaw a diversified array of businesses, some not even focused on health care.[37] Hospitals also engaged in product line management, often a disguise for cultivating profitable clinical services and jettisoning unprofitable ones. Hospital executives focused on cost management in their dealings with physicians—for example, through educational seminars and physician leadership training. Some went so far as to use "economic credentialing," evaluating physicians' privileges partly on the basis of their contribution to hospital profits. This engendered physician complaints about diminished clinical autonomy and the corporate practice of medicine.

Hospital forays into the ambulatory care market represented an extension of the outpatient department strategy discussed in chapter 1. Hospitals developed freestanding ambulatory services such as imaging, emergency or urgent care, surgery, and rehabilitation and occupational medicine, as well as remote physician office complexes. In some cases, aggressive ambulatory development brought hospitals into direct competition with the community-based physicians on their medical staff. In such cases, hospitals began to develop joint ventures with medical staff members to manage these potential conflicts.

IDNs in Action

By the late 1990s, IDNs had thoroughly transformed the health care landscape, as local health providers had morphed into giant businesses. An IDN encompassed one or more anchor hospitals and several feeder hospitals, hundreds of physicians, and either an in-house health plan or risk contracts with external plans.[38] Some IDNs diversified across geographic boundaries, making them quite complex to operate and manage. We provide a few examples of giant IDNs below, but save our discussion of the biggest of them all—the ill-fated Allegheny Health Education and Research Foundation (AHERF)—for the next chapter.

Hospital-Led IDNs

Most of the giant systems were created by hospitals, and often had labyrinthine structures reflective of a seemingly random history of prior deals. Allina Health System, one of the first and most prominent IDNs, exemplified this model. Allina was the result of the merger of HealthSpan Health Systems and Medica HMO in 1993, each the product of prior mergers. Allina included seventeen hospitals, six thousand network physicians (organized into fifty-five to sixty clinics with more than four hundred employed physicians), two nursing homes, and HMO and PPO health plans that covered one-quarter of the Minnesota population.

The story of how Allina emerged is typical for many IDNs of the time, especially those in "stage 3" and "stage 4" markets. First, two purchasing groups formed among Minnesota employers to exert pressure on providers to rein in spending. The State of Minnesota Employees Health Benefit Program formed a purchasing group in 1985 on behalf of 144,000 enrollees. In 1991, fourteen large Twin Cities employers formed the Buyers Health Care Action Group to purchase coverage on behalf of 250,000 members through an exclusive contract with one delivery system. Second, the state legislature enacted MinnesotaCare in 1993, which further encouraged providers to develop "integrated service networks" to provide a continuum of services in a cost-efficient manner. Third, the Twin Cities market had undergone a rapid and massive expansion of managed care enrollment from 500,000 in 1984 to nearly three million by 1994. The market now featured a heavy presence of managed care, with over 70 percent of the population in PPOs, commercial HMOs, and Medicare and Medicaid HMOs. These developments were so rapid and massive that many observers felt that the Twin Cities was becoming a "stage 5" marketplace.

The creation of Allina was also noteworthy for the assumptions underlying the merger—assumptions that motivated many other vertical integration efforts during the decade. Foremost among these was that health care reform was imminent: it had already happened at the state level in 1993, and everyone assumed it was going to happen in 1994 at the federal level. Thus, the merger anticipated future regulatory controls and positioned the delivery system to deal with them. Second, everyone believed that common ownership of the continuum of care (e.g., physicians, hospitals, and health plans) was the only way to achieve a truly integrated system. Only by combining all components of health care financing and delivery under one corporate roof could a system achieve real improvements in community health, live up to the name "health maintenance," and achieve real "economic integration," whereby all components could be rewarded for their contribution to efficient, high-quality health care. The merger provided sufficient scale to manage the risk of a population and reap operating efficiencies. Third, the merger provided unified governance and "single signature authority" to contract as one with purchasers (employers, government). Such purchasers were believed to prefer a single point of accountability.

Sutter Health, based in Sacramento, is one of today's largest and most successful systems, consisting of twenty-four hospitals, several medical foundations, and close partnerships with giant medical groups including Brown and Toland and the Palo Alto Medical Foundation. Sutter consisted of only two hospitals in 1983, and neither one held a dominant market position. Eager to emulate the Kaiser model, by 1993 Sutter encompassed thirteen hospitals and five medical foundations employing more than four hundred physicians.[39] For a time during the 1980s, it also co-owned a health plan; and in the 1990s it re-invested in another plan. Sutter's goals were to develop the leading regional health system in northern California; counter the threat posed by Kaiser, which was gaining market share, avert the threat of investor-owned hospital systems; and respond to the "managed competition" message of Paul Ellwood and of Alain Enthoven, who was preaching integration from his nearby office at Stanford.

Physician-Led IDNs

Large physician groups also jumped on the IDN bandwagon. The Fargo Clinic in North Dakota, one of the largest multispecialty clinics in the United States with 250 physicians, expanded rapidly during the 1980s with the addition of several primary-care practices. The clinic provided more than 90 percent of the admissions to St. Luke's Hospital, located next door. A series of joint ventures between the two organizations during the 1980s (outpatient surgery center, MRI service, home health agency, cancer center) culminated in their merger in 1993 as MeritCare, partly in response to anticipated health care reform.

Nearby in central Wisconsin, the Marshfield Clinic, with four hundred physicians, likewise accounted for more than 90 percent of admissions to St. Joseph's Hospital. Founded in 1916, the multispecialty clinic grew organically and opened a center next to the hospital in 1975. The clinic also operated its own HMO in 1971, which supplied about one-third of clinic patients and one-quarter of its revenues, as well as imaging, outpatient surgery, and other ancillary services. During the next fifteen years, the clinic expanded aggressively into primary as well as specialty care practices in the region. The clinic and the hospital worked together through a joint conference committee without actually merging.

Four hundred miles south in Urbana, Illinois, the Carle Clinic and the Carle Foundation Hospital followed a similar blueprint. The Carle Clinic consisted of 240 physicians in a multispecialty group formed initially in 1931 by two physicians trained at the Mayo Clinic, and complemented by six more Mayo physicians by 1935. A year later, the physicians formed the hospital. The Carle Clinic and Hospital are both physician-led, physician-centric organizations that are economically interdependent. Like the other physician organizations profiled above, the clinic operates profitable ancillary services such as radiology and a laboratory. Carle also opened its own in-house HMO health plan in 1980 which capitated physicians in the clinic; nearly all of the HMO's patient care costs generated by in-house providers.

To the east in Danville, Pennsylvania, lies the Geisinger Health System, now a famous system with unusual origins. A benefactor donated $500,000 in 1915 to build a small sixty-three-bed hospital. The hospital's first medical staff member, another physician trained at the Mayo Clinic, convinced the benefactor to reorient the facility to emulate Mayo's multispecialty model. That clinic enjoyed stable, long-tenured physician leadership for the remainder of the century. In 1972 Geisinger started its own health plan, spurred on by President Nixon's HMO Act. During the 1980s, Geisinger began to aggressively market its health plan, but it needed more physicians to do so. In 1982 the Geisinger Clinic had 207 physicians; over the next ten years, it added another 300, including about 150 PCPs to complement the traditional specialist mix. The expansion consisted of joint development of a multispecialty clinic and affiliated nearby hospital in other northern Pennsylvania cities (e.g., Wilkes-Barre). Health plan enrollment rocketed from 12,000 lives in 1985 to 144,000 lives by 1993. Nearly all medical care of health plan enrollees was rendered by physicians in the Geisinger system.

These and many other physician-led IDNs differed from the hospital-led models in some significant ways. First, their roots lay in large multispecialty groups founded early in the twentieth century; in this manner, they were physician-centric, collaborative provider organizations. Second, they developed health plans prior to the managed care era, oftentimes in the 1970s. They thus had more experience and comfort with risk contracting and assumption of risk. Third, they primarily operated in rural areas of the country, sheltered from the demands of more urban-based Blue Cross and commercial plans. This enabled them to develop dominant market shares that inhibited entry by other payers and providers.

Private Sector Investments in Physician Practices

Physician-led IDNs represented one end of the spectrum of physician involvement in management. Most physicians wanted less involvement. They had become doctors to save lives, not to run businesses. Their challenge was to focus on patient care while dealing with burdensome administrative requirements and facing growing capital needs for new office management technologies, including electronic billing and fledgling electronic health records. While many physicians were thrilled when IDNs offered guaranteed incomes plus generous upfront buyouts, others wanted to retain some degree of autonomy. This created a market opportunity for independent firms to offer to manage physician practices while otherwise leaving the doctors to be doctors. This was the rationale behind physician practice management (PPM) companies.

PPMs began in the late 1980s, as government regulations and the demands of HMOs and PPOs began taking their toll on physicians. PPMs offered physicians what seemed to be a win-win proposition. PPMs would handle all of the administrative aspects of practice management, including billing and collections and negotiations with insurers, while offering low-interest loans for capital equipment. Some PPMs secured capitated HMO contracts on behalf of a pool of physicians. In this way, PPMs resembled large group practices that accepted capitated risk for the group, although in this case the physicians often did not even know who else was in the pool. In exchange for handling the financial side of medical practice, PPMs kept roughly 15 percent of practice revenues.

By the early 1990s, thousands of physicians had signed over their practices to PPMs. Eager for more rapid growth, several PPMs—including PhyCor, FPA Medical Management, and relative newcomer MedPartners—raised capital by going public. They soon became Wall Street stars. MedPartners shone the brightest. Richard Scrushy, a former respiratory therapist who had previously founded the rehabilitation services company HealthSouth, cofounded MedPartners in 1992. A medical professional with a proven entrepreneurial track record, Scrushy was hailed as a business genius. He spoke at countless management school forums, describing his vision for bringing management rigor to medical practice. Scrushy and his PPM brethren convinced investors that the business model was easily scaled. With financial backing from Wall Street investors, PPMs eventually recruited more than ten thousand physicians. Share values skyrocketed, and MedPartners cracked the Fortune 500.

Many analysts, including both authors of this book, were having a hard time figuring out how PPMs could be so profitable. They offered essentially the same deal as hospitals—they would buy physicians' practices, and put the physicians on fixed salaries—but hospitals offered two advantages over PPMs. First, physicians who were nervous about selling out to investor-owned corporations felt no such compunction about selling out to hospitals. Second, and probably more important, hospitals could afford to pay more than PPMs, because they expected the acquired physicians to bring their patients with them.

Within a few years, PPMs were going bankrupt. So were some IDNs. The term "integrated delivery," once on everyone's lips, swiftly fell out of favor, with mentions in *Modern Healthcare* plummeting from eighty-three in 1998 to twenty-one in 2000. In the next chapter we describe how and why things went so terribly wrong with integrated health care.

3

WHY INTEGRATION FAILED

"What's past is prologue."

ANTONIO IN SHAKESPEARE'S
THE TEMPEST, ACT 2, SCENE 1

As the integration wave started to form in the early 1990s, IDN advocates pushed hospitals to get ahead of two related trends: the ongoing spread of managed care, and the anticipated purchasing pressures from the Clinton Health Plan. They told hospital executives that integration would allow them to cope with an uncertain future that seemed to include declining inpatient admissions, lower payment rates, capitated payments, narrow networks, downsizing of specialist provider capacity, and the need for more primary care physicians. Advocates argued that horizontal consolidation of hospitals and vertical integration with physicians would enhance bargaining leverage against more powerful and better organized payers. They also played up the scale and scope economies and other efficiencies that would be necessary for success in a competitive marketplace. Such efficiencies would assure that IDNs were a win for hospitals, payers, and patients. As hospital executives took up the challenge of forming IDNs, they took it for granted, or at least did not openly doubt, that they could efficiently manage an entire continuum spanning primary care, inpatient and outpatient surgery, and postacute care. Throw in some risk contracting, and ambitious executives could imagine themselves leading the next Kaiser.

Some of the assumptions underlying the arguments of IDN advocates proved accurate. HMO and PPO enrollments swelled during the early-to-mid 1990s, with a corresponding rise in both steeply discounted fee-for-service and partially capitated payments. This put a financial squeeze on provider revenues, exacerbated by a decline in inpatient days and stagnating admissions.

Most of the remaining assumptions did not bear out, and provider organizations that acted upon them paid the price. The Clinton Plan died on arrival in early 1994. Closed networks and global capitation, both widely anticipated in the early 1990s, were quickly scuttled by the managed care backlash of the late 1990s, when enrollees objected to the tight access controls in many HMOs. In his last year in office, President Clinton even proposed a "Patient Bill of Rights," which died amid opposition from conservative Republicans who felt it meddled too much, and liberal Democrats who felt it didn't meddle enough.[1] Horizontal and vertical integration failed to yield scale and scope economies. Finally, the strategy of "moving with speed" often resembled "moving on speed," with disastrous consequences. IDN executives were confronted with the realities of trying to change culture and processes in complex hierarchical organizations, a challenge made more difficult by their inability to get on the same page with their key decision makers, their medical staff.

While IDN formation accelerated in the mid 1990s, the movement quickly slowed due to financial losses on several fronts: the weight of sprawling operations, poor returns on investments in physician employment and alliance models, and losses sustained from capitated contracts. The Medicare fee schedule reductions built into the Balanced Budget Act (BBA) of 1997 and contemporaneous reductions in Medicaid payments only poured salt on the wounds. The BBA also gutted the long-term care sector, prompting many bankruptcies of nursing home chains, which put a serious dent into efforts to develop a care continuum in the postacute segment. By the end of the decade, the IDN movement was on life support.

This chapter sorts through the rubble of failed IDN development during the 1990s. We begin by discussing Kaiser, which stood as a role model for health care organizations in a fully evolved stage 4 market. Many IDNs attempted to replicate Kaiser's West Coast successes in other parts of the country. None succeeded; not even Kaiser. As an example of what could go horribly wrong with integration, we then present a case study of the Allegheny Health, Education and Research Foundation (AHERF). After some shorter case studies of IDNs that faced a variety of struggles, we critique the strategies of horizontal and vertical integration pursued more broadly, presenting results from academic studies. Along the way we point out what executives hoped to accomplish, and why they failed.

Kaiser: The Gold Standard, or Fool's Gold?

It is not impossible to successfully integrate hospitals, doctors, and insurance. Kaiser has been getting it right for more than seventy years, and by the 1980s the entire country was aware of its success. The economist Harold Luft was an important chronicler of Kaiser's success. His 1978 *New England Journal of Medicine* study opened some eyes, finding that the premiums charged by Kaiser and other integrated HMOs were 10 to 40 percent lower than comparable indemnity health insurance.[2] Most of the savings was attributed to lower hospitalization rates. It seemed that health maintenance organizations were living up to their name. Not everyone was convinced by this evidence, because it did not establish causality. Was Kaiser really keeping its enrollees healthy, or did it have healthier enrollees in the first place? If the latter, then perhaps Kaiser wasn't saving any money at all. It was not until the randomized control trials of the RAND National Health Insurance Experiment that naysayers started accepting that fully integrated HMOs (in this case, the Group Health Cooperative of Puget Sound) had lower spending.[3]

As hospitals formed IDNs in the 1990s, hoping to become the next Kaisers, the genuine article was hardly watching and waiting. At the same time that new IDNs were forming, Kaiser expanded from its West Coast base, entering seven new markets east of the Mississippi. But even Kaiser found that creating a successful IDN was hard work.

By 1998 it had withdrawn from many expansion markets except Baltimore, Washington, and Atlanta, where today it still struggles to turn a profit. Although there may be a secret sauce to Kaiser's success, not even Kaiser is sure of the ingredients.

To understand what went wrong, economist Kate Ho conducted interviews with Kaiser officials and performed her own statistical analyses to provide further insight into the factors that affected Kaiser's expansion.[4] Three factors rose to the top: scale, brand, and relationships with physicians. In its home West Coast markets, Kaiser has a sterling reputation; it was one of the few HMOs to survive the managed care backlash unscathed. Kaiser used its own hospitals, each carrying the Kaiser brand, and enrollees believed that Kaiser quality was equal or superior to other providers. In fact, government statistics on provider quality, available today (though not at the time of Kaiser's eastward expansion), show that Kaiser-branded providers in California systematically offer average or above-average quality.[5] But the Kaiser brand meant very little outside of the West Coast. Nor could Kaiser's Eastern affiliates tout their own hospitals, as Kaiser accelerated its expansion by contracting with existing hospitals, often relying on less prominent hospitals in order to keep its costs down. Potential enrollees saw Kaiser as just another HMO with questionable provider networks.

Each new Kaiser plan needed about one hundred thousand enrollees to reach scale economies. Building a critical mass of enrollees is a chicken-or-egg problem. Without enough enrollees, you cannot manage risk and form networks, and this makes it more difficult to get more enrollees. Had Kaiser grown even larger, it might have built its own hospitals—something it has not yet done in its expansion markets. Kaiser entered Atlanta and Washington by acquiring existing plans, so scale was not so much of an issue. In the other five expansion markets, Kaiser entered de novo, and the results speak for themselves.

Kaiser's remaining problem was perhaps the thorniest. Kaiser physicians on the West Coast are simply different from other physicians. They have more conservative practice styles, yet the data suggest that their patients are more than satisfied and that quality does not suffer. While part of this is chalked up to recruitment and training, part of it is hard to define. Richard Rumelt coined the term "causal ambiguity" to describe situations where the source of a firm's ability to do what its rivals cannot is hard to set down in words.[6] Kaiser's ability to manage physicians is a clear example: even Kaiser could not find a way to materially change how physicians in these new markets practice medicine. Perhaps that is the secret sauce. We will offer a few possible ingredients in chapter 10.

AHERF: Is This Any Way to Run a Health System?

As Kaiser's experience shows, hard work and good intentions were not enough to guarantee the success of new IDNs. At the time, most hospital executives believed the opposite: none more so than Sherif Abdelhak, the CEO of the Allegheny Health Education and Research Foundation (AHERF).[7] Headquartered in Pittsburgh, AHERF rose to prominence in the 1990s as one of the largest and fastest growing IDNs. In a January 1998 speech, Abdelhak boasted of the system's phenomenal growth, sprawling organization, and productivity improvements, and he mused about the system's bright future. Who could blame him? At the time, AHERF owned fourteen hospitals in the Pittsburgh and Philadelphia metropolitan areas, operated two medical schools, and counted more than 550 physicians among its 30,000 employees. It also held risk contracts for 750,000 lives. Abdelhak was a rising figure in health management circles. Hailed as a visionary and a genius, he delivered the prestigious 1996 John Cooper Lecture to the Association of American Medical Colleges. He was flying too close to the sun. In July 1998, AHERF ran out of cash and declared bankruptcy, leaving 65,000 creditors with unpaid debts of $1.3 billion.

The AHERF system originated with Allegheny General Hospital (AGH), a 670-bed tertiary hospital in Pittsburgh. AGH enjoyed a modest teaching affiliation with the University of Pittsburgh Medical Center (UPMC). AGH played second fiddle to UPMC, however, as the latter enjoyed a reputation as one of the nation's leading academic medical centers and was an international referral center for transplants. AGH's valuable teaching status was threatened when UPMC withdrew some residency positions.

Sherif Abdelhak took control of AGH in the mid-1980s and, with the support of board members, set out to top the prestige enjoyed by UMPC. He embraced every tenet of the IDN movement. Within a decade, AHERF (1) developed the first statewide IDN grounded in academic medicine, (2) built regional market share to leverage managed care payers, (3) garnered capitated contracts, (4) pursued—more accurately, desperately sought—synergies and efficiencies among the assets acquired, and (5) used community and suburban hospitals to try to refer private-pay patients to teaching hospitals and fill their beds.

A big believer in scale economies and first-mover advantage, Abdelhak expanded AHERF's physical plant, physician operations, geographic footprint, and risk exposure all at once. Part of this rapid response was based on the desire to get ahead of managed care and market stages, part of it reflected the CEO's fear that others might outbid AHERF for the acquisitions, and part of it reflected the CEO's general disposition to get things done quickly. Abdelhak was quoted as saying, "You cannot stop a freight train traveling seventy miles per hour."

While the simultaneity of these strategies suggests that AHERF was opportunistically exploiting synergies, more often than not the strategies were necessitated by circumstances. AGH sought a medical school affiliation to compete with its local Pittsburgh rival UPMC. In 1987, AHERF acquired the Medical College of Pennsylvania (MCP), situated across the state in Philadelphia, which involved buying two hospitals and an affiliated medical school. In 1991 it acquired the four-hospital United Hospital system. In 1993, having barely digested MCP and United, it acquired the struggling Hahnemann Medical College and its hospital. Acquisition of these local hospitals necessitated the acquisition of community physician practices to feed them; physician practice acquisitions were also needed to support burgeoning capitated contracts. Because of the desire to move quickly, AHERF conducted inadequate due diligence in the valuation of these assets. The hospitals it acquired were losing money and encumbered with debt; the two medical schools were poorly endowed; and it paid far more for the physician practices than they could hope to generate in profits, while giving the physicians guaranteed compensation and no productivity incentives. AHERF also miscalculated its financial exposure in capi-

tated contracts by accepting a low "percent of premium" reimbursement at a time when the underwriting cycle was in a downswing. All
of this occurred at the same time that AHERF's cash cow, Allegheny
General Hospital, was feeling the effects of the nationwide trend away
from inpatient care.

The speed and scale of this IDN growth strategy, particularly in the
face of investments in underperforming hospitals and medical schools,
could not be financed by the declining revenues of a single teaching
hospital. Moreover, AHERF made strategic blunders in entering a very
competitive Philadelphia market with several other academic medical
centers and two large insurers with heavy HMO enrollments. When
the Commonwealth of Pennsylvania mandated HMO coverage for
Medicaid beneficiaries in 1996, and the federal government cut Medicare reimbursements to hospitals as part of BBA 1997, AHERF's future
was sealed. As its hospital revenues shrank, its financial situation de-
teriorated. Abdelhak still believed in scale economies, and he doubled
down on his IDN bets by acquiring additional physician practices and
taking on more risk contracts. The scale economies never happened
and the capitated contracts never turned a profit, and in July 1998 the
system declared bankruptcy. The $1.3 billion owed creditors consti-
tuted the largest nonprofit health care bankruptcy in history.

Was this any way to run a health care system? In retrospect, certainly not. That was less clear to many observers at the time. And when
it came to struggling health systems, AHERF had plenty of company.

Detroit Medical Center

Detroit Medical Center (DMC) performed almost as poorly as AHERF.
DMC formed in 1985 as a nonprofit system affiliation of several hospitals (Harper University Hospital, Grace Hospital, Hutzel Women's
Hospital, Children's Hospital of Michigan) along with the city's main
safety net facility (Detroit Receiving Hospital), which was located near
and affiliated with Wayne State University. Like other hospitals, DMC
suffered from declining inpatient utilization, cuts in reimbursement
from private managed care payers, BBA 1997 cuts in hospital reimbursement, and freezes on Medicare payments for graduate medical

education. Its financial situation was exacerbated by the economic decline of the Motor City, high levels of hospital competition (six systems: among them, three academic medical centers including the prestigious Henry Ford Health System), excess bed capacity, high levels of
unionization, high levels of Medicare and Medicaid patients, aggressive cuts in the state's Medicaid budget, and state efforts to migrate
Medicaid beneficiaries over to HMO plans. DMC was further stung
by suburban hospital competitors that raided its medical staff. Some of
DMC's wounds were also self-inflicted, including the unprofitability
of the nineteen clinics it acquired in 1997 to build an ambulatory care
network to appeal to managed-care payers; additional hospital acquisitions, which brought with them costly physician contracts; and the
costs incurred in trying to consolidate its sprawling physical plant,
now eight hospitals. After suffering operating losses of $53 million in
1998 and $106 million in 1999, and after watching its credit rating fall
to junk-bond status, DMC eliminated two thousand full-time positions in January 1999 — roughly 20 percent of its staff. According to re-
porters, DMC was suffering from "AHERF-like symptoms."[8]

Allina Health System

Like AHERF, Allina sought to be ahead of market evolution. By some
accounts, the Twin Cities in the early 1990s was already in early stage 4.
Everyone thought that global capitation was just around the corner
and only IDNs would survive. Allina assembled an enormous system with nineteen hospitals and more than four hundred employed
physicians. Its Medica insurance company had more than one million
members. If Allina could work with its medical staff and align the diverse incentives among its hospitals, physicians, and health plans, it
could make capitation work and become the Kaiser of the Midwest.
This never happened.

By the end of the 1990s, there were already signs of trouble. Used to
broad networks, residents of Minneapolis wanted provider choice, not
a closed Kaiser-like system. No more than 30 percent of enrollees in
Allina's Medica HMO plan used Allina hospitals and clinics, making it
difficult for Allina to alter provider behavior and achieve scale econo-

mies through consolidation. High out-of-network (i.e., outside Allina) utilization also meant high costs to Medica. Medica might have restricted out-of-network utilization to Allina providers, but the HMO backlash was in full swing and enrollees would have rebelled.

Allina might have succeeded, had it managed to transform how medical care was practiced in its own hospitals. A longitudinal study conducted by University of Minnesota researchers showed that Allina's acquired primary care physicians were not "aligned" with the system.[9] While the physicians' commitment to the medical profession increased, their commitment to the hospital system decreased, and they expressed little willingness to cut costs to boost Allina's profits. This would prove to be a common theme at IDNs.[10] It was a lot easier to talk the alignment talk than walk the alignment walk, for reasons we will explore later on.

Starting in 2001, Minnesota's Attorney General Mike Hatch pressured Allina to jettison the Medica HMO on the basis that it incurred excessive administrative expenses and used the in-house plan's premium revenues to prop up the IDN's wasteful expenditures. Hatch claimed that as much as 47 percent of the health insurance premiums paid to Medica were spent on Allina's administration rather than on medical care for its members, greatly exceeding the 10 percent that Medica had reported.[11]

While Allina remained a hospital system, it was out of the risk contracting business and its dreams of emulating Kaiser had died.

California IDNs and Sutter Health

California served as the seedbed for many of the IDN models that were supposed to serve as the template for stage 3 and 4 markets. Yet no one bothered to ask what happened to the exemplars from the Golden State. California's health systems followed the IDN playbook, expanding horizontally and vertically and taking on risk contracts. Operating in Kaiser's shadow, California's new IDNs could not match its performance and soon underwent the same shakeout as observed elsewhere. Physician groups and IDNs that formed in response to managed care were not prepared for risk contracting, and incurred huge losses. Many of the medical groups closed between 1998 and 2002, and IDNs pulled out of their disastrous risk contracts.[12]

Sutter Health, today one of the nation's biggest IDNs, had considerable growing pains. Sutter consolidated numerous physician practices to form the Sutter Medical Group (SMG). SMG's origins lay in an independent multispecialty group that affiliated with Sutter Health in 1992 as part of a foundation model and then merged with three other medical groups in 2011. SMG encompassed five thousand physicians organized around eight groups, with roughly half of physicians in medical foundations and the other half in IPAs. This was an enormous panel of physicians that Sutter managed to retain and grow.

Things did not go so well on Sutter's insurance front. Sutter's HMO plan (Omni Healthcare, jointly owned with St. Joseph's Regional Health System) grew to 160,000 enrollees, giving it the second largest market share in the area, after Kaiser. Despite its size, Omni Healthcare was heavily reliant on the state's Medi-Cal program for business; it also incurred enormous administrative costs in marketing to and serving a rural population base, leading to a reported $2 million loss in 1998. In May 1999 it announced that it was pulling the plug on operations, designating Blue Cross of California as its successor.

The Broader Picture

We have offered a handful of case studies in which IDNs struggled. Academics published additional case studies documenting the problems in aligning incentives among hospitals, physicians, and health plans.[13] Much of the impetus for the IDN movement came from more optimistic case studies, structured interviews, and surveys performed by respected academics such as Stephen Shortell and Robin Gillies.[14] These studies suggested that IDNs could align incentives, reduce costs, and improve quality. As we have previously discussed, case studies (including our own) are not very good for prediction. Executives trying to figure out whether integration would work for their hospitals would have been better served had academics conducted large-scale studies using actual data on cost and quality. Some systematic studies did make it into print, including qualitative analyses of vertical integration and specific IDN models such as physician-hospital organizations and studies documenting that capitated payment failed to influence hospital costs. The latter helped to explain why hospital-sponsored health plans performed less than spectacularly.[15] A handful of subsequent empirical studies reached conflicting conclusions about the effects of IDN on spending, but they all suffered from poor data quality, and none proved to be convincing.[16]

With the benefit of hindsight, it is clear that there was inadequate research evidence on IDN performance, allowing academics on both sides of the IDN debate to push their theories for and against integration. It is perhaps unsurprising, then, that many executives made the leap of faith into integration, rather than let market evolution pass them by while they waited for academics to come up with the answers. All too often, that faith was misplaced. AHERF, which followed the IDN playbook to the letter, may have been the most visible evidence that something was wrong. AHERF had plenty of company, as IDNs across the country were in retreat. By the end of the decade, hospitals had stopped acquiring physician practices and many were divesting from them. At the same time, hospital-physician alliances, as exemplified by PHOs and MSOs, were on the wane.[17] The idea that hospitals could turn themselves into local versions of Kaiser was all but abandoned. The handful of successful provider launches of HMOs (Carle Clinic, in Urbana, Illinois; Marshfield Clinic, in central Wisconsin; Geisinger Clinic, in central Pennsylvania; Scott and White, in rural Texas) could be attributed to unique locational and historical advantages.[18] To this day, these provider-sponsored plans remain largely confined to their original local markets and surrounding rural communities.

From a broader health policy perspective, the effects of IDNs on cost and quality were hard to discern. National health spending did moderate in the early to mid-1990s, but this was more likely due to one-time gains made by employers in migrating their workers to HMO and PPO plans, gains by insurance companies using their market share and negotiating leverage to reduce hospital payments, and one-time savings from pharmaceutical firms voluntarily holding down price increases in response to threats by the Clinton Health Plan to regulate them. IDNs were also supposed to give us better outcomes, but two reports issued by the Institute of Medicine at the end of the decade highlighted alarming deficiencies in hospital quality.[19] It remains difficult to find a single data point suggesting that IDNs made a positive impact on the 1990s US health economy. Hailed as saviors, IDNs failed to generate profits for their owners, or to lower costs and improve outcomes for consumers. What went wrong? Let us count the ways.

Acquiring Physician Practices: Losing by Winning

Vertical integration with physicians is perhaps the defining feature of IDNs. The rapid divestiture of physician practices in the early 2000s highlighted the failure of this strategy.

Hospital executives have long desired to control physician practices, and for good reason. Researchers have long noted that physicians control about 85 percent of all health care spending, either directly or indirectly.[20] A solo physician who generates practice revenues of a few hundred thousand dollars also orders drugs and tests and makes referrals to specialists and hospitals. The resulting revenue stream, often in the millions of dollars, does not redound to the solo practitioner, but instead goes to the specialists and facilities where the work has been referred.

The prevailing "managerial logic" was, and still is, that whoever controls the physician controls the "pen" and gets the revenue stream that comes with it. In theory, hospitals and specialists could have directly paid physicians for their referrals. This has always been considered unethical, and it is a felony under federal Stark and Anti-Kickback statutes. Unable to directly pay for referrals, hospital executives instead resorted to other strategies to lure physicians. During the 1970s and 1980s, executives equipped their hospitals with the latest technologies and staffed them with the best trained nurses and technicians, on the theory that physicians would go to the hospitals that allowed them to make the most money for the least effort, while simultaneously providing state-of-the-art quality for their patients. Never mind that this often led to overspending, and prevented hospitals from realizing scale economies. (Because every hospital was making the same investments, no one could ramp up their volumes.) At this time, insurers largely paid hospitals on a cost basis, so it was enrollees who paid the price of this medical arms race.[21]

IDNs provided hospitals with a more direct way of controlling physicians. With the potential for millions of dollars in future revenues, hospitals fell over each other to purchase physician practices—especially PCPs who were at the top of the referral chain and were in relatively short supply. When AHERF began shaking up the Philadelphia market, some physicians reported having breakfast with representatives from one hospital system, lunch with a second, and dinner with a third. Similar scenes must have played out across the country. Some systems offered to pay PCPs $1 million or more upfront, a vast sum for the typical PCP netting $150,000 in practice income. This was on top of a guaranteed salary that matched their prior income, not to mention regular hours, freedom from much administrative work, and even payments for "goodwill" (intangible assets).

How did things get so far out of hand? Most savvy managers are familiar with the winner's curse.[22] This is the tendency for the winning bidder in an auction to overpay what the item is worth, because the winning bidder is usually the most optimistic about its value. All too often, it means that the winning bidder is overoptimistic, and the item is worth less than they thought. Experienced bidders shade their bids to avoid falling victim to the curse. The competition to acquire physician practices was nothing less than an auction, and hospital executives, fueled by their belief in IDNs, suffered from excessive optimism.

Here is how it played out in market after market, physician practice after physician practice. Hospitals "bid" against other hospitals and physician practice management companies for each physician practice by offering huge upfront payments and generous guaranteed salaries. To determine how much they were willing to offer physicians, each hospital estimated the value of the practice, based on the number and perceived loyalty of patients and the expected revenue generated through tests and referrals. Whichever hospital had the highest valuation would make the highest bid. But these valuations were merely informed guesses. The cruel implication is that the winning hospital's valuation was invariably overoptimistic. Hospital executives in the 1990s were not experienced bidders. Rather than shading their bids, they got caught up in the bidding frenzy and paid a heavy price for their naivete. With the growth of MCOs and the demise of cost-based reimbursement models, it was hospitals, and not enrollees, who were stuck footing the bill.

Even if hospitals accounted for the winner's curse, they could not escape another problem, which took the form of a prisoner's dilemma.[23] This is best explained by a highly stylized example. At the time that AHERF was expanding into the Philadelphia metropolitan area, there were roughly four thousand PCPs serving an area of about four million residents. AHERF was not the only nascent IDN in the area; three other local academic medical centers were growing their own health systems. Roughly speaking, each of the four health systems could rely on referrals from about one thousand physicians. Bear in mind that prior to IDNs, hospitals paid these physicians absolutely nothing for their patients and their "pens." In short order, AHERF and each of the other three IDNs had employed about four hundred PCPs at an average cost of about $400,000 per doctor. Each IDN still received referrals from another six hundred independent PCPs. In other words, each of the Philadelphia IDNs was receiving referrals from a total of about one thousand physicians, the same as before the acquisition spree. Only now, each IDN was out roughly $160 million, having paid for what used to come for free. In this way, integration allowed physicians to monetize their pens. The hospitals' collective loss was the physicians' collective gain.

What happened in Philadelphia was almost unavoidable. Every system thought it had to join in the acquisition battle, lest it see a sharp reduction in referrals. This is the essence of the prisoner's dilemma — what is best for each system individually is worst for the collective. Once AHERF started buying up physician practices, they all had to do so. It takes discipline for competing hospitals to agree not to start a bidding war, and AHERF lacked discipline. With everyone beating the drums for integration, AHERF would not have been alone, and it is quite possible that the remaining systems would have entered a bidding war without prodding from AHERF. Similar scenarios played out in market after market, and with seemingly every pundit advocating for integration, hospital executives across the nation fell victim to the prisoner's dilemma.

Hospitals were soon facing other costly problems stemming from the related issues of moral hazard and adverse selection. Moral hazard describes predictable yet undesirable responses to incentives, such as the excessive risks taken by executives at banks deemed "too big to fail." Moral hazard struck hospitals when they converted physicians from independent entrepreneurs to salaried employees. In their rush to outbid others, hospitals gave physicians guaranteed multiyear contracts with no productivity incentives. With guaranteed incomes, physicians did not put in the same effort to build their practices. One consulting report suggested that physicians reduced their productivity by as much as 10 percent after they became salaried employees.[24] Adverse selection occurs when the product you buy is worse than you expect. This plagues used-car markets, where every buyer fears getting a lemon; and it plagued IDNs, which found that the physicians most eager to sell their practices were the ones most eager to reduce their effort. As one study put it, "physicians hit the beach."[25]

To make matters worse, hospitals could not assure that acquired physicians would change their referral patterns and send their patients to the mother ship. The Department of Justice believed that the Stark and Anti-Kickback Statutes applied to acquisitions, and sent "Stark letters" informing hospitals that they could not reward acquired physicians for increased admissions unless it benefited patients. The DOJ loosely enforced this rule, however; so referrals did increase, but not always by as much as hospitals had planned. AHERF reportedly attracted only 20 to 25 percent of the referrals of the physician practices it employed. Contrast this with Kaiser, whose employed physicians refer nearly 100 percent of their patients to Kaiser facilities. But Kaiser had it easy. In its West Coast markets, Kaiser employed physicians straight out of residency, which meant that it did not have to overbid for established practices or try to get physicians to change referral patterns. Moreover, enrollees in Kaiser's health plans had to stay in network and use Kaiser hospitals and physicians. Kaiser had no such luxury in its new markets, and struggled to acquire practices and influence referrals. Other IDNs faced the same struggles.

This raises a question: Why didn't the newly integrated physicians change their referral and admission patterns to the degree that IDN executives believed they would? One likely reason is that physicians had well-developed referral networks that were not easily disrupted. Physicians were and perhaps still are more interested in referring their patients to colleagues they trust than in helping executives they likely have not met, and who are located in some corporate building they likely have not visited. Moreover, the referral network often consisted of colleagues from medical school or residency programs—ties built up over time.[26] Another reason is that patient and physician choice of hospitals is governed by a "gravity model" in which physicians admit to hospitals that are closest to their patients' homes and their own offices.[27] To change referral patterns, IDNs had to defy gravity. Finally, either out of respect to Stark or out of deference to the physicians they were trying to attract, IDNs did not write employment contracts specifying requirements on where to admit or whom to refer.

Misalignment

While the direct and immediate goal of physician integration was control of referrals, many IDNs sought to produce all facets of medical care and take full responsibility for the costs, just like Kaiser. The president and CEO of the Carilion Clinic in Virginia, Ed Murphy, stated his intention to be the Kaiser of the East.[28] To that end, he built a six-hundred-member multispecialty clinic. And why not emulate Kaiser? If IDNs succeeded, a pot of gold would await. To achieve this, IDNs needed to change how physicians used their pens. Most of them failed.

The odd thing is that many physicians believed in integration. In 1996, David Hartenbower, CEO of a large California IPA, shared a growing view among physicians: "We believe integration is a foregone conclusion because aligning the financial and patient-care incentives of hospitals and our physician groups is the only logical way to get us working together."[29]

Aligning incentives proved an elusive goal. Part of the problem lay in the conflicting motivations of hospitals and physicians to enter into vertical integration arrangements.[30] Hospitals sought to capture market share, increase revenues and margins, gain leverage over pricing, improve care processes and outcomes, and increase physician loyalty. For their part, physicians sought increased access to capital and technology, greater job satisfaction, increased patient service quality, and increased incomes with reduced business risk. These often conflicting objectives created an obvious management problem for hospital executives: How do you get self-interested physicians to do what is best for the hospital?

The creation of IDNs was supposed to be all about aligning incentives, a problem that was a long time in the making. Hospitals and physicians had developed separately for the past century, were independent of one another organizationally, and historically were paid out of separate buckets (physicians did not want hospitals to mediate their reimbursement). As physicians came and went, they did not necessarily care about hospital goals; and the hospitals could have hundreds of physicians on their medical staff whose goals they could not fathom. There was little basis for any trust and cooperation to develop between hospitals and physicians. And yet they were entirely interdependent. Aside from PCPs, most physicians made most of their income from patients who required hospital care. Physicians authorized or influenced most hospital spending; if they were not attuned to cost containment or quality improvement, hospitals would have a hard time satisfying the dictates of managed care. IDNs could not profit from risk contracts without reducing health spending, and this required changing the profligate ways of physicians used to the rewards of fee-for-service medicine. How exactly would IDNs do this?

Many IDNs had previously experimented with the physician-hospital organization model of integration. The early experience of PHOs should have provided a cautionary tale.[31] Recall that the PHO represented a joint venture between hospitals and physicians to attract covered lives, accept risk contracts, and thereby prepare for capitation. The PHO also represented an effort on behalf of hospitals to foster collaboration, especially by jointly negotiating managed-care contracts with members of their medical staff. Hospital executives told physicians that if they could work together to improve quality and reduce costs, joint contracting would yield higher reimbursement rates and higher profits, allowing both the hospital and its medical staff to prosper.

PHOs failed miserably at all of these tasks. As collaboration vehicles, PHOs failed to improve physician alignment with the IDN.[32] As contracting vehicles, PHOs failed to garner any managed-care contracts, let alone risk-based (e.g., capitated) contracts.[33] The result was that PHO physicians saw few new managed care patients, and came to see the PHO as a vehicle that benefited the hospital but not them. PHOs also failed to reduce costs. Survey data showed that fewer than half of all PHOs were profitable; several declared bankruptcy, while others experienced physician defections.[34]

At the root of the problem was the lack of managed-care infrastructure inside the PHO chassis. To execute all of their intended strategies, the PHOs needed to attract a new type of physician willing to drive efficiencies, while excluding expensive physicians who were unwilling to change their behavior. This meant that PHOs should try to selectively contract with higher-quality, lower-cost physicians who would populate their physician panels. This also meant that PHOs should incentivize appropriate physician behavior by using either financial incentives (such as capitation or equity participation in the PHO) or nonfinancial incentives (such as monitoring utilization, quality assurance, or clinical pathways). None of this happened.

In reality, the IDNs allowed virtually their entire medical staff inside the PHO panels; open-panel PHOs included 95 percent of physicians, while so-called closed-panel PHOs included 80 percent of physicians.[35] The PHO panels were deliberately inclusive up front, with the philosophy of "Prune later." Moreover, the criteria used to select physicians were basically the same as the criteria for joining the medical staff (e.g., medical license, liability coverage, breathing). By diluting membership, managed-care patients under the control of the PHO were distributed across a large number of physicians, thus barely penetrating each physician's practice and providing them little incentive to adjust their overall practice styles. Without risk contracts, the PHOs had no basis on which to share economic risk and reward. In the handful of cases in which the PHOs did obtain risk contracts, the risk remained at the PHO level while the physician was paid a fee for service. Finally, the PHOs lacked full-time staff in critical managed care areas such as marketing, provider relations, medical director, and finance, and often lacked information to track utilization and costs.

The result of all this was that physicians had little skin in the game, and kept using their pens as if nothing had changed. While supposedly a "joint venture," most PHOs were heavily capitalized by the hospital partner, while physician members contributed a nominal amount (e.g., one thousand dollars) and had little to gain. The joke on the street at the time was that the PHO was "little p, big H, and no O" (i.e., no organization).

Had they had the contracts, PHOs could have enjoyed some success in changing the incentives facing PCPs by offering them capitated payments. Capitating PCPs had limited potential for cost cutting, however, because the capitated rate mostly covered primary-care services, which represent only a small piece of the health-spending pie. PHOs would only succeed if they could influence specialists, who accounted for the lion's share of medical spending. One idea was for the PCPs' capitation payment to cover specialists' referrals; some HMOs were already doing this. This would encourage PCPs to serve as gatekeepers, keeping an eye out for expensive specialty care. PCPs and specialists alike pushed back against this. PCPs felt that it would put them at great financial risk, since specialist bills could be quite volatile. PCPs also lacked the information they needed to manage specialist expenses. In the absence of electronic health records (EHRs), which were in their infancy in the 1990s, PCPs could not identify specialists with less costly practice patterns, nor could they monitor and potentially influence specialist decision making. By the same token, specialists did not want the scrutiny of PCPs, who they felt had inadequate data to evaluate whether they were doing too many surgeries or ordering too many tests. Even today's EHR systems are not up to the task.

Specialists had even more cause for concern, as they viewed PHOs as an effort to eat into their hefty incomes. The specialists threatened to take their practices to other hospitals, so hospital executives treated them with kid gloves. PHOs continued fee-for-service payments and offered specialists a share of PHO profits. Simple math shows the limitations of profit sharing. A surgeon might make five thousand dollars performing a surgery that costs the hospital an additional twenty thousand. The surgeon who recommends watchful waiting instead of surgery will see only a tiny fraction of that twenty thousand dollars in shared savings, hardly enough to offset the loss of five thousand in direct billing. With little changed from their old fee-for-service incentives, surgeons kept on doing what they were doing, and PHOs failed to hold down costs. In the end, PHOs pitted PCPs against surgeons, and PCPs and surgeons against hospitals.

Most IDN executives knew about the incentive problems that plagued PHOs. Many reasoned that if joint-venture PHOs did not align incentives, formal employment arrangements would do the trick. However, these contracts were typically five-year "no cut" contracts without any productivity incentives to motivate physician behavior. Such contracts were typical, since other potential bidders for the practices (e.g., PPMs) offered similar terms. The same incentive problems quickly emerged, and IDNs had no solutions; they had no better luck than PHOs in moving PCPs to expansive capitation contracts that covered specialist expenses. IDNs continued to give specialists fee-for-service incentives with limited profit sharing. Employed physicians had even less skin in the game than physician joint venture partners. EHRs had not appreciably improved; managers and physicians alike were in the dark about physician productivity. IDN executives should have known all of this before drinking the Kool-Aid, but the pressure was on to do something in response to managed care and to keep up with evolving health care markets. Integration was the thing to do.

Unable to change incentives, IDN executives fatally focused on "structures" to integrate with their medical staffs.[36] Structures were easy to portray in PowerPoint presentations shown in the ubiquitous IDN symposia; they easily fit into the growing IDN bureaucracies being erected as "physician divisions" or "physician subsidiaries." As structures, they were also perceived to be easy to control. Unfortunately, IDN executives did not appreciate that structures fail to motivate physicians. Quite the opposite, as it is commonly observed that physicians hate bureaucracy. Moreover, the structures that were developed were not accompanied by the needed EHR infrastructure. IDNs learned the hard way the management adage "No contract language, no control," but they could not find contract language that would appease physicians while simultaneously changing their incentives. And they could not find noncontractual ways to convince physicians that they would eventually share in the good fortune of the system. Today's systems are faring only a little better, as we will see.

Multiple studies during the 1990s showed that physicians were more interested in "processes" such as involvement in decision making, a role in IDN governance, and respect from and trusting relationships with management.[37] IDNs eager for rapid growth could not easily create such processes. Instead, many executives neglected to include physicians in IDN planning and development. They rationalized this behavior by stating, "We will bring the physicians along later," not recognizing that such exclusion likely killed physician trust. Rather than align hospitals and physicians, IDNs pitted them against one another. Today's health systems are still feeling the consequences.

Physicians were not the only ones alarmed by the prospects of new incentives. It is important to remember that IDNs created a new layer of bureaucracy, one that sits above the individual hospitals. While those sitting in the IDN C-suite were looking to be the next Kaiser, the administrators of their member hospitals saw things differently. Although system executives could see the benefits of cutting back on inpatient expenses, administrators viewed these cutbacks as threats to their domains and balked at the prospect of cost containment. If the system needed to reduce beds, lay off staff, or consolidate services, so be it—as long as it happened to a sister hospital.

Just as AHERF illustrated what can go wrong when IDNs buy up too many physician practices and take on too many covered lives, the ill-fated 1997 merger of the Stanford University and University of California, San Francisco (UCSF), hospital systems shows what can go wrong when physicians and hospital administrators are not on the same page as system executives. The four-hospital Stanford/UCSF system hoped to save more than $250 million through scale and scope economies, mostly by consolidating high-end services such as cardiology and cancer care. Doctors and hospital administrators had other ideas. Hardly anyone liked the idea of relocating and working for new division heads, and the cultures at the two flagship hospitals could not have been more different: think San Francisco urban sophistication versus Stanford academia. With top physicians threatening to bolt the system, executives backed off from consolidation plans. After two years and no scale economies to show for their efforts, the system had lost nearly $100 million, most of which was due to the costs of integrating EHRs and the hiring of a thousand employees to manage the new bureaucracy. Unable to weather the worsening storm, Stanford and UCSF had a hasty divorce, and angry Stanford University trustees forced the resignation of President Gerhard Casper. Many other hospital mergers suffered from the same problem of physicians protecting their turf. This helps explain why it was so difficult for hospitals to realize economies of scale.[38]

The IDNs of the 1990s lacked the ingredients that made Kaiser and other HMOs successful: careful selection of a narrow physician panel willing to work for the HMO as much as for themselves, use of financial incentives to further motivate desired physician behavior, a closed system of care delivery and financing, and use of nonfinancial mechanisms to monitor and influence physician practice patterns.[39] We will return to these themes in chapter 5 when we discuss the performance of today's integrated systems, which we find repeating many of the mistakes of the past.

Managing Risk

If IDNs were to fully emulate Kaiser, they would need to either sell health insurance or come close by assuming full capitated risk; the challenges are similar. It took Kaiser decades to hone its expertise predicting and managing risk. IDNs did not have the luxury of time. They entered the risk-bearing market as neophytes and it showed; they experienced widespread failures with insurance products as a result of low capitalization, conflicting capital needs between hospitals and health plans, lack of expertise in actuarial science and marketing, and competition from larger and more savvy insurers.[40] By the end of the decade, hospital systems and networks began shedding their PPO and HMO products.

Lacking the business expertise to sell health insurance, some IDNs hired managers from insurers and formed their own HMOs. A few of today's successful provider-sponsored health plans (e.g., UPMC) originated in this way, but many others failed.[41] Other IDNs struck deals with local insurers that they should have run away from. It was common knowledge that about 80 percent of insurance premiums went for medical costs, so IDNs embraced a "can't miss" strategy. They took full responsibility for all medical costs in exchange for 80 percent of the premiums. If IDNs could reduce medical spending, as they widely expected, they would pocket the entire savings. It is easy to see why insurers were happy to sign these deals. Insurers could cover their administrative costs and profit margins without bearing any financial risk. It was even better for insurers, in a way that would prove the undoing of many IDNs. One of the biggest expenses for any insurer is medical underwriting, which entails forecasting the medical needs of enrollees and using those forecasts to set premiums. Under these new arrangements, insurers no longer bore any financial risk, so they could take a pass on medical underwriting. If they underestimated medical needs, the IDNs would bear the financial losses.

Risk does not go away; it is the inevitable consequence of the unpredictability of illness. Regardless of who bears the risk, underwriting is necessary for pricing. If insurers were not going to bear and underwrite risk, IDNs would have to do so. IDN executives missed this crucial point and failed to recognize the need for underwriting expertise. Most systems did have marketing departments, however. When it came to selling new insurance products, hospital marketing departments did what businesses always do: they targeted their own customers—that is, their current patients. This was a disastrous move, since these were high users of inpatient care, exactly the people whom insurers do not want to enroll if they are trying to make a buck. It was no surprise when IDNs took a beating on their risk contracts. What was surprising is that they failed to see this coming. Today's provider-sponsored plans have learned from these mistakes, with limited but more promising results.

The PPM Debacle

IDNs were not the only ones to stumble during the 1990s. An entire industry of publicly traded physician practice management firms (PPMs) such as MedPartners, FPA Medical Management, and PhyCor developed in the 1980s and 1990s. Despite predictions that they would dominate many health care markets, they collapsed in the late 1990s, taking nearly $12 billion in investor equity with them. Like their IDN counterparts, this industry suffered from exaggerated expectations and hype that should have cautioned investors—much of it fostered by the same pundits who had trumpeted the arrival of the IDNs.[42]

Like PHOs, the PPMs sought to consolidate a fragmented physician market in order to negotiate with managed-care payers on an equal footing, gain scale economies, and develop a strong managerial orientation and infrastructure, all to build solo physician offices into a coherent, organized business. They hoped to achieve further economies by sharing best practices across physician sites and through attendant organizational learning, development of a cadre of physician leaders, and use of data across sites to control practice variations.

Such hope springs eternal. In reality, PPMs tried to combine a management culture, often dominated by accountants, with a clinical culture. The former was focused entirely on acquisitions, usually through roll-ups of many similar practices to satisfy Wall Street expectations of earnings growth; the latter was focused more on clinical issues and patient care. Like the IDNs, PPMs focused on structures and deals to get physicians on board. Unlike IDNs, PPMs focused even less on building infrastructure and what to do with the physician assets once they had been acquired to make them more productive. Another problem was that in their search for growth, PPMs acquired lots of practices across the country, often boasting about the number of markets and states in which they operated. What they failed to grasp is that they needed critical mass within a given market to have any bargaining leverage with hospitals or MCOs.

Mostly, the central problem with PPMs was the unrealistic belief in scale economies and the price they paid in search of them. Like other business roll-ups, PPMs needed to keep growing to satisfy investors, but many physicians balked at the 15 percent commissions while others were nervous about turning their practices into profit centers. PPMs offered physicians $200,000 to $300,000 in upfront payments, combined with guaranteed salaries equal to their prior practice earnings. As more physicians took the bait, PPMs fell victim to the same problems of moral hazard and adverse selection that affected hospital systems. All the while, scale economies remained elusive. At best, PPMs could offer some purchasing discounts on basic supplies. Sharing of best practices never materialized, as PPMs lacked the EHR infrastructure to make it a reality.

If PPMs were to meet investor expectations for growth, they would have to throw good money after bad. As Uwe Reinhardt pointed out, the PPM sector became a giant Ponzi scheme that used later investors to pay off earlier investors—a scheme fueled by the groupthink of Wall Street analysts.[43] Wall Street soon wised up, and the flow of investment funds dried up. By 1998, PhyCor, FPA, and countless smaller PPMs were bankrupt. MedPartners left the PPM business but carried on for another decade in other sectors of the health economy.[44] The PPMs were darlings of Wall Street no more; *Fortune* magazine described them as "vulgarians at the gate" that had cost investors billions.[45] In a telling postscript, a federal court in 2006 convicted MedPartner's founder, Richard Scrushy, on multiple felony counts, including money laundering, racketeering, and bribery, in conjunction with his work at HealthSouth.

It is easy to see the risks in the PPM business model. Some were predictable; it is difficult to realize scale economies in labor-intensive activities like medicine, and more difficult to motivate employees than entrepreneurs. Others were less obvious; it was never possible to predict just how many physicians would be willing to sign up with PPMs, especially when PPMs faced unexpectedly stiff competition from a potentially worthier adversary, IDNs.

Coup de Grace

In the pursuit of scale economies and risk contracts, and desperate to become the next Kaisers, IDNs took on boatloads of debt. They felt confident that generous payments from Medicare would cover up some of their losses—until they couldn't. In 1997 Congress passed the Balanced Budget Act, and for the next few years—and for the only time since 1970—the federal government operated at a surplus. This required massive cuts in spending. With defense spending and Social Security largely off limits, Congress looked to slash the next biggest piece of the budget: Medicare. The BBA cut $30 billion over five years in spending for hospitals, with an additional reduction of $6.5 billion in medical education payments to teaching hospitals. Many states got on the cost-cutting bandwagon, lowering Medicaid fees. These cuts hit the biggest IDNs squarely in the jaw. AHERF estimated revenue losses of $30 million annually, while others saw losses in excess of $10 million. If realizing scale economies was just a matter of time, Medicare and Medicaid cutbacks meant that for many IDNs, time had run out.

A Washout

IDNs were once touted as a tidal wave that would wash away the old fragmented health care system. Hospitals embraced the movement as a strategic response to managed care, a way to increase referrals, and a step toward becoming the next Kaiser, deemed essential in a world where health care markets were inexorably evolving through "stages." Their dreams were quickly shattered as IDNs encountered a bevy of problems: competition for acquisitions, moral hazard, adverse selection, the prisoner's dilemma, balkanization of the market, and ineptitude with risk contracting and medical underwriting. While many of these problems could have been anticipated, none were effectively managed. It was as if hospital executives believed that IDNs would manage themselves. The combined weight of these management failures dragged the IDNs down by the end of the decade. The rest of the health economy sunk with them.

Most of the IDN models did little to reduce costs or improve quality. The health care cost curve bent upward rather than downward during the late 1990s and early 2000s. Quality concerns continued due to IDN executives' obsession with structures and integration rather than with doing the hard work changing what was happening in the clinical trenches. IDNs and PPMs served as vehicles for executing roll-up strategies designed to quickly build up scale with the hope of garnering managed-care contracts and exerting bargaining leverage under them. Such strategies largely failed to achieve anything except to consume a great deal of capital. The large IDNs that developed included more levels of bureaucracy, corporate offices separate from the facilities that treated patients, highly paid system executives, greater dependence on expensive external consultants, slower decision-making, an emphasis on the front-office mentality over the frontline mentality, little effort to make system changes meaningful to frontline staff, and no real efforts to reduce costs or improve quality. Broad-based health plans, such as PPOs and point-of-service (POS) plans, triumphed over closed-panel HMO plans. This meant that IDNs could not offset their development expenses, physician practice acquisition costs, and operating losses with additional patient enrollment.

As the 1990s wore on, many health plans wound down capitated contracts and hired disease management firms to carve out troublesome subsets of cost risk—particularly mental health and prescription drugs. The emergent and consolidating pharmacy benefits management companies (PBMs) served to manage prescription drug costs, contract with pharmaceutical companies, and impose protocols on health plan members. Health plans also developed their own disease management programs, or delegated them to new companies such as COR Solutions and American Healthways. These activities had the effect of bypassing the provider relationship, and attempting to manage cost risk directly.

The failure of IDNs and PPMs left a bad taste in physicians' mouths and increased their cynicism and suspicion of the corporate practice of medicine. Despite the rhetoric about aligned incentives, these efforts failed to improve physician-hospital relationships. Though some larger systems retained their provider networks, the late 1990s were characterized by dissolution of many physician-hospital contracts. As a result of the failed 1990s experiment with global capitation, few providers wanted to assume risk.

Epitaph

Through the creation of IDNs, hospitals transformed themselves from doctors' workshops, where physicians controlled the medical side and CEOs worried about reimbursements, into complex hierarchies requiring a deft management touch. Successful executives in these complex health systems needed to know how to combine contracting expertise with managerial discretion and, in the process, to command respect and trust from all key stakeholders. Many of the era's health care executives lacked these skills, and their systems floundered. Some prominent scholars and consultants, including Mark Pauly, Regina Herzlinger, Jeff Goldsmith, and the authors of this book, wrote about these dangers. It didn't matter. Once a tidal wave starts gathering force, there is little a handful of contrarians can do to stop it. As we shared our concerns with small audiences, those who proselytized in favor of integration spoke to larger and largely unsuspecting crowds.

In the short run, IDNs failed to alter the dangerous trajectory of the US health care system, and many suffered financially. They attempted to undo the damage they had caused, spinning off some of their physician practices and exiting the risk-contracting business. Yet IDNs held on to many physician practices and all of their hospitals. They found that despite everything, having a system of local hospitals provided a path to profitability. Whereas insurers seemed to have all the bargaining leverage at the start of the 1990s, the tables had turned by the end of the decade. Hospital systems now held sway; and for this, we are still paying the price.

4

THE FALL AND RISE OF
THE ANTITRUST AGENCIES

"As freak legislation, the antitrust laws stand alone. Nobody knows what it is they forbid."

ISABEL PATTERSON[1]

The rise of the IDNs posed a new challenge to the nation's antitrust agencies. Prior to 1990, most hospital mergers involved national for-profit systems such as Hospital Corporation of America, National Medical Enterprises, American Medical International, and Humana.[2] These systems provided smaller hospitals with management expertise and purchasing economies, and largely avoided vertical integration. With a few exceptions, they rarely owned more than a couple of hospitals in any one metropolitan area and owned few if any academic medical centers or other "must have" hospitals. They offered little pushback against managed care purchasers, at least in large urban markets where MCOs thrive. Despite their size and for-profit status, these national chains posed little threat to competition. If anything, the efficiencies that they brought helped to keep prices down.[3]

Although few people understood it at the time, the threat to competition would come from local nonprofits. Prior to 1990, nonprofit hospital mergers were few and far between, and most nonprofits remained independent. The IDN movement changed that, as local community hospitals merged in the name of scale economies and "systemness," and urban academic medical centers acquired suburban feeder hospi-

Table 4.1. The emergence of hospital systems: numbers of hospitals, by year

System	Home	1990	2000	2019
Advocate	Chicago	DNE*	8	12
Allina	Twin Cities	DNE	11	13
Atrium**	Charlotte	DNE	9	10
Aurora	Wisconsin	2	11	15
Banner	Phoenix	DNE	8	15
BJC	St. Louis	DNE	11	14
Cleveland Clinic	Cleveland	DNE	10	11
Inova	Northern Virginia	DNE	4	6
Memorial Hermann	Houston	DNE	9	17
Northwell***	Long Island	DNE	6	19
NY Presbyterian	New York City	DNE	11	12
Orlando Regional	Orlando	2	6	9
Partners	Boston	DNE	9	11
RWJBarnabas	New Jersey	DNE	10	15
Sentara	Southeast Virginia	3	5	12
Sutter	Northern California	6	23	25
UPMC	Pittsburgh	DNE	12	40

* DNE = Did not exist

** Formerly Carolinas Health

*** Formerly Northshore-LIJ

tals. Table 4.1 shows how nearly all of today's largest regional systems came of age during the 1990s.[4]

Most of these systems did not come close to fulfilling the dreams of integration enthusiasts. Not only had vertical integration failed to generate efficiencies, but economies of scale were proving hard to come by. Academic research showed that by the early 2000s, local systems did eventually develop one important competitive advantage: they were able to leverage their dominant positions in local hospital markets to charge higher prices to private payers.[5] This helps explain the rapid increase in medical prices that has occurred in recent years. Since 2004, price inflation has accounted for the lion's share of overall medical spending growth.[6] Insurers pass these price increases on to employers through higher premiums, and employers pass them on to employees through a combination of higher premium contributions, less generous policies, and smaller wage increases. Simply put, the creation of IDNs in the 1990s was bad news for consumers, who are still feeling the pinch two decades later.[7]

This raises the question that is the focus of this chapter: If hospital mergers have been so bad for consumers, why didn't federal and state antitrust agencies nip the merger trend in the bud? The short answer is that they tried but failed. After enjoying some initial success in the courtroom using economic arguments lifted from studies of competition in coal markets, hospitals turned the tables, successfully using the same arguments in their defense. By the end of the 1990s, the agencies had lost seven consecutive merger challenges and put further merger challenges on hold. The agencies emerged from the decade with new and winning strategies; but by that time dominant local systems were firmly entrenched, and they have remained so to this day.

Pyrrhic Victory: The Rockford Merger Case

Two federal agencies enforce antitrust laws in the health care sector: the Department of Justice (DOJ) and the Federal Trade Commission (FTC).[8] States may also weigh in on local mergers through the efforts of their attorneys general (AGs). As health care merger activity ramped up in the late 1980s, the federal agencies sprang into action. In June 1988, the DOJ filed suit to block the merger of Rockford Memorial and Swedish American Hospitals in Rockford, Illinois. The DOJ won the battle but lost the war. Thanks in no small measure to the Rockford case, it would be almost fifteen years before any antitrust agency would successfully challenge a hospital merger.

The DOJ seemed to have the facts on its side. Rockford is a midsize city (population in 1990: 144,000) located sixty miles from Chicago's northwest suburbs. Rockford Memorial and Swedish American were the two largest of three hospitals in the city, and their merger would leave Rockford with only two hospital competitors. In any other sector of the economy, a "three-to-two" merger would raise eyebrows. The hospital sector proved to be different. With the prevailing mantra that "health care is different," and the growing view that system integration was an essential part of market evolution (see chapter 2), many questioned the application of antitrust law to hospitals. The conventional wisdom at the time among noneconomists was that competition led to higher health care prices.[9] Even today, after twenty-five years of overwhelming evidence to the contrary, many observers still cling to this discredited view. The DOJ ignored the skeptics, and approached the case much like any other merger. So did the court, for better or worse.

The DOJ sued under the Clayton Act, which prohibits mergers that "lessen competition." Over the years, the agencies had successfully used the Clayton Act to block mergers in industries as diverse as banking, shoe manufacturing, and grocery retailing. Based on legal precedents, the DOJ knew that it could only win a Clayton challenge if it established that the merging hospitals had substantial market shares. As a first step toward doing this, they would have to define the market in which they competed. This proved to be far more important, and far more challenging, than anyone had anticipated.

The Horizontal Merger Guidelines and Market Definition

In August 1996 the FTC and the DOJ issued a revision of their 1993 "Statements of Antitrust Enforcement Policy in Health Care." More than half of the 142-page document was devoted to joint ventures among physicians and between physicians, hospitals, and other types of providers. At the time, many independent providers were creating new entities—independent practitioner associations (IPAs) and other types of organizations—to negotiate with health insurers. Statements 8 and 9 in the document clarified when these entities crossed the line from efforts to foster integrated care into illegal collusion. In the ensuing decades, the agencies investigated nearly fifty of these joint ventures, forcing most to unravel. Only four pages of the statements dealt with hospital mergers. Statement 1 established a safety zone for small and underutilized hospitals. Otherwise hospital mergers would be reviewed according to the agencies' horizontal merger guidelines (HMGs).

The agencies issued the first HMG in 1993. Using input from leading academic economists, subsequent revisions have established a protocol for assessing whether mergers in any industry are anticompetitive.

Importantly, both the agencies and defense attorneys and economists accept the HMGs, and judges base their decisions on them. The HMGs in place in the 1990s put a heavy emphasis on "structural analysis" of mergers. This requires economic experts to compute the market shares of the merging parties and their largest rivals, and to compare them to established thresholds. If the merging parties are too big, the merger is deemed "presumptively anticompetitive"; this is also known as the "structural presumption." Unless there are extenuating circumstances such as provable efficiencies, the court will normally reject the merger.

Economists cannot compute market shares without first knowing who is in the market. This requires market definition, a topic so obscure outside of antitrust that most of our academic colleagues in business schools have never heard of it. Yet time and again, market definition is key to the outcome of merger cases. In 2009 Whole Foods abandoned its ambitious plan to acquire Wild Oats, and arguably became a more attractive target for Amazon, when a court found that it competed in the market for natural and organic groceries rather than all groceries. Office Depot and Staples scrapped their merger plan in 2016 when a court found that they were in the business of selling office supplies to commercial customers looking for one-stop shopping convenience. This narrow definition excluded online retailers as well as mass merchandisers like Walmart. In allowing Oracle's acquisition of PeopleSoft in 2004, the court rejected the DOJ's proposed market consisting of firms selling enterprise resource planning (ERP) software targeted to large businesses, favoring a broader definition that included firms selling ERP to midmarket as well as large customers.

In no sector of the economy has market definition proved more important than in provider merger cases. Trying to understand health care competition without knowing about market definition is like trying to understand genetics without knowing about DNA. In most provider merger cases, the agencies will argue that hospitals compete in narrow markets, so that the merger concentrates power among only a handful of hospitals. The merging hospitals invariably define broad markets with many competitors, so that the proposed merger would hardly put a dent in the level of competition. It is up to the courts to determine whose definition more closely reflects economic realities. If the court finds that the market in which the merging providers compete is narrow, with just a few competitors, then the merger might seriously lessen competition and violate the Clayton Act. If the market is broad, with many competitors, then the merger probably does not materially lessen competition.

Market definition requires answering two questions: What do the hospitals sell, and where do they sell it? There is general agreement that the "what" is inpatient services. For a wide range of medical procedures, there are no meaningful alternatives to a stay in the hospital.[10] Defining the "where" has always been more challenging. Did Rockford hospitals compete only among themselves? Did they compete with hospitals throughout northern Illinois, including Chicago? If the former, then this was a three-to-two merger, and the court would likely block it. If the latter, then Rockford Memorial and Swedish American would face dozens of competitors, the merger would not materially "lessen" competition, and the Clayton challenge would fail. Needless to say, the DOJ attempted to convince the judge that the relevant "where" was closer in scope to Rockford than all of northern Illinois. The DOJ could not win its case through mere assertion; it would have to prove it with data. This is where it made a fateful decision.

Coal and Elzinga-Hogarty

If we are to understand how the outcome of the Rockford case ultimately helped health care markets became so concentrated, we need to know a little bit about coal markets in the early 1970s. The Organization of Petroleum Exporting Countries (OPEC) had recently gained control over oil markets, and America's concerns about energy policy turned inwards, leading to an intense focus on coal. The DOJ invoked the Clayton Act to force the breakup of industry giant General Dynamics, which had recently acquired Freeman Coal. The DOJ argued that there were separate regional markets for coal, and that the merger harmed competition in Illinois, where General Dynamics and Freeman were major players. General Dynamics argued that it competed in a larger regional market with many more competitors. Neither party provided much more than anecdotal evidence to support its claims.

The court sided with General Dynamics and complained, "The Government's own economist testified that he had 'concluded that the State of Illinois was the most appropriate market' *without explaining why* [emphasis added]."[11]

This was not the first time geographic market definition was critical to a merger case, yet the courts often seemed to rely more on anecdote than rigorous analysis. To fill this void, legal scholars developed new data-intensive analytic frameworks. In two research studies, Kenneth Elzinga and Thomas Hogarty developed a way to test a market definition that was highly intuitive and easy to implement.[12] Little did they know that their test would eventually cost health care consumers hundreds of billions of dollars.

Here is how the Elzinga and Hogarty (E-H) test works. Suppose you want to show that Illinois constitutes a distinct market for coal. First, you calculate the total amount of coal consumed in Illinois. Next, you calculate the amount of that coal that is produced elsewhere. Divide the first figure by the second to get the "inflow" percentage. For example, suppose that Illinoisans consume ten million tons of coal and that six million tons are mined outside the state. The inflow percentage is 60 percent. Next, calculate the fraction of coal that is mined in Illinois and consumed elsewhere. Use these to compute the "outflow" percentage. In their first paper, Elzinga and Hogarty argued that if either the inflow or outflow percentage exceeded 25 percent, then the proposed market fails the test. In this case, that would mean that the proposed "Illinois market" is too narrow to be a properly defined geographic market. The geographic market would have to be expanded until both imports and exports fell below 25 percent. In their second paper they tightened this threshold to 10 percent—yet another fateful decision.

Looking for an analytic hook it could use to dangle a market definition before a judge, the DOJ used the E-H flow test in the Rockford case. But instead of examining flows of coal, it examined the travel patterns of patients. The data showed more than 25 percent of patients in Rockford hospitals came from outside the city. This meant that the immediate "Rockford market" was too narrow to be a proper geographic market. By slightly expanding the geographic bounds to in-

clude nearby suburbs, the DOJ reduced both the inflow and the outflow percentages to nearly 10 percent. In the resulting six-hospital
region, Rockford Memorial and Swedish American were still the two
largest—big enough for the court to conclude that the merger would
lessen competition. The hospitals appealed to the US Seventh Circuit,
which upheld the lower court decision, implicitly endorsing the E-H
test. While not having the same authority as a Supreme Court decision, the Seventh Circuit decision was written by the noted antitrust
scholar Richard Posner and set a precedent for future merger cases.
Courts love precedents.

Hospitals Gain the Upper Hand

In the decade following Rockford, antitrust agencies would lose seven
consecutive merger challenges and reluctantly give approval to countless more. Seemingly shell-shocked, the agencies eventually took a
break from hospital merger enforcement before returning with a ven-
geance in the early 2000s. Given what we now know about the impact
of mergers on the health economy, it is rather depressing to look back
at these seven cases, not to mention the many deals that went unchallenged, and consider the damage they wrought.

UKIAH ADVENTIST HOSP. V. F.T.C (1992)

Fresh off the Rockford win, the FTC set its sights in 1992 on an apparent
two-to-one merger between Ukiah Adventist Hospital and Ukiah Valley Medical Center.[13] Situated sixty miles north of Santa Rosa and more
than one hundred miles north of San Francisco, Ukiah is even more
isolated than Rockford. With E-H inflows of 9 percent and outflows
of 25 percent, the FTC was fairly confident of victory—overconfident,
as it turned out. The judge thought the 25 percent outflows too high,
especially since many of those patients could have received similar
treatments in Ukiah. He ruled that the geographic market extended at
least to Santa Rosa, a market in which the two Ukiah hospitals had a
relatively small market share. With this ruling, the FTC failed to show
the structural presumption, and the case was lost. The Ninth Circuit

Appellate Court upheld the decision, adding that the E-H test should not be dispositive, though it did not mention what other evidence might be used to complement or even supplant it.

FTC V. FREEMAN (1994)

Joplin is a small metropolitan area in extreme southwest Missouri, far from any big city. In 1994 Joplin had three hospitals, and the two smaller hospitals, Freeman Memorial and Oak Hill Hospital, proposed to merge. Joplin's third hospital, St. John's Regional Medical Center, was larger than the other two combined, so the merger challenge was no slam dunk, even if the FTC could persuade the court to accept a narrow geographic market. The FTC applied the E-H test using the liberal 25 percent thresholds. This expanded the market to include two neighboring counties with two additional hospitals owned by Freeman, strengthening the FTC's case. The court was troubled by the FTC market, however. While outflows were low, inflows accounted for nearly 20 percent of admissions. The data also seemed to be incomplete. The defendants presented their own analysis using arguably richer data. Using a 10 percent inflow threshold, the defendant market contained thirteen counties and seventeen hospitals. In such a large market, the Freeman merger would not be likely to diminish competition. The court approved the deal.

US V. MERCY (1994)

While the FTC was busy in Joplin, the DOJ took on a case in Dubuque, Iowa. The closest metropolitan area of any size is Cedar Rapids, seventy miles away. When the only two hospitals in Dubuque, Mercy Health Center and Finley Hospital, announced their merger in 1995, the case against the merger seemed like a slam dunk. Once again, E-H patient flow analysis said otherwise. A geographic market with inflows and outflows below 10 percent extended far outside Dubuque, all the way to Cedar Rapids. Based on the E-H test, this was hardly a two-to-one merger. It was more like a ten-to-nine merger, and the court refused to block it. Shortly after winning the case, Mercy and Finley abandoned their merger plans. This did not placate the antitrust agencies, which were wondering what it would take to win another case.

Economists were particularly galled by the Joplin and Dubuque decisions, as these mergers looked, walked, and sounded anticompetitive. Yet the E-H test stated otherwise, due to two disturbing patterns that were emerging in health economics research. Whenever a small city was within about fifty miles of a large metropolitan area, at least 10 percent of the small city's residents traveled to the big city for hospital care. By the same token, hospitals in isolated metro areas usually drew at least 10 percent of their patients from surrounding small towns and rural communities. This meant that hospitals in these metro areas could engage in any anticompetitive conduct, including merging with each other, knowing that if sued for antitrust violations, they would be bailed out by the E-H test. E-H was also a boon to hospitals in larger metro areas, where neighboring hospitals could merge with impunity, even if that meant they would dominate a large swath of downtown or a slice of suburbia. The geographic market under E-H would encompass the entire metropolitan area, so unless the system controlled most hospitals across the entire region, they would likely be safe from prosecution under the Clayton Act. The agencies would soon learn this lesson well.

Most economists believed that E-H was painting a misleading picture of hospital competition, and they turned their attention to discovering why. Several economists conjectured that patients who traveled from small towns to big cities might not be like those who stayed close to home. Perhaps they had difficult cases, or perhaps they had family or business dealings in the big city. In other words, while one lump of coal may be pretty much like another, no two patients are alike. This hinted at a reason why E-H was poorly suited for defining hospital markets, and it would eventually open the door to new and vastly improved analytic methods that we will discuss later on in this chapter.

US V. LONG ISLAND JEWISH MEDICAL CENTER (1997)

In 1996, North Shore Health System (NSHS) agreed to merge with Long Island Jewish Medical Center (LIJ), a major academic medical center. NSHS was the largest health system on Long Island, with eight hospitals, plus a ninth on Staten Island. Its flagship hospital, North Shore Manhasset, was just two miles from LIJ, and in 1997 the DOJ sought to block the consummation of what the court agreed were "fierce competitors." Unfortunately for the DOJ, the court also cited evidence that local patients could receive treatment for relatively routine cases from several nearby hospitals, and that local patients often obtained complex tertiary care services from hospitals in Manhattan. Thus, the court rejected DOJ claims that the merging hospitals dominated any relevant geographic market.

The hospitals also defended the merger by describing the IDN wave, which had largely passed over New York, and the purported benefits of integration. They called on Dr. Michael Stocker, the CEO of Empire Blue Cross, who offered this revealing testimony at trial:[14]

Q: And tell us, what is your opinion as to the benefits of this merger?

A: I think it is a good idea. I think it would help drive down costs. I think it is consistent with what I talked about previously about integrated delivery systems. If it doesn't happen I think our chances in this area of the market are less likely that we will be able to control costs, and that's my job, to control costs.

This was 1997, so we will cut Dr. Stocker some slack for buying into the IDN mythology. One would be hard-pressed today to find a single insurance industry executive who has anything nice to say about dominant health systems (at least in public; insurers need to stay on good terms with providers). Dr. Stocker also testified that he believed prices would fall for all insurers, thus leaving the court little choice but to approve the merger.

FTC V. TENET (1999)

This one had a familiar ring to it. Lucy Lee Hospital (owned by the Tenet system) and Doctors' Regional Medical Center were the only two community hospitals in Poplar Bluff, Missouri, an isolated metropolitan area situated 150 miles south of St. Louis. Tenet wished to acquire Doctors' Regional and the FTC objected, arguing that this was, for all intents and purposes, a two-to-one merger. The court rebuffed this argument, relying instead on patient flows to conclude that the relevant market encompassed all of Southeast Missouri. Little notice was given to the geographic market proposed by the defense econo-mist—an E-H market encompassing the entire state of Missouri. By this time, academic economists were getting used to such absurdities.

CALIFORNIA V. SUTTER HEALTH SYSTEM (2000)

This one stung. While the FTC and the DOJ are the best-known anti-trust agencies and handle most of the high-profile merger cases, states can also file antitrust actions under federal and state laws, and some state Attorney General offices have active antitrust divisions. Cali-fornia is busier than most. With the FTC and the DOJ licking their wounds, it was up to the state to try to stem the growth of the high-flying Sutter system.

At the time of this deal, Sutter already operated twenty-six hospi-tals in northern California, including six in the Bay Area. As the largest hospital system in the state—not counting Kaiser hospitals, which patients could only access if they had Kaiser insurance—Sutter was on everyone's radar screen. Insurers were worried that if Sutter grew too big, it could demand higher prices than other hospitals. Sutter was not yet an eight-hundred-pound gorilla, at least not in the Bay Area, but this deal would help it put on weight.

In 1992, Sutter owned Alta Bates Medical Center in Berkeley and proposed to purchase the Summit health system, which included two Oakland hospitals, Merritt Peralta Medical Center and Providence Hospital. Berkeley and Oakland border each other in the East Bay, just over the Bay Bridge from San Francisco. At first blush the merger may have seemed like a nonissue, as there were at least twenty hospitals in the East Bay. Upon closer examination, things were not so simple. Alta Bates and the two Summit hospitals were situated just a few miles apart and were each other's closest competitor. Alameda County Medical Center was bigger than all three, but it was a government-run hospital "of last resort" that was not considered attractive by privately insured enrollees. Most of the other hospitals in the vicinity were either much smaller, highly specialized, or both.

In making its case, the state followed the DOJ and FTC playbook and presented patient flow data. The state presented inflows and outflows in a narrow market centered on the "Inner East Bay," in the range of 10 to 25 percent. The court held that a proper E-H market must have flows below 10 percent. This nearly impossible standard meant that the market was as large as the entire Bay Area. This decision opened the floodgates for further expansion by urban health care systems. Most urban systems grow piecemeal: a hospital here, a physician group there. Each acquisition makes only a small addition to the system's power, making it difficult to challenge in court. If the relevant market is the entire metro area, as the E-H test dictates, then urban behemoths like Sutter, New York Presbyterian, Advocate, and Partners still fall short of a 50 percent market share.

FTC V. BUTTERWORTH AND BLODGETT (1997)

This case is discussed out of chronological order because the outcome hinged on a very different issue. The proposed 1995 merger of the two largest hospitals in Grand Rapids, Butterworth Hospital and Blodgett Memorial, to form Spectrum Health provided a unique set of challenges to antitrust enforcers and economists. On the surface, the case resembled the others. With a population of close to two hundred thousand, Grand Rapids is the second largest city in Michigan and a local commercial hub. The closest city of any size is Kalamazoo, forty miles south with fewer than eighty thousand residents. The FTC challenged the merger, alleging that it would diminish competition in the Grand Rapids area. Butterworth/Blodgett's expert economist, Bill Lynk, used patient flow analysis to expand the geographic market. Coupling flow analysis with qualitative arguments about patient travel patterns, FTC expert Keith Leffler argued for a smaller market. For once, the court accepted the narrower market definition. Still, the hospitals prevailed.

In defending the merger, Lynk claimed that the local boards controlling these nonprofit hospitals would assure that they maximized benefits to the community and not the bottom line. Local executives testified in support of the merger, and Lynk presented research evidence showing that nonprofit hospital prices were unrelated to their market shares. To further sway the courts, Butterworth and Blodgett offered a "community commitment" to freeze prices at the current levels, with only an adjustment for inflation.[15] The Lynk evidence, support from the community, and the promised price freeze swayed the district court judge, who approved the merger.

Of immediate concern in the Butterworth Blodgett case was Bill Lynk's contention that there is nothing to fear from monopoly nonprofits. This benign view stood in sharp contrast with the theory that nonprofits are "for-profits in disguise."[16] Skeptics had some justification, since the managers of nonprofit hospitals cannot be immune from self-interest. Given that their salaries and prestige grow in proportion with the revenues and prestige of their institutions, it would be hard to resist exploiting profit opportunities. Perhaps this was purely an empirical matter, one in which the data would speak louder than the theory, and Lynk was the only one who had a voice. Not for long. Within a year of the court decision, two teams of economists published separate analyses raising serious doubts about Lynk's methods and conclusions. Today there is a strong consensus in the academic, policy, and practitioner communities that when it comes to exploiting monopoly power, nonprofits do behave like for-profits in disguise. Hospitals may save lives, but hospital managers are not exempt from the same venal motives that afflict all of us. We may as well throw doctors into the mix. After Butterworth-Blodgett, no hospitals have successfully used the nonprofit defense to support their mergers.

The court's evaluation of the evidence on nonprofits may have reflected a bit of confirmation bias, as evidenced by this statement from the opinion: "Hospitals are in the business of saving lives and managed care organizations are in the business of saving dollars."[17] This is just a variation of the old refrain, which probably occurred to more than one judge, that "health care is different" from normal markets. How often economists have put up with this statement! Of course, health care is different. Patients have poor information about price and quality. Doctors take the Hippocratic Oath. Most hospitals are nonprofit. Lives are on the line. There is no other market like health care. So what? This only implies that the textbook model taught in the first few weeks of Econ 101 does not adequately describe health care markets. Well, that textbook model describes hardly any markets. This does not mean we should throw out the rest of the book.

In the next section we will introduce some of the research showing that provider mergers in concentrated markets harm consumers. In chapter 7 we will present similar evidence about insurance mergers. As Martin Gaynor put it before Congress: "Extensive research evidence shows that consolidation between close competitors leads to substantial price increases for hospitals, insurers, and physicians." Hence the near universal consensus among academic economists: Competition throughout the health care value chain is the best way to serve the interests of consumers.

Economists Strike Back

Most health economists were suspicious of the E-H test, which seemed to have been invented out of whole cloth. For one thing, there was no particular reason for choosing a threshold of 10 percent, or any other number, other than the initial instincts of Elzinga and Hogarty. Even if 10 percent seemed like a good threshold for coal, the extension to hospitals seemed a gargantuan reach. Most importantly, it seemed to give cover to what were, on their face, obviously anticompetitive deals. Economists set their sights on destroying E-H, with a three-front assault:

1. Economists would show that there was no theoretical basis for using E-H.

2. Economists would show that E-H markets lacked face validity. They were implausibly large, stripping the method of any intuitive appeal.

3. Through retrospective analyses of consummated mergers, economists would show that mergers that had passed muster using E-H had in fact resulted in higher prices.

The economists would prevail and, for the time being at least, would change how courts view hospital mergers. This would prove to be one of those rare cases in which you could draw a straight line from the work of academic economists to a real-world policy impact.

Challenging the Theory of E-H

Antitrust economists use data and models to predict the future. Plaintiff experts usually predict that mergers will lead to excessively high concentration and higher prices. Using different data and models, defense experts predict the opposite. It is up to the court to decide which side has the better data and models and, therefore, whose predictions are more likely to bear out.

Early on, economists pointed out that Elzinga and Hogarty offered an intuitive defense of their model but little in the way of formal analysis. Based on what they wrote, it was difficult to know exactly what flows say about pricing power in markets for homogeneous goods like coal, and even harder to say anything about markets where products are highly differentiated, like health care. Nor could anyone figure out how Elzinga and Hogarty came up with their inflow and outflow thresholds. Should it be the same in all contexts? Is 10 percent the right number? A good theoretical model would have lent much needed precision, but the E-H test was based on informal arguments, not rigorous theory. It was a leap of faith for the DOJ in the Rockford case to draw precise conclusions from such informality. Unfortunately, once the DOJ jumped, there was no turning back.

In two studies published *prior to* the agency's losing streak, the FTC economist Greg Werden used formal economic models to illustrate the folly of relying on specific E-H thresholds. In titling these papers, Werden did not hold his punches: "The Use and Misuse of Shipments Data in Defining Geographic Markets" and "The Limited Relevance of Patient Migration Data in Market Delineation for Hospital Merger Cases."[18] Both papers show that even if a region experiences very low inflows and outflows, sellers may face substantial competition from other areas.[19] Werden also demonstrated the flip side: a region can have large flows, as high as 40 percent or higher, and yet a local merger could be anticompetitive. It all depended on the degree of product differentiation and transportation costs. Taken together, Werden's studies showed that almost any flow percentage could be consistent with a broad geographic market, a narrow one, or anything in between.

Face Validity

Three economists with extensive experience testifying both for and against hospitals in antitrust cases made a remarkable discovery about E-H markets. In a 2004 publication, Ted Frech, James Langenfeld and Forrest McCluer revisited the Sutter case.[20] They observed that there is considerable leeway for implementing the E-H test, both in the choice of the flow percentage thresholds and in the choice of methods for expanding the market in order to get below the thresholds. They tried several alternatives and always reached the same conclusions: "These methods pick up large numbers of hospitals and large geographic areas, leading to E-H markets that are truly breathtaking; they are approximately 400–600 miles long and 200 miles wide." Had they used a stricter 10 percent threshold, the E-H market likely would include almost the entire state. In this worldview, Sutter's East Bay hospitals compete with hospitals from the Oregon border to Mexico. No one could take this seriously, except the economists who worked on behalf of merging hospitals, and the judges who were prisoners of precedent.

Taken together, these academic studies represented an all-out assault on the E-H test. If the assault succeeded, E-H would be dead. This was not necessarily a good thing. Without a replacement, antitrust enforcement would return to pre-Rockford days, with market definition based on assertions rather than hard facts. It was one thing for economists to tear down E-H; it was now their job to find something better. Two teams of economists were well on their way to doing just that.

Retrospective Merger Analyses

Like weather forecasts, economic predictions are better than nothing, and some predictions of antitrust economists are pretty good. Few would argue that monopolists charge higher prices than competitive firms, all else equal.[21] How good is E-H as a predictive tool? To answer this question, several teams of economists performed retrospective studies. They examined mergers that had passed muster using the E-H test. If E-H is any good, none of these mergers should have resulted in unusually large price increases.

It is not easy to perform these studies, for the simple reason that hospital pricing data are hard to come by. Government agencies collect data on charges, which are not the actual prices negotiated by insurers.[22] If researchers were to put E-H to the ultimate test, they would have to find a way to get pricing data. Cory Capps and David Dranove published one of the first retrospective studies.[23] They obtained actual transaction prices from "one or more insurers in several markets." These included markets in which the agencies had reviewed and/or challenged mergers. In every market they studied, the mergers passed the E-H test. If the test was valid, the mergers should have had no impact on prices. In fact, all but one merger resulted in statistically significant price increases. Showing the caution that is typical of academic publications, Capps and Dranove conservatively concluded: "The results presented here suggest that on balance, recent court rulings on hospital consolidations may have been overly permissive." Translated, they were saying that E-H is wrong and that the courts should stop using it!

While academics had to appeal to insurers for data, the FTC had it easier. They could subpoena pricing data directly from insurers and providers. Using these data, economists published studies of three consummated hospital mergers. One study looked at the Alta Bates/ Summit deal that expanded the Sutter system, concluding that "Summit's price increase was among the largest of any comparable hospital in California, indicating this transaction may have been anticompetitive."[24] A second study examined the merger of Dominican Hospital and Community Hospital in Santa Cruz, a deal reviewed by the FTC and given a pass, despite appearing to be a two-to-one merger. The authors found that "controlling for casemix, input prices, and other cost- and demand-side characteristics, our results suggest that both hospitals raised prices in the aftermath of the transaction."[25] So did the closest rival, Watsonville Community Hospital. A third study of a merger in coastal North Carolina found mixed effects on prices.[26] With apologies to Meat Loaf, two out of three ain't good.

A New Approach

By the early 2000s, economists had effectively destroyed patient flow. Looking for an alternative, they began exploring "structural models" that took seriously the unique institutional features of different markets. Rather than use a model lifted from an undergraduate textbook or graft a model of coal market competition onto hospitals, economists developed models that recognized the unique role played by health insurers. In the textbook market, it is the consumer's price elasticity that constrains seller pricing. In managed care markets, prices are determined in *negotiations* between insurers and providers. Consumers are largely insensitive to any seller price differences, provided that the sellers are in-network. Thus, all the pricing action occurs during the negotiations.

This raises a fundamental question: What might give providers the upper hand in negotiations? Would providers be powerless if some local customers traveled elsewhere for care, as suggested by flow analysis? Cory Capps, David Dranove, and colleagues argued that the "silent majority" of consumers who do not travel may have a strong preference for local access, even if others do travel.[27] This strong preference would force insurers to negotiate with local providers. If the local provider market was concentrated, providers would have the upper hand. They dubbed this the "silent majority fallacy," a term that would loom large in the next big merger case, where Kenneth Elzinga would testify against the use of his own method.

The FTC took note of all these developments, and met with many of the economists whose work cast doubt on Elzinga/Hogarty. Combining the insights from Capps et al. and others with the knowledge gleaned from retrospective studies, the FTC reentered the antitrust arena, and this time emerged victorious.

Evanston Northwestern

In 2003 the FTC relaunched its campaign to assure competitive hospital markets when it brought action to undo the recently consummated merger between Evanston Hospital and Highland Park Hospital that created Evanston Northwestern Healthcare (ENH). The FTC knew that through precedent, E-H had become the de facto test for market definition. The E-H test would show that ENH competed in a gigantic Chicagoland geographic market, with dozens of competitors. If the court relied on E-H, this would be the eighth consecutive defeat for the agencies. Despite this, the FTC felt confident of victory.

Following the script that had proved so successful, ENH presented evidence about patient travel patterns, confident that the court would embrace a broad geographic market. The FTC surprised everyone by arguing that the relevant geographic market was extremely narrow, encompassing just a small slice of Chicago's North Shore suburbs. In this market, ENH was dominant. To defend the market definition, FTC's expert economist Deborah Haas-Wilson drew on recent research and argued that competition among hospitals occurs in two stages.[28] In the first stage, hospitals compete to be included in insurers' networks. In the second stage, hospitals within networks compete to attract patients. Prices are determined in the first stage, through provider-insurer bargaining. If a merger increases the bargaining leverage of providers, they will command higher prices.

Several fact witnesses, including representatives from health insurers, argued that they could not successfully market their networks to local employers unless they had at least one major North Shore hospital—either Evanston or Highland Park, and preferably both. Prior to the merger, they could credibly threaten to drop one of these hospitals from the network as long as they included the other. This threat gave the insurers the upper hand in negotiations. Once the hospitals merged, insurers could no longer make this threat, and hospitals would increase their prices. In current terminology, the combined ENH would be a "must-have" hospital system and thus would be able to price accordingly.

This wasn't just ivory tower speculation. It was backed up by facts on the ground. ENH had already merged in 2000; the deal came during the time when the agencies were licking their wounds and letting all mergers go through. The FTC had kept their eye on this deal, however, and had subpoenaed pricing data from the hospitals. Haas-Wilson analyzed the data and showed that after the merger, ENH had raised its prices significantly faster than peer hospitals in the area. Although ENH's economics experts quibbled over exactly which data to use, they ultimately reached a similar conclusion.[29]

In going after ENH, the FTC had two objectives. The first was to undo the merger. The second was to get a court to agree that the E-H test was flawed. The retrospective pricing evidence was the first step toward meeting these objectives. As far as undoing the merger, the facts on the ground about pricing trumped any speculation about market definition. The court heavily relied on the pricing in ruling that the merger violated section 7 of the Clayton Act. As far as the E-H test, if it was valid, then ENH competed in the vast Chicago-area market, and we would not have expected ENH to raise prices after the merger. Yet ENH did raise prices, by at least 10 percent relative to peer hospitals. The E-H test had made the wrong prediction, just as it had in the published retrospective studies. If E-H was consistently making wrong predictions, the courts would look for other models, making other predictions. The FTC also had an ace up its sleeve. It called on Kenneth Elzinga, who cited the silent majority fallacy in testifying that the E-H test was not appropriate for hospital markets.

Both the District Court and the Seventh Circuit Appellate Court ruled in favor of the FTC. The FTC could have ordered the dissolution of the ENH merger. Instead, in what many considered a political decision, the agency allowed ENH to remain intact. To limit the exercise of market power, the FTC required Evanston and Highland Park Hospitals to enter into separate contracts with insurers, with no sharing of pricing data. Many economists were skeptical that this would meaningfully limit ENH's prices. Without access to confidential contracting data, such skepticism remains. ENH has subsequently added one neighboring hospital, and even tried to merge with another suburban health system—a story we save for chapter 7.

Too Little, Too Late

ENH gave the FTC a framework for future merger challenges. It would attack the validity of the E-H test and discuss the importance of two-stage competition. It would get payers and employers to testify about the importance of filling geographic niches in provider networks, and the dangers of allowing hospitals to merge into must-have systems. As the FTC moved from retrospective analyses to challenging proposed mergers, it lacked one luxury it enjoyed in ENH. It would not have retrospective pricing data. If the FTC were to predict the impact of proposed mergers, it would need a new analytic tool.

Once again, academic economists provided the answer, with two independent teams reaching nearly identical solutions. Robert Town and Greg Vistnes were first to publish, offering a structural economic model that emphasized the price negotiations between insurers and hospitals.[30] Cory Capps, David Dranove, and Mark Satterthwaite formulated a similar model that was a bit more intuitive and easier to use.[31] They developed a measure, which they called willingness to pay (WTP), that could be computed from data on hospital admission patterns. WTP captures a hospital's ability to negotiate higher prices, and the extent to which two hospitals can command higher prices than they can when they are separate. If the hospitals attract similar patients—from the same locations or with the same illnesses—then a merger will have a bigger impact on prices. FTC has used WTP in all recent hospital merger challenges, with great success, blocking local mergers in northern and southern Virginia, Toledo, Rockford (again!), north suburban Chicago, and central Pennsylvania.

The Chicago and Pennsylvania cases happened nearly simultaneously. Both deals were announced in 2015 and wound their way through the courts in 2016. For a while, both cases left many wondering if the courts were easing off of antitrust enforcement. In the Chicago case, the region's largest system, Advocate, sought to merge with NorthShore University Health, the new name given to an ever-growing ENH. Although the merger would enhance their already dominant positions in the northwest and north suburbs respectively, the district court judge overseeing the case rejected the FTC challenge, questioning the very legitimacy of the horizontal merger guidelines. The Pennsylvania case featured the merger of the two largest systems in Harrisburg, the Penn State Hershey Medical Center and PinnacleHealth. Although this merger would seemingly turn the combined system into a monopoly juggernaut, the district court judge in this case also rejected the FTC challenge, this time citing high patient inflows. For the moment it seemed as if the two judges had turned back the clock on antitrust enforcement.

The moment was fleeting. The FTC appealed both cases. A three-judge panel of the Seventh Circuit Appellate Court unanimously reversed the Chicago decision, essentially finding that the lower court judge's criticisms of the HMGs were illogical and unfounded. When the panel ordered the district court to reopen the case, Advocate and NorthShore saw the writing on the wall and abandoned the deal. A three-judge panel of the Third Circuit Appellate Court similarly reversed the lower court decision in Penn State/Pinnacle. In their decision, the panel admonished the judge for accepting flow analyses that had been so widely discredited by academic economists.

Physician Mergers

At the same time that hospitals were merging with hospitals, physicians were also consolidating—but in their own quiet way. There were few actual mergers of large medical groups. Instead, groups grew organically and incrementally over time by adding on more practitioners and specialties.[32] Any large-scale mergers of physicians with other physicians were brokered by the PPMs described above, or by hospitals acquiring medical groups.

Antitrust agencies did little to block the initial merger wave, for reasons best left until chapter 7. Where physicians ran into trouble with the agencies is when they negotiated prices collectively but otherwise retained their financial independence. IPAs were frequently behind this, negotiating managed care contracts on behalf of their member physicians. In recent years several prominent medical groups and IPAs have actually merged, though the member physicians remain independent.[33] Hospitals also have served as brokers. For example, the ENH merger described above also entailed a merger of the ENH Medical Group and Highland Park Hospital's IPA.

The problem is that the Sherman Act clearly prohibits "conspiracies in restraint of trade," which is an apt description of what happens when independent physicians jointly set prices. In more than seventy cases over the past forty years, the FTC has charged independent physicians and other health care professionals with conspiring to restrict competition. FTC action ramped in the late 1980s, and the agencies devoted fifty-five pages of the 1996 Statements of Antitrust Enforcement Policy in Healthcare to "physician network joint ventures." In the ensuing decade, the FTC successfully challenged forty-eight conspiracies among independent physicians.

Mesa County IPA provides a good example. In the late 1990s, this IPA comprised 85 percent of all physicians in Mesa County in western Colorado. Like the rest of the country, western Colorado was being swept up in the managed-care revolution, with rapidly growing enrollments in HMOs and PPOs. Mesa County IPA offered its members a vehicle for contracting with health plans, setting both fee-for-service and capitated rates. The IPA thought it was contributing to the revolution, but it overstepped its bounds when it refused to deal with insurers that balked at its terms and refused to allow its members to negotiate separate contracts. The FTC accused Mesa County of violating the Sherman Act; the IPA accepted a consent decree banning these practices. Similar scenarios played out all across the United States, from Alamogordo, Austin, and Berkeley to Tahoe, Tulsa, and Yakima—and seemingly across all specialties, from anesthesiology to urology.

The FTC did not dismiss the potential benefits of coordination among independent physicians. The statements include guidelines for physician negotiations with MCOs. Independent physicians could fix prices and refuse to deal with payers, provided that they took meaningful steps to either clinically integrate (e.g., use care guidelines, EHRs, coordinate care), financially integrate (e.g., use alternative payment models like capitation), or both. The AMA broadly publicized these issues to its members, and many physician groups sought guidance from the FTC in the form of "advisory letters" before taking collective action with insurers. The FTC authorized only a small percentage of these efforts, and rightly so. Few groups were able to demonstrate successful integration, however, either clinically or financially. Such was the case with the ENH Medical Group–Highland Park IPA, which the FTC successfully challenged. When it came to transforming health care delivery through IPAs and alliances, physicians talked the talk but did not walk the walk.

Pyrrhic Victories

The FTC had a mixed record of antitrust enforcement in the 1990s. The agency blocked several blatantly illegal physician price-fixing schemes, but failed to convince the courts to stop hospital mergers even when they seemed to create monopolies. The FTC used new economic models to turn the tables in the 2000s. With the recent appellate court decisions in Penn State / Hershey and Advocate / North Shore, the FTC has proven that it can consistently block hospital mergers in concentrated markets. It may be too little, too late, however. By 2000, health systems were firmly entrenched and there was little the FTC could do to break them apart. The FTC victories did not stop systems from expanding. As we describe in the next chapters, systems have found new ways to grow while staying just beyond the reach of antitrust enforcers. In the process, they have expanded into today's megaproviders.

5

HISTORY REPEATING: THE SECOND WAVE OF INTEGRATION

"It's déjà vu all over again."

YOGI BERRA

During the 1990s, hospitals tried to perform alchemy. By creating integrated delivery networks (IDNs), they hoped to transform a fragmented and costly health care system into one that was aligned and efficient. Instead, they mostly transformed black ink into red. It seemed that the magic of integration was gone. A decade later, everyone believed that the magic was back.

As we described in chapter 3, many factors contributed to the demise of IDNs, none more than the failure to change how physicians used their "pens." IDNs spent heavily to acquire physician practices, but did not give them the incentives or information needed to change their practice patterns. They instead relied on bureaucratic structures that only served to alienate physicians. Hospitals also tried to add structure to relationships with independent physicians, through an alphabet soup of strategic alliances. While adding costly layers of management, these alliances were impotent and empty as vehicles for contracting. Unable to make these relationships work, hospitals put a hold on physician integration. A few hospitals engaged in widespread divestment. Others tried to make a go of it, correctly reasoning that most of the costs were sunk, and optimistically reasoning that they would eventually be able to wring economies out of their growing systems.

IDN forays into risk contracting proved equally inept. Recall that in the fourth and final stage of market evolution, providers would organize into integrated systems that accept full financial responsibility for their patients' medical expenditures. Hospitals failed to appreciate that this would oblige them to assume the role of health insurer, which required a very different skill set. The dream of population health management was also put on hold.

One part of the IDN strategy proved successful for hospitals, if not for anyone else. By merging with erstwhile competitors, hospitals gained valuable bargaining leverage against managed care organizations (MCOs).[1] This gave them the revenues they needed to offset their losses from physician integration and risk contracting, and to fund further growth. Hospital executives were smart enough to stick with a winning strategy, and the horizontal merger wave continued unabated until the FTC victory in the ENH case. Even after ENH, hospitals continued to consolidate local markets in Illinois, Ohio, Virginia, and elsewhere, only to be rebuffed by the courts. Hospitals have since learned to avoid the most obvious anticompetitive mergers, and have expanded outside their immediate home markets. Partners expanded into southern Massachusetts, UPMC into western—and, more recently, central—Pennsylvania, Sutter spread across northern California, and so forth. Throughout the decade, the number of hospital systems, the number of hospitals in a system, and the percentage of community hospitals in systems all continued to grow.

By 2010, hospitals had begun reassembling the vertical components of IDNs. They ramped up physician acquisitions and installed costly electronic health records (EHRs) to try to control the physician's pen and maximize reimbursement for what they did. They pursued many of the same structures witnessed in the 1990s, and also developed a new type called an "accountable care organization" (ACO). ACOs put hospitals back into the business of managing risk, offering the opportunity of capturing a portion of any savings they generated, while giving back a portion of any excessive costs. Hospitals could choose how much risk they wanted to bear; larger rewards entailed larger risks. Some hospitals jumped back into the deep end of risk management, offering their own provider-sponsored health plans.

To many observers, hospitals have gone "back to the future" with strategies, graphics, and buzzwords reminiscent of prior efforts. Was this a reaffirmation of the 1990s' strategies to develop IDNs, this time armed with new tactics (ACOs) and tools (EHRs)? Or was this a mindless retreading of old and discredited strategies? Were IDNs prospering by creating value for their patients, or were they merely finding new ways to exploit market power? To some extent, the correct answer is "all of the above." We are more than a bit pessimistic, as we explain in the next three chapters. The evidence for market power is stark and depressing. The evidence for value creation is mixed and troubling. All is not yet well in the health care world.

Doppelgangers

By 2010 the industry was repeating many of the integration themes, both horizontal and vertical, that were so pervasive in the 1990s. Table 5.1 shows that many of the important concepts central to health care in the 1990s have their 2010s counterparts.[2] Capitated payment models morphed into risk-contracting models. Cost-effective care is now value-based care. Integrated delivery networks are bigger than ever, but nowadays we talk about their close cousins, ACOs. And for some reason, perhaps to mask past failures, we have replaced the lofty "iron triangle" (access, quality, and cost containment) with a new trinity, the "triple aim": patient experience (which includes access), population health (which includes quality), and cost containment.[3]

Why does history seem to be repeating what was regarded as unsatisfactory the first time around? One can make the case that integration was an idea before its time, lacking only the infrastructure and supporting systems to make it work. With EHRs, real-time patient information, data analytics, and other innovations, the health system might be poised to implement the desired changes that were heretofore elusive. There are also important differences in the "prime mover" of integration. The private sector initiated and implemented the 1990s transformation, with the government as a passive observer, particularly after the failure of the Clinton Health Plan. This time around, the Affordable Care Act of 2010, popularly known as "Obamacare," pro-

Table 5.1. History repeating

1990s concept	2010s doppelganger
Capitation	Risk contracting
Cost-effective care	Value-based care
Integrated delivery network	Accountable care organization
Hospital-physician alliances	Hospital-physician networks
Physician practice management	Physician equity models
Health maintenance organizations	Narrow provider networks
Iron triangle	Triple aim

moted the formation of ACOs, and with it came a potential financial windfall for integrated providers.

Another view is that there has been a single twenty-five-year trend toward integration, albeit with a brief hiatus. Three factors may have contributed to the hiatus. First, provider systems lost more money than they expected, and needed time to regroup. Second, the Balanced Budget Act of 1997 prolonged their misery by sharply cutting Medicare hospital reimbursements. Finally, systems may have needed time to renegotiate managed-care contracts for each newly acquired provider. It was not until the early 2000s that systems had completed these renegotiations and fully began to reap the financial rewards of their growing market power, which they plowed back into further acquisitions.

A less charitable explanation draws on the insight of John Kenneth Galbraith.[4] Galbraith wondered why investors repeat the mistakes from prior financial crashes, seemingly having learned nothing from the past. He concluded that old ideas were respun by newer generations of managers and policymakers every twenty years or so. As the prior generations who were chastened enough not to repeat those ideas died off or retired, new generations came in believing they had discovered something afresh. Health care executives may have fallen victim to the same trap, putting old wine in new bottles.

Perhaps all of these interpretations have some element of truth. Which interpretation one prefers likely reflects one's ideology and ingrained level of cynicism. As academics who have studied IDNs since their inception and produced a healthy chunk of research revealing lackluster performance, we lean toward the "market power" and "old wine in new bottles" explanations while still trying to keep an open mind. We actually admire some IDNs (see chapter 10) and have written articles with their executives. In the remainder of this chapter we will describe the startling resurgence of megaproviders and offer some of the most likely reasons for their growth. In the next chapter, we will document that big systems have failed to constrain health spending—if anything, they are more expensive—and we will offer some explanations for these distressing facts. In the last chapter on the topic, we will examine how powerful megaproviders continue to evade punishment by the antitrust agencies.

Highlighting the Trends

The integration movement that began in the mid to late 2000s may have seemed reminiscent of the 1990s, but there was a clear difference in one respect: there was a lot more going on in the new millennium. Integration was apparent everywhere one looked, taking place on a much bigger scale and at a faster pace.

HOSPITAL MERGERS

With a few exceptions such as AHERF, the IDNs of the 1990s survived with their hospitals intact. Hospitals took a break from horizontal mergers in the early 2000s, when the number of annual deals fell from a merger wave of over one hundred to just thirty-eight in 2003. Merger activity has since rebounded, with more than one hundred mergers every year since 2014.

HOSPITAL-PHYSICIAN INTEGRATION

Many, if not most, hospitals quickly discovered that they would be unlikely to pay back the huge upfront bonuses doled out during the bidding wars for physician practices. With most practices incurring operating losses, enthusiasm for further acquisitions quickly waned.

This was an overreaction. Once hospitals accounted for the profits generated by physician referrals, they realized that some specialties and practices were making operating profits for the system. Integration therefore reached a kind of stasis, where hospitals were neither acquiring nor divesting physician practices.

Instead of acquiring more physicians, hospitals turned their attention to making their existing practices more profitable. Learning some lessons from the 1990s, hospitals rewrote contracts to exclude goodwill payments and guaranteed salaries, and to include productivity clauses. The prevalence of "integrated salary models" (ISM, the label used by the American Hospital Association to denote physician employment) in hospitals increased thereafter, as did the number of hospital-employed physicians, especially after 2003. While the number of employed PCPs slowly increased, the number of employed specialists took off. While hospitals mainly acquired PCPs in the hope of winning referrals, they started employing specialists to exploit changes in Medicare payment rules that hurt physician reimbursement, as we will explain in the next chapter.

At the same time, a new class of employed specialist emerged: the "hospitalist."[5] Specialists work full-time in the hospital to cover specific patient services (e.g., an "intensivist" to cover the intensive care unit; a "laborist" to cover the maternity unit; a "surgicalist" to cover the operating room) and to provide broad oversight of the treatment of inpatients admitted by community-based physicians. Today, there are an estimated forty-four thousand hospitalists, and hospitals employ a third of them.

Why did hospitals become interested in "hospitalists"? One reason was to cater to the needs of admitting physicians in the community who did not want, or financially could not afford, to leave their busy office practices to see their patients in the hospital. A second reason was the perceived need to have one in-house physician to help coordinate the patient's care and journey through the institution. An influential 2002 case study in the *Annals of Internal Medicine* bolstered support for hospitalists.[6] Subsequent research evidence on their effectiveness is mixed, however: there is no consistent impact on quality of care or patient satisfaction, mixed evidence on cost, and a minor effect on shortening lengths of stays.[7] One study suggests that hospitalists may reduce inpatient costs by facilitating early discharge, only to see patients spend even more money after they leave the hospital—a situation reminiscent of the "quicker but sicker" problem that plagued the DRG system in its early years.[8] Still, belief in hospitalists remains strong.

INTEGRATION INTO HEALTH PLANS

After a long withdrawal, hospitals are again taking a dip into the waters of full risk contracting. Between 2010 and 2017, at least seventeen hospital systems started their own health plans, although many are barely profitable and at least six have already closed.[9] This is partly an extension of the risk taking inherent in ACOs, but mainly is a reaffirmation of the view, widely held in the 1990s, that vertical integration will lower costs. Through their own provider-sponsored plans, hospitals hope to fully reap the benefits of integration efficiencies.

INTEGRATION INTO POST-ACUTE CARE

Hospitals have returned to the post-acute care business by developing both vertical and virtual linkages with hospices, long-term care facilities, and home health agencies. Both strategies resembled the 1990s IDN effort to prepare for risk contracting and to develop the continuum of care.

PAYER INTEGRATION WITH PHYSICIANS

Not to be outdone, private insurers are vertically integrating into the physician practice business. With thirty thousand physician employees as of spring 2018, UnitedHealthcare and its Optum division is the largest employer of physicians in the United States. With its recent merger, Aetna/CVS has also combined insurance and medical practice under one roof. We will have much more to say about these arrangements in chapter 9.

PHYSICIAN PRACTICE MANAGEMENT

Since the time of the PPM "crash and burn" in the late 1990s, private equity firms have reentered the business. This time around, they are targeting hospital-based practitioners in such areas as emergency medicine, radiology, and anesthesiology, rather than primary care.

Causes of Integration

A confluence of factors has led to the resurgence of health care integration. While one can point to a single government policy—the failed Clinton Health Plan—as a catalyst for integration in the 1990s, integration in the new millennium is perhaps the unintended consequence of no less than seven federal policy developments that bolstered forces already at play in the private sector.

PUBLIC SECTOR DRIVERS

In an effort to address the problem of enforcing the sustainable growth rate formula in Medicare payments, during 2004 and 2005 the Centers for Medicare & Medicaid Services (CMS) pivoted to "pay for performance" (P4P) as an alternative strategy to reduce spending by rewarding providers when they achieved quality benchmarks.[10] P4P programs were increasingly implemented by both public and private payers to control hospital and physician costs. Hospitals responded by trying to work with their physicians to simultaneously reduce cost and improve quality. As with efforts to deal with managed care pressures in the 1990s, hospitals believed that the best way to change the behavior of physicians was to employ them.

At the same time that CMS was offering bonuses for efficiency, the Deficit Reduction Act of 2005 reduced Medicare payments by 20 to 40 percent to cardiologists, orthopedists, and medical oncologists for in-office imaging procedures.[11] The financial impact motivated many of these specialists to seek safety in hospital employment. A few years later, the "meaningful use" provisions of the HITECH Act of 2009 incentivized physicians to incorporate EHRs into their practices, initially to gain extra reimbursement, and later on to avoid financial penalties. EHRs were very expensive, however, costing as much as $1 million or more for a small medical group practice. While HITECH provided physicians some financial assistance in purchasing EHRs, hospitals that employed physicians could help them offset the costs of EHR adoption and the associated overhead. So, in a sort of reversal from the 1990s, physicians began seeking out hospitals, and not the other way around. As a result, the price of acquiring physician practices plummeted.

Another important driver of integration resulted from an obscure change to an obscure payment calculation. When an independent physician bills Medicare (or most private insurers) for a given service delivered in their medical office, they receive a single fee meant to account for their time and office expenses. When a hospital-employed physician provides the identical service, even in an identical office, they submit two bills: one for "professional fees," meant to cover physician costs, and one for "technical fees," meant to cover overhead. Historically, the total reimbursement to hospitals has exceeded the total paid to independent physicians, even for the same service performed in the same location. The purported reason for this is to help hospitals defray their higher overhead costs. (Note that this reason casts doubt on claims that hospitals enjoy scope economies.) This meant that if a hospital acquires a physician practice, payment rates increase formulaically, and at faster rates over time.[12] In 2008, CMS changed the survey it used to measure costs, with the result that the differential between hospital and independent physician payments mostly increased, with especially large increases in some specialties such as cardiology and radiology. This made it that much more attractive for hospitals to employ physicians. A recent study shows that this change in surveys and the financial windfall it created are responsible for about 25 percent of all recent hospital acquisitions of physician practices.[13] CMS has taken some steps to close this loophole, but has not gone far enough.

Finally, the ACA expanded hospital eligibility for the 340B Drug Discount Program, which allowed hospitals to purchase drugs at a 25 to 50 percent discount. Hospitals now had an incentive to employ community-based oncologists who obtained 70 to 77 percent of their revenues from chemotherapy drugs.

ACCOUNTABLE CARE ORGANIZATIONS

If there was any doubt about the need to integrate, a key provision of the ACA helped put it to rest. And for once, IDNs would have to cut costs in order to fully reap the benefits. The ACA created a new organizational model for providers, called accountable care organizations (ACOs). ACOs can be formed by hospitals, physician groups, or even independent physicians. There are several key ingredients to the ACO program.

1. CMS assigns Medicare enrollees to ACOs. While the assignment rules are complex, they essentially boil down to this: CMS assigns Medicare beneficiaries to an ACO if they receive the majority of primary care from providers who belong to the ACO. This means that beneficiaries do not choose an ACO; CMS chooses it for them.

2. During the year, CMS pays hospitals and other providers using its standard fee schedules. At the end of the year, it compares the actual spending for patients assigned to ACOs—including expenses incurred by providers who do not belong to the ACO—against expected spending based on patient demographics and prior health status.

3. The ACO can receive "shared savings" reimbursements if its actual spending comes in below the expected level. At the start of the year, the ACO can choose one of several risk-bearing tracks. ACOs that want to dip their feet into the waters can agree to a small percentage of any savings. More ambitious ACOs will receive a larger portion of the savings if they agree to return to CMS a portion of any excessive costs. The actual rules are much more complicated, and have recently changed to include "advanced payment" and "next generation" models with even stronger financial incentives.

4. ACOs receive pay-for-performance bonuses based on successfully hitting dozens of quality metrics.

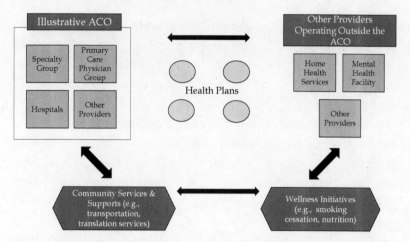

Figure 5.2. Boundaries of the ACO. Adapted from the Dartmouth Institute for Health Policy and Clinical Practice.

Sensing a chance to reap financial windfalls, providers have eagerly formed ACOs, with nearly one thousand ACOs responsible for the costs of caring for more than thirty million Americans. There are few restrictions on who can participate, and a wide array of provider organizations offer them. Figure 5.2 depicts the organizational boundaries of a typical system-led ACO.[14] The ACO is a nexus of providers, services, and initiatives, such as wellness. Some are offered by the integrated system, shown in the upper left of the figure, while others are secured by contract, as shown on the upper right and below. Remove the hospitals from the upper left and place them with the "other providers" on the right, and you have a physician-led ACO. In practice, ACOs range from fully integrated systems to virtually integrated networks and strategic alliances.

As IDNs learned in the 1990s, risk bearing can be a difficult business. By handling most of the difficult financial transactions, CMS has minimized the administrative burden of risk bearing and, in the process, has done us all a favor. ACOs might have been a catalyst for hospital-based megaproviders to further extend their stranglehold; but instead, physician-sponsored Medicare ACOs and joint-venture ACOs between independent physicians and hospitals both outnumber hospital-sponsored ACOs.[15] The largest ACOs, however, are usually organized by large IDNs.

In promoting ACOs, CMS had one other trick up its sleeve. In the 1990s, HMOs fell victim to the managed-care backlash against perceptions of substandard quality and restricted choice. To avoid the HMO stigma, CMS chose a very different name and used some important new rules. Start with shared savings: critics contend that HMOs have a financial incentive to skimp on care; ACOs have only a fraction of those incentives. Or take a look at access to care: HMO enrollees must choose from providers in mostly narrow networks. In principle, Medicare beneficiaries have free choice of providers both within and outside the ACO's provider network, though ACOs make every effort to keep them from going outside. Finally, HMO members know they are enrolled, whereas Medicare beneficiaries have no idea they have been assigned to ACOs. For all these reasons, there is little chance of a backlash against ACOs.

ACOs may be little more than "HMO-lites"—less restrictive, with half the incentives. But they are politically viable HMO-lites, and they have been very successful in the marketplace. After just seven years, ACOs already serve half as many Americans as HMOs. Unfortunately, the evidence we present in the next chapter shows that they are not saving any money. The authors of this book fully support the experiments in incentives embodied both by HMOs and ACOs. For now, however, most ACOs are sucking wind.

From the Deficit Reduction Act to the ACA, a decade of federal rules and regulations have catalyzed the new IDN movement in two distinct ways. Congress and CMS intended that many of these policy changes would correct unfair payment practices, but instead they had the unintended consequence of promoting physician-hospital integration. Other changes, especially the formation of ACOs, more directly rewarded cost cutting, and they all promoted the further growth of powerful megaproviders. It is all reminiscent of the late Harold Demsetz's two systems of belief about the rise of monopolies.[16] Under the "self-sufficiency" theory, efficient firms outcompete their rivals and dominate markets, to the benefit of all. Under the "interventionism" theory, monopoly power arises from government intervention, to the benefit of no one except the monopolists. As we explain in the next chapter, thus far the interventionism theory carries more weight.

Private Sector Motivators

Neither the self-sufficiency theory nor the interventionism theory might have gained much traction were it not for the encouragement of health policy gurus, who once again viewed IDNs as the elixir for all that continued to ail the health economy. In 2008, the policy analyst—and head of CMS, under President Obama—Don Berwick and his colleagues published an influential paper titled "The Triple Aim," which called on providers to simultaneously address population health, per capita cost, and the patient's experience of care. Hospitals jumped on the bandwagon and treated Berwick as their guru. The president-elect of the American Hospital Association proclaimed in 2016, "It's all about the triple aim." Hospitals believed that integration was necessary to achieve the triple aim, even though hardly anyone could tell you what "population health" meant (health status), how Berwick actually measured it (life expectancy and morbidity levels), or what hospital executives could actually do about it (not much).

Second, between 2006 and 2008, researchers at the Commonwealth Fund and elsewhere began to herald the twofold "transformation" of the health care system: (1) move away from fee-for-service (FFS) to alternative payment models, including pay-for-performance, bundled payment, episodes of care, and capitation; and (2) move away from fragmented delivery sites (e.g., solo practice of physicians, freestanding hospitals) to more integrated provider systems such as IDNs, ACOs, and Kaiser-like IHOs.[17] This transformation was not only advocated; it became normative, and was already underway. The ACA was a huge step in this direction, due to its encouragement of ACOs and its new methods of paying them. This transformation was alternatively billed as the movement "from volume to value," where value was defined as quality divided by cost.[18]

The transformation narrative was repeated so often that everyone believed it was true, inevitable, and a positive development. Part of the narrative involved moving from less integrated to more integrated models of health care delivery. Of course this meant bigger size, bigger networks of hospitals and physicians, and bigger bargaining power,

all cloaked in the name of having the ability to manage risk and population health. Thus, integration now served as *the* vehicle to achieve
the triple aim, and to achieve a host of lofty goals. Of course, no one
bothered to articulate the process by which forming megaproviders
increased one's life expectancy or made one feel better. As in the IDN
wave of the 1990s, there was an element of "proof by assertion": saying
it so made it so.

Provider Justifications for Integration

Even without a push from the ACA and policy wonks, hospitals had
many reasons to renew the integration wave. Some hospitals foresaw
shortages in certain specialties and thought it best to employ physicians in these fields, rather than risk being short-staffed. Other hospitals partnered with physicians in an attempt to mitigate competition
with entrepreneurial physicians who set up competing imaging facilities and ASCs. Hospitals also hired star physicians to lead "centers of
excellence," in an effort to distinguish themselves from competitors
and embrace the growing movement in pursuit of quality care.

By and large, the most important justifications for integration
echoed those from the 1990s. Hospitals sought to increase their share
of the growing outpatient market, to increase their revenues through
risk contracting, and to increase their leverage over payers. They still
believed that employment would increase physicians' loyalty and alignment. In further echoes of the past, many health-services researchers
again claimed that physician-hospital integration might confer several benefits.[19] These included the efficient production of hospital services, improved communication and coordination of care across sites,
development of an in-network continuum of care, aligned incentives,
preparedness for new payment models and organizational models,
reduction in wasteful spending, and ability to make investments in
population health. As in the 1990s, the goals espoused by researchers
often bore little resemblance to the motivations of providers.[20] And as
we will explain in the next chapter, the goals espoused by both often
had little basis in economic and organizational realities.

The Elusive Goal of Physician Alignment and Engagement

As part of this effort to integrate, hospitals now began talking about "engagement" with physicians to transform care delivery—for example, to reduce waste and variation, and to embrace care protocols and evidence-based medicine—and thereby demonstrate "value" to payers.[21] It was not clear what "engagement" really meant, or how it differed from the "alignment" sought during the 1990s integration effort. Researchers have noted that, like alignment, the concept of engagement is broad and indistinct."[22] Some researchers view it as the opposite of "burnout"; others tailor the definition to specific activities such as reducing disparities in treatment styles, coordinating care, or improving safety. Most definitions are reminiscent of alignment, including physicians' commitment to the enterprise, willingness to exert effort, emotional attachment, trust, decision-making voice, conflict resolution, motivation to perform, ability to suggest and implement improvements, and willingness to advocate for the organization in which they work. Some organizations, like Press-Ganey, tried to separate the two terms by distinguishing physician alignment (perceived strong partnership, or connection with the organization's leadership) from physician engagement (appraisal of the work environment, emotional experiences, and attachment to workplace).[23] The literature conflicts on whether alignment leads to engagement or vice versa.[24]

Not only was there confusion about what the outcomes of integration were, but we soon discovered that the types of integration between hospitals and physicians were also incredibly varied. The Health Systems Integration Study (HSIS) of the 1990s talked about three types of integration in "organized delivery systems": functional, physician-system, and clinical.[25] The first type applied only to the hospitals in a system and the degree to which they standardized their back-office functions (e.g., accounting, finance, human resources). The other two types applied to physicians and their relationships to hospitals.

In the 2000s, research muddied the waters by specifying *three* types of physician-hospital integration: nonfinancial, financial, and clinical.[26] The "nonfinancial" mechanisms spanned a whole array of hospital efforts to market their physicians to patients and beef up their practices, all without monies changing hands. There was nothing new here; hospitals had been doing these things for years. The "financial" mechanisms involved economic transfers from hospitals to physicians, and spanned a wide array of arrangements; one study listed nearly fifty ways that organizations may contract with and compensate physicians.[27] Nowadays, many health care executives treat integration like a checklist. (Create medical executive positions? Check. Offer an imaging center through a joint venture with radiologists? Check. Use hospitalists? Check. And on and on and on.) This is no way to manage an integrated system; the next chapter will develop this theme.

Expectation: Things Will Be Different This Time Around

In his 1936 novel *The Last Puritan*, the philosopher George Santayana famously warned, "Those who cannot remember the past are condemned to repeat it."[28] This has become a catchall phrase used to condemn nearly any effort to dredge up a previously failed strategy. It is not always true. What once failed might now succeed, provided that the surrounding circumstances are conducive. If there is any hope that 2010s integration will succeed where 1990s integration failed, then some things must have changed. The good news is that there have been important changes, allowing us some room for optimism.

For starters, hospitals have learned some lessons from their past failures. Hospitals that eagerly embraced risk contracting in the 1990s enjoyed the return to fee-for-service medicine in the 2000s, and did not return to risk contracts until ACOs offered them shared savings with minimal downside risk. Hospitals have also largely managed to avoid overbidding for physicians. One reason for this is that hospitals are a lot better at valuing practices. They also take more time to woo physicians, thereby avoiding the bidding frenzies that once drove practice values through the roof. The lack of an active private equity market vying for physician practices (at least until recently) has also helped.

Perhaps the most important change is in the attitude of physicians. In the 1990s, hospitals had to pay premiums to pry physicians away from their private practices. A decade later, physicians were eager sellers. They had grown tired of ever-increasing administrative hassles in dealing with payers, they were fed up with malpractice premiums, and they were facing big expenses for EHRs. Demographic changes in the medical profession further worked in favor of hospitals. An ever-increasing number of women entering the profession, combined with a growing number of households with two working spouses, meant that more physicians were looking for regular hours and guaranteed incomes.

There were now enough potential physician-employees to satisfy the growth objectives of every system, and bidding wars became a thing of the past. Moreover, with the majority of physicians now working as employees, the threat from adverse selection (in which only the worst physicians seek employment) has abated. It seemed as though hospitals could avoid the worst losses associated with physician employment. What was less clear was whether they turn a profit when the physician's desire for income stability stood in conflict with the hospital's desire to get into risk contracting, or the physician's desire for normal hours stood in conflict with the hospital's drive for volume. Simply put, how could hospitals manage risk without pushing that risk down onto physicians? This is yet another key issue we will address in the next chapter.

Looking around the health care landscape, the biggest change by far is the improvement in information technology, embodied by the widespread adoption of EHRs. With 20-20 hindsight, we can see why the absence of EHRs doomed the systems of the 1990s. How could one integrate care without an electronic record that could track the patient's movement across the sites of the IDN? How could PCPs direct patients to cost-effective specialists in the IDN without knowing who those specialists were? They couldn't. Just having the different providers who cared for the patient under one administrative structure did not do the job. EHRs promised to solve this problem. This was not lost on health care executives at that time; even AHERF had been heavily investing in a first-generation EHR.

Perhaps no single element of today's health care systems has received as much attention, funding, and enthusiasm as the EHR and its various components, such as clinical decision support systems (CDSS) and computerized physician order entry (CPOE). CDSS might increase quality and reduce costs by improving physician decision making, reducing medication errors, and facilitating the prevention and use of evidence-based recommended therapy. CPOE can reduce costs and improve quality by reducing medication error rates. The entire EHR could be used to evaluate the performance of individual providers and to develop recommendations for improvement.

While there were other important differences between the 1990s and 2010s, EHRs are supposed to be a game-changer, the "silver bullet" that solves all IDN problems.[29] Armed with advanced EHRs, hospitals could operate disease registries, improve care coordination, perform data analytics, and thereby advance population health management. The presence of EHRs helped to resurrect the promises at the heart of integration: "coordinated care," "seamless continuum of care," "patient transitions," and "the right care at the right time at the right place." Independent providers could neither afford to invest in EHR systems (which cost upwards of $20 million for a hospital, or $1 million for a physician group practice, plus annual maintenance costs) nor assure interoperability with EHRs used by other providers, even EHRs purchased from the same vendor. Megaproviders could at least pay for them. Armed with a system-wide, fully interoperable (at least in theory) EHR, surely things would be different this time around. How did we know? Everyone said it was true.

Today's megaproviders believe they have an additional advantage. Unlike in the 1990s, they have developed infrastructure (to what actual degree is unknown) to accept alternative payment methods, including bundled payments and shared savings, and to work with incentives to lower costs. This infrastructure requires systems to push high-level incentives down into the organization, so that individual physicians and other decision makers share the same goals of the triple aim as does the organization. As we will discuss in the next chapter, today's systems have struggled with finding the best way to achieve this alignment.

Whole Lotta Shakin' Going On

It is obvious that things are really cooking in both the payer and the provider worlds during the new millennium. There is so much integration happening on so many fronts that surely things will now be different. Yet the more things change, the more they stay the same. While many managers have learned from past mistakes, and while innovations like ACOs and EHRs mean that today's systems have opportunities unavailable to 1990s IDNs, it is difficult to find systematic empirical evidence that today's systems are bringing us any closer to the triple aim than yesterdays' systems brought us near the iron triangle. The next chapter will tell the sad tale of unmet expectations.

6

INTEGRATION IS STILL FAILING

"Success is stumbling from one failure to another with no loss of enthu-siasm."

WINSTON CHURCHILL[1]

The 1990s effort to integrate hospitals with hospitals, hospitals with physicians, and hospitals with health plans led to some rather unspec-tacular results. One would have hoped, and perhaps even expected, that hospital integration in the new millennium would demonstrate some impact on cost and quality. Hospitals now have powerful finan-cial incentives to succeed, thanks to accountable care organizations and the gradual spread of alternative payment models. Hospitals also have new tools for influencing the physician's pen, including electronic health records, data analytics, and new contracts to better align in-centives. Perhaps integration really is the magic elixir, and it just took more time than expected. We are still waiting. Dozens of academic studies have assessed the impact of integration and, for the most part, the news for consumers is all bad. Prices are up, quality is unchanged at best, and the quest for efficiencies continues. To quote the old Wendy's commercial: "Where's the beef?"

Impact of Hospital Mergers

The academic literature has virtually nothing good to say about the impact of hospital mergers. In 2012, the Robert Wood Johnson Foundation summarized the research evidence as follows:

> Hospital consolidation generally results in higher prices. This is true across geographic markets and different data sources. When hospitals merge in already concentrated markets, the price increase can be dramatic, often exceeding 20 percent.[2]

A comprehensive 2018 study echoes these findings, reporting that prices at monopoly hospitals are 12 percent higher than prices in markets with four or more competitors.[3] The RWJF study also reports that lower levels of hospital competition are tied to lower quality. A 2020 study in the *New England Journal of Medicine* finds that mergers have no impact on two key quality measures, and a modest negative impact on patient satisfaction.[4]

The evidence on whether mergers reduce costs is mixed. Some studies suggest that hospitals do achieve savings when they consolidate under a single license, which is not the situation in most systems. The most favorable recent academic study of hospital mergers finds that they sometimes reduce the costs of supplies, likely through purchasing discounts.[5] These savings are mainly apparent when national hospital systems such as Community Health Systems and HCA acquire small, mostly rural hospitals. Mergers between competing hospitals do not appear to generate cost savings.[6] Even when mergers do reduce hospital costs, this is of little comfort to patients who still end up paying higher prices.

Hospital mergers may also affect referral patterns, though not always in ways that benefit patients. One study found that after UPMC acquired suburban hospitals, the system's flagship hospital saw an increase in referrals of profitable commercially insured patients from the affected suburbs, while rival Allegheny General Hospital saw an increase in referrals of less profitable patients.[7] We doubt whether UPMC is the only tertiary care hospital to design its feeder network in this way.

The Impact of Physician-Hospital Integration

The research evidence on physician-hospital integration is more volu-
minous and more nuanced than the evidence on hospital mergers,
though at the end of the day it is nearly as depressing. Integration advocates claim that it will lead to more efficient use of medical services.
That hasn't happened. Vertical integration of hospitals with physicians
often leads to more hospitalizations, especially when physicians are
salaried.[8] Some studies also indicate that employment of physicians
leads to more outpatient tests, outpatient procedures, and postacute
services.[9] There is even evidence that patients of employed physicians
are treated at higher-cost, lower-quality (i.e., low-value) hospitals, and
receive a higher use of low-value services.[10] There do not appear to
be any care coordination efficiencies flowing from physician employment. Moreover, there is some evidence that physician productivity
declines after employment.[11]

Advocate Health System, the largest IDN in Chicago, provides an
excellent case study. When it comes to creating an IDN, Advocate
seems to do most things the right way. It was an early adopter of the
most advanced EHR system, and it makes sure that its physicians are
on the same EHR platform. It offers performance bonuses to physicians, and includes physicians at the highest levels of corporate decision making. For everything it gets right, Advocate has not generated
consistent savings under the Medicare ACO program. What makes
Advocate an especially interesting case is that of its six thousand affiliated physicians, only about one thousand are employees. Yet Advocate
is hard pressed to find meaningful differences in performance between
the two sets of physicians.

As with hospital mergers, integration of hospitals with physicians
has mixed effects on quality. On the one hand, vertical integration is
associated with higher levels of several process quality measures, including health promotion activities, EHR adoption, use of chronic disease registries, and use of reminders for both patients and physicians.[12]
On the other hand, vertical integration is associated with lower levels
of several other metrics, including avoidable hospitalizations and in-
appropriate ER visits.[13] There is no consistent impact on mortality rates

and patient safety.[14] None of this says that integrated systems have low quality. What the research does say is that integration does not lead to higher quality; these physicians and hospitals would probably deliver care that is every bit as effective if they had remained independent. Maybe it would have been a bit higher in some cases, maybe lower in others, but there would be no systematic difference.

Overall, the evidence on physician-hospital integration is unambiguously ambiguous. It seems that, for every study that finds that integration works, there is another that finds the opposite, and a third that finds it makes no difference. To make matters worse for those looking for answers, very few of the studies we have cited have proper statistical controls, so that measured differences in performance may reflect unobserved differences in the types of patients who are treated by integrated providers, or in the types of physicians who choose to become employees. In other words, most of these studies are prone to biases, but we cannot determine the direction of the biases.

There are fewer studies of the effect of hospital-physician integration on prices. Fortunately, the methods are usually free from bias and the results are clearer. The most prominent recent study examines what happened after hospitals across the country acquired hundreds of physician practices.[15] On average, physician prices increased by 14 percent. Total medical costs also increased, and there is no evidence that acquired physicians saved money elsewhere by reducing unnecessary utilization. A separate case study found that when two IDNs acquired three multispecialty physician groups in the Twin Cities, average physician prices rose by 32 to 47 percent.[16] The researchers found limited evidence of quality improvements, and cautioned about disruptions in referral patterns.[17]

As we discussed in the last chapter, some of the price increase stems from the payment of higher technical fees when physicians are employed by hospitals. Some of it is also contractual. The typical hospital has more bargaining leverage than the typical physician, and the large megaprovider has a lot more leverage, which the hospital uses to negotiate higher prices for services performed by its employed physicians. Thus, the moment the hospital employs the physician, the fee automatically goes up. Research confirms that physician prices increase more when the acquiring hospital has more market power.[18]

Impact on Clinical Integration

The thirty-thousand-foot view of integration provided by academic research on cost and quality leaves much to be desired. The view on the ground, where we look at the steps that organizations are taking to effect change, is not much better. If integrated systems are to transform health care delivery, the payoff will come from enhanced clinical integration, which is supposed to lead to speedier and more accurate diagnoses, eliminate duplicative services, and improve handoffs of patients from one provider to another. Integrated systems are supposed to engage in disease management, implement unified electronic patient records to facilitate decision making, track patient utilization throughout the year to promote population health, and track provider decision making to provide feedback and incentives for quality improvement. While these are all promising ideas, systems are not translating them into reality. Research shows that vertical integration has had little systematic impact on the extent of clinical integration.[19] Nor are patients in vertically integrated systems more likely to perceive that they are receiving "integrated" care.[20]

Why do we not observe elements of clinical integration in the presence of physician-hospital integration? One explanation is that hospitals are focused more on growing patient volume than on changing clinician behavior or practice patterns. Another explanation is that physicians enter into integrated arrangements in order to escape market risk and volatility. For both of these explanations, the reason we do not see clinical integration is that it was never the reason for physician integration in the first place. Advocates of integration argue that the infrastructure necessary to support clinical integration, especially interoperable EHR systems, requires more time. True believers are always patient.

It is always possible that physician-hospital integration actually inhibits clinical integration. Several studies show that many desirable attributes of physician group culture (e.g., collegiality, organizational identity, trust, autonomy) suffer under bureaucratic structures and ownership by hospitals.[21] The attenuation of such group attributes can be tied to lower quality of care.[22]

Impact on Medical Group Performance

Despite charging higher prices, physician-hospital integration is associated with poorer physician group performance and larger group operating losses.[23] During the 1990s, analysts commonly observed that hospitals lost an average of one hundred thousand dollars per acquired physician per year.[24] Most of these were PCPs working under guaranteed salaried contracts with no performance incentives. More recent data suggest that hospitals' operating losses on physician practices have widened well beyond inflation. One survey of nearly two hundred hospital-owned multispecialty group practices found that over 90 percent were losing money, with an average annual loss of nearly two hundred thousand dollars per physician.[25] Conversely, physician-owned groups reported a small net profit. More recent data suggest the losses on hospital-owned multi-specialty groups continue to rise.[26]

Why have the hospital-owned groups incurred such large losses compared to physician-owned groups? The answer does not appear to be the different financial environments they face. Recent survey data gathered by the Medical Group Management Association (MGMA) indicate that physician-owned and hospital-owned groups identify (1) financial management as their greatest challenge and (2) the same financial issues as most challenging.[27] These issues include dealing with rising operating costs, preparing for reimbursement models that place a greater share of financial risk on the practice, and managing finances with the uncertainty of Medicare reimbursement rates. Groups of different size also cite the same financial challenges.

Upon employment, hospitals assume responsibility for physician salaries and benefits, malpractice coverage, office staff salaries and benefits, office space rental and equipment, and infrastructure investments needed to fulfill regulatory billing requirements. Hospitals also offer physicians higher compensation to induce them to join employment relationships, and may pay them the same compensation regardless of the patient's insurance status. This model of physician compensation is linked to higher resource use.[28]

Another possible explanation lies in the structure of the two sets of group practices and their management. MGMA Cost Survey data reveal that hospital-sponsored groups have a higher percentage of primary care physicians who generate less revenue than specialists. Such groups also have more Medicaid patients, provide more charity care, and treat fewer commercially insured patients. Crucially, physicians salaried by hospitals exhibit 16 to 29 percent lower productivity. Collection rates are negligibly lower for employed physicians. These facts suggest that when it comes to acquiring physician practices, today's hospitals are suffering the same problems experienced by hospitals in the 1990s: poor incentives associated with salary guarantees and perhaps adverse selection of less productive physicians.

In another repeat of the 1990s, hospitals in a hurry to integrate may exercise less due diligence in rapid practice acquisitions. Hospitals may lack good information about the acquired group's clinical and financial performance due to the lack of robust information technology inside the practice.[29] Beyond due diligence, hospitals may overpay physicians to avoid losing them to competing hospitals. To secure the transactions, hospitals may also acquiesce to the physicians' desire to remain in their current locations and retain their current staffing and systems.

MGMA Cost Survey data further reveal that while the top quartile of hospital-owned groups (in terms of overall performance) resemble physician-owned groups in many aspects of staffing and operations, they both differ substantially from the bottom three quartiles of the hospital-owned groups.[30] Lower-performing groups employ fewer support staff per full-time equivalent physician, provide less square footage of space per physician, and have more branch clinics with fewer physicians per clinic. Such differences in management and operational efficiency may explain the financial performance differences between hospital-owned and physician-owned groups. Many hospitals actually operate their "groups" as dispersed collections of solo and partnership practices where the only things that really change after acquisition are the nameplates on the doors, the source of the physicians' and office staff's W-2s, and, of course, the billing rates.

The Impact of Physician-Hospital Integration on Hospitals' Financial Performance

The data reviewed above suggests that hospitals lose money on their physician employees. The situation may be even worse than it appears. Physician-related costs incurred by hospitals extend beyond the direct cost of employment to encompass physician subsidies for taking calls, administrative fees for serving as medical directors, and higher compensation under professional service agreements. For hospital systems with many such employed physicians, their physician operations are generating nine-figure operating losses.

There is another side to the story. Most hospital systems report that employing physicians does not sap their financial health.[31] The discrepancy between physician-level performance and system-level performance may be partly explained by accounting. Hospital-owned physician groups have much lower revenues from ancillary tests (e.g., lab, X-ray) and nonprocedural items (e.g., infused drugs, durable medical equipment).[32] This is because the hospital accounts for those revenues separately. Much of the economic impetus for salaried employment of physicians by hospitals has been to charge for ancillaries under the hospital's banner, increase these so-called "ancillary revenues," and generate a significant fraction of hospital profits. At the same time, employed physicians are more likely to refer their patients to their hospital employers, generating potentially massive financial windfalls for their systems. Looking at it another way, systems could not afford not to own physician practices, lest they lose out on their share of referrals.

The only problem with this "referral defense" is that, with competing systems all buying up practices, the resulting balkanization of the market leaves every system with roughly the same market share as before, only now they are paying the price. This too is a replay of the 1990s. There is nothing systems can do about it except try to figure out how to minimize the losses.

The Bottom Line

Fueled by even higher prices, systems are enjoying record-high revenues. Sutter Health had operating revenues of $12.4 billion in 2017, up 4.8 percent since 2016 and a whopping 41 percent since 2010. Partners Health saw 2017 revenues grow by 7 percent to $13.4 billion, and UPMC saw revenues grow by 16 percent to $15.6 billion. This growth is partly the result of higher prices, and partly the result of continued expansion: more hospitals, more physicians, and more outpatient facilities for those physicians to practice in. If you think that every abandoned bookstore and electronics shop in your neighborhood has been converted to an immediate care facility or diagnostic imaging center, you are not alone. An estimated 20.5 million square feet of new medical office buildings were constructed in 2018, shattering records set in 2016 and 2017.[33]

The executives who run these huge systems reap substantial rewards. According to Medicare cost reports, more than thirty systems pay their CEOs more than $5 million annually. While these salaries are in line with those paid to CEOs of comparably sized, publicly traded businesses outside health care, the hospital systems are nearly all nonprofit. Someone is clearly prospering. We pay for all these sky-high system revenues and executive salaries through higher insurance premiums, higher out-of-pocket payments, and higher taxes (both general revenue and social security taxes). While it is difficult to precisely connect system revenues and consumer expenses, one carefully conducted study estimated that the increase in hospital-employed physicians alone translated into a 12 percent increase in premiums for patients covered under the California ACA health insurance exchange.[34]

Even as systems continue their decade-long buying spree, they have enough money left over to post solid profits. Through much of the 2010s, the typical system enjoyed operating margins of 3 to 4 percent, which is well above the long-term average for hospitals. Some systems enjoy margins in excess of 5 percent, which rankles state regulators who question why highly profitable "nonprofit" systems should enjoy tax breaks that amount to 6 percent of revenues.[35] Ironically, the fact that all the megaproviders are nonprofit may contribute to their growth, and not just because they avoid paying property and other taxes. We can only speculate, but it seems that in order to limit their profit margins and thereby avoid bad publicity and punitive taxes, nonprofits may be "burying their free cash flows" by spending their excess revenues on further expansion.

All is not rosy for megaproviders, however. As fast as revenues have increased, expenses have increased even faster.[36] From 2015 to 2017, average system operating margins dropped from 4.2 to 2.6 percent.[37] Systems have failed to develop cohesive physician organizations, standardized staffing, and standardized operational support functions (e.g., purchasing, supply chain, scheduling systems, and centralized office locations). They have failed to contain expenses for electronic health records, the formation of accountable care organizations, and the operation of physician practices.[38] Fitch analysts expect continued deterioration.[39] This will give systems incentives to further increase prices if they haven't already pushed them as high they can. Unless systems can figure out how to make integration work, consumers might be paying even more for their failures.

The "Black Box" of Integration: Physician Alignment as the Missing Ingredient

So how are we to explain twenty-five years of mediocre performance (at best!) in hospital-physician integration? Integration advocates often work with an implicit causal model in which hospital-physician integration fosters physician alignment with the organization which, in turn, helps promote collaborative efforts to improve quality and reduce costs. It all sounds so easy. The problem is that no one seems to know what alignment is, no one can show that integration fosters alignment, and no one can show that alignment leads to better quality or lower costs. Aside from that, the causal model makes sense.

PHYSICIAN ALIGNMENT

Researchers and managers alike have for decades talked about the importance of physician-hospital alignment. Researchers have devoted countless pages in academic journals to describing how best to achieve alignment, and whether integration is necessary for it. Yet there is no clear understanding of what alignment means. Many people discuss alignment without defining it; and when they do, the definitions differ. Alignment has alternately been described as

- shared purpose, shared vision, shared goals, and shared efforts to achieve them;

- cooperation, collaboration, and trust;

- consistent financial incentives;

- psychological attachment and identification with the hospital;

- commitment and organizational identification — being a "good citizen"; and

- shared governance.

A handful of studies empirically measure alignment using physician surveys. The dimensions studied, and some of their items, include organizational identification, affective commitment, teamwork, co-operative behaviors (e.g., controlling cost and improving quality), trust, voice in decision making, conflict resolution, perceived partnership, continuance commitment (willingness to continue admitting patients and to exert effort to help the organization), citizenship (participation in committees), physician autonomy, and quality of support services.[40] Alignment seems to be a catchall term to describe any and all of the above.

NEW KID ON THE BLOCK: PHYSICIAN ENGAGEMENT

Over the past fifteen years, integration discussions also mention "physician engagement" and "physician empowerment," two terms often used interchangeably.[41] Like alignment, the concept of engagement is broad and imprecise, and most definitions of engagement resemble alignment: commitment to the enterprise, willingness to exert effort, emotional attachment, trust, and so forth. Physician burnout is the opposite of engagement and, according to some health system CEOs, burnout is a "national health crisis."[42] Evidence does suggest that physicians are quite pessimistic regarding the practice of medicine, that such pessimism is widespread and extends to value-based payment, and that dissatisfaction can be tied to characteristics of the medical practice (e.g., financial stability of the practice, administrative burden of practice management, time and complexity of using EHR).[43]

RESEARCH ON ALIGNMENT AND ENGAGEMENT

From the 1990s IDN gurus until today, advocates of hospital-physician integration have put the blame for high costs and subpar quality on fragmentation—every provider out for themselves. Integration is supposed to end fragmentation by promoting alignment. If only it were that easy.

Research suggests that integration only marginally improves physician alignment with the hospital. One study found that salaried physicians show a marginally higher identification with their system.[44] Another study reported that any alignment between hospitals and employed physicians declines over time.[45] Still other researchers found that hospital acquisition of medical groups negatively impacts most dimensions of group culture (e.g., collegiality, organizational identity, trust, autonomy).[46] One recent study indicates that physicians report greater alignment with independent physician-led practices than with system-led practices.[47] Another recent study summed up its findings this way: Hospital-physician alignment is only a matter of degree, is somewhat tepid, and may occur along some dimensions but not all.[48] This is not a ringing endorsement of integration.

What explains the historical lack of alignment between hospitals and physicians? One reason is the historical tension between hospitals and medical communities—something that has persisted for nearly a century.[49] Medical professionals and health care executives have profoundly different cultures and norms. Many physicians are suspicious of the motives of managers with MBAs and MHAs, while managers believe that physicians are ignorant of economics and care little about efficiency. As a result, both groups often close ranks when, in fact, they have a lot to learn from one another. Such suspicions are fueled by hospital efforts to infringe on the physicians' traditional turf: outpatient care. A second reason is that hospital executives sometimes feel that the integration process ends when physicians have signed their contracts, while sometimes ignoring the hospital processes that physicians find most dissatisfying. This gives physicians further reason not to trust hospital management.[50]

The lack of trust manifests itself in a variety of ways. We frequently speak before groups of physician leaders, mostly department chairs or leaders of clinical or research teams. Nearly all of them work in large integrated systems, and nearly all of them are frustrated, leaders in name only, with little sense of how they are contributing to the success of their organizations. To get a better sense of how well they feel integrated into their organizations, we always ask the same questions: Suppose you were to invest your time and effort into an initiative that will improve the performance of your system. Maybe you assist the information technology team in finding ways to make the EHR more user-friendly. Or perhaps you develop a new protocol for dealing with morbidly obese patients. Whatever the investment, how many of you feel that you will be recognized by the senior leadership of the system? How many expect to receive additional compensation, or funds to enhance clinical practice and/or research? How many believe that virtuous behavior today will lead to rewards tomorrow?

We are still astonished by the virtually unanimous negative responses. Unless physicians do something that is singled out in their contract—serving as department head, for example—then they can probably forget about any tangible rewards for their efforts. A recent survey of physicians by Deloitte supports our experiences.[51] The majority of physicians receive productivity-based bonuses, and nearly half are rewarded for measurable quality of care indicators. Only 18 percent of respondents are rewarded for contributing to their hospital's teaching, research, or community activities; and only 7 percent are rewarded on the basis of the "satisfaction of other physicians." Compensation seems to be entirely based on a checklist of a few easy-to-measure aspects of medical practice. Do anything that is not on the checklist, and the most the physician can expect is a pat on the back. The result is that physicians feel unappreciated and have some reluctance to go out of their way to help their hospitals. It is as if the turf wars that divided hospitals and physicians in the mid-twentieth century have never ended. This is not how things work in other businesses, especially where professional services are key to success. We will return to this problem in the final chapter of this book.

Once again, surveys back up our experiences. Physicians are demoralized and pessimistic about their role within large systems. Many say they plan to retire early rather than endure life in an unappreciative bureaucracy.[52] The three most satisfying attributes of their practices—patient relationships, protection of the health of individuals, and intellectual stimulation—do not seem to be emphasized in integrated or employed relationships. Instead, systems ask their physicians to become team leaders and help administer complex organizations, two attributes that physicians rank as least satisfying. It is hard to imagine how hospitals might develop "alignment" among such a disillusioned group, particularly given the historic lack of trust between the two parties.[53]

In the 1990s, physicians sold their practices to hospitals because they received offers that were too good to be true. Today, they enter into these unhappy relationships out of financial necessity. Physicians face a revenue squeeze from Medicare and Medicaid, and pricing pressure from managed-care organizations. At the same time, the cost of medical practice keeps going up. Added to all of this, a new generation of physicians seeks predictable hours of work. Integration has helped physicians gain economic security and job stability at the cost of their clinical autonomy and many of the practice attributes they find most satisfying.[54] They are not aligned with their hospitals. They are not satisfied with their jobs. It does not bode well for the integrated system.

Over the longer term, both hospital and physician partners may find these relationships further strained by a double whammy: continuing cuts to Medicare and Medicaid, and a gradual shift in enrollments to these public programs. While hospitals will continue to squeeze what they can from commercial insurance contracts, even monopolists face limits to their pricing power. In the future, hospitals may have difficulty financing their investments in physician practices; hospital margins are already beginning to shrink, as we have discussed. Hospitals may be faced with the prospect of unwinding some of these acquisitions, as they did once before, or of dramatically restructuring the employment contracts with physicians to reduce operating losses. Hospitals may pressure their employed physicians both to do more (see more patients per hour, admit more patients from the ER, refer more patients in network) and to do less (reduce lengths of stays, reduce inpatient costs in bundled payment and gain-sharing programs). Managing these often conflicting incentives and economic pressures will create new strains in their rocky relationships. Under the pressures of health reform, many hospitals may transition from their former role as "physician's workshop" to a new role as "physician's sweatshop."

Summing up: Many hospitals have employed physicians as a quick and easy way to try to develop closer working relationships with them. They hope that in time, physicians will change how they use their pens. We believe that this hypothesized causal chain of aspiration has too many untested and weak linkages to ever bear real fruit. Thus far, the empirical evidence is on our side. Yet all of our major health care stakeholders, including Medicare, private insurers, and hundreds of provider systems, are staking the future on it. Relying on ACO payments and other alternative payment models, payers are dangling the carrot of financial incentives in front of health care systems that can figure out how to make integration work.

Vertical Integration: The Strange Case of Accountable Care Organizations

With so much at stake—and so much freely available data, courtesy of CMS—it is no surprise that academics have saturated the market with research on ACOs. Research appeared almost immediately after the first Medicare Pioneer ACOs began operating. As the Pioneer program unfolded, the news that emerged was not good. Among the Pioneer models, twenty-three of thirty-two had dropped out of the program by the time of its sunset in 2016. Program year 2015 data showed an average savings of $2.7 million among the remaining twelve participants. Of the $34 million earned, however, one ACO accounted for

72 percent of the savings.[55] Between 2012 and 2014, many showed improvement on the thirty-plus quality metrics. Even so, fewer than 30 percent sufficiently reduced costs to earn shared savings. The Pioneers were having a hard time making a go of it.

There is now a large body of research on the full Medicare ACO program. The results are no better. Roughly half of the ACOs reduced spending. The percentage of ACOs achieving savings was correlated with earlier start years and higher initial spending levels per beneficiary, implying that much of the ACO "savings" might merely have been regression to the mean that would have been realized anyway. ACOs led by physicians achieved a higher savings rate than hospital-led ACOs; smaller ACOs (with a mean number of beneficiaries less than ten thousand) achieved greater net savings per beneficiary than larger ACOs. Medical group participation in Medicare ACOs failed to change use of either high-value or low-value specialty care.[56] Additional research suggests little or no impact on hospital readmission rates.[57]

The ACO movement has been beset by notable failures and continuing dropouts. Cornerstone Health Care was one of the few ACOs that succeeded in achieving both higher quality and lower cost than its peers. By December 2016, however, Cornerstone had ceased to operate as an independent entity, plagued by the amount of personal debt assumed by its physicians to finance the ACO's infrastructure, as well as the defection of seventy of its specialists after CMS changed payment rules in 2015.[58]

In the fall of 2016, a range of stakeholders and analysts engaged in an interesting exchange on the savings potential of ACOs. In August 2016, CMS pronounced that it had reaped $1.29 billion in total savings since 2012. That same month, Harvard researchers replied that half of the ACOs made money while half lost money in 2015. After paying providers their bonuses, CMS lost a net of $216 million, which did not include CMS program costs.[59] In September 2016, Leavitt Partners reported that there was considerable variation in ACO cost and quality, and that quality was unrelated to both spending and savings. They also raised concerns about mean regression. Moreover, several managed-care veterans dropped out of the ACO program, in part because they claimed they were already efficient and were given unfairly low benchmarks. By the end of 2016, the commissioners of MedPAC, an academic advisory board to CMS, called the ACO savings "incredibly unsatisfying."

As the research evidence piled up, things looked especially bad for hospital-led ACOs, which were supposed to be the exemplars for integration supporters. In September 2018, Harvard researchers reported that savings were roughly three times higher in physician-group ACOs versus hospital-integrated ACOs.[60] Another study is less damning, finding that ownership type explains only 5 percent of the variation in ACO performance.[61] Among those ACOs that reduced costs, the biggest reductions were in inpatient care and postacute care.[62] Savings in hospital-led ACOs were restricted to postacute care. These ACOs seemed unable or unwilling to cut into the core business of their system owners.

CMS continues to report that ACOs are saving money, now approaching $700 to $800 million annually. Based on a Medicare budget in excess of $2 trillion, this translates into a whopping .04 percent saving in total Medicare spending.[63] What none of these analyses addressed was how much money, time, and energy providers had to invest up front in ACOs to reap these savings. According to one survey, ACOs spent an average of $1.62 million to participate in the Medicare program.[64] Multiply this by the nearly one thousand participating ACOs, and the provider cost is twice the estimated savings to CMS. That is the optimistic view. The American Hospital Association estimates the cost of participation of hospital-led ACOs at about ten times this amount.[65]

Advocates of ACOs offer a range of explanations for their limited success.[66] They are still new. Physicians still have not bought in. Just give them more time. Perhaps the most obvious problem is that a program predicated on the power of economics doesn't actually provide very strong incentives. The vast majority of ACOs are in the safest version of the program, in which they receive modest bonuses if they cut costs, but pay no penalty if costs increase. ACOs in this program can do nothing to cut costs, and random chance alone will guarantee them the occasional "shared savings." In 2018, CMS announced plans to move ACOs away from this safe option. The AHA and other provider groups warned that such a change, if enacted, would spur a hospital exodus from the program. So much for having more time.

There is also the question of whether the incentives reach the individuals who matter most: physicians. Few if any systems push the shared savings down the organization. If doctors are adjusting their decisions to save money for the ACO, they are not seeing any of the returns. CMS might as well offer the shared savings to academics instead of hospitals. We seem to have the same control over physicians, which is to say none at all.

It is the same old story. ACO advocates claim that they need more time to move down the learning curve. Time alone will not be enough. As we will explain in chapter 10, managers must find a new way of working with physicians.

Vertical Integration and Its Discontents

We put a lot of blame on hospitals for the current crisis in American medical care. Physicians are their willing co-conspirators. Happy to enter into integrated arrangements, physicians are blunting the kinds of changes that integration could make possible. Physicians prefer fee-for-service payments over any of the alternatives promoted by payers and policymakers, even though they recognize that it is a more expensive model.[67] Overall, as little as 5 percent of physician compensation may be at risk for quality and other factors.[68] Why is this so? Back in the 1950s, physicians objected to HMOs on the grounds that fee-for-service payment led to better patient care and better financial rewards, while alternative payment models led to more uncompensated work and an incentive to not treat complicated conditions. Little has changed since then. Physicians remain allergic to alternate payment models, and believe that value-based payment worsens the quality of care.[69]

A large percentage of physicians are unaware of how much their profligacy detracts from their hospital's bottom line. Physicians may not know whether their hospitals participate in ACOs or other risk contracts, and almost certainly do not know if their patients are attributed to an ACO.[70] This is also partly because ACO financial incentives exist at the contract level, not at the individual physician level, and because practice organizations shield physicians from direct risk-based or quality-based compensation. Practice-level financial incentives, including bonuses, are usually small and rarely based on cost of care. While physicians may receive performance feedback, less frequently are they released from contracts on the basis of quality or efficiency. This situation has remained unchanged for several years.[71]

Not that it would be simple for hospitals to push the incentives harder. Enforcing complex pay-for-performance contracts involves costly documentation that is sure to foster physician dissatisfaction. A hospital may also wish to avoid drastic income reallocation among its medical staff, many of whom will blame their income shortfalls on data integrity and measure validity, further sapping physician enthusiasm. If hospitals push physicians, the physicians will push back. Physicians report being on a treadmill in their hospital practice. They have been forced to be more productive to avoid stagnating incomes, while simultaneously facing rising patient complexity that demands more of their time. They also feel that quality metrics are "the bane of their existence," and are what managers want to extract from EHRs, rather than what doctors or their patients perceive as quality care—for example, listening to patients.[72]

The roll-out of the Medicare Access and CHIP Reauthorization Act in 2015 has only added to physicians' woes.[73] MACRA introduces a pay-for-performance scheme known as the Merit-Based Incentive Payment System, or MIPS. MIPS is so complex that physicians must hire consultants to interpret and prepare for the changes, only to be frustrated as the Medicare Payment and Advisory Commission recommends substantial changes.[74] Overall, there is a high degree of risk aversion in the medical community toward these new payment models. Many practices have seen these models eat into their incomes. Others lack the capital to finance investments in infrastructure that may or may not help them to successfully manage under these new models.

Physicians are not blind to the presence of waste in the system. Rather, they see it as the fault of someone else: insurers, drug makers, system executives.[75] This may explain why physicians are reportedly averse to contracting for risk they feel they cannot control, and are skeptical about new organizational models to improve quality or reduce cost. In a 2016 survey, only 34 percent of physicians "somewhat" or "mostly" agreed that hospital employment would enhance quality of care and decrease costs.[76]

There is a strong disconnect here between the views of hospital executives and those of physicians. For example, when asked about the impact of value-based care delivery on quality, 62 percent of executives responded favorably, compared to 59 percent of clinician leaders and only 47 percent of clinicians. Executives and physicians also differ in their views about how to reduce costs.[77] Rank-and-file clinicians are least likely to see value-based reimbursement as their primary revenue model (37 percent), and see value-based contracts as significantly improving the quality of care (38 percent) or significantly lowering its cost (36 percent).[78] With the growing size and bureaucracy of hospital systems, physicians feel that hospital executives with their overhyped MBA degrees are increasingly detached from the reality of medicine at the frontline of care delivery, and are increasingly focused on data, metrics, and policies (e.g., standardization, in-house referrals).[79]

Despite payer efforts to promote value-based purchasing, physicians continue to over- and underutilize care. Part of the problem is that of staying current with the sheer growth in the scientific literature. New medical practice that is widely cited is often contradicted by subsequent evidence. It is no wonder that physicians are often slow to change their practice patterns. Physicians also make low use of data on quality or cost in referrals.[80] Growing physician "burnout" at the frontline of care delivery may further increase as payment reform receives greater impetus and the physician supply shortage worsens.[81] Some analysts have called for a quadruple aim that includes improving the work lives of providers.[82]

While alignment and engagement remain elusive goals, hospital executives continue to try to work with their medical staff in "the old fashioned way": kickbacks. The trade press is replete with stories of executives offering bribes to surgeons and other providers for patient referrals, and then covering up the kickbacks in hospital corporate tax filings.[83] Other scams involve (1) waiving patients' out-of-network payments (illegal under Medicare, but legal for commercial payers in some states) and concealing the discounts as uncollected bad debt; (2) bribing physicians to refer patients to the hospital's in-house diagnostic testing; and (3) swapping referrals for ancillary management contracts with outside testing and treatment centers.[84]

We Have Met the Enemy and He Is Us

Patients' beliefs and behaviors can also undermine the success of payment reform and new organizational models. More than half of the US population assigns low importance to personal health.[85] When it comes to taking better care of their health, more than a third are either "aware but struggling" or "disengaged and overwhelmed."[86] As a result, not enough Americans engage in healthy behaviors, take proper preventive care measures, or engage in disease-specific self-care behaviors. Few care about medical costs unless it hits them in the pocketbook.

More generally, there is a problem with health literacy. Like physicians, patients may not be aware of what "low value care" is, let alone be intelligent consumers of high-value care, partly because they face limited exposure to costs. As many as one-third of patients have difficulty envisioning benefits from avoiding low-value care. Among the less educated, the proportion is as many as one-half. One report describes "an unhealthy truth": only one in six Americans comprehends the magnitude of the problem of chronic disease and its impact on mortality and spending.[87] Another suggests that patients are uncertain about how to manage their chronic conditions.[88]

To be sure, there is hope that giving patients more skin in the financial game, through higher deductibles and the information necessary to compare provider prices, will foster greater shopping and use of high-value services. However, some studies suggest that when patients pay more out of pocket, they cut back on all types of high-value and low-value care. By the same token, early efforts to promote price transparency have had limited success.[89]

Electronic Health Records to the Rescue?

In a 2008 study, the Congressional Budget Office estimated that electronic health records could reduce spending by as much as $1 trillion over the course of a decade.[90] Vertical integration supporters argued that large systems would be best positioned to generate these massive efficiencies. The evidence says something quite different. Numerous studies have found mixed evidence about the benefits from EHR.[91] There may be a slight improvement in outcomes at hospitals that have adopted the most advanced EHR technologies, but there is no systematic reduction in costs. There are many reasons for these disappointing results. For one thing, vendors have been slow to assure interoperability, even among providers using the same vendor platform. Industry leader Epic has made strides with its "Care Everywhere" initiative, which in theory allows patients to share information with providers. Epic's "One Virtual System Worldwide" facilitates direct data exchange among providers—allowing them, for example, to share test results (potentially eliminating duplication) and make appointments for patients on each other's calendars. Epic's systems may be state-of-the-art, but providers tell us that many inconsistencies and incompatibilities remain. Sharing data across Epic platforms, even within the same health system, is no piece of cake. Even as Epic irons out its problems and rolls out more features, its system will still have limited use for providers on platforms other than Epic. Unless Epic takes over the currently fragmented market, there will be a Wild West aspect to EHR for the foreseeable future.

More problematic is the reluctance or inability of physicians to integrate the vast storehouse of information available from EHR into their practices. Not without reason, many physicians find that the time required to use the EHR is excessive, while the information contained within is overly simplistic, and the treatment recommendations are not always relevant to the needs of their patients. According to a 2018 Harris/Stanford University survey, half of all PCPs believe that EHRs detract from their practice, and 59 percent believe that EHRs need a "complete overhaul."[92]

A recent article in *Fortune* magazine provides a cautionary tale, recounting how the EHR was rushed to market too fast and engendered several unintended and harmful consequences for US physicians.[93] Indeed, a recent Medscape poll reveals that more primary-care physicians believe EHRs have decreased the quality of care in their workplace than believe it has increased it. Tellingly, the vast majority of these physicians had no input in the choice of the EHR used.[94]

Physicians pour out their frustrations in a recent article published in the popular trade magazine *Becker's Hospital Review*, titled "25 Quotes That Show Just How Fed Up Physicians Are with EHRs."[95] Here are just two of the juiciest quotes: "Too often I pull up a record ... and it's almost impossible to really get an understanding of the story line. On a daily basis I can't find the information ... that is really valuable to me. In a sense it's turned us into data entry clerks." "The haughty, overbearing audacity of our federal government and hospitals which forces us to absorb millions of dollars in lost time is maddening." Patients have their own complaints. One of the authors of this book recently visited the same specialty-care facility twice in one week for a diagnostic procedure and follow-up discussion of the results. Despite the health system's use of Epic's Care Everywhere EHR, the medical staff had to request and enter the same personal information both times, as the patient wryly smiled.

EHRs not only exact a toll on physician and patient time, but are fraught with misleading, hard to use, and even inaccurate data. Doctors will tell you—as they have certainly told us—that EHRs are primarily in place for billing purposes. Not surprisingly, providers are encouraged to enter more data in order to earn more. This places an enormous burden on analysts to determine whether the data really reflect what is happening with the patient at the point of care. Remember this the next time a consultant says that "analytics" based on EHR data are "a game changer." Moreover, the increased data flow requires additional information on the evidence-based responses that providers and other caregivers should undertake in acting on the data. A related problem is that only 20 to 30 percent of clinical data are structured (e.g., computable numbers); the rest are encoded in messy and often inconsistent language. Yet another problem is the shortage of tech staff with data analytic skills (e.g., database experts, computational scientists, data scientists). Without such added capabilities, organizations have difficulty turning data into actionable information.

Patients have their own stories about EHR data. In the aforementioned pair of visits for a diagnostic procedure, just about the only information shared across the two offices was prior drug use. For some reason the team that performed the procedure entered the wrong drug information, and the team that handled the follow-up care did not correct it, even when the mistake was pointed out. From now on, medical providers using this Epic system will scratch their heads as to why one of us is using an obscure drug that, according to WebMD, has no known practical use! Again, this is hardly an isolated anecdote.

When analysts explain why integrated delivery systems might succeed today despite the colossal failures of the past, they often point to EHR, which was not available to the AHERFs of the 1990s. We are still far from realizing the trillion-dollar promise of EHR. Everyone is waiting for full interoperability. Without the ability to share information across providers, there is little opportunity to scale data and coordinate patient care across care sites. Most importantly, physicians are fed up. As with much else that is wrong with health systems, meaningful change is impossible without physician buy-in.

Chasing Kaiser: Provider-Sponsored Plans

The most audacious move made by IDNs in the 1990s was to get into the health insurance business. Very few IDNs directly sold insurance, instead opting to contract with traditional health insurers to accept full financial responsibility for the health spending of enrollees. Twenty-five years later, this still seems like a reasonable strategy, provided that IDNs can really control costs. It would also help if they could adequately predict patient health care risks so as to avoid adverse selection. Hundreds of health systems have dipped their feet in the water by participating in accountable care organizations. A few dozen have jumped in at the deep end, once again offering what we today call provider-sponsored health insurance plans.

There are currently about 150 provider-sponsored plans. Several plans that began in the 1980s or earlier, including the Geisinger Health

Plan (north-central Pennsylvania), Presbyterian Health Plan (New Mexico), and the Marshfield Clinic Health Plan (central Wisconsin) are market-share leaders and very profitable. In contrast, most of the plans introduced by IDNs in the 1990s barely got off the ground, lost money, and were quickly divested. A few IDNs kept the faith, and between 2010 and 2016 they sponsored thirty-seven new health plans.

Yet again, history seems to be repeating. As of 2015, only four of the new plans were profitable.[96] This is not too surprising; new health plans usually incur losses as they build market share. The losses in some systems have been too painful for many plan sponsors. The giant Northwell Health System in New York opened its Care Connect Insurance to much fanfare in 2013. By 2015 enrollments had swelled to over one hundred thousand, but took $32 million out of Northwell's bottom line. When losses swelled to $157 million the following year, Northwell had had enough, and it shut down the plan.[97] Ohio's Mercy Health System tried to avoid growing pains by acquiring Kaiser's local health plan in 2013. Kaiser had suffered five consecutive years of losses. Mercy did no better, and after losing $115 million in the first nine months of 2015, it shut down the plan for good. Other recent high-profile failures include Piedmont/WellStar, Catholic Health Initiatives, Inova, and even the Mayo Clinic.

The facts on the ground provide some damning evidence about the potential for provider-sponsored plans to transform health care delivery. There is only a smattering of systematic research evidence on provider-sponsored plans, and results are once again discouraging. One study found that states with a large concentration of provider-sponsored plans experienced faster growth in per-capita health spending.[98] Another found that provider-sponsored plans serving the Medicare Advantage market have higher premiums, controlling for quality and plan benefits.[99] The most recent study finds no consistent relationship between sponsorship, costs, and quality.[100] Higher spending does not seem to be helping the plans; nearly half of provider plans suffered negative margins in some or all of the period from 2011 to 2014.[101] Not all the studies paint such a negative picture. One found that provider-sponsored Medicare Advantage plans provided higher-quality care with greater patient satisfaction, while another found that hospitals with provider-sponsored plans had higher bond ratings (the latter study does not consider which is cause and which is effect).[102]

To a large extent, today's provider-sponsored plans are falling victim to the same problems that plagued IDNs in the 1990s. Some are financial: provider-sponsored plans are often undercapitalized, and lack reserves to weather financial losses or unforeseen regulatory changes. Other barriers are managerial: health care providers continue to lack the expertise required to run insurance companies. They are unskilled at designing and marketing insurance. They lack underwriting expertise, which leads to underpricing and adverse selection. To make matters worse, some provider-sponsored plans do not contract with providers outside the system. The resulting narrow-network plans have limited appeal in the commercial insurance marketplace. If that were not bad enough, some provider plans are finding that incumbent insurers may drop them from their networks in retaliation for starting rival health plans.[103] McKinsey concluded there is no guarantee for value creation by provider-payer integration, since the costs incurred may outweigh the cost savings.[104]

One particular issue—the inability to reach a minimum efficient scale (i.e., enough enrollees)—is especially important. There is a broad industry consensus that a plan must have at least one hundred thousand members in its local market to reap the benefits of scale economies for things like sales and administration. An even larger size allows a plan to negotiate deeper discounts with independent providers. By contrast, health plans operated by providers have an average enrollment of only thirty thousand lives, and many of these are system employees who prefer to be treated at system hospitals, leaving the system little leverage with other providers in its market.

The heart of the problem is the failure of IDNs to control costs. We have talked about this ad nauseam, and in chapter 10 we will offer some suggestions for achieving efficiencies. Even if systems could not trim the excess fat from medical care delivery, they could save money for their plans by charging lower internal transfer prices for hospital and physician services. Done right, this can lead to a more competitive insurance product and more overall profits for the system.[105] Add some efficiencies and the plan could effectively compete against larger rivals.

The problem is that transfer pricing creates a big management problem. What the insurance division of the IDN calls efficiencies, the provider divisions call a loss of revenues. Providers have been at odds with payers for the better part of the past century. Can IDN executives navigate this tension any better within their own systems? It would be easy for them to set lower transfer prices; but few, if any, appear to be doing so. We do not yet know how IDNs will pacify hospitals that create efficiencies to the benefit of the integrated insurers, largely because those efficiencies are just not happening.

Winners and Losers

For nearly a hundred years, dominant hospitals have pursued strategies to secure their market positions, more often than not at the expense of consumers. Integration into IDNs is just the latest effort. If we look today at the flagship hospitals of the largest systems, we find that they are more expensive, both on a cost-per-case and on a total-cost-of-care basis, than the services of their most significant in-market competitors.[106] This, despite operating in purportedly competitive health care systems that should be rewarding efficiency. To understand why power persists, we must revisit the role of antitrust law and enforcement in protecting health care competition. This we will do in the next chapter.

7

NEW ANTITRUST CHALLENGES

"Power is neither good nor evil. It just is. It's what people do with power that matters."

C. J. REDWINE[1]

As providers continue to merge, health spending continues to climb. There is little doubt about causality. Economists attribute the bulk of the growth in spending to higher provider prices.[2] Providers raise prices because market forces cannot stop them. The failure of courts to block mergers in the 1990s is partly to blame, as the systems that formed during that decade wield considerable power today. Starting with its 2004 victory in the ENH case, the FTC went on a long winning streak, successfully blocking proposed mergers in Virginia, Ohio, Pennsylvania, and Illinois.[3] Even so, merger activity continues, and despite its successes, the FTC lets most deals go through. So do state antitrust agencies. Some of these deals appear to further diminish market competition, yet they still go unchallenged. The result is that systems continue to accrue power. Systems also engage in conduct that further limits competition, such as imposing gag rules that prevent patients from comparison shopping. While the agencies picked at the edges of this conduct, they again largely remained on the sidelines. The Trump administration recently stepped in to force some disclosure of prices. As of this writing, it remains to be seen whether regulation will sufficiently substitute for insurer efforts to publicize prices.

It would be easy to blame the agencies for sleeping at the wheel, but the story of how megaproviders accumulate and exploit market power is far more complicated. It begins with systems that were already big before the pendulum of antitrust swung in favor of the agencies. Add in mergers that, for a variety of reasons, the agencies are unable or unwilling to challenge, and toss in some questionable conduct. The resulting witches' brew defies consumers and defines our health economy. How did we allow this to happen? A good place to start is by examining the megaproviders that have received the most antitrust scrutiny: Partners, UPMC, and Sutter.

Partners Health. Partners established its dominant position in Boston in the late 1990s. At its core are Brigham and Women's Hospital and Massachusetts General Hospital, the original "partners" and the two largest academic medical centers in Massachusetts. Partners has hospitals throughout the state, mostly in the east. Partners's physician network includes 6,700 physicians, of which about 2,500 are employed by Partners subsidiaries. Partners also offers its own health plan, Allways, which it sells to Medicaid and commercial enrollees. Partners's growth has largely been piecemeal—a hospital here and a medical group there. Add it all up and today Partners is the dominant force for medical care delivery in eastern Massachusetts.

According to a 2018 report by the Massachusetts Health Policy Commission (MHPC), "Partners hospitals and physicians garner some of the highest prices in the state and its primary care patients have among the highest health status-adjusted medical spending."[4] There is little doubt that Partners relies on market power to inflate prices. For example, MHPC calculates Partners's inpatient market shares in "primary service areas," which represent the areas from which hospitals draw 75 percent of their patients. While derived from patient flows rather than the two-stage model discussed in chapter 4 of this book, primary service areas can be a useful screen for establishing market power. MHPC reports that "within the primary service areas for its hospitals, Partners' shares of inpatient services were higher and often substantially higher than those of other systems."

The two-stage model provides a more obvious reason for Partners's power. With control of two prestigious academic medical centers, plus many well-regarded community hospitals and more than 6,700 physicians, Partners is a must-have provider for many employers. Insurers that do not contract with Partners risk losing enrollees. Partners knows this and drives a hard bargain in contract negotiations. Ask Tufts Health Plan, which Partners brought to its knees in contract negotiations undertaken in 2000.

Policy makers and the public are aware of Partners's powerful position, and the Massachusetts attorney general's office scrutinizes every major acquisition. In 2014, the state attorney general reached a consent agreement whereby the state agreed to Partners's acquisition of three hospitals in eastern Massachusetts, in exchange for Partners subjecting its prices at these three hospitals to legal review. A year later, a skeptical state judge blocked the deal and the merger. Judge Sanders's opinion reflected the concerns of many of Partners' critics:

By permitting the acquisitions, the settlement, if adopted by this Court, would cement Partners' already strong position in the health care market and give it the ability, because of this market muscle, to exact higher prices from insurers for the services its providers render.[5]

Since then, Partners has acquired Massachusetts Eye and Ear Hospital in Boston and has also expanded into New Hampshire, while continuing to acquire physician practices and opening more outpatient facilities, including the rollout of a dozen Partners' urgent care centers.

Sutter. Sutter started out as a small multihospital system in Sacramento before expanding into the Bay Area. It arguably has a dominant market position in San Francisco and the East Bay, where its acquisition of Alta Bates Hospital in the mid-1990s drew an unsuccessful antitrust challenge from the state attorney general's office. Sutter subsequently acquired hospitals throughout the region, including several rural counties where it faces no direct competition. It also acquired or opened dozens of outpatient facilities and hundreds of physician practices. Sutter also contracts on behalf of the roughly one thousand physician members of the Palo Alto Medical Foundation (PAMF), the second largest medical group in the Bay Area, and receives the vast majority of referrals from the 2,500 independent members of Brown and Toland Physicians IPA.

By 2018, the state of California joined several private parties in an antitrust suit against Sutter. The plaintiffs contended that Sutter hospitals possess market power in San Francisco, the inner East Bay area, and several smaller northern California communities, and that Sutter used this power to negotiate higher prices for all of its member providers as well as PAMF physicians. The plaintiffs did not challenge Sutter's accumulation of market power; this would have required revisiting the Alta Bates merger discussed in chapter 4, as well as dozens of piecemeal acquisitions. Instead, they challenged several of Sutter's contractual demands that allegedly allow Sutter to sustain its high prices across the system, even at member providers that seemingly lack market power:

1. As a condition for the participation of Sutter's most desired hospitals in payer networks, Sutter received 95 percent of billed charges for services delivered at non-contracting Sutter facilities.

2. Sutter refused to participate in tiered networks unless all of its contracting providers are in the top tier.

3. Sutter refused to allow payers and employers to disseminate information about Sutter prices and quality of care.

The first demand was a clever bit of blackmail. Normally, payers limit out-of-network prices to usual, customary, and reasonable rates, which may be 50 to 75 percent of billed charges. By threatening to withhold its must-have hospitals from the network, Sutter forced providers to agree to pay 95 percent of billed charges for care at Sutter's other hospitals. This was so onerous that providers agreed to include all of Sutter's hospitals and outpatient facilities in the network, even "run-of-the-mill" facilities that face a lot of competition. This was just a complicated form of "all-or-nothing" contract requirements imposed by other systems, whereby insurers must include every system provider in their networks, or none.

Even at in-network rates, prices at Sutter's run-of-the-mill providers were vastly higher than those of the competition. Insurers would have liked to encourage patients to use lower-cost alternatives, but were stymied by the second and third of Sutter's contract demands. Insurers call these "anti-steering" provisions, because they limit patients' incentives and ability to shop among in-network providers. Put all three provisions together, and Sutter had a recipe for sustaining high prices across its network without losing market share.

UPMC. By the time AHERF channeled Icarus and burned through all of its cash in 1998, UPMC had become the dominant hospital system in Pittsburgh. Since that time, UPMC has steadily grown to become the dominant health care provider in Western Pennsylvania, and is rapidly expanding in central Pennsylvania. UPMC operates forty hospitals including Children's Hospital of Pittsburgh and Presbyterian Shadyside; in 2020, *US News* ranks UPMC Shadyside number one in Pittsburgh and number two in Pennsylvania. UPMC employs 4,800 physicians and operates dozens of outpatient, rehab, and long-term care facilities. By all accounts, it has market power. It controls about 60 percent of discharges in the Pittsburgh area, and its premier academic medical centers make it a must-have for insurers.

UPMC also sponsors a highly successful provider-sponsored health plan, making it the third largest insurer in Pennsylvania, with 3.4 million members. Perhaps because of its dual role as provider and insurer, it has been engaged in a decade-long dispute with Highmark Blue Cross, the largest insurer in western Pennsylvania. To make things more complicated, Highmark owns the West Penn Allegheny Health System (WPAHS), a Pittsburgh-based health system second in size only to UPMC, which emerged from the ashes of the AHERF bankruptcy.

In an effort to bolster its fledgling health plan, UPMC had every reason to drive up costs at Highmark. Initially that meant charging higher prices. Because UPMC is both the biggest provider in the Pittsburgh area by far, and the unique provider of many complex services, Highmark faced enormous pressure to accede to its demands. For its part, Highmark was still the dominant insurer and it had an extra incentive to support its struggling WPAHS providers. This meant using its purchasing clout to lowball UPMC. By 2012 the two were at an impasse, and UPMC announced that it would pull out of Highmark's network when its contract expired in 2014.

The state attorney general stepped in, forcing both UPMC and Highmark to sign a consent decree that expired in June 2019. This required UPMC to provide Highmark subscribers full access to "unique or exceptional" UPMC providers and services. Highmark patients being treated by UPMC providers may need to switch insurers or providers. While no one wants to switch providers in the middle of treatment, switching plans may be even more difficult, especially for those enrollees covered by their employers.

We wonder what the academics who proposed the market evolution theories of the 1990s would have made of all this. In many ways, Pittsburgh is on the verge of reaching the fourth and final stage of evolution, with two fully integrated competing systems accepting full financial risk while offering every part of the health care value chain, from health insurance to primary care to complex surgeries. It would be as if Pittsburgh had two competing Kaisers, something that would make Alain Enthoven and Steven Shortell proud. Employers and patients see it differently. They want to mix and match insurers and providers. If they have UPMC insurance, they want access to Allegheny providers. Most especially, if they have Highmark insurance—or Aetna, United, or Cigna—they really want access to UPMC providers. Unless you subscribe to UPMC's health plan, that access comes at a price. It is not even clear if you will save money by enrolling in the UPMC plan. By raising its rivals' costs, UPMC can jack up its own premiums and remain competitive.

To make matters worse, UPMC has expanded across western and central Pennsylvania where it dominates many local markets. After a lengthy investigation, the state attorney general in 2017 approved UPMC's acquisition of Pinnacle Health, making it the largest health care provider in Harrisburg. UPMC has grown from being the must-have system for Pittsburgh-area employers to being a contender for a must-have system for larger employers across all of central and western Pennsylvania.

Recent antitrust cases in Illinois and Pennsylvania confirm that courts will block horizontal mergers within the same geographic market, especially if the merging parties already have considerable market clout. So, instead of stockpiling local hospitals, Partners, Sutter, UPMC, and other megaproviders are acquiring new outposts outside their home market while vertically integrating across the value chain. All the while, they protect their fiefdoms by engaging in a range of behaviors that seem blatantly anticompetitive.

Twenty years ago, when systems first starting amassing power, hardly anyone was raising antitrust alarms. Now it seems that everyone not associated with a hospital is calling on the antitrust agencies to do something. They may be disappointed. To understand the limits of antitrust law, we need to take a closer look at how megaproviders continue to grow.

Cross-Market Mergers: Spooky Pricing at a Distance

By the mid-2000s, the agencies had convinced the courts that geographic markets for hospital services are local—no bigger than metropolitan areas and often far smaller. The impact has been broadly felt, from mergers that were successfully blocked to others that were never attempted. Many economists wonder if these successes came at a price. Consider the recent FTC victory against the proposed merger of Penn State and Pinnacle, the two largest systems in the Harrisburg, Pennsylvania, area.[6] After the deal fell apart, Pinnacle was still looking for a deep-pocketed acquirer. A few months later, UPMC stepped into the breach and the FTC did not challenge them. After a lengthy investigation, the Pennsylvania attorney general also signed off on the deal. The agencies had little choice. Although UPMC may dominate Pittsburgh, it had no presence in Harrisburg. If markets are local, as the agencies had successfully argued in Penn State/Pinnacle, then the UPMC/Pinnacle deal affects two distinct markets—Pittsburgh and Harrisburg—and does not increase concentration in either one.

There are countless cross-market mergers like this one. Prior to acquiring Pinnacle, UPMC had grabbed hospitals across western Pennsylvania. Sutter grew by expanding into Sacramento, San Francisco, and the East Bay, each a distinct geographic market. Partners has expanded in southeast Massachusetts and New Hampshire. Many other megaproviders have expanded outside their original markets.

If we follow the traditional economic model of health care competition, it is difficult to complain about cross-market mergers. How would adding hospitals in Harrisburg allow UPMC to raise its prices in Pittsburgh, or vice versa? These are different markets, and the merger leaves the structure of each market unchanged. Yet two recent studies provide tantalizing evidence that cross-market mergers lead to higher prices. Matthew Lewis and Kevin Pflum find that "the prices of hospitals acquired by out-of-market systems increase by about 17 percent" relative to trend.[7] Other hospitals in the same markets also raise prices, suggesting an overall weakening of competition. Leemore Dafny, Kate Ho, and Robin Lee also find significant cross-market merger effects.[8] Dafny et al. drill deeper, finding that the effect is present when the merging hospitals are in the same state, even if they are at opposite ends of the state. There is no similar price increase when hospitals in different states merge. It is almost as if a Ford dealer in Los Angeles merges with a Chevy dealer in San Francisco, and both raise prices. Not only that, but other car dealers in both cities also raise prices! Einstein coined the term "spooky action at a distance" to describe the impossibly weird behavior of subatomic particles.[9] We might describe the evidence on cross-market mergers as "spooky pricing at a distance."

We should not get carried away by these remarkable findings. Both studies rely on relatively old, highly aggregated price data that commingle Medicaid prices and whatever payments are made by the uninsured with the actual prices paid by commercially insured patients. This makes the price data noisy in ways that may introduce subtle but important biases. Many of our colleagues suspect that the results will not stand up with newer, more accurate commercial insurance pricing data. The pattern of results in both studies also presents some curiosities suggesting that there is more going on than meets the eye. That said, it is hard to ignore these findings. If true, they shake to the core our understanding of how health care competition works.

There are two plausible explanations for cross-market merger effects, neither of which requires an understanding of quantum physics. According to one theory, it all stems from insurers trying to sell their networks to employers. We call this the "good network" theory. It is one thing for a network to exclude one or two hospitals and a handful of large medical groups, because no employer expects universal access. It is quite another thing to convince an employer to sign up for a network with many geographic holes. If a system has a presence in many different markets, any insurer that has failed to include that system in its network would be offering a Swiss cheese plan. In some cases, the need to fill holes is quite explicit, because many employers require networks to meet minimum access standards. Some megaproviders are so large that insurers cannot easily meet these standards without them. Employers might relax these standards to allow for an "everyone but Sutter" network. Doing so would risk angering their employees. Employer demands for access have thus put insurers over a barrel. This theory helps explain how the expansion of Partners into southeast New Hampshire, which is now part of Boston's exurbs, would enhance its leverage with insurers selling to Boston-area employers.

According to the second theory, some providers have so much power that they could charge a lot more than they currently do. The problem for these powerful providers is that if they raise their prices even higher, they might draw the attention of regulators, and that might lead to price controls or other retaliation. We call this the "unseemliness theory." What it lacks in economic rigor it makes up for in plausibility. Many state government officials with whom we have spoken have raised the potential return of rate setting, and hospitals do not want to call attention to their high prices. In this theory, these powerful hospitals acquire other less powerful ones and raise prices there. So, rather than charge extremely high prices where the systems truly have power, they only charge very high prices across the board. This theory may help explain UPMC's expansion outside of Pittsburgh. UPMC remains under the microscope and must feel pressure not to raise prices too high. By expanding, it can spread a smaller price increase over a larger base of providers, generating the same overall increase in revenues.

As economists develop these theories and offer more refined evidence on "spooky action," the agencies might eventually have what it will take to block cross-market mergers. Following the blueprint of the ENH case, they could present a parade of insurance executives and employer health benefit managers, all testifying to their need to include the megaprovider in their network, and how this latest merger makes it that much more difficult. An economist could describe the latest research and make dire predictions about future prices. With just two published papers as evidence, such litigation is premature.

The upshot is that academic studies of cross-market effects will only go so far in the courtroom. In every successful merger challenge, the agencies have narrowly defined geographic markets. In prosecuting a cross-market case, the agencies would have to argue that direct evidence of merger effects should trump two decades of legal precedents. The courts may simply think that when it comes to market definition, the agencies are trying to have it both ways: narrow when it suits their interests, and broad when that serves them best. The agencies must also acknowledge that while recent research finds that cross-market mergers usually lead to higher prices, there is considerable variation in the data. The results in the Lewis/Pflum and Dafny et al. papers indicate that many mergers have no effect, or even lead to lower prices. Thus far, economists offer no way to sort the good cross-market mergers from the bad. While this is also true for local mergers, there are a number of bellwether indicators, such as the degree to which the local hospitals substitute for one another. There are no such indicators for cross-market mergers, at least not yet—which means that there is no "limiting principle." We cannot block every cross-market merger. While monopoly may be bad, forcing every health care provider to remain independent may be worse. We will return to this question of balance in chapter 10.

A new study by Matt Schmitt is even spookier.[10] He looks at what happens when hospital systems overlap in multiple markets. For example, both Sutter and Dignity Health have hospitals in Sacramento, California. Currently, only Sutter has a hospital in the Oakland-Berkeley region. On the basis of Schmitt's observations of nationwide hospital merger and pricing trends, if Dignity were to open its own hospital in Oakland-Berkeley, both Sutter and Dignity would raise their prices in Sacramento! The apparent reason is that, as the two systems gain points of geographic overlap, they become wary of trying to undercut each other's prices in one market, for fear of retaliation in another. If future studies confirm Schmitt's results, the case against cross-market mergers gets stronger.

As always, hospital systems defend these deals by appealing to scale economies. This explanation does not hold water, especially when mergers involve systems that do not overlap. Consider the recent merger between South Dakota's Sanford Health and Iowa's Unity-Point Health. These systems are already large enough to reap whatever scale economies are available, and are too far apart to achieve any meaningful clinical integration. Sanford's CEO Kelby Krabbenhoft touts the deal because it will improve patient access. He says that insurers always ask, "Where are your clinics? Where are your hospitals? Where are your doctors?"[11] The answer is that the clinics, hospitals, and doctors are all in the same places they would have been had the two systems remained separate. In Krabbenhoft's defense, the merger might make it easier for the combined system to command higher prices, which it could use to fund more hospitals, and so on, thus feeding the vicious cycle of higher health care spending.

Despite the depressing evidence emerging from recent studies, the concerns of academic economists may be beside the point for the simple reason that the agencies lack the wherewithal to police every transaction. Consider that if a merger case makes it all the way to trial, the agencies may spend well over one million dollars for internal staff plus outside experts. (The hospitals may spend twice this much or more in defense.) The federal agencies do not have the resources to challenge more than a tiny handful of the more than one hundred hospital mergers that occur every year. State attorneys general might jump in, but they have even smaller budgets—and besides, few seem interested. While states have scrutinized the most egregious offenders, such as Partners, UPMC, and Sutter, this has mainly resulted in a lot of investigating and very little litigating. The California attorney general has taken action against Sutter, as part of a case initially funded by a private class of plaintiffs. Most of the other state attorneys general seem to have ignored health care antitrust. Cost is one reason. Risk aversion may be more important. Megaproviders are among the biggest employers and political donors in their states, and most voters have failed to connect the dots between local megaproviders and rising medical bills. Local officials who challenge megaproviders may fear retribution at the polls.

A few attorneys general are fed up and might be willing to challenge the megaproviders. Some seem to prefer regulation over litigation. A few have mused about obscure laws that would allow them to block nonprofit mergers without proving antitrust harm. Others would like state legislators to impose price controls. When we point out that price controls have failed in the past, and that the courts are the best place to judge whether a merger is anticompetitive, they seem to acknowledge our concerns. Other attorneys general are even worse, still subscribing to the view that competition is the last thing we need in healthcare. The alarming conclusion is that federal agencies, which are further re-moved from local and regional political considerations and have fully bought into the latest economics research on provider mergers, remain our best hope for taking on the megaproviders. Unfortunately, federal agencies lack the wherewithal to stop the majority of anticompetitive deals. For now, state attorneys general and legislators are watching and waiting. If megaproviders continue to gain power, they may impose regulatory solutions, for better or for worse.

The good news is that recent research has opened a lot of econo-mists' eyes, more studies are on the way, and the FTC is engaging with key researchers, much as it did in the early 2000s when it retooled its approach to within-market mergers. The FTC is also probably con-ducting retrospective studies of cross-market mergers and, as it did with ENH, it will soon pick one or two test cases in which it can trot out its new theories and evidence. Without additional resources or help from the states, the FTC might not stop the flood of anticompeti-tive mergers, but it can stick a few fingers in the dike.

Consolidation of Physician Practices

Physicians dislike competition as much as any other business owners and have long taken steps to avoid it. Sometimes they step over the line, as happened in the 1950s when state medical societies organized boycotts of HMOs like Kaiser. As we reported in chapter 4, physicians got into trouble with the FTC again in the 1970s when they chose to negotiate collectively while retaining their independence. This is blatantly illegal. Ironically, the same physicians could have avoided conspiracy charges by merging. As a single legal entity, a merged group cannot conspire with itself. This legal distinction may have encouraged physician mergers.

Until the 1990s, the vast majority of physicians were self-employed.[12] Most physicians today are employees (of other physicians, hospitals, insurers, and others), and most physician-employees work for large organizations. Somewhat surprisingly, United Healthcare is the largest, employing more than thirty thousand physicians as of spring 2018, including thirteen thousand it picked up in 2018 when it acquired the nondialysis portion of DaVita. No other large insurer has taken such a big plunge into the physician market, unless you count Kaiser and the twenty-two thousand physicians employed by Permanente Medical Groups. Independent medical groups employ hundreds and even thousands of physicians. The biggest, each with over a thousand employed physicians, include the Kaiser Permanente Medical Group, the Cleveland and Mayo Clinics, and the Palo Alto Medical Foundation, which negotiates jointly with Sutter Health. Megaproviders are also mega-employers, either directly or through affiliated medical foundations. UPMC employs nearly five thousand physicians, while dozens of other systems, including Partners, Sutter, and Northwell (North Shore–Long Island Jewish) employ nearly one thousand or more. Despite these big numbers, only one-third of all physicians work in groups of one hundred or more. Megaproviders have lots of room to grow.

Working in groups, physicians enjoy economies of scale by sharing office space, staff, and equipment, especially the cost of electronic health records. Older research studies, some of which admittedly suffer from questionable methods and data, suggest that scale economies peter out pretty rapidly—at group sizes of five to ten physicians.[13] With today's demands for costly equipment and electronic health records, we speculate that figure might be closer to twenty-five to fifty, although there are no definitive studies. The key takeaway is that smaller and midsize groups usually are more efficient than solo doctors. Larger groups may not enjoy additional scale economies, and may entail costs of bureaucracy and free-riding, but they do gain added bargaining leverage against payers.

Economists have long suspected that physicians use their heightened leverage to raise prices. As data on physician prices become available to academics, research evidence is emerging to back this up. Three recent studies show that physician prices are higher in more concentrated markets.[14] The findings suggest that competition among physicians in a given specialty is limited to duopolies or triopolies, and that prices are roughly 10 to 30 percent higher than they would be if the same physicians faced substantial competition. One case study found that after six orthopedic groups in southeastern Pennsylvania merged to create a virtual monopoly, they raised prices by 10 to 25 percent.[15] If the orthopedists or any other powerful physician groups did manage to achieve scale economies, they do not appear to be passing on the benefits to their patients.

Despite the anticompetitive threat posed by larger physician groups, physician mergers largely fly under the antitrust radar, for three reasons. First, merging parties do not have to inform antitrust agencies unless they exceed a generous threshold (currently $84 million) that vastly exceeds the size of pretty much all groups. The agencies may still learn about these deals and challenge them, especially if disgruntled payers object. The second problem is that physician groups usually grow piecemeal, adding one or two physicians at a time, thereby failing to cross the thresholds established in the horizontal merger guidelines. This is death by a thousand cuts. Finally, the agencies lack the resources to challenge even a tiny fraction of the thousands of mergers and acquisitions of physician practices that occur every year.

Using several sources of previously confidential data, Cory Capps, David Dranove, and Chris Ody show how physician mergers fly under the antitrust radar even when the physicians gain substantial market power.[16] They looked at nine major specialties—including primary care, surgery, and cardiology—in more than a hundred metropolitan areas. What they found was deeply discouraging. Based on the agency merger guidelines, over 40 percent of physician markets (defined as a specialty/metro area pair, such as "cardiology in Chicago") are at least moderately concentrated, while over 20 percent are highly concentrated. In one of every six markets, the largest physician group has more than a 50 percent market share. In almost every situation, medical groups got big via many small deals rather than via one or two big ones. It is rare for even the largest groups to acquire practices with more than ten physicians. Not only do small deals exempt the groups from antitrust reporting requirements, but they barely change market concentration and are not presumptively anticompetitive under the merger guidelines. Through such gradual accretion, small groups become dominant groups, with the demonstrated power to raise prices and dictate contract terms.[17]

The agencies are not completely blind to the exercise of market power by physicians. Some insurers alert the agencies to deals that they view as troublesome. If the deals are large enough, the FTC will step in. In 2011 it successfully challenged a deal to create Keystone Orthopaedic Specialists in Berks County, Pennsylvania, which would have united nineteen of the county's twenty-five orthopedists.[18] In 2016 the FTC prevented St. Luke's Health System in Idaho's Treasure Valley (the area encompassing Boise and its surroundings) from acquiring the Saltzer Medical Group in suburban Nampa.[19] St. Luke's already owned several physician practices in Nampa, and the deal would have made the Nampa primary-care market highly concentrated. Notably, the state of Idaho joined in the FTC suit and even funded an independent testifying expert. For every Keystone and St. Luke's, there are hundreds or even thousands of deals that pass through the net. The FTC either remains in the dark about the deals or lacks the wherewithal to act, and most states prefer not to get involved.

Vertical Deals

The St. Luke's case probably had more to do with the system's existing market power throughout the Treasure Valley than it did with the threat to competition among PCPs in Nampa. St. Luke's four hospitals dominate the metropolitan area. It dwarfs the rival St. Alphonsus system, which owns the area's other two hospitals. Over the course of about a decade, St. Luke's acquired more than two hundred physician practices, opened fifteen emergency and urgent care facilities, and added another ten hospitals across the state. Insurers have long complained about St. Luke's market power and high prices. While the St. Luke's antitrust case was nominally about stopping the horizontal merger of St. Luke's and Saltzer PCPs, no one could miss the vertical elements. The case put the entire system on trial.

One wonders why the FTC based its formal case against St. Luke's on the relatively small horizontal merger in Nampa. As we have noted, it is much harder to use antitrust law to block vertical mergers, let alone undo them. Almost by definition, vertical mergers between hospitals and physicians affect two distinct markets, because hospitals and physicians do not normally compete head-to-head against one another. This means that vertical mergers between hospitals and physicians do not increase concentration in either hospital or physician markets. The same is true when hospitals expand into intermediate and urgent care. Unless there is some horizontal overlap, as there was with primary care in Nampa, the agencies cannot use traditional merger enforcement tactics to block vertical deals. So, while the FTC has recently blocked Bismarck-based Sanford Health from acquiring the Mid Dakota Clinic, arguing that there was overlap in primary care and general surgery, and similarly prevented Santa Barbara-based Cottage Health from acquiring the Sansum Clinic, it has not directly challenged vertical deals. It thus remains open season for most mega-provider acquisitions.

The Horizontal Merger Guidelines are considered the "bible" for antitrust analysis of horizontal mergers, and for good reason. Well-established economic theories, some dating back two centuries, relate horizontal mergers to consumer welfare. There is a lengthy empirical literature that consistently shows a direct relationship between price and concentration. There is also a long and consistent case law, providing important precedents. The same cannot be said for vertical mergers.

The agencies published the Non-Horizontal Merger Guidelines in 1984. Few hold these in the same regard as the Horizontal Merger Guidelines, again with good reason. The economics of vertical integration is relatively new and still evolving. Economists offer a range of competing theories and empirical evidence, often with conflicting conclusions about the merits of vertical mergers that vary widely by industry. While it is difficult to organize diverse economic theories and evidence into a coherent set of guidelines, the 2020 rechristened Vertical Merger Guidelines do offer some straightforward recommendations. They exempt mergers in which both parties have less than 20 percent market shares. They highlight the potential for efficiencies, especially by eliminating "double marginalization," which drives up the final price to consumers and can be eliminated through merger. In other ways, the Vertical Merger Guidelines are controversial. The two Democratic appointees to the FTC claim that they do not go far enough to stop mergers, while some Republicans complain that they fail to recognize the special economic circumstances of many high tech businesses. What all parties agree to, and this is reflected in the Vertical Merger Guidelines, is that the economics of vertical mergers vary across industries. The guidelines are terse, just nine pages (versus thirty-seven pages for the Horizontal Merger Guidelines), leaving much discretion to economists studying the specific circumstances of the industry in question.

So what do health economists have to say about vertical mergers? They have developed theories of vertical mergers that focus on provider/insurer bargaining; unfortunately, these yield mixed results.[20] Some health economists suggest that we should treat vertical mergers much as we treat cross-market horizontal mergers. Thus, we might invoke the good network theory, arguing that if a powerful hospital merges with a large physician group, it could make it difficult for insurers to exclude them both from their networks. Or perhaps the unseemliness theory applies, and powerful hospitals expand vertically so that they can spread out their price increases. Maybe hospitals just want to exploit generous facilities fees, as we discussed in the last chapter, in which case antitrust laws are the wrong remedy. Yet another possibility is that hospitals acquire physicians in order to gain referrals, again suggesting that enforcement of antitrust law may be the wrong remedy. Economists also appeal to traditional vertical issues such as tying and bundling, which we discuss below.

Although theory may be ambiguous, the empirical evidence seems pretty clear—the studies we presented in the last chapter show that vertical mergers usually drive up physician prices without improving quality. Not all vertical mergers are harmful, of course, and we have few signposts to distinguish good from bad. For now we might conclude that, in the absence of any obvious efficiencies, we should be skeptical. On the other hand, are we really better off if all physicians remain independent? As with cross-market mergers, we need limiting principles. And just as with cross-market horizontal mergers, it will take better theory, more evidence, and a few retrospective studies before the agencies can confidently challenge vertical deals. Providers themselves will benefit from such studies, as they may pinpoint when and why some physician acquisitions are more successful than others.

We have had positive experiences working with federal and state antitrust agencies, and admit that we may be biased fans. We have also seen clear examples of bias among some agency lawyers and economists, who have gone beyond healthy skepticism to outright dismissal of any and all efficiencies defenses. There is a fine line between enforcing antitrust law and zealotry against big firms. While the evidence suggests that today's megaproviders have failed to generate consistent savings, we are hardly reassured that a fragmented system is best in the long run. If the next generation of research shows when integration works and which megaproviders are most efficient, the antimerger zealots would need to give way. Heretofore, we have allowed too many bad mergers to go through. We must take care in the future that we do not block the good ones.

Provider-Sponsored Plans

UPMC is not just the largest provider of health services in western Pennsylvania; it is the second largest insurer. Presbyterian Health System is the largest provider and insurer in New Mexico. Had it acquired Harvard Pilgrim, Partners would have been the second biggest insurer in Massachusetts. At first blush these do not seem like antitrust concerns, as health care provision and health insurance are distinct markets. Upon closer inspection, these provider-sponsored plans (PSPs) can diminish competition, and the agencies have considered challenging some of them. As is too often the case, economic theory does not offer a clear answer about how they will affect consumers. Fortunately, economists have tools they can use to help predict the effects of any particular deal. These were on full display in a major merger case from another sector of the economy, the ATT/Time Warner case.

In 2016, AT&T announced plans to merge with Time Warner. Two years later, a federal judge approved the deal.[21] This was a quintessential vertical merger. Time Warner produces content that it sold to AT&T and other content distributors, notably cable providers such as Comcast and Charter Spectrum. The US Department of Justice challenged the deal, arguing that it would harm competition in the content distribution market.

This was the biggest litigated merger case on record, whose outcome could potentially affect tens of millions of Americans. The DOJ assigned its top staff to lead the investigation, and retained a talented team of independent economists to predict how the merger would affect consumers. Citing established economic theories, the DOJ's experts argued that AT&T would have an incentive to raise the cost of Time Warner content sold to rival cable providers, as this would confer a competitive advantage on its own Direct TV platform. AT&T spared no expense in its defense. Their experts countered that the deal would benefit consumers in two ways. AT&T would immediately have access to Time Warner content at marginal cost, rather than paying a markup, and could pass these savings onto its subscribers. In addition, the deal would allow AT&T to learn more about its customers and coordinate future product development with Time Warner. On June 13, 2018, US District Court Judge Richard Leon issued his opinion. The judge was keenly skeptical of the DOJ's "raising rivals' costs" theory, in part because AT&T had not previously increased content prices after it acquired NBC Universal. Judge Leon was also strongly supportive of the need for innovation in the value chain, and approved the merger.

This decision must have given pause to the staff of federal and state antitrust agencies as they contemplated taking action against PSPs such as UPMC. The central issues in AT&T/Time Warner and PSPs are virtually identical. On the one hand, a PSP might charge higher prices for medical care sold to rival insurers, anticipating that this would encourage some enrollees to switch to the PSP's health plan. On the other hand, a PSP would be able to secure its own provider services at marginal cost and pass on some savings to enrollees. The PSP might also argue that vertical integration would facilitate innovation, though there is thus far little evidence to support this. With Judge Leon casting doubt on the "raising rivals' costs" theory, the agencies know they will face considerable uncertainty if they challenge PSPs. This may explain why the DOJ took a pass on the CVS-Aetna deal, which we will describe in the next chapter.

Abdicating Responsibility

In November 2015 the FTC filed a complaint to stop the merger between Cabell Huntington Hospital and St. Mary's Medical Center in Huntington, West Virginia, a deal that had the blessing of the Vatican.[22] The hospitals prevailed, but only with the help of the state. In July 2016, the West Virginia Senate passed legislation granting the state Health Care Authority the power to invoke "state action immunity," which rendered the FTC powerless to intervene.

State action immunity dates to a 1943 Supreme Court decision. In *Parker v. Brown*, a raisin producer called Brown challenged the California state agriculture commissioner (Parker) and a state program that facilitated a market division and price fixing scheme.[23] The Supreme Court allowed it, concluding that states had authority to regulate local matters so long as they met two conditions: (1) the regulations do not materially obstruct interstate commerce, and (2) the states engage in active supervision to assure that consumers are not harmed. In a sort of bandwagon effect that may have been a response to the growth of managed-care organizations (MCOs), twenty states between 1992 and 1995 enacted Certificate of Public Advantage (COPA) laws that met these conditions, thereby allowing merging hospitals to avoid antitrust scrutiny by the federal agencies. Soon thereafter, Mission Health obtained a COPA to become the dominant system in Asheville, North Carolina; and the only two hospitals in Wichita Falls, Texas, used their COPA to form United Regional Healthcare. As MCOs thrived and market competition began to heat up, states grew reluctant to grant COPAs. In recent years, the tide has turned. Rural hospitals are struggling, and many view mergers as necessary for their survival. Some state governments seem to agree. In addition to West Virginia, New York, Virginia, and Tennessee have granted COPAs to rural hospital systems, and three more states have passed COPA laws, thus suggesting that more hospitals will soon be getting a pass on antitrust enforcement.

States know that COPA creates monopolies; their own antitrust agencies are often the loudest critics. In its press release for the Ballad Health COPA, the Tennessee Department of Health could not have been more explicit, stating that the "merger would create a public benefit . . . that would outweigh any downsides of the creation of monopoly services."[24] It is difficult to balance the known evils of monopoly against the ambiguous benefits of mergers and come down in favor of monopoly, but that is just what Tennessee and other states are doing. They have bought into the holy writ of care coordination and clinical integration. Never mind that academics are still turning over rocks trying to find any evidence of the benefits. At least some states require rate regulation as a quid pro quo. A lot of good that does; two states have dropped rate regulations at the request of the monopoly systems. It is one thing for government to regulate monopoly pricing; sometimes there is no other choice. It is another for government to sanction the monopoly and then fail to regulate it. That is nothing less than legislative malpractice.

There is another, more subtle explanation for COPA. To the extent that rural hospitals are struggling, a major reason is underfunding by Medicaid. States could solve this problem by increasing Medicaid payments, which would require raising taxes. Instead, they give rural hospitals monopoly power, which allows them to raise prices to commercially insured patients. Either way, taxpayers end up subsidizing rural hospitals; except that with COPA, it is the insurers who take the blame, as people see their ever-increasing insurance premiums. By sweeping things under the rug, legislators seem to have chosen just about the worst way to resolve the issue of how to fund rural healthcare.[25]

State action immunity returns us to the stone age of the 1970s, with states relying on price regulations to rein in spending. As we discussed in chapter 1, the research is not kind to supporters of state price regulations on hospitals. It failed in the 1970s, and we doubt there is any reason to suspect greater success today. Even if states figure out how to limit price increases, rate setting is still a bad idea because it locks in the method of payment. Whatever that might be—per diem pricing in the 1970s, perhaps DRG-based prices today—that will be the basis for payment far into the future. What a mistake that would be! At a time when providers and payers are moving forward with new payment models that reward efficiency and quality, COPA would freeze us in place. It won't help if states forgo price regulation. By granting monopolies, COPA eliminates all hope of meaningful payment reform, as it gives hospitals the power to choose the payment model that best serves their own interests, rather than allowing the market to experiment and find the model that best serves the interests of patients. With COPA we are damned if states regulate prices, and damned if they do not.

The FTC vigorously opposes COPA, routinely sending cautionary letters to states considering COPA. The FTC has little more than a bully pulpit on this matter and despite its efforts, COPA remains popular. Our only conclusion is that many states seem content to help their hospitals (which contribute to political reelection campaigns, and are laser-focused on this one issue) and to punish their patients (who are unlikely to even know what a COPA is). The FTC has challenged several COPA mergers, with just one success to show for its efforts. In 2012 the Supreme Court declined Georgia's COPA for Phoebe Putney Health Systems.[26] The court was concerned that the merger between the only two hospitals in Athens, Georgia, would cause competitive harm, and noted that Georgia law did not clearly articulate a regulatory strategy that would replace competition.

Why would any state wish a return to the 1970s, with archaic payment models, double-digit annual health care inflation, and no incentives for quality? We asked several of our colleagues, including some who have had leadership positions at the federal antitrust agencies. They offered explanations that range from overly optimistic and frustrating, to cynical, and even cynically clever:

1. *The overly optimistic reason*: When it comes to economics, health care is different. In this view, providers are not just angels of mercy, but paragons of virtue. Providers do not merge to exploit market power. Rather, they merge to realize economies of scale and pass the savings on to their patients.

2. *The frustrating reason*: Legislators are either ignorant of, or refuse to accept, three decades of economic research showing that scale economies are few and far between, and that medical providers fall victim to the same venal impulses as the rest of us.

3. *The cynical reason*: Providers have captured the regulatory process.

4. *The cynically clever reason*: Most hospitals provide charity care, which they pay for out of profits they earn on commercially insured patients. Take away those profits, and the burden of paying for charity care shifts to county hospitals, which means higher taxes. Some legislators may prefer to surreptitiously fund charity care by granting hospitals monopoly power. By the same token, hospitals usually do not receive enough money from Medicare and Medicaid reimbursements to cover the total cost of care. Again, they rely on the profits they earn from commercially insured patients. Legislators may prefer to look the other way as hospitals use monopoly profits to fund their Medicare and Medicaid shortfalls. If hospitals keep some of the profits for themselves, that is OK, as long as consumers are duped into thinking that the legislators had nothing to do with it.

It is difficult to know which explanation to believe. The last is at least partially satisfying, inasmuch as providers are giving something back to their communities. There are three problems with this explanation, however. The first is that, thanks to Obamacare, there are far fewer uninsured and there is a concomitant reduction in the demand for charity care. Second, recent research finds that when hospitals experience financial windfalls, they do not increase charity care.[27] Third, the solution is myopic. Monopoly hospitals may shirk their responsibilities to become more efficient and offer better quality, and that leaves all patients worse off in the long run.

Systems Behaving Badly

While antitrust agencies have largely stayed on the sidelines, insurers have done what they can to undo the damage caused by powerful megaproviders, largely by encouraging patients to shop around for providers offering the best value. They do this through a combination of tactics including tiered networks, narrow networks, and price and quality transparency tools. In response, high-priced megaproviders are flexing their muscles, engaging in tactics of their own expressly designed to thwart patients who want to save money. Collectively, these are known as *antisteering provisions*. We briefly review and assess these tactics below.

Insurer Tactics

Most insurers accept the need to include megaproviders' must-have hospitals in their networks. Many of these hospitals are excellent and deserve to be reimbursed at above-market rates. Even so, insurers would prefer to exclude at least some of the megaproviders' high-priced, run-of-the-mill system members. As a result, some insurers have introduced tiered networks and narrow networks, which reimburse patients far more generously if they choose the most preferred providers. Research finds that when network structure is clear, these strategies can be very effective in getting patients to choose less costly providers.[28] This in turn encourages providers to give bigger discounts in order to get into the most preferred tier.

To further encourage patients to choose low-priced providers, insurers are promoting price transparency—roughly 80 percent of health plans offer online provider-selection tools that incorporates price information.[29] Between deductibles and coinsurance, the out-of-pocket price difference between a high-priced megaprovider and everyone else can be substantial. Even so, researchers have yet to turn up compelling evidence that transparency tools are making a difference. One study suggests that health spending actually increased slightly in the first year that a transparency tool was available.[30] Another study found that those who used the tool reduced spending, thus suggesting that transparency tools can work once patients learn about them and use them.[31] Some insurers, including United, have been aggressively experimenting with different disclosure formats in order to identify the best ways to measure and report usable pricing information. In late 2020 the Trump administration mandated that insurers disclose provider price information. As we write this, it is unclear what form that disclosure will take, and whether it will be an adequate substitute for the best practices of private insurers.

While tiering and transparency should eventually help patients find the lowest price providers, they may not be the boon their supporters make them out to be. Facing the possibility that insurers may place some of their hospitals on a lower tier, megaproviders might raise the rates of their must-have hospitals and still get them on the most preferred tiers. Transparency might be even more problematic. Hospitals may be unwilling to grant deep discounts to one insurer knowing that other insurers will find out about them. Hospitals may also discover that they are far cheaper than their neighbors, and adjust their prices accordingly. Even so, pressure for transparency is likely to intensify, and it seems that megaproviders will not have enough fingers in the dike to hold back the flood of pricing information.

Megaprovider Tactics

Whether these tools are working for consumers or not, megaproviders will have none of it. Many insist on "all-or-nothing" contracts or the equivalent, and also insist on gag rules preventing insurers from publicizing their prices.[32] Needing the systems' must-have providers, insurers cave. These tactics seem blatantly anticompetitive. All-or-nothing contracting is tantamount to tying, allowing powerful systems to prop up their least attractive providers at the expense of potentially superior competitors. Banning price transparency also props up high-priced megaproviders at the expense of less costly rivals — or at least it will, once payers work out the kinks. Even with federally mandated disclosure, gag rules will prevent insurers from providing more detailed price information or offering the information in potentially superior formats. Although megaprovider tactics appear to diminish competition, unless plaintiffs can show that the must-haves have monopoly power — a higher hurdle than is required in a typical merger case — they will lose in court.[33] A private lawsuit against Presbyterian Health System in Albuquerque (no relation to Presbyterian in Pittsburgh) languished for years, with the plaintiff struggling to show that Presbyterian has monopoly power. This might be a surprise to those who note that Presbyterian has a 40 percent share of the inpatient market (and an even larger share among the most prosperous demographics) as well as a provider-sponsored plan that is the largest insurer in New Mexico.[34] Unfortunately, the duck test does not cut it in the courtroom.

The tide may be turning. In 2016, the Department of Justice challenged several antisteering provisions in contracts with Carolinas HealthCare (since renamed Atrium Health), a $10 billion behemoth that, the DOJ alleged, controls 50 percent of the Charlotte hospital market.[35] The DOJ further alleged that Carolinas used its status as a "must-have" provider to obtain top-tier network placement and to impose gag rules. Carolinas sought dismissal of the suit, citing precedent from other industries, such as the credit card industry, in which courts have refused to block similar provisions.[36] In November 2018 the DOJ and Carolinas reached an agreement whereby Carolinas agreed to end antisteering practices in all current and future contracts.

In perhaps the most closely watched health care antitrust case of the past few years, Sutter Health has reached a settlement agreement with plaintiffs. Pending court approval of the agreement, Sutter will limit or abandon all of the practices described above, unless Sutter can demonstrate that it is clinically integrated in ways that benefit patients. Sutter also agreed to a substantial financial settlement. As reported earlier in this chapter, plaintiffs in the case against Sutter seem to have won major concessions that would limit many of Sutter's anticompetitive practices.

Nota Bene

Through unbridled growth and business tactics seemingly borne out of arrogance, megaproviders have placed themselves under the antitrust spotlight. They do not have our sympathy. Many economists, policy makers, and insurers and a growing number of employers want the antitrust agencies to throw the book at them. While we have been part of this antisystem crowd, some caution is advised. Megaproviders maintain that integration is still the key to achieving the triple aim. While we remain skeptical, we have not abandoned hope. In chapter 10 we will explain how fundamental changes in how managers work with physicians might yet unleash the potential envisioned by Enthoven, Shortell, and other true believers.

For now, megaproviders seem incapable of driving efficiency, and impregnable to market forces. The antitrust agencies have taken a go-slow approach to enforcement, reflecting a combination of risk aversion, resource limits, and rules of the legal system. If the agencies are to take on the megaproviders, they will need better theories and evidence. The rules themselves may need changing. We will return to these themes in our final chapters. Before we get there, we need to discuss how established insurers and new market participants might disrupt the status quo.

8

COUNTERVAILING POWER

"Money and power by themselves are like a two-legged stool—you can balance on them for a while, but eventually you're going to topple over."

ARIANNA HUFFINGTON[1]

We have told a story of powerful megaproviders running roughshod over the US health economy. If you asked the providers about abuses of power, they would say that we have it all wrong, that provider power is nothing in comparison with the power wielded by insurers. Insurers would scoff, insisting that they need power to resist providers. Countervailing power seems to be the name of the game. While both sides are fighting for the upper hand in this battle, it is consumers who wear the scars.

The Concentrated Health Insurance Marketplace

At first blush, the health insurance market seems fairly competitive.[2] The largest carrier, Anthem, has a nationwide share of just 15 percent, well below the level necessary to cross the merger guidelines threshold, and well below the shares of many megaproviders in their local markets. There are dozens of other large insurers and hundreds of smaller competitors.

These numbers are misleading, however. One minor quibble is that enrollment data are derived from imprecise surveys. A bigger problem

is that the data often combine many distinct insurance markets, mask-
ing considerable concentration within each one. For example, Humana
and Centene are strong in the Medicare and Medicaid managed-care
markets, yet do not provide meaningful competition in the private
commercial insurance market. An even more serious problem is that
many of the largest health insurers—including Anthem, Health Care
Services Corporation, Highmark, and Wellcare—are Blue Cross and
Blue Shield licensees that operate in different parts of the country. By
mutual consent, they keep to their own territories and do not compete
against one another. In any given city or state, the local Blue may have
as much as an 80 percent market share.

Just as was true for providers, insurance markets are local. When
an employer shops for an insurance plan for its employees, it looks at
plans that have strong local networks of providers. It would be point-
less for our employers, Northwestern University and the University of
Pennsylvania, to offer Kaiser to their faculty and staff, for the simple
reason that there is not a single Kaiser provider anywhere near our
campuses. Likewise, Stanford University's benefits manager could
hardly expect faculty and staff to travel three thousand miles to Harvard Pilgrim Health Plan's New England-based providers.

When we home in on local markets, national market shares become
almost meaningless. The consulting firm HealthLeaders estimates insurer market shares in every state and metropolitan area, based on a
combination of state insurance commission data and proprietary surveys. Eager to document the power of health insurers, the American
Medical Association publishes a summary of the HealthLeaders data.[3]
According to the most recent AMA summary, local Blue plans have
the largest market shares in nearly two out of every three metropolitan statstical areas (MSAs). The local Blue share exceeds 50 percent in
nearly half the MSAs, and in one out of every ten MSAs the local Blue
share exceeds 70 percent. United tends to be the second largest insurer
behind the local Blue, though United is sometimes first, and United's
share exceeds 50 percent in just three markets.

Many employers have employees doing business all across the nation. These "national accounts," as the insurers label them, need insurers that have a presence in every location in which they operate. Only

a few insurers—mainly United, Aetna, and Cigna—can service these national accounts. Local Blue plans also service national accounts through a cooperative arrangement known as the "Blue Card," and the Blues collectively are the largest insurer of national accounts. National accounts sometimes add a local HMO, such as Kaiser or Harvard Pilgrim, to give employees an additional option.

Once we account for location, the market share data look bleak. Based on the Horizontal Merger Guidelines, two-thirds of local insurance markets are highly concentrated. The important national accounts market is also highly concentrated. This is partly due to Aetna, Cigna, and United's many acquisitions, but is mostly due to the long-standing dominance of the Blues.

The Perpetually Powerful Blues

From its inception, Blue Cross Blue Shield dominated the health insurance landscape.[4] As early as 1940, the Blues had 50 percent of all enrollees nationwide. Blue shares fell slightly in the 1950s and 1960s after for-profit insurers such as Aetna and Prudential entered the market. United Healthcare entered in the 1970s, growing rapidly through a combination of aggressive pricing and acquisition of smaller plans. Only a handful of other carriers have meaningful market shares— mainly Cigna, Kaiser, and, in a few places, local provider-sponsored health plans like Presbyterian in Albuquerque and UPMC in Pittsburgh. This raises three questions. Why do the Blues dominate? Why haven't other insurers made inroads? And, most important, is there anything wrong with concentrated insurance markets?

Why Do the Blues Dominate?

Hospitals and physicians sponsored the health insurance plans to prop up demand during the Great Depression. Dozens of local plans eventually organized their activities under the aegis of the Blue Cross and Blue Shield Association. (The hospital plans were Blue Cross; physician plans were Blue Shield.) Association members must restrict sales of Blue-branded insurance products to employers headquartered in their own territories. With a few exceptions—notably California, where there are two competing Blue plans—there is just one Blue per market. Several Blue plans have merged, often through a parent corporation that does not have Blue in its name. Anthem is the Blue Cross licensee in fourteen states, including California and Indiana, while Health Care Services Corporation is the Blue Cross licensee in five states, including Illinois. Most of their member Blue plans—indeed, nearly all Blues—are the largest insurers in their states.

Much of the current success of the Blues can be traced to decisions made decades ago. The first Blue plans were designed to benefit their hospital and physician sponsors. Plans featured free choice of provider with minimal cost sharing, and always stayed out of medical decision making. Blues also lobbied states to enact insurance "enabling laws" with several key features that resonated for decades. The laws established the Blues as nonprofits, exempting them from local taxes. In exchange, the Blues agreed not to experience-rate enrollees. The laws also required all insurers, not just the Blues, to cover all licensed providers. This meant there would be no networks, and it effectively gave all pricing power to providers.

With the Blues enjoying unbridled support from providers, tax exemption, limits on networks, and favorable brand recognition, competing insurers had only a few options for competing. They emphasized customer service, which proved to be a hard way to stand out. They also experience-rated low-risk groups—a strategy not initially followed by the Blues. Some commercial carriers offered plans with high patient cost sharing, in an attempt to attract cost-conscious employers.

The managed care revolution that legitimized HMOs in the 1970s threatened Blue dominance. In the 1980s, states repealed enabling laws and allowed insurers to create narrow networks. Seizing the opportunity to transform themselves, the Blues claimed full independence from providers, and then used their size to go after their former sponsors. They wielded their dominant market shares to secure large discounts in their newly formed HMO and PPO networks. The large discounts allowed them to maintain their dominant shares, in a virtuous cycle for the Blues and a vicious one for providers.

Why Haven't Other Insurers Made Inroads?

The health insurance marketplace used to be crowded with more competitors. Networks changed everything. Size translates into purchasing clout, which translates into better networks. In short order, Aetna, Cigna, and United rolled up a highly fragmented market, giving them big market shares in many MSAs and making them formidable competitors for national accounts. Even so, they still could not match the size of the Blues and have since resorted to different positioning strategies. United emphasizes data analytics through its very successful Optum division, and has also vertically integrated to become the nation's largest employer of physicians. Aetna and Cigna rely on sophisticated wellness programs and enhanced provider relations.

The big four are the only serious competitors for national accounts employers. National accounts sometimes offer Kaiser or another regional HMO to complement the big four, never to replace them. Regional HMOs, including many provider-sponsored plans such as Presbyterian in New Mexico and UPMC in western Pennsylvania, vie to be "carved in" to national accounts as well as to get the business of local employers. There are also dozens of small "third-party administrators" (TPAs) which "rent" networks from larger insurers. They pay providers the fees negotiated by the large insurer, plus a rental fee to the insurer. TPAs also process claims for self-insured employers, but otherwise provide few of the additional services expected from large insurers, such as wellness programs and data analytics. While TPAs have no chance of selling to larger firms, they can compete for the business of smaller firms by offering bare bones coverage. Despite the presence of dozens of competitors, both the national accounts market and most local markets are highly concentrated. High concentration can be a sign of a healthy marketplace, if firms have gained their high shares by building better mousetraps.[5] Health insurers, especially the Blues, cannot be let off so easily. The problem with dominant insurers was on full display in the Department of Justice's successful challenge of the proposed merger between Anthem and Cigna. One author of this book, Dranove, was the economics expert for the DOJ in this case, and had a front-row seat at the proceedings.[6]

The Anthem/Cigna Merger Case

The DOJ focused much of its case on the national accounts market, where customers had four main options: Blue, United, Aetna, or Cigna. The Anthem/Cigna merger would remove one option, making this a "four to three" merger. Anthem wanted the court to treat the Blues as separate firms, implying dozens of potential competitors. This flew in the face of the Blues' market division rules, and the court dismissed this claim as well as Anthem's claim that TPAs provided meaningful competition. Anthem successfully argued that a large fraction of national accounts customers offered more than one plan to their employees, often including Kaiser or another regional HMO. The DOJ countered that these carve-outs complemented rather than substituted for a big-four plan. Based on market share data obtained directly from insurers, the DOJ concluded that the merger was presumptively anticompetitive according to the Horizontal Merger Guidelines. Anthem complained about data quality—yet, when given the chance, it offered little data that would contradict the self-evident duck test: this merger looked, walked, and talked anticompetitive. The court sided with the DOJ.

The two sides reenacted this dance when they analyzed local markets. The DOJ argued that midsize and large local and regional employers also tended to favor one of the big four insurers. Unlike national accounts, where there were basically four insurers among which to choose, large employers in some regional markets had additional local options including HMOs and provider-sponsored plans. In many other markets, however, local options were few. The DOJ identified nearly three dozen MSAs where the merger was presumptively anticompetitive. Anthem again complained about data quality, and made additional noises about the threat from potential entrants. The court was a bit more equivocal about the impact of the merger in local markets, concluding that it would be harmful in "at least one" MSA (Richmond, Virginia), and potentially in more than one.

With the court siding with the DOJ's claim that the merger would increase concentration for at least some customers in some markets, the case now hung on whether this would harm consumers. The DOJ argued that there was much to learn from past mergers, and it presented the results of published research studies. Somewhat surprisingly, there is not a lot of compelling historical evidence about whether high insurer concentration is bad for consumers. This is not for want of highly concentrated markets, but rather for lack of good data and the difficulty of finding the right statistical methods.[7] One study looked at the 1999 merger of Aetna and Prudential, finding that insurance premiums increased by an average of 7 percent in those markets where both insurers had nontrivial shares.[8] At the same time, physicians in those markets saw their incomes decline. Another study found that premiums in Nevada increased by 13 percent after the 2008 acquisition of Sierra Health Plan by United.[9] A third study convincingly finds that premiums are lower in more competitive markets, but the methods are indirect, and it is difficult to say how much premiums will fall if the number of competitors increases.[10] That is about it for credible research; though the findings are consistent, there is not a lot to go on.

With no studies speaking directly to the facts of the Anthem/Cigna case, the DOJ's expert presented a model showing the merger would allow Anthem/Cigna to raise its prices, costing consumers nearly $1 billion annually. This was based on theoretical modeling rather than historical evidence. The DOJ separately argued that the merger would also harm providers when Anthem/Cigna used its enhanced purchasing power to drive down the prices it paid to hospitals and doctors by as much as $500 million. Anthem responded by playing a trump card. Its economics expert, Mark Israel, agreed that provider fees would fall, calculating that Anthem/Cigna would obtain additional discounts of nearly $2.5 billion. He further claimed that Anthem would pass nearly all of these "efficiencies" on to enrollees. When Dr. Israel incorporated this into his own economic model, the merger ended up saving consumers more than $1 billion annually. Anthem further argued that it would incorporate some of Cigna's most innovative business practices, such as its industry-leading wellness programs, into its own insurance offerings. Anthem called this the "best of best" integration outcome.

This was when the DOJ pulled an ace from its sleeve. The HMGs are clear that courts should not credit merging firms with efficiencies unless the firms have a realistic plan to achieve them. Any plan would require Anthem and Cigna to work together. Yet courtroom observers could not help but notice that, while Anthem was conducting a vigorous defense of the merger, Cigna was largely silent. When it came time for Cigna CEO David Cordani to testify, the reason became clear. Cordani expressed serious reservations about the deal, stating that Cigna stopped work on merger integration. He worried that the merger could weaken Cigna's insurance offerings and drive away loyal customers. Cordani acknowledged a letter in which Cigna's general counsel, Nicole Jones, complained to her counterpart at Anthem: "Your approach to the regulatory strategy, when coupled with your approach to integration and other matters, appear [sic] to be designed to cause commercial harm to Cigna while simultaneously strengthening your fellow Blues."[11] Cordani's testimony was a bombshell. How was Anthem supposed to achieve the "best of best" when Cigna was not cooperating? How could Anthem even know what savings were feasible when it had yet to decide whether it would seek further discounts from providers in Cigna's plans? As we explain below, such discounts might harm Cigna's strong provider relationships, one of the "best" things Cigna had to offer to Anthem.

Anthem's status as a Blue plan further complicated matters. Recall that Blue plans cannot sell their Blue-branded products in each other's assigned territories.[12] They can, however, compete outside their home territories by selling non-Blue-branded products, something they often do after acquiring other insurers. The Blue Cross and Blue Shield Association limits the extent of this competition by capping the sale of non-Blue branded products relative to the size of the parent Blue. This is known as the "best efforts" rule and it played a huge role in the Anthem/Cigna trial. If the court approved the merger, Anthem would immediately be in violation of the rule and would face fines potentially exceeding $2 billion. To come into compliance, Anthem would have to shift customers from Cigna plans to Anthem plans. Once again, Anthem had no strategy for doing so, and Cigna was not helping it find a solution.

We can speculate about why Cigna had soured on the deal. Perhaps it anticipated difficulties in merging two very different corporate cultures (more on that in a moment). Perhaps top executives at Cigna were disappointed by the diminished responsibilities they would have after the merger. Or perhaps Cigna realized there were opportunities to turn the tables and become an acquirer instead of a target, as would soon happen when Cigna acquired the pharmacy benefits management giant ESI (see chapter 9). All of this is reminiscent of the problems faced by merging hospitals: different cultures and differing incentives often stand in the way of realizing efficiencies.

Anthem/Cigna and Innovation

The Department of Justice pushed one additional argument. The debate about market shares and provider discounts focused on what antitrust experts call "static effects." The debate assumed that everything else about the insurers would remain unchanged. The DOJ raised strong concerns about "dynamic" effects, which are long-term changes. The DOJ argued that harmful dynamic effects would dwarf the static effects.

If you ask a health policy expert what needs to change in the US health system, they might echo the 1932 report of the Committee on the Cost of Medical Care, pointing out the need for innovations in payment reform, care coordination, and prevention. As we have discussed, innovation threatens the sovereignty, incomes, and power of providers. Is it any wonder that organized medicine has objected to HMOs, payment reforms, quality reporting, electronic health records, increase in convenient access at minute clinics, and virtually every other effort to disrupt the status quo? If the long deceased members of the Committee on the Cost of Medical Care could see how little has changed in our health care system, they would roll over in their graves. Or they might look for outside innovators to disrupt the system—the subject of the next chapter.

While health care providers have played their part in this sorry story, we should not let insurers off the hook. Nearly a century after the first Blues appeared on the scene, HMOs and PPOs represent about the only meaningful innovations launched by commercial health insurers, and renegade providers are responsible for some of the most important HMOs. This is not to say that insurance practices today are the same as they were a half century ago. Insurers use third-party review to assure the appropriateness of treatment protocols. They use prospective payment to set budgets, bundled payments to change hospital incentives, and the relative value scale to standardize physician payments. For the most part, Medicare deserves the credit for these innovations. The same can be said for today's value-based payments and accountable care organizations; private insurers saw how well these worked, and followed with their own versions, closely modeled after the Centers for Medicare and Medicaid Services. It is as if insurers require proof of concept before disturbing the status quo, and Medicare is willing to experiment and provide that proof. The Blues, which had the most to lose from disturbing the status quo, are among the most prominent followers.

For a while during the 1990s, innovative HMOs and PPOs seemed to be doing well. Health care spending flattened, and that contributed to broader macroeconomic growth. After the managed care backlash of the late 1990s, insurers backed away from the tightest managed care controls (including HMOs), enrollees migrated to less restrictive PPOs, and health care spending spiked. Forced to expand networks and lift utilization controls, insurers raised premiums. Under President George W. Bush, Medicare also seemed to stop innovating. Unwilling to wait any longer for solutions from Washington, some insurers took matters into their own hands. Cigna was at the forefront of the movement.

When David Cordani took the reins at Cigna in 2005, the insurer was at a crossroads. Although Cigna had become a national insurer through a series of acquisitions, its position was precarious. This was a time when PPOs ruled and insurers could not succeed without strong low-cost provider networks. With their dominant market shares in most markets, the Blues were sitting in the catbird seat. United was a strong second and, having established a reputation for tough bargaining, often paid less than the Blues. Aetna had regional pockets of strength, especially in the growing Medicare managed care market. Cigna was the weakest of the four, and its relatively poor networks made it a victim of the same virtual cycle that fed the success of the Blues.

Cordani asked an existential question: If Cigna could not compete on network strength, how could it compete? Bearing in mind that the total amount spent on health care is the product of the amount you buy and the price you pay, the answer was apparent. Cigna could not hope to outcompete its larger rivals on price; it lacked the purchasing clout to get the same deep discounts. Instead, it would compete by cutting quantities.

Through a combination of internal development and acquisitions, Cigna beefed up its wellness programs, which many consider the best in the industry. Cigna also pursued innovative partnerships with providers that further set it apart from its competitors. Cigna launched its collaborative accountable care (CAC) initiative in 2008, through a partnership with the Dartmouth-Hitchcock health system. Today Cigna has more than six hundred CAC partnerships with hospital systems and physician groups across the country, including Sutter. Cigna pays its partners a care coordination fee that places Cigna's reimbursements well above those of other insurers. In exchange, the partners employ nurses who serve as care coordinators for Cigna enrollees, and purchase data systems to link with Cigna's own data. Through sharing of data and care coordination, Cigna helps its partners identify patients at risk for high costs and adverse outcomes, and recommends courses of treatment based on data-driven treatment protocols to keep patients out of the hospital. Care coordinators may educate patients about lifestyle, medication, and potential gaps in care, and may refer difficult cases to specialists in medical or behavioral case management. Cigna also provides feedback about cost and quality. Cigna may add a bonus to the care coordination fee to reward high-performing providers.

Cigna is not the only insurer using CACs; Aetna uses them as well. United directly employs about thirty thousand physicians (through its Optum division) who have access to similar data and receive similar pay-for-performance incentives. Tellingly, the Blues have generally opted not to form such partnerships (southern California is one exception). While the jury is still out on the performance of CACs, this is exactly the kind of innovation that has the potential to bend the cost curve. Cigna plans to expand its CACs to two hundred more locations. The more experimentation, the merrier.

Cigna has also partnered with a handful of provider systems that want to offer their own health plans but lack the requisite capabilities in the insurance business. Cigna provides medical underwriting, claims processing, and marketing expertise while allowing providers to offer full-risk contracts. These arrangements stand in stark contrast to Anthem's ACO contracts. Anthem contracts with multiple providers in each market, offers only shared savings arrangements, and attempts to make money by driving down provider fees. Cigna's partnerships avoid the patient assignment problems inherent in ACOs, ratchets up the financial incentives for cost cutting, and turns adversaries into partners. Again, the jury is out as to whether these arrangements will bear fruit.

The contrast between Cigna's and Anthem's approaches to cost containment is a case study in business strategy. Each has chosen a different market position. Cigna tries to reduce the amount of inefficient care. In strategy parlance we might describe it as a "quantity leader," because it is trying to reduce health spending by reducing the quantity of unnecessary services. Anthem is a "price leader." Each relies on different tactics to achieve its strategic goals. Cigna's success depends on its wellness programs as well as its successful partnerships with providers, giving them the information they need to avoid costly overtreatment and the incentives to act on that information. This has often meant paying higher fees than anyone else, in order to subsidize care coordinators and information technologies. In contrast, Anthem's success hinges on paying lower prices than anyone else. When Anthem does pay attention to inefficiency, it is as a second mover, observing and adopting some of the best practices of the competition. For example, Anthem has its own wellness programs and manages a large number of ACO contracts.

A key insight from business strategy is that when firms pursue two broadly different strategic objectives at once, they risk being "stuck in the middle" and succeeding at neither.[13] By acquiring Cigna, Anthem risked being in this unenviable position. How could Anthem sustain Cigna's CACs while stinting on provider reimbursements? Would Anthem be interested in partnering with a small number of systems that wanted to offer full-risk products, when Anthem was the leader in low cost, *broad* networks? When pushed at trial, Anthem executives had no answers to these questions.

These strategic concerns sowed further doubts about Anthem's "best of best" arguments. There was a related issue raised at trial pertaining to the future of the overall health economy. Anthem acknowledged that one reason for the deal was to benefit from Cigna's innovative strategies. What if, instead of leveraging those innovations, the deal squelched future innovation? The negative consequences for the entire health economy could easily dwarf any benefits from reducing payments to providers. The United States spends $3 trillion annually on health care. An innovation that reduces spending by just 1 percent would save $30 billion. Might we dare to dream that innovative payment reform and use of big data might even bend the cost curve, leading to a permanent decline in health spending? We need to do everything we can to encourage innovation. Although Cigna's CACs and exclusive provider partnerships might or might not work, perhaps Cigna's next innovation will. (Cigna's merger with ESI is a promising new direction, as we will discuss.) It would be a mistake to let Cigna, an independent driver of innovation, be subsumed into Anthem, a consistent second mover.

This case reminds us of the St. Luke's merger case discussed in the previous chapter. The St. Luke's Health System in Boise, Idaho, attempted to purchase the Saltzer Medical Group in suburban Nampa. While the FTC mainly objected on the grounds of static price effects, the FTC expert (Dranove, an author of this book) questioned whether the deal might eliminate a potential innovator. After the court rejected the deal, there was some doubt as to whether Saltzer would survive. These doubts were quickly erased when Saltzer was purchased by Change Healthcare, a subsidiary of the giant medical supply firm McKesson Medical. In 2018, Saltzer announced ambitious plans to more than double in size, expanding into nearby suburbs as well as

192 * CHAPTER EIGHT

rural areas in western Idaho. Having another thriving competitor can only be good news for the Boise community.

Postscript

The court had several good reasons to block the Anthem/Cigna merger. The market is already highly concentrated, and the deal would only make things worse, pushing the national accounts market and at least one local market into highly concentrated territory. It was not clear whether the merging parties could successfully achieve "best of best" savings, and the deal posed a threat to innovation. Based on these considerations, a lower court judge ruled against the merger, and by a two-to-one vote, the District of Columbia Circuit Appellate Court upheld the decision. The dissenting appellate court judge Brett Kavanaugh (yes, that Brett Kavanaugh) raised a key issue that the other judges had largely ignored. Suppose that Anthem had credibly showed it would achieve $2.5 billion in additional provider discounts. Should the court have put this on the positive side of the ledger? As we now discuss, we think the answer is no.

What's So Bad about Countervailing Power?

There was another striking similarity between the Anthem and St. Luke's cases. Both merging parties claimed that the deal would give them "countervailing power." Anthem argued the providers use their market power to raise prices above competitive levels, and it was only right that insurers should have enough power to bring prices back down. St. Luke's argued that insurers used their market power to drive its own prices below competitive levels, and it was only right that it should have enough power to bring prices back up. By evening up the sides, seemingly anticompetitive mergers could make markets more competitive. To paraphrase Stanley Kubrick, we might even learn to stop worrying and love monopolies.

Antitrust experts have long debated the merits of the countervailing power argument. In a famous presentation to the American Economic

Association in 1954, John Kenneth Galbraith offered what could have been used, nearly verbatim, as a defense of the Anthem-Cigna merger:

> One important manifestation of countervailing power ... is that of the modern mass buyer. The gains from this bargaining ... are, in turn, passed along to the consumer. The consumer, as a result, is in a far happier position than were he or the small independent merchant to bring his negligible bargaining power to bear on the characteristic market power of the large manufacturer.

If powerful buyers get great deals for their customers, why should the courts stop them?

One answer is that the Clayton Act condemns any merger that diminishes competition. This obviously includes competition among firms setting prices to consumers. It also includes competition among firms paying wages to suppliers. In the former, we worry about the harm done by monopolists. In the latter, we are concerned about "monopsonists." The textbook theories of monopoly and monopsony are mirror images, and are best understood by remembering that monopolists have control over output and monopsonists have control over input. Thus, monopolists produce less output, resulting in higher output prices, while monopsonists hire fewer inputs, resulting in lower input wages. In other words, monopolists diminish competition in the output market, at the expense of consumers, while monopsonists diminish competition in the input market, at the expense of suppliers. In principle, the antitrust laws should prevent both monopsony and monopoly.

Galbraith says, Not so fast. If the monopsonist passes on some of its input market savings to consumers, then the exercise of monopsony harms suppliers but helps consumers. Perhaps the Clayton Act goes too far in protecting suppliers, especially when those suppliers are exploiting their own power to harm consumers. In these cases, Galbraith says, monopsony works in the best spirit of competition by mitigating the exercise of power. If a monopsonist is not constrained by competitors, then perhaps it is necessary for buyers to mitigate its power.

Many economists have taken issue with Galbraith on a number of dimensions. Galbraith himself acknowledges that we should only tolerate a powerful monopsonist if it is to pass on the gains from bargaining. Often the monopsonist is also a monopolist, and it is unclear how much of its gains it would share with consumers. The Anthem-Cigna case very much has this flavor, with the deal increasing both monopoly and monopsony power. Although Anthem claimed that it would pass on nearly all the savings from lower provider prices, it produced little hard evidence to support this conjecture, just as the DOJ had little evidence to refute it. Subsequent theoretical work suggests that it is only in the rarest of market conditions that these sorts of mergers, in which both input and output markets are concentrated, result in lower consumer prices.[14] The conditions facing Anthem/Cigna suggested that consumer prices would almost surely go up.

The Galbraith argument seems to depend on some notion of a "just price." The idea is that markets thrive when prices are at or near the just price: consumers pay no more than a product is worth, and efficient producers earn competitive rates of return. In terms of basic economics, the just price might be where supply equals demand. Monopolies usually charge more than that price, whereas monopsonists generally pay less than the price. You can see how some combination of monopoly and monopsony might split the difference and get us to the just price. At least that is the idea.

Galbraith offers up regulation as another way to achieve the just price. In doing so, he exposes two flaws in his argument. First, it presupposes that we know what the just price is. This presupposition clearly plagues regulatory enforcement. It also plagues antitrust enforcement, where the question is how to find the right balance of power. Suppose that we believe that providers are more powerful, and we allow an insurer merger. What happens if we then discover that the insurers have become too powerful? Do we allow another provider merger? Do we only stop approving deals when we have one insurer and one provider?

Suppose some government agency is able to calculate the just prices for provider fees and insurance premiums. Do we just hand over pricing power to the agency? In such a regulated market, dominant firms will wield undue political influence. Providers will try to convince regulators that they have underestimated the just price for medical services. Insurers will do the opposite while also arguing for higher premiums. Both will waste resources lobbying for their cause, and it would be rather surprising if regulators responded to this lobbying by favoring consumers. Perhaps, or maybe most likely, the regulator will raise the "just price" and raise the "just premium."

Or suppose that the market is unregulated, and the handful of providers and insurers have perfectly countervailing power. Why not let the monopoly megaprovider and monopoly insurer duke it out, eventually settling on the "just price" or something near it? This is what megaproviders and big insurers seem to be asking for. The question raises another: Why would we expect them to choose those prices? They could make far more money by doing what they would have lobbied regulators to do: simultaneously raise provider fees and insurance premiums. With no competition, no one could stop them. Powerful providers and powerful insurers currently exploit their power at the expense of consumers. Why would we expect that to change for the better if we concentrated these markets even further? To make matters worse, long before the monopolist and monopsonist emerge, competing buyers and competing sellers will do everything they can to become the dominant firms. They will lobby governments for favors, or advertise to excess, or expand capacity beyond what is needed to serve the market. Such rent seeking can be incredibly wasteful, and there is no guarantee that the most efficient firms will be the ones who survive. Our future hospitals and insurers may be the best lobbyists. Does anyone really want that?

If we consider innovation, the case against countervailing power is sealed. If there is one thing we have learned from studying health care markets over nearly four decades, it is that we are still trying to figure out how things work. We are now in a period of great experimentation, with organizations of different shapes and sizes, at all points in the value chain, taking different approaches to bending the cost curve. Some will be more successful than others and, if competitive conditions allow, they will grow their market shares as a result. Others will learn from these successes and either match them, exceed them, or fade away. For all this to happen, we need more experimentation, not less. If a market consists of just one dominant insurer squaring off against one dominant provider, there will be at most two chances at experimentation. Given their exalted market positions, it is more likely that neither insurer nor provider would take risks. Why would these monopolists bother making investments with uncertain payments when their dominance is already assured?

Break Up the Blues?

"Agreements among competitors to divide sales territories are almost always illegal."[15] So says the FTC, which successfully ordered Chicago-based FMC and Japan-based Asahi to stop dividing the market for microcrystalline cellulose. FMC had agreed not to sell in Japan while Asahi agreed to stay out of the United States. The Blues agree to divide sales territories, and the Blues would potentially compete with one another were it not for this agreement. Shouldn't antitrust law apply to them? In the early 2010s two classes of plaintiffs, representing insurance enrollees and providers, claimed that it should.

Plaintiffs had little trouble proving two important facts: Blues plans are independent companies, rather than divisions of some overarching Blue corporation, and the market division (and associated best efforts) rules are binding. In April 2018, a US District Court judge presiding over the enrollee class ruled that the Blue market division should be analyzed under the per se standard, rather than under a rule of reason standard that would have been more favorable to the Blues. In a nutshell, the judge would not let the Blues offer the Blue Card in defense of market division. A panel of the 11th Circuit Appellate Court upheld this ruling in December 2018.

Despite this setback, the Blues initially carried on in court. It was one thing for plaintiffs to prove that the Blues had violated antitrust law. It would be another for plaintiffs to prove that they had suffered damages. The Blues argued that market division and best efforts rules are procompetitive because they enable each local Blue to assemble a national provider network by piggybacking off the networks of other Blue plans; this is what the Blue Card is all about. Plaintiffs countered that independent Blues could easily form national networks without central coordination by the Blue Cross and Blue Shield Association. Plaintiffs also argued that in the absence of market division and the best efforts rules, independent Blues plans would enter each other's markets The Blues countered that the economic model that predicted the impact of entry was divorced from market realities.

In September 2020 the Blue Cross Association reached a tentative settlement agreement with the enrollee class. If the settlement is approved by member plans and the court, the Blues would eliminate best efforts rules, relax other aspects of their market division agreement, and pay $2.7 billion in penalties. There is already speculation that Anthem will become a national player. Health Care Services Corporation might follow suit. Whether they will build out their existing networks or acquire other plans remains to be seen. In any event, this is likely to be good news for consumers. Insurance markets have been highly concentrated for many decades, something that was unlikely to change without a dramatic shock to the system. This settlement could be that shock.

9

WILL DISRUPTORS SAVE THE HEALTH ECONOMY?

"Anything you can do, I can do better."

FROM *ANNIE GET YOUR GUN*; SONG BY IRVING BERLIN

The lure of profits is a siren call to innovators. Fifty years ago, General Motors was the largest and most profitable business in the world. Enter Honda, Toyota, and Nissan, whose lean manufacturing techniques revolutionized car making and made a mockery of GM's high costs and uneven quality. Or consider Kodak, which once sold more camera film than all other companies combined, until digital cameras turned it into a dinosaur. And then there is Toys "R" Us, the poster child for all the big box stores that lost out to online retailers. Virtually every industry is replete with stories of once dominant firms cut down to size by innovative competitors.

Health care is the big exception. One is hard pressed to find a dominant provider or insurer that started less than seventy-five years ago. The Blues, Kaiser, Johns Hopkins, Mayo, New York Presbyterian, and Massachusetts General are among the most obvious exemplars of endurance. From coast to coast, yesterday's dominant health care organizations are today's dominant health care organizations. There are a few relative "newcomers" like United Healthcare, Sutter, and Intermountain, but even they are forty years old.

This seems very puzzling. Strategy gurus preach about how inefficient firms are ripe for disruption. So where is the disruption in health care, whose providers and insurers seem rife with inefficiency? Recent surveys of health care leaders suggest that certain sectors of health care (hospitals, information technology, primary care, pharmaceuticals, and payers) are desperately in need of disruption.[1] Change does seem to be in the air, with organizations at the periphery of the health economy attempting to take center stage, while successful firms outside of health care place seemingly bold bets that they can turn around this "broken system." If only it were so easy. The US health economy is a stubborn thing, and we are pessimistic about the potential for outsiders to transform it.

Destruction and Disruption

The "theory" of disruption stems from Joseph Schumpeter's discussion of "the gales of creative destruction" in his 1942 book *Capitalism, Socialism, and Democracy*.[2] Schumpeter argued that innovative entry by entrepreneurs sustains economic growth while destroying the value of incumbent firms. Although today's business leaders may be unfamiliar with Schumpeter, they are very aware of the concept of "disruptive innovation."[3] This term was coined by the late Harvard Business School strategy guru Clayton Christensen, originally in *The Innovator's Dilemma* (1997) and then in his application to health care, *The Innovator's Prescription* (2009).

Most people familiar with the concept know that it refers to new approaches with the potential to create or transform an industry. What they don't often recall is that Christensen's disruptors start off by offering bottom-tier products that are cheaper and of inferior quality. They target the "low end" of the market that has been underserved or not served at all. Left alone by the large incumbents, the disruptors grow market share, allowing them to further reduce costs through scale economies and improve product quality through learning by doing. The disrupters move up the value chain and attack the next lower-tier product market, eventually and successfully challenging the large incumbents in the higher end of the market.

In a 2000 article published in the *Harvard Business Review*, Christensen and his colleagues asked the question "Will disruptive innovations cure health care?" The "cure" he proposed was "the iron tri-angle" of health care: improved access, lower costs, and higher quality.[4] Seventeen years later, Christensen and colleagues published a report titled "How Disruptive Innovation Can *Finally* Revolutionize Health-care" (emphasis added), in which the ever-optimistic Christensen ad-mits that disruption in health care, to quote Bob Dylan, is a "slow train coming." Over time, Christensen proposed a succession of possible disruptors. Initially his list included retail clinics, ambulatory surgery centers (ASCs), and single-specialty hospitals. These all failed to dis-rupt, for a variety of reasons.[5] More recently, Christensen identified the following "likely suspects": diagnostics, Kaiser-like models of inte-grated care, home-based care, care teams, health coaches, community health workers, and even Medicare Advantage plans. Not only is the train slow, but the train cars, like the times, "are a-changin'."

This chronicle suggests the need to rethink the potential for out-siders to transform health care markets. Think of it as "the disruptor's dilemma." It would look very different from "the innovator's dilemma," because while Christensen's disruptors initially target the low end of the market, it is hard to see how this would work in health care. As the economist Mark Pauly succinctly put it, "We're not quite as good, but we sure are cheap" is not likely to win over the average patient.[6] It almost sounds like an invitation to get sued. Nor does this sound like the approach taken by the new entrants profiled below. While some of these newcomers may try to disrupt health care markets, they are not following Christensen's prescription. Nor do we think they are likely to succeed.

A Different Paradigm

In many ways, Christensen's view of disruption runs counter to two fundamental economic principles. The first is associated with the school of thought in corporate strategy known as the resource-based view of the firm. The second is associated with the "make or buy" problem. When we view potential disrupters through these economic lenses, the reasons for the health care "disrupter's dilemma" come into focus, and the few meaningful changes truly stand out. We discuss these principles here, and then use them to assess several of the most highly publicized attempts to disrupt the market.

According to the resource-based view of the firm, no firm can out-compete its rivals unless it possesses unique resources and capabilities. Amazon disrupted traditional retailing through a unique combination of a user-friendly online interface and sophisticated distribution logistics. Facebook disrupted traditional advertising through software that keeps users' eyes glued to their screens and by creating highly differentiated, customer-specific messaging. Many of today's so-called disrupters in health care do not bring new resources and capabilities to the table. Instead, they reorganize existing resources through mergers and acquisitions of previously independent firms. As we will discuss, this makes it likely they will remain niche players. In a $3 trillion market, even niche players can generate outsized financial returns, but they are unlikely to transform the health economy.

The decision to merge or remain independent is known as the "make or buy" problem, in which "make" means "do it yourself" and "buy" means doing business through market transactions. The economics of the make or buy problem suggest that "make" is the right answer under very limited conditions. These include (1) the presence of several firms in the value chain, each with some degree of monopoly power, which often leads to inefficient pricing; (2) the existence of severe coordination problems in production that cannot be resolved by contract; or (3) the need for firms to make upfront investments whose value is contingent on maintaining their relationships with specific trading partners. In the latter case, firms may be reluctant to make these investments out of fear that their trading partners will extract all the profits. While any of these conditions might justify integration, there is an offsetting benefit to remaining independent—namely, that independent market specialists are often more efficient than integrated firms. This is because independent firms face harder-edged financial incentives—ask any entrepreneur—and because independent firms often develop specialized expertise to serve multiple customers upstream or downstream that larger firms find hard to match.

With these ideas in mind, we now examine some of the most prominent recent attempts to disrupt health care markets.

202 * CHAPTER NINE

The 2,400-Pound Upstart Gorilla

In January 2018, Jeff Bezos, Warren Buffett, and Jamie Dimon announced a joint venture among their firms—Amazon, Berkshire Hathaway, and JPMorgan Chase—which they referred to as "ABC." Its stated goal was to find ways to control costs and improve the quality of health care offered to their one million employees and dependents. Although many observers of the health care sector hailed these business leaders as saviors, Bezos et al. stressed the need for patience. They had no idea how to effect meaningful change; they only knew that they had lots of money and the determination to change the status quo. They made a good start in June 2018, when they tapped the physician and Harvard professor Atul Gawande to be CEO of their joint venture. Gawande's books and articles in the *New Yorker* and elsewhere have drawn attention to many of the problems facing our health care system.[7] He recognizes that physician decision making is at the heart of the crisis; however, he has sometimes been a cheerleader for large hospital systems.[8]

Three years in and there is little to report, other than that Bezos, Buffett, and Dimon named their venture "Haven"—ostensibly to signal to employees that this is their new home, one that will explicate the intricacies of health care and health insurance. One immediate goal was the redesign of health insurance benefits for their own employees. Amazon and JPMorgan would offer new plans to employees in 2020 that feature wellness incentives, no deductibles or coinsurance, flat copays, and out-of-pocket maximums; Berkshire tested a similar pilot in a few of their companies. The plans would be administered through the major MCOs (e.g., Cigna, Aetna). ABC hired Dana Safran away from BlueCross BlueShield Massachusetts to help. If they were going to disrupt the industry, they needed to do a lot more than this, and they knew it. Other espoused goals included making it easier to access primary care, making it easier for primary care doctors to provide good care and spend more time doing it, and making pharmaceutical costs more affordable.[9] This sounds like just another way of saying that they want to solve the iron triangle. Who doesn't? The leaders of ABC suggested they had more ambitious long-term plans to address the iron triangle for the country, not just for their employees.

What could one expect from the ABC initiative? We start by asking what resources and capabilities ABC brought to the table. Special expertise in understanding how to influence physician decision making? While Gawande was no slouch, he had no unique insights. Innovative information technologies? No. New approaches to data science? Again, no. To us, it smacks of the hubris shared by many managers who believe that past success in one industry guarantees success in others. The idea that great managers have some sort of Midas touch is the stuff of legend. In the real world, however, success in one area does not guarantee success in another, no matter how deep the pockets. ESPN sold a mobile phone called the Mobile ESPN. Microsoft once offered the Zune, and Google released a game called Lively. Removed from their comfort zones, these successful firms all found ways to fail.

Don't get us wrong; ABC possessed many resources and capabilities that conveyed powerful advantages in its native markets. No one is better than Amazon at distribution and cloud computing. JP Morgan Chase excels at selling financial instruments while navigating financial regulations, while Warren Buffett has been a preternaturally good stock. The problem is that ABC lacked the expertise required to transform health care delivery. None of its principals had experience managing health care professionals or dealing with customers at the height of emotional engagement, which is what it will take to fix the doctor-patient relationship. Nor did Dr. Gawande have any meaningful management experience. Collectively, these executives might provide new insights into how we use data, but it is not as if they were inventing the wheel. Many industry analysts argue that they would come up with solutions by thinking outside the box. With health care consuming nearly 20 percent of GDP, there are already thousands of entrepreneurs doing just that. To their credit, the three business superstars acknowledged that the health care system is "enormously complicated" (echoing President Trump), that fixing it was "not going to be easy," and that we should not "expect any miracles out of us soon."[10] This is not the first time that firms which have enjoyed massive success in other industries have made forays into health care. Their track record is not reassuring: Microsoft Vault's and Google Health's failure with "personal health records" come to mind. (Google is giving it another try, by entering a joint venture with megaprovider Ascension Health. Whether this will allow Ascension to use Google's data analytics to improve care delivery, or whether Google will use Ascension's patient records to better target advertising, remains to be seen.) ABC should have been cautious.

Amazon does possess one potentially valuable capability, which it may use to disrupt retail pharmacy. In June 2018, it purchased Pill-Pack, an online pharmacy startup. With Amazon's considerable expertise in home delivery (imagine drones dropping off pills at your door), this seems like a logical extension of its business model. Investors took note, as shares of retail pharmacy giants CVS and Walgreens plunged 10 percent after the deal was announced. Investors quickly determined that there was less here than met the eye, as Amazon has no obvious plan for turning PillPack into a mainstream competitor. By August 2018, CVS and Walgreens were trading at or above their all-time highs. Amazon may soon use PillPack as an online supplier to its own employees. It remains a long way from threatening the retail pharmacy giants.

Even if Amazon successfully disrupts retail pharmacy, it would make little more than a dime's worth of difference to the overall health economy. Pharmacists have little input into medical decision making, and online pharmacies have almost none. Smart technology and big data may allow pharmacies to identify drug use patterns suggestive of health problems, and might flag these for physicians. Walgreens and CVS are already doing this, as we discuss below. If Amazon does the same, the benefits to consumers will be incremental at best. Given Amazon's business model, it seems equally likely that Amazon will use big data to improve how they market and sell other goods. Just imagine filling a prescription for a cholesterol blocker and then finding that Amazon sends you advertisements for diet books and exercise equipment. Not everyone will think this a boon.

We would be remiss if we did not mention one other resource that ABC possessed in great supply: cash. This means that it could afford to lose massive amounts in new ventures. And we can never rule out succeeding through dumb luck. If you play the lottery often enough, you might hit the jackpot, even if the odds are heavily stacked against you.

As this volume goes to press, we can conclude the story. Haven's early history was rocky. In its first three years of operation, it saw the turnover of its CEO, Atul Gawande; its chief operating officer; its chief technology officer, and its data scientists and software engineers — in all, about 14 percent of the workforce with public profiles on LinkedIn. The CEO said he wanted to spend more time on policy and advocacy work (e.g., in relation to COVID) — perhaps not too surprising, given that he never left his academic position at Harvard. Haven's ambitions to shake up health insurance likely exceeded its ability, especially given the geographic dispersion of the three founding companies' work forces, the lack of any concentrated presence of these employees among any set of providers, and the numerous stakeholders in the US health care ecosystem that they would need to engage. It also did not help that Amazon has pursued its own provider initiatives (e.g., virtual care). In January 2021, ABC shut down altogether, disrupting the lives of its remaining fifty-plus employees.

Smaller Newcomers

While ABC entered the fray with deep pockets, many smaller companies hope to disrupt the market by exploiting modern technology. One of the most interesting is a newcomer to the insurance market. Others are small companies that hope to change the health care world one web app at a time.

And Who Goes to Oscar?

Oscar, which bills itself as a "new kind of insurance company," wants to do for health insurance what Geico and Progressive have done for car insurance — sign up millennials over the Internet with little hassle and at a low cost. Founded in 2012, Oscar has more than 400,000 members as of 2020, and was valued at more than $3 billion. It started in New York and has expanded to nearly twenty states including California, Florida, and Texas. Some of our MBA students think it is the next big thing. If only they could articulate why—especially since most of Oscar's growth comes from geographic expansion, with relatively modest within-state growth. With its heavy reliance on ACA exchange enrollments, Oscar has been blindsided by the repeal of the "individual mandate," which reduced the appeal of the individual market. With ongoing losses ($131 million in 2017, $57 million in 2018), Oscar is now moving into the crowded Medicare Advantage and small business markets.

By all appearances, Oscar's online platform makes all the other health insurers seem very twentieth-century, providing an experience that works well for its targeted audience. Oscar boasts the highest member engagement of any insurer. Unfortunately, Oscar's positioning strategy, to the extent it has one, pretty much stops there. Oscar does not do anything else particularly well, and in most important respects it remains at a deep disadvantage relative to the competition. As a result, it is likely to remain a niche product. We are skeptical as to whether Oscar will ever remotely resemble UnitedHealthcare, the last great startup insurer.

Why such skepticism? Think about the tasks performed by traditional insurers. They employ actuaries and underwriters to estimate risk and price it. They assemble networks. They adjudicate claims, analyze data, and manage care. They offer wellness and disease management programs. The best insurers work proactively with providers to reduce costs and boost quality. They have dedicated sales forces that sell to and service the needs of employer groups. What does Oscar do? Other than marketing on the Internet, not much. It rents its broad networks from other insurers, which immediately puts it at a cost disadvantage. To offset this, Oscar has begun forming its own narrow networks. This allows Oscar to get reasonable discounts as well as funnel care to low-cost providers. Young and healthy enrollees, especially those who rarely engage in the health care market, do not mind these choice limitations. Small businesses looking for cheap health insurance solutions might also buy in. Midsize and large employers, which account for the bulk of commercial insurance enrollments, will steer clear. Oscar also outsources care management and wellness, again driving up its costs. And despite its "high tech" image, Oscar lacks the sheer volume of data, let alone the data analytics capabilities, to match those of its bigger rivals. Again, this might not matter to its core market, but it necessarily limits the size of the core. Is it any wonder that Oscar largely thrived on the ACA exchanges, whose participants skew young, healthy, and inexperienced as health care consumers? Oscar has room to expand its model to more states, but is unlikely to achieve substantial market penetration in any of them. This quote from a dissatisfied customer posting to Bestcompany.com sums up Oscar's problem: "Oscar has some nice bells and whistles for millennials—a phone app, a decent web site, a wellness center in Brooklyn. None of this is a substitute for good coverage, which they definitely do not offer."[11]

Oscar is hardly the only insurer that steers away from the employer marketplace. Centene, Molina, Neighborhood Health Plan, Amerigroup, and others have all fared well in the exchange and in Medicaid managed-care markets with plans that often feature narrow networks with few bells and whistles. Executives at the Blues, United, Aetna, or Cigna do not lose any sleep over them.

Oscar partnered with Cleveland Clinic on a cobranded health plan, launched in 2018, to offer individual coverage to five counties in northeast Ohio. Enrollees get access to Cleveland Clinic primary care physicians and care managers, as well as an Oscar Concierge nurse and three care guides, and 24/7 access to telemedicine. The plan enrolled 11,000 members for 2018 and is now engaged in rolling out to additional counties in Ohio. Oscar also announced partnerships with both Humana and Cigna to provide services to small business owners. Essentially, Oscar can bring its technology-enabled health care services to small businesses in concert with the large health care networks that employers are used to working with. For 2020, Oscar plans to expand into nineteen new markets and four new states—which would bring its total footprint to forty-seven markets in nineteen states. Part of the expansion will rest on Oscar's "Virtual Primary Care," which offers digital and in-home services (e.g., lab draws) at no cost in selected markets to respond to the COVID-19 crisis.

Oscar faces stiff competition in all the new markets it is trying to enter. Medicare Advantage (MA) is an increasingly saturated market, with an estimated 2,700 MA plans open for enrollment in 2019; this is 18 percent higher than the 2,300 offered in 2018. Over the same period, MA enrollment is projected to grow 11.5 percent. If growth in new plans continues to outpace growth in new enrollees, Oscar may struggle to grab any market share. Oscar also has to compete with the largest insurers, which account for a large share of MA enrollees and have disproportionate underwriting gains. Oscar may not find the small business market any easier, given the large number of players.

Ultimately, Oscar envisions a health care industry where employer-defined plans will disappear as more consumers turn to individual coverage, HDHPs, and health reimbursement arrangements (HRAs). From a small base of only 70,000 enrollees several years ago after retrenchment and withdrawal from several markets (e.g., Dallas, New Jersey), Oscar Health has grown to roughly 400,000 enrollees, including around 375,000 individual members and another 20,000 coming through small-group insurance and Medicare Advantage. Fueling this expansion is a massive capital infusion of $540 million raised from Alphabet, Founders Fund, Capital G (Alphabet's later-stage investment firm), and Verily (Alphabet's investment firm focused on life sciences). Overall, Oscar has raised $1.3 billion, with plans announced in December 2020 to file for an initial public offering.

What App, Doc?

Every year, a few of our MBA students believe that the path to reforming the health care system goes through their smartphone. They want to use big data and little phones to facilitate price shopping, allow patients to self-diagnose every sort of ailment, track physical activity, and send real-time reports to nurses at monitoring stations, who can send feedback to the users, alert primary care physicians, or even call for an ambulance. Another set of apps creates a video interface between patients and doctors, while allowing both to access the patient's medical history. This cross between Skype and electronic health records allows patients to obtain urgent care without leaving home — a virtual return to the good old days when doctors made house calls.

The field is very crowded. A 2016 study reported more than 250,000 available consumer apps for dozens of medical conditions.[12] However, there is very little regulation and quality control in this space; the US

Food and Drug Administration has vetted only a fraction of a percent of the mobile apps available. There are also concerns over security of the private information conveyed through these apps, an issue rarely addressed in consumer-written reviews. Despite this, many of these ideas are catching on.

Even more concerning is the evidence base on mobile apps. A 2018 study identified twenty-three randomized trials evaluating twenty-two available apps that mostly address diabetes, mental health, and obesity.[13] Most trials were pilot studies with small sample sizes and limited durations. While eleven of the twenty-three trials showed a meaningful effect on health or surrogate outcomes attributable to apps, the overall paucity of evidence showing app effectiveness makes it difficult to be confident about their future.

We see several reasons why smart technology will have limited impact on megaproviders. The first two are related to the 80/20 rule of medicine, also known as the Pareto Principle: 80 percent of spending can be traced to 20 percent of the population. Patients with cancer, on dialysis, or in need of joint replacement surgery will have little to gain from these new technologies. This is backed up by a recent study of twenty digital health companies with more than $2.5 billion in private equity funding.[14] The study found a total of 156 published studies on these companies' products. Of these, only 29 studies pertained to "high-burden" conditions such as cancer, stroke, or heart disease. Even these products may have a hard time reaching their target audience, which consists mainly of older patients who, at least for now, are less tech savvy and are unlikely to replace the traditional doctor-patient relationship with the impersonal cell phone. Ultimately, the key question is whether smart technology will substitute for or complement the traditional provider-patient relationship. While many patients may want to participate in medical decision making, we suspect that few will want to be their own doctors.

Direct Contracting

If big insurers face a nonregulatory threat, it may come from their biggest customers, who are directly contracting with providers. The most prominent of these is Walmart, which caught everyone by surprise in 2012 when it announced a "Centers of Excellence" (COE) program to serve its own employees. Walmart offered to cover 100 percent of medical costs, plus travel expenses, for selected spine and cardiac surgeries performed at one of six selected health systems across the country, including the venerable Mayo and Cleveland Clinics. Walmart has since doubled the number of participating providers. It only pays for spine surgery at its Centers of Excellence, and may tightly narrow its networks for other procedures. Walmart does not disclose the prices it pays to these systems, but it seems likely that it is getting a pretty hefty discount. It also claims that its designated providers avoid unnecessary procedures, and when they do perform surgery, they are delivering better outcomes, which gets Walmart's employees back to work sooner.

Walmart also directly contracts for diagnostic services, paying for some employees diagnosed with cancer to fly to the Mayo Clinic in Rochester, Minnesota. Walmart reports that 10 percent of employees referred to Mayo had been incorrectly diagnosed by their local providers. Thanks to Mayo, these employees receive more appropriate and usually less expensive treatments. (This does not imply an overall false positive rate of 10 percent, as only selected employees make the trip to Mayo.) Walmart has expanded this program to a half-dozen Centers of Excellence. Through its Centers of Excellence programs for surgery and diagnostics, Walmart is doing exactly what had made it so successful as a retailer: it is bypassing the middleman and contracting directly with suppliers.

Walmart is not the only big company involved in direct contracting. In a 2018 survey of some of the nation's largest employers, 18 percent said they expected to directly contract with hospitals.[15] A broader survey found that 6 percent of large employers were directly contracting with hospitals and an additional 16 percent were considering it.[16] The most popular procedures for direct contracting included transplants, bariatric surgery, and spine surgery. Despite this trend, we doubt whether direct contracting poses an existential threat to big insurers.

Simple economics seems to weigh against direct contracting. For most things it sells, Walmart is its supplier's biggest customer, which allows it to negotiate the best deals. This is rarely the case for medical care, where Walmart is hard-pressed to match the purchasing clout of a local Blue or United plan.[17] Walmart succeeds here by tightly narrowing its network—usually just a handful of providers across the entire nation. This allows it to drive market share and command larger discounts. Only a handful of large employers will be able to copy Walmart before overwhelming Mayo and the other top centers. Future success will require narrowing networks within local geographies rather than concentrating patients in just a few national centers. Thus far, most employers seem reluctant to offer narrow local networks.

Direct contracting is also largely restricted to a handful of discrete surgical procedures, as well as some diagnostic procedures. This is no accident. It is fairly easy to negotiate a price for bariatric surgery, which involves a relatively fixed and predictable bundle of services and lends itself to a fixed bundled price. It is far more difficult to identify a common bundle of services for patients with chronic conditions—or with conditions, such as cancer, whose course is difficult to predict. This makes bundled pricing all but impossible for many costly conditions.

When it comes to direct contracting, the size of the purchaser matters. The more covered lives in the contract, the bigger the discount, and even modest-sized insurers control more covered lives than all but the biggest employers. Many insurers offer narrow networks for the selected surgical procedures, and for every large employer that directly contracts with providers, there are four that rely on insurance-sponsored narrow networks.[18] Even if more employers choose to go the narrow-network route, it will still be more economical for insurers to offer them. By combining the purchasing clout of their many clients, insurers will be able to strike better deals, and perform more effective care management, than even the largest employers.

Making New Connections

Another potential source of disruption comes from new combinations of existing firms, many of which possess ample resources and capabilities that support their current success. Will integration lead to further success, or just a rearrangement of the deck chairs? As our discussion of the economics of "make or buy" suggests, there are often complex economic factors on both sides of the ledger.

DRUG STORES, INSURERS, AND

PHARMACY BENEFIT MANAGERS

In December 2017, CVS Caremark announced its merger with Aetna. Four months later, Cigna and Express Scripts tied the knot. Observers predict big things for both deals. Before we tone down these expectations, we should point out that there is a genuine make/buy efficiency in play. Each deal brings a traditional medical insurer (Aetna and Cigna) and a pharmacy benefit manager (CVS Caremark and ESI) under one roof. Properly designed, health insurance should encourage the proper balance of medical and drug treatment. Patients should not have to face high copayments for drugs that substitute for more expensive medical care. When drug coverage is divorced from medical coverage, however, pharmacy benefit managers (PBMs) may have less incentive to promote substitution toward expensive drugs, even if the alternative is more expensive medical care. The result is a formulary that reduces drug costs but raises overall treatment costs. Research confirms that when medical and drug coverage decisions are coordinated by an integrated firm, cost sharing is rationalized, and total spending goes down.[19] The benefits of this coordination might be enough to justify these enormous deals. They had better be enough, because it is difficult to find any other sure-fire efficiencies.

We focus on the CVS-Aetna deal, which drew the lion's share of market and regulatory attention. CVS consists of (1) a large chain of nearly 10,000 CVS retail pharmacies; (2) a large PBM, Caremark, with 90 million members; (3) a chain of more than 1,100 retail clinics (MinuteClinics) that reside within some of its pharmacies; and (4) a staff of 4,000 nursing professionals working in the retail clinics and home health care. For its part, Aetna is a large health insurer covering roughly 22 million enrollees with Medicare Advantage, Medicaid, and commercial insurance.

According to a CVS Health statement, the merger will "integrat[e] more closely the work of doctors, pharmacists, and other health care professionals and health benefits companies to create a platform that is easier to use and less expensive for consumers."[20] In so doing, "the combined company [will serve] as America's front door to quality health care." Not quite the iron triangle, but close.

According to the announcement, the merger will have thirteen specific aims:

- Combine CVS Health's clinical capabilities with Aetna's analytics.

- Connect Aetna's provider network with CVS Health's community access model.

- Remake the consumer health care experience.

- Improve understanding of patients' health goals.

- Guide patients through the health care system.

- Put consumers at the center of health care delivery and empower them.

- Avoid unnecessary hospital readmissions & emergency department visits.

- Help members achieve their best health.

- Complement the care provided by patients' physicians.

- Help meet the health needs of members with chronic conditions.

- Use analytics together with broader patient information to reduce cost of care.

- Provide face-to-face counseling to patients between doctor visits.

- Provide remote monitoring of patients' health status indicators.

It is the triple aim on steroids. Anyone who can deliver on all of these benefits deserves Nobel Prizes for medicine *and* economics! Thus far, the firms have been a bit vague about how they will meet these goals. At the JP Morgan Health Care Conference in San Francisco in January 2019, CVS's CEO, Larry Merlo, summarized the value proposition in a simple statement: "Create a uniquely powerful new platform that will enable us to transform the consumer health care experience." Aetna's chief digital officer, Firdaus Bhathena, summarized it even more simply as "one-stop shopping," a label also applied by Harvard Business School economist Leemore Dafny.[21] Such labels are designed to conjure up the image and imagined benefits of Kaiser. More recently, Larry Merlo confirmed the primacy of its "healthHUB" pharmacy store concept during CVS's investor day.

While there are lots of moving parts here, much of the enthusiasm for this deal rests on CVS's retail clinics, Aetna's claims database, and the espoused belief that "data is king in today's economy." These supposed advantages are fraught with problems, as outlined below.[22]

RETAIL CLINICS

CVS Health operates MinuteClinics in roughly 1,100 pharmacies. Following the merger, these retail clinics will purportedly become mini-health centers that expand access to lower-cost health care services and improve care convenience. Some liken them to new community health centers. As we have detailed in earlier chapters, health care is local, and there are few firms offering more local options; 71 percent of Americans live within five miles of a CVS.[23] Patients who visit nearby Minute Clinics will have faster access to lower-level care that can increase earlier management of illness and reduce unnecessary use of hospital emergency rooms. In this fashion, retail clinics will help solve the iron triangle of health care by simultaneously delivering on improved access, improved outcomes, and lower costs.

Proponents have long hailed the potential for retail clinics to transform the health care industry. Such expectations began with Christensen's futuristic view of retail clinics as a disruptive innovation.[24] This helped to propel a rapid rise in the number of clinics that, in turn, led consultants to forecast growth in the sector to nearly three thousand by 2021.[25] Proponents also claim that enhanced retail clinics can cure many of the ailments plaguing the health economy. We disagree.

When viewed through the lens of "make or buy" economics, it is difficult to see the value proposition in pharmacy-based retail clinics. While it is true that the health care value chain is often poorly coordinated, combining pharmacy with primary care seems like an odd way to address the problem. Megaproviders, which integrate nearly the entire value chain except for retail pharmacy, have struggled to improve care coordination, so it is difficult to see how pharmacy/PCP integration is going to do any better. Avoiding hold-ups and promoting investments—the other potential benefit of make versus buy—seems like a total nonstarter. Retail pharmacies offer one real asset: convenient locations for patients who require basic primary care. That will only take the concept so far.

Not surprisingly, the hoped-for expansion in the retail clinic sector has yet to happen. The number of clinics plateaued just below two thousand sites by 2015, with a slight decline by 2018.[26] The average clinic sees only ten to thirty patients per day, and loses forty thousand dollars annually.[27] The trend holds for both CVS Health, which operates roughly half of all such clinics, and Walgreens, which operates roughly one-fifth. If anything, Walgreens has shifted its strategy away from in-house clinics to partnerships with local health systems that own and operate the clinics inside Walgreens—effectively moving away from a vertically integrated model to a strategic alliance model. Other retail clinic chains have also stopped their expansion. For its part, CVS Health has concentrated its efforts in recent years on horizontal integration and on transforming the pharmacy operations acquired from Target. Contrary to the hype, retail clinics are not a booming industry. Even one of Christensen's colleagues has admitted this.[28]

There are other explanations for the stalled growth of retail clinics. CVS Health's pharmacies have experienced slow overall growth.[29] This may be partly attributable to its efforts to swallow two recent acquisitions: long-term care pharmacy Omnicare, and Target's in-store pharmacies. With top management focused on internal integration issues,

CVS would naturally take a go-slow approach to expanding elsewhere. The stalled growth also reflects the maturation of the retail pharmacy business, with annual growth of only 1 or 2 percent. Retail pharmacies also face mounting competition from mass merchandisers, mail-order prescription providers, online pharmacies, convenience stores, and other health clinics. Indeed, some speculate that CVS plans to use its retail clinics to play catch-up with UnitedHealthCare's Optum subsidiary and its MedExpress urgent care centers. In contrast to retail clinics, the number of these centers grew by 8 percent between 2017 and 2018. There is some speculation that the retail pharmacy market suffers from excess capacity and that consolidation is likely, due to falling drug reimbursement rates, mandatory mail-order plans, the growth of generic drugs, and the growth of narrow networks.[30] Drug volumes and general margins in retail pharmacies, including CVS Health, remain stagnant at best.[31]

CVS also faces competition from Amazon/PillPack. CVS has funded a pilot at 350 of its drugstores in Boston to compete with Amazon called "Care Pass," which offers free delivery on most online purchases and prescription drugs, a 20 percent discount on CVS-branded products, 24/7 access to a pharmacist helpline, and a monthly ten-dollar coupon, all in exchange for a $5 monthly or $48 annual subscription. In various cities, CVS is also offering same-day delivery of prescription drugs. This pricing and these benefits are not sustainable.

One final problem with CVS's strategy is the issue faced by all firms that seek to vertically integrate: a mismatch in capacity across stages in the value chain. For example, CVS has 135 pharmacies in the state of Minnesota, comprising roughly 10 percent of that market. It has only twenty-five retail clinics, indicating that more build-out is required. More importantly, Aetna has a small share of the Minnesota private health insurance market. Thus, the company will be challenged in steering enough Aetna enrollees to retail clinics in CVS pharmacies to keep them busy, and will be required to attract enrollees from rival insurers and PBMs.

ANALYTICS AND BIG DATA

One of Aetna's major contributions to this merger is its analytics capability. CVS-Aetna's chief financial officer, Eva Borato, announced that the merged company will invest up to $350 million in 2019 on analytics and digital capabilities to improve chronic care management and enhance its "clinical platform."[32] The goal? To engage enrollees, improve outcomes, and lower costs (shades of the iron triangle). In recent testimony, Aetna counsel Thomas Sabatino stated that his company's "analytics team can identify members who are at high risk for developing health complications and share that information with providers to help them prevent catastrophic health events before they happen."[33] There is less here than meets the eye. Insurers have been developing predictive modeling capabilities since the early 2000s. Aetna was already a leader in this area. Predictive modeling has had limited success thus far, and it is not clear how an additional $350 million will make much of a difference. The problem is that prediction is not enough. Even if CVS-Aetna can identify high-risk individuals, it must (1) contact and alert them, (2) activate them to seek care, and (3) change their behavior to prevent further complications. The problem here is that those at highest risk are among the least motivated to take care of their own health, and may also be least able to take corrective action. It is not clear how Aetna's linkage to a chain of pharmacies, some of which have retail clinics, will ameliorate this situation.

There is also growing recognition of the "oversell" of digital health technologies. A recent issue of *Health Affairs* is devoted to this topic.[34] There is scant evidence of clinical impact on any of the corners of the iron triangle. Moreover, most digital companies do not seem interested in studying the impact of their technologies on clinical endpoints. This may reflect the fact that technologies that work in a laboratory setting have trouble working in the real world, as Google has discovered in its effort to apply artificial intelligence to treating blindness in India.[35] While algorithms can be trained on sample images, real-world photos of patients' eyes can be a whole different ballgame. The same may prove true for all sorts of conditions.

Like retail clinics and digital technologies, the whole field of health care analytics has suffered from excessive hype. Big data requires "big analysis" and "big understanding" to test hypotheses about what the data suggest and to discern signal from noise. We can use big data to identify associations, and we can apply machine learning for predictive modeling. These are valuable tools, as they allow us to make informed guesses about which patients are at risk for what outcomes. This is the starting point for positive change, but more must be done. As noted by John Halamka, chief information officer at Beth Israel Deaconess Medical Center, someone has to "ask the right questions."[36] What big data does not easily allow us to do is make causal inferences so that we can understand how to improve outcomes. Consider patients who are at risk for heart disease. Thanks to big data, we are better able to identify these patients. Once we know who they are, we might want to encourage them to change their diets and exercise regimens. The question is how. Should we provide patients with more information about their health? Nudge them with reminders to exercise? Incentivize them? Inform their physicians and let them do the nudging? To answer these questions, we need to figure out what causes what, something all the terabytes in the world may not tell us (though a carefully designed randomized trial of just a few dozen patients might). Even if we come to these deep understandings, we have to get patients and physicians to buy in. Can Aetna achieve buy-in where integrated health care systems have failed? It is definitely worth the effort, even if we are skeptical of its success.

Progress is slow. Recent research shows that predictive analytics using a claims-based algorithm to compute member health care utilization risk scores can help in the treatment of high-risk elderly patients with chronic conditions.[37] Such targeting can reduce some types of utilization (specialist visits, emergency room visits) but not the most expensive types of utilization (hospital admissions). The impact here is due more to care coordination for the chronically ill rather than to the artificial intelligence technology, however. In other words, AI helps identify patients who need help, but old-fashioned personal attention is required to deliver that help. Thus, any new technology may owe its impact to the accompanying social structures to help implement them—a fact long ago observed as the "sociotechnical system." It's not certain that the new tech entrants understand this. Based on the growing isolation of younger Americans, it appears that social media companies emphasize the technical side more than the social.

Nearly two decades after the introduction of electronic health records, there is no evidence that big data is reducing costs, and only scattered evidence that quality of care is improving.[38] A more recent illustration of such overblown expectations is IBM's aggressive promotion of its Watson supercomputer as a revolution in precision medicine and cancer care. Analysts suspect that IBM marketed the product to providers without any evidence base, in order to bolster its flagging revenues.[39] We might summarize this critique by reminding everyone that, like EHRs, artificial intelligence and big data are "tools" and not solutions.[40] Tools do not transform companies, let alone industries.

OTHER RATIONALES FOR THE DEAL

When the ESI/Cigna deal was announced just months after CVS-Aetna, any informed observer of the health care industry should have immediately asked, "Why them, why now"? One cynical answer was that the Department of Justice had just blocked horizontal mergers of Aetna and Humana, and of Anthem and Cigna. Given the well known adage that public companies need to show growth to their investors, the two health insurers looked to other companies with which they might merge and thereby boost their earnings. What gives credence to this cynical view is that within one month of a US District Court blocking its merger with Aetna, Humana courted the nation's largest postacute care provider, Kindred—a deal consummated in June 2018.

Another explanation for the CVS-Aetna merger is that it is a defensive strategy undertaken by both parties. Many suspected that CVS Health moved on this deal to counter Amazon's entry into pharmacy distribution; in hindsight, this rumored entry did not occur. Moreover, CVS Health has been facing declining performance over the past few years, in part due to a loss of pharmacy customers to Walgreens. In 2014, Walgreens formed a strategic alliance with Prime Therapeutics, the PBM serving Blue Cross Blue Shield plans in several states. As a result of this alliance, BCBS members were steered away from other pharmacies, including CVS, and toward Walgreens as their national preferred pharmacy network.

For Aetna, the merger may be a defensive move to counter growth challenges. Much of the growth in managed care enrollment has occurred in three market segments: Medicare Advantage, Medicaid, and, until recent years, the state health insurance exchanges. Aetna had lower market share in the more profitable Medicare Advantage market, and sought to correct that weakness through its proposed 2016 merger with Humana. Aetna was looking for growth in all the wrong places as the Department of Justice successfully blocked the merger.

Aetna also watched as the Optum Health subsidiary of its major competitor, UnitedHealthcare, announced in December 2017—the same month as the announced CVS-Aetna deal—its plan to merge with a large provider, the DaVita Medical Group. The deal would add significant physician capacity (DaVita has three hundred clinics with a reported thirteen thousand affiliated physicians) to Optum's burgeoning provider network (thirty thousand physicians, both employed and affiliated) serving its MA plans. It would also augment its large ambulatory care business; DaVita has 35 urgent care centers. United already operates 250 MedExpress urgent care centers, and a chain of surgery centers. Aetna is thus looking to respond to the growing provider presence of a major competitor.

We will leave it to the financial analysts to explore the benefits of growth for growth's sake, although we suspect they are not pleased. We will observe that this seems a lot more like rent seeking than value creation. There may be some benefit to CVS-Aetna, but where is the benefit to the health economy?

THE ANTITRUST WRINKLE

Some critics of the CVS-Aetna merger complained that it represented a further concentration of power, and asked for antitrust relief. For example, the American Medical Association opposed the deal on the grounds that it would lead to excessive concentration in Medicare Part D and PBM markets.[41] The Department of Justice took nearly a year to review the merger, during which time market analysts questioned whether it would go through. They need not have worried, as the antitrust concerns were overstated. The two firms overlapped in a few markets, and the DOJ did require Aetna to divest its Medicare Part D drug insurance business as a condition for approval. There was also some concern about vertical aspects of the deal, namely that Aetna might tailor insurance benefits and provider fees to favor CVS Minute Clinics while CVS might raise its Minute Clinic prices to other insurers, so as to favor Aetna. The DOJ looked long and hard at this "raising rivals costs" argument, but took a pass. The DOJ may have felt that neither Aetna nor CVS Minute Clinics had the market size necessary to make the theory plausible. Critics also protested that Aetna would push enrollees to visit CVS clinics. This would be a product feature or product defect, depending on one's point of view, and not an antitrust violation. If consumers didn't like it, they could choose another insurer. What probably cemented the DOJ decision to approve the deal was that US District Court Judge Richard Leon, who was hearing the CVS-Aetna case, had just ruled in favor of the AT&T/Time Warner merger. The two deals have similar economics, especially the raising rivals costs argument, with the facts favoring CVS-Aetna at least as much as AT&T/Time Warner. Surprisingly, after the DOJ allowed the deal to go through, Judge Leon raised new questions concerning the growth of CVS's PBM, at a time when the US Senate was looking into alleged anticompetitive practices of the PBM sector.

WALGREENS HAS A GO AT IT

Not to be outdone, CVS's major competitor, Walgreens, has entered the fray. In mid-2018, Walgreens launched a digital marketplace in partnership with sixteen local health systems and national providers. The website Find Care Now lists cash prices for a range of health care services. This is hardly a new idea. Led by the late Uwe Reinhardt, academics and policy wonks have been calling for health care price transparency for years.[42] Many private insurers offer transparency tools, as have a handful of entrepreneurs whose smartphone apps give prices for everything from prescription drugs to MRIs and ultrasounds. The problem is that no one has figured out how to consistently translate price transparency into lower health spending.[43] Individuals who use price transparency tools tend to be young and healthy—hardly the desired target audience if one is trying to bend the cost curve. Users also tend to have big deductibles, which makes sense; but once they exhaust their deductibles, the benefits of price shopping disappear or are attenuated. Someone may yet figure out how to get high-cost patients to respond to prices, but Walgreens's effort does not strike us as the answer.[44]

Walgreens is looking for other ways to expand. It is collaborating with McLaren Health Care to offer new health care offerings in its Michigan drug stores, and it has formed a partnership with Laboratory Corporation of America to open six hundred medical testing locations in its stores. It announced a partnership with Humana, called Partners in Primary Care, to develop senior health clinics. As noted above, Walgreens has developed a pilot with UnitedHealthCare's MedExpress unit to develop urgent care centers next to its pharmacies—with separate entrances, but with a connector between them and the pharmacies. The stated goal, according to David Wichmann, United HealthGroup's CEO, is to develop a "higher-performing local health system," whatever that means.[45] In January 2019, Walgreens announced a seven-year pact with Microsoft to develop new care delivery models that leverage Microsoft's Azure cloud and artificial intelligence platform, including "digital health corners" in some stores to sell health care–related hardware and devices. Walgreens is also now working with Microsoft scientists to create the "store of the future," and "health care breakthroughs" to be named later. In classic corporate speak, Walgreens's CEO, Stefano Pessina, stated that the "strategic partnership with Microsoft demonstrates our strong commitment to creating integrated, next-generation, digitally-enabled health care delivery solutions for our customers, transforming our stores into modern neighborhood health destinations."[46] He also called the partnership an effort to create a "seamless ecosystem of participating organizations" (e.g., providers, insurers, and pharmaceutical firms) "that will be able to facilitate the life of our customers." We await the translation.

Like those of many other would-be disrupters, Walgreens' strategy includes a heavy emphasis on "bricks and mortar" in the local community. Such an emphasis serves as a contrast to, and hopefully a competitive advantage over, Amazon's more virtual approach. That said, both Walgreens and CVS also emphasize their digital approaches to compete with Amazon. At the same time, Amazon has bought up Whole Foods as perhaps a foothold in the bricks-and-mortar space, with an option to open even pharmacies or retail clinics in its grocery stores. It may also open thousands of AmazonGo cashierless stores. It sounds like everyone is hedging their bets and moving into one another's spaces. It does not sound as though they have anything new to offer to health care consumers, except more places to spend the same health care dollars.

UNITED'S BIG BET ON BIG DATA

We have previously commented on the importance and limitations of big data for predictive analytics. United Healthcare has placed a big bet on doing more than just predicting illness. Its spinoff company, Optum, holds the largest private claims database and employs a large team of computer scientists and social scientists to mine the data for all they are worth. While that seems like yet another (albeit large) bet on data analytics, Optum is also the nation's largest employer of physicians. After its recent acquisition of DaVita's medical groups, United employs and affiliates with roughly fifty thousand physicians, or about 5 percent of all physicians in the United States. Optum also owns labs, outpatient surgery centers, and urgent care centers. The obvious question is whether the two strategies—data analytics and vertical integration—are linked. At a minimum, United can assure that its vertically integrated physicians are equipped with the latest EHR technology, something that independent physicians often lack. After mining its data, Optum can also keep its providers informed about the latest discoveries. Optum could even conduct experiments in which some of its physicians employ new treatment options. Optum would be well positioned to rapidly change treatment pathways in response to new discoveries. Optum's vertical integration strategy might ultimately pave the way for discoveries about treatment processes (as opposed to specific drugs or medical procedures) that have been out of reach in our fragmented system. Of course, what sounds good in theory often falls apart in practice, as megaproviders have discovered. Whether Optum can deal with physicians as effectively as it deals with data remains to be seen. Still, this seems far more promising than merely amassing terabytes of medical records.

Optum has one other reason for buying up providers in the value chain that may be more about rent seeking than about value creation. These acquisitions give United leverage when bargaining with powerful providers, including some of the megaproviders we have profiled. Optum could also use its data analytics capabilities to experiment and identify ways to steer enrollees to the lowest-cost treatment options. Pushed to the limit, this might mean that United enrollees are steered to United providers. In this way, United may be on its way to being a Kaiser with a national scope, albeit without Kaiser's culture or deep knowledge about how to work with physicians to manage patient care. If this is all that Optum ultimately accomplishes, it will serve United's interests, it may serve the interests of United's enrollees, and it may promote competition across value chains. It will also further balkanize our health care system. This bears watching.

Taking Stock

A basic tenet of business strategy is that high profit margins are an invitation for new firms to disrupt the market. Health care is a huge and hugely profitable business, so it is no surprise to see so many organizations joining the fray. While many may succeed at grabbing a piece of the pie, overall health care spending will only fall if these newcomers reduce the size of the pie. We are skeptical about many ongoing efforts. Consider the themes mentioned in this and other chapters: disruption, transformation, platforms, silver bullets, and gurus. These are quintessential examples of the types of BS that are commonly found in the health care industry.[47] Such BS may be covering up the main reasons for many of the strategies discussed here: rent seeking and growth. This suggests that everyone should swallow all these would-be disrupters with a huge grain of salt.

There is some cause for hope. We are seeing more new ideas for transforming the health care value chain than ever before, from a wider scope of players. The good news is that one success may be all that is required for radical change. Disruption of health care markets is a lot like venture capital in Silicon Valley. Nearly all venture capital bets fail. But occasionally a Google or Facebook comes along, and the venture capitalists make more than enough to cover their losses. While we are doubtful whether any of the efforts described in this chapter will prove to be the Google of health care reform (including Google itself), it is still early days for the disrupters. So fasten your seat belt, as it could be a wild ride.

10
RECOMMENDATIONS FOR COMPETITION POLICY

"Vigilant and effective antitrust enforcement today is preferable to the heavy hand of government regulation . . . tomorrow."

FORMER US SENATOR ORRIN HATCH (R-UT)[1]

In the four decades since we authors of this book started our academic careers, we have witnessed many trends, including the rise of (and near fall and then renewed interest in) HMOs, the growth of hospital systems, and the emergence and ultimate dominance of integrated delivery networks.[2] We have also seen CONs, DRGs, PPOs, PPMs, ACOs, EHRs and the increasing use of big data. With every new TLA (three-letter acronym), enthusiasts promise accountability, alignment, and coordination. If the enthusiasts are to be believed, then we are poised to reach the goals for an ideal health system laid out by the Committee on the Cost of Medical Care nearly a century ago, and more recently articulated in the iron triangle and the triple aim.

These have not been totally empty promises. The quality of American health care is better than ever, and arguably better than what is available anywhere else.[3] While health care providers have played a key role in the development of many new treatments, we doubt whether the arc of technological change has benefited from the growth of mega-providers. There have also been meaningful improvements in the consistency of medical practice, thanks to the promulgation of evidence-based medicine, but even this is still not that widespread.[4] Again, we doubt whether megaprovider systems have played much of a role in this welcome trend.

While our health system has improved along several dimensions, in other ways things have gotten worse. When we began our academic careers, people complained about health spending accounting for 7 percent of GDP. Today it eats up 18 percent. Too many people still receive the wrong care at the wrong time in the wrong place. Some are priced out of care entirely, or go bankrupt trying to pay their bills. Physicians have never been less satisfied, and patients have never placed less trust in the system. Is it any wonder that Americans are fed up with the status quo?

The need to fix our health care markets has taken on a sense of urgency. Some critics, including President Trump, have offered a slew of ideas for reforming markets, some of which we discuss below. Others have concluded that markets do not work and instead embrace "Medicare for All." Although we will largely steer clear of this volatile debate, we acknowledge that if we do not soon find a way to fix health care markets, there may be no markets left at all.

In these last two chapters we offer some partial fixes. Two principles guide us. First, competitive markets must have competitors. In this chapter, we take a close look at competition policy and antitrust law. In developing our proposals, we picked the brains of two of our academic colleagues, Leemore Dafny, former deputy director for health care and antitrust at the Federal Trade Commission, and Martin Gaynor, former director of the Bureau of Economics at the FTC.[5] They are responsible for some of our best ideas and none of our worst. The second principle is that competition will not do us any good unless competitors know how to create value for their customers. To this end, the next and final chapter will consider steps that managers and physicians can take to mend the health care value chain. As hospitals, doctors, and insurers experiment with new ways to deliver and finance health care, the cauldron of competition will assure that consumers reap the benefits.

228 * CHAPTER TEN

Preserving Competition among Value Chains

Our current health care system took shape in the 1990s in a climate of fear. Facing the uncertainty of proposed federal health reform (the Clinton health plan) and enormous cost-cutting pressures from Medicare, Medicaid, and managed care, hospital executives bought into the idea that bigger was better. By 2000, hospitals had learned that big was not good enough, so they got bigger still, expanding horizontally and vertically to become today's megaproviders. Decades of research leave us scratching our heads. We were told that big integrated systems would "transform" (whatever that means) our health care system for the better, but where is the evidence for that assertion? When it comes to reducing costs and raising quality, there is little to choose between our megaproviders and everyone else. (That is not entirely true; megaproviders are more costly.)

At long last, there is growing recognition that health care providers have too much market power. Where it used to be that a handful of academics were tilting at windmills with their complaints about mergers, we now see major foundations such as Robert Wood Johnson and the Commonwealth Fund issuing health care antitrust policy briefs. Health policy forums, including *Health Affairs* and *NEJM Catalyst*, run frequent stories about provider market power, and major news outlets are giving extensive coverage to antitrust cases involving Sutter, Partners, and other megaproviders. Even Congress seems interested, with the House Judiciary Antitrust Subcommittee starting work on new legislation. Most importantly, megaproviders are in the crosshairs of federal and state antitrust agencies. Now that those agencies have the megaproviders in their sights, should they pull the trigger? Do they have the right ammunition? In this chapter we identify the promises and pitfalls of relying on antitrust law to fix our health care system.

Some of our academic colleagues think that the proper way to deal with megaproviders is to break them up, or to make blanket prohibitions against them by changing the standard presumption of anticompetitive harm in antitrust law. It is foolish to rely on antitrust laws, even if we reform them. The agencies are understaffed. Megaproviders enjoy too much local support. And besides, haven't past antitrust efforts been rather toothless? There is something to be said for throwing the bums out. If power is the problem, then why take half measures?

The truth is that we have had equally bad experiences with fragmented markets (think US health care through the 1980s) and consolidated markets. There are arguments to be made for and against both approaches. While we have seen how megaproviders abuse their market power, we have also seen many of them do things in terms of information systems and provider incentives that markets are hardpressed to copy. We believe that the integration experiment deserves to continue. We also believe that we can curb many of the worst megaprovider abuses through selected, albeit limited, reforms to antitrust law. This will require us to rethink what it means to have competitive health care markets. As we will explain, thinking of competition in traditional terms—competition among hospitals, competition among doctors, competition among insurers—fails to address the real benefits of competition. What matters for value creation is whether we have competition among health care *value chains*. We should allow megaproviders to play an important—if circumscribed—role in such competition.

What Is a Value Chain?

In general, a value chain for a product tracks the flow of goods and services from raw materials through production and sales. For example, the value chain for an automobile would progress from steel, glass, and other raw materials to component parts and assembly, and finally to distribution to dealerships and sales to consumers. Firms may belong to one or more value chains. Independent car dealers often sell just one car brand. AC Delco is a vertically integrated, dedicated parts supplier to General Motors. Many other suppliers sell to several automakers. These include Bosch, which makes antilock brakes, and Bose, which makes car stereos.

In health care, the value chain represents the formal and informal linkages among payers and providers that govern the entire medical care process. As such, it is not necessarily based in an integrated delivery network that owns all the pieces. A patient who chooses to have a medical procedure done at a particular hospital is effectively choosing the entire value chain, including the doctors, nurses, therapists, post-acute care service providers, and even the IV fluid and bedpan manu-facturers. Some providers belong to just one value chain. These include independent doctors who exclusively admit patients to one hospital, and physicians who have vertically integrated into hospital systems. Some providers belong to more than one value chain. These include physicians who practice at more than one hospital. In these ways, the health care value chain is much like any other.

Breaking Up Is Hard to Do

Megaproviders offer the full gamut of services in the health care value chain. Given that they have so much under their control, many expert policy analysts have argued that they should be placed under greater antitrust scrutiny. Here is what the Brookings Institution had to say in a 2013 report:

> [Policy makers should] enhance the current antitrust enforcement practice of imposing higher standards and greater scrutiny for mergers relative to clinical/financial integration contracts. Financ-ing and delivery reforms that do not require full integration of pro-viders are easier to modify or undo than provider mergers if they do not work. They may also permit more flexibility in health care organization as further innovations occur in health care delivery.[6]

This statement stems from two key points made in the Brookings re-port. First, we still do not know the best way to organize health care delivery. Should providers merge into a single entity, or is virtual inte-gration preferred? Should hospitals organize systems, or should physi-cian groups take center stage? Are insurer-provider alliances the way to go? What about exclusive Kaiser-like arrangements? We still do not know the answers, and can only find out through constant experimen-tation. Second, megaproviders are like black holes. They pull indepen-dent providers into their orbit and never let them go. Once a hospital system comes to dominate a community, there is no turning back, even if hospital-controlled integrated systems prove to be the least efficient way to deliver high-quality medical care. The same is true for physician-led systems. It is far easier to put systems together than to take them apart.

Brookings concludes that competition policy should promote experimentation, but that doing so requires us to err on the side of maintaining independent providers. If we learn how to make mergers work, we can easily allow more integration. If we confirm that integrated systems do not work, it will be difficult to break them apart. It is sort of like choosing between renting or buying a house. Until you know for certain where you want to settle down, you should probably rent.

The Brookings report stresses the importance of innovation in health care delivery. Supporters of megaproviders might argue that integration is the innovation and that it will prove itself in time. We can live with this viewpoint, provided it is subject to a market test: let megaproviders prove themselves against competing visions for organizing care delivery. In many big metro areas, local megaproviders face some serious competition. In Chicago, several prominent systems compete head-to-head (thanks in no small measure to the FTC's successful challenge of the NorthShore/Advocate merger). Amita Health's recent acquisition of Presence gives it nineteen hospitals in Chicago, more than any other system. Even so, Amita faces considerable competition and the FTC made the correct call in not challenging the deal. There is similarly vigorous competition in Los Angeles, the Washington, DC, metropolitan area, New York City, and elsewhere. In all these areas, there are regional pockets where competition could be more intense, often a legacy of court rulings dating back to the 1990s. As we have chronicled, other large metropolitan areas—including Boston, Pittsburgh, and the San Francisco Bay Area—are much less fortunate, as are smaller metro areas that may be permanently stuck with just one or two dominant megaproviders. Roanoke, Virginia, has the Carilion hospitals. Peoria, Illinois, has OSF St. Francis. Boise, Idaho, has St. Luke's and St. Alphonsus. These megaproviders can sustain themselves on higher prices, regardless of whether or not they are efficient.

We must have some standard for evaluating mergers in all market environments, a standard that promotes innovation in the organization and practice of medicine. This will require us to rethink how we define health care markets. Instead of thinking about competition among hospitals, or competition among physicians, we should think about competition among value chains.

Competing Value Chains

When two firms have different visions for organizing the value chain, the market often reveals which vision is clearer. For decades, General Motors believed in vertical integration. Japanese and European carmakers took a different approach, preferring to work with networks of semiautonomous and independent parts suppliers. We know how that competition played out. Chrysler tried the Japanese approach in the US, but still lagged behind GM and Ford (maybe best practices in Japan are not best practices here). Likewise, Advocate Health is more integrated than Edward-Elmhurst Health, a two-hospital system in Chicago's western suburbs. When patients choose between one system or the other, they are also choosing among competing visions of how to organize the value chain. It is this competition that we seek to preserve.

While competition policy tends to focus on specific levels of the value chain—think competition between parts suppliers, or competition between hospitals—competition between value chains can be far more important, especially in health care. When hospitals compete with hospitals, they offer lower prices to consumers. The savings may amount to one or two percentage points of total health spending. That is nothing for us to sneeze at, but it is not revelatory either. When value chains compete with value chains, they also have to offer lower prices, again saving a percentage point or two. They must also efficiently organize health care delivery, and that unlocks the door to far larger savings. An effective value chain will find the best ways to use big data, develop treatment protocols, reward high quality, punish unnecessary duplication, match patient needs to the right specialists, pass patients from one provider to another, and so much more. These decisions have the potential not only to lower medical spending by many percentage points, but to bend the cost curve so that future costs stop rising.[7]

Two recent merger cases illustrate the relevance of value chains to competition policy. The Anthem/Cigna case involved two insurers with very different visions for organizing the value chain. Anthem prefers a hands-off approach, leveraging its size to pay lower provider fees and thereby enjoy higher profits. Lacking Anthem's bargaining leverage, Cigna prefers a collaborative approach, working with providers to cut health spending and profit from a share of the savings. Consumers should have an opportunity to choose between these alternatives. Cigna's approach is especially important as it represents something truly novel, which admittedly may fail. The merger would have narrowed the number of alternative value chains, eliminating a potentially important alternative for many consumers. In the process, it would have stifled Cigna's innovative approach to care delivery.

The St. Luke's Health System, in Idaho's Treasure Valley, had a hospital-centric view of how to organize the value chain. Saltzer was the region's largest independent physician group practice and could emerge with its own vision, perhaps by starting a physician-led PHO. Saltzer had not yet taken this step, but its recent growth suggested that it was getting ready to compete head-to-head against St. Luke's by being a major component of an alternative value chain. The FTC argued against the merger on narrow grounds, claiming that the deal would limit competition among PCPs in suburban Nampa, near Boise. There was far more at stake here than primary care in Nampa, however. Fortunately, the two arguments against the merger were in alignment.

In both cases, the agencies successfully blocked deals using traditional market definitions: commercial health insurance and physician services. One might ask why we need another nontraditional market definition. The answer is that under slightly different circumstances, the courts might have approved both mergers, even though both would have greatly diminished competition among value chains. If Anthem had been a bit smaller, and other insurers such as United a bit larger, then the market concentration measures might not have exceeded Horizontal Merger Guideline thresholds. If St. Luke's had no PCPs in Nampa, the merger would also have passed muster under the HMG guidelines. Once we think about competition among value chains, and not just individual insurers or individual PCPs, we realize the enormous dangers inherent in both deals.

The stakes involved in competition among value chains are huge. Annual health care spending in the Boise area is approaching $10 billion. Imagine if a physician-led accountable care organization could reduce spending by just 5 percent, and that half of Boise's population enjoyed the benefits. That would translate into $250 million in annual savings, or $333 for every resident of the metropolitan area. This exceeds by a factor of fifty the worst-case estimates of the direct harm from diminishing competition among PCPs in Nampa. Or consider the Anthem/Cigna merger. The Department of Justice estimated that the merger would increase insurance premiums by about one billion dollars annually. This works out to about twenty dollars per enrollee. Imagine instead that Cigna's innovations led to a mere 1 percent reduction in commercial health spending, which other insurers, including Anthem, would eventually copy. Now we are talking about annual savings in the tens of billions of dollars.

Thinking about value chains puts the emphasis of antitrust law where it needs to be: on long-run dynamic changes to the health care industry, and not just on short-term price changes. Thinking about value chains is also very much in the remit of the Clayton Act, which prohibits mergers that diminish competition. Mergers that diminish competition in provider or insurer markets are bad enough. Once we take dynamics into account, mergers that diminish competition among value chains can be far worse. The courts should continue to worry about the former. They need to worry a lot more about the latter.

A New Approach to Competition Policy

We are not proposing to abandon antitrust analyses based on traditional market definitions. Our recommended approach considers both competition among individual firms and competition among value chains.

COMPETITION POLICY AND VALUE CHAINS

If markets are to thrive, we believe that competition policy should strive for two goals:

Goal 1: Maintain at least three competing value chains.

Goal 2: Make sure that at least one value chain consists mostly of independent providers.

Why three value chains? Research from a variety of industries suggests that competition intensifies as markets add additional competitors, at least until there are four or five.[8] The research most relevant to health markets suggests that we may need six or more competitors for markets to be fully competitive.[9] It is unrealistic to expect more than three value chains in all but a handful of markets, however, as this might require costly duplication of facilities and services. It may even turn out that bigger really is better, so that the extra efficiencies of having fewer and larger value chains would offset the loss of additional competition. It follows that merger policy should be fact-intensive, with an eye toward answering two questions:

1. Can the market support three value chains?

2. Are there three organizations that could serve as foci for organizing the chains?

If the answer to both questions is currently yes, then the agencies should scrutinize any deal that threatens to reduce the numbers to two. If the answer to either question is no, then the market is already concentrated, and all deals involving focal organizations should be scrutinized.

Again, the St. Luke's case provides useful guidance. The facts on the ground made the case for the Federal Trade Commission. There are two major hospital systems in Idaho's Treasure Valley (the other is St. Alphonsus). Saltzer is a large multispecialty group practice. Although at the time of the case there was little reliable information about Saltzer's strategic intentions, similar medical groups around the nation have organized ACOs and entered into other risk-bearing relationships with payers, thereby creating a physician-led alternative to the hospital systems. By keeping Saltzer independent, the court assured that Salter would remain free to do the same. As it turns out, there have been a few twists to the Saltzer experience which confirm the wisdom of the court decision. In 2017, McKesson purchased Saltzer and planned expanding outpatient offerings in the Treasure Valley. In 2019, local developer Ball Ventures Ahlquist purchased Saltzer from McKesson, adding the medical group to its portfolio of new medical centers and thus building out a third value chain. The future of competitive health care in the Treasure Valley looks bright. While it may be difficult to predict the path of any health care organization, we do know that integration forecloses opportunities for competition.

A similar situation recently arose in Santa Barbara, California, a market dominated by the Cottage Health system. The vertically integrated Cottage owns the only two hospitals in town, as well as imaging centers, outpatient clinics, and ambulatory surgery centers. When Cottage announced its intention to acquire the Sansum Clinic in 2013, the FTC challenged the deal on the grounds that it would lead to excessive concentration in several outpatient services markets, such as surgery and radiology. This put the FTC on solid ground in terms of the merger guidelines. It was also concerned about the impact on value chains, as it had been in the case of St. Luke's. Sansum operates twenty-four outpatient clinics in the county, and is by far the county's largest independent provider of ambulatory surgery and other outpatient services. If the merger had gone through, Santa Barbara residents would be stuck with just one vision for delivering medical care: the Cottage vision. Monopoly value chains are as problematic as any other monopoly, and it was good news in 2017 when Cottage backed down and agreed not to acquire Sansum.

Although we envision competing value chains, the reality is that competitors will often need to contract with one another. Should Saltzer choose to accept full-risk contracts, it would need to arrange and pay for hospital services. Rather than build a costly new hospital, Saltzer should be able to contract with St. Luke's and/or St. Alphonsus for inpatient services. Likewise, physician groups and community hospitals should be able to contract with tertiary-care providers for high-fixed-cost low-volume services, such as transplants and proton beam therapy, rather than waste money through unnecessary duplication. The tertiary-care hospital might set excessively high prices, so we may need to suck it up and treat these as the natural monopolies they are. If this requires price regulation, so be it.

As much as we hate to admit it, there are limits to what we can accomplish through unfettered markets. We are even tempted to revive certificate of need (CON), despite its many shortcomings. As we see it, the theory of CON—in some situations, hospitals may enjoy significant scale economies—still has some merit. It was the application of CON that was fatally flawed in two ways. First, CON applied to nearly all hospital services, not just the handful with demonstrably high fixed costs. Second, CON decisions were made by local boards, and were subject to the political pressures imposed by big local hospitals that favored incumbents and blocked new entry. We propose restricting CON to the handful of services for which duplication really can be a problem, such as transplants. A national board would be responsible for granting CON, which should offer some protection against local political concerns. In exchange for CON, incumbents must agree to offer their protected services to all insurers, at regulated prices. There are a few natural monopolies in health care. We should acknowledge them, regulate them, and move on.

As much as we are skeptical about government regulation, we must also acknowledge the facts on the ground. There are must-have hospital services, and the hospitals that offer them command high prices. To make matters worse, these hospitals use the resulting profits to expand operations and further increase their power. Rather than let these hospitals take over entire markets, we should regulate the prices of their monopolized services. Perhaps a modest markup above the Medicare rate would do the trick. This will be especially effective in midsized markets where there may only be one high-end provider. Eventually, some payers may create national networks for the high-end stuff, just as Walmart has already done for cardiac care and spine surgery. Payers could then play one formerly must-have against another, resulting in prices that beat the government price. Once we carve out the rare but important high-end stuff, we suspect that some hospitals may lose their must-have status, thus leading to more intense competition for all the other services that they provide. If we were sure this would happen, we would not consider the next step. But we are not sure.

TURN BACK THE CLOCK?

In a recent speech before a congressional committee, Fiona Scott Morton, former chief economist in the Antitrust Division of the Department of Justice, called for the agencies to undertake extensive reviews of powerful hospital systems with an eye toward breaking them apart. This seems to be an increasingly popular view among our academic colleagues who believe that megaproviders have no redeeming qualities. As we have described, retrospective review is not unprecedented, and it even led to the successful challenge of the Evanston Northwestern Healthcare system. Many of today's megaproviders only exist because of the flawed court decisions of the 1990s. Retrospective review is likely to identify more than a few ripe for dissolution.

Wholesale retrospective review would potentially allow the agencies to restructure the entire industry by turning back the clock to the period before the courts' permissive merger opinions. We have had positive experiences working with the agencies, and we admit that we are fans. We have also heard some agency lawyers and economists go beyond healthy skepticism of big firms to scorning their motives and dismissing out of hand any and all efficiencies defenses. There is a fine line between enforcement of antitrust law and zealotry against big firms. While the evidence suggests that today's megaproviders have failed to generate consistent savings, we are hardly reassured that a return to the market structure of the 1980s through a restructuring process overseen by regulators is best in the long run.

Then there is the question of whether it is practical to break up the megaproviders. This might not be too difficult if it was just a question of splitting the Smith and Jones System into Smith Hospital and Jones Hospital. The reality is that the Smith and Jones System owns numerous outpatient facilities, diagnostic facilities, and extended-care facilities. It would take Solomonic wisdom to figure out how to equitably divide them all. Then there are all the employed physicians. Having gotten used to salaried jobs with regular hours, physicians may not want to return to private practice. Many will struggle with their new lives as entrepreneurs. Some inevitably will seek shelter in large physician groups and physician practice management companies. At least this could create a potential competing nexus of power.

As long as markets support competition among three or more value chains, we would leave the megaproviders alone. That is all well and good for Chicago and New York, but what about Peoria, Syracuse, and all the other midsize and small markets where a single provider threatens to dominate? Come to think of it, we cannot assume that there will always be enough competition in the biggest cities. In Chicago's northern suburbs, Advocate and NorthShore vie for market leadership, Northwestern is strong is selected areas, and a few smaller systems and independent hospitals are also in the mix. The Advocate/NorthShore merger which the FTC blocked in 2016 would have eliminated each system's closest competitor and left only one potentially meaningful competitor to Northwestern.

In smaller markets, or in markets where decades of antitrust neglect have allowed megaproviders to take over, divestiture should be on the table. We should give dominant provider systems an option: divestiture or regulation. Again, a modest markup above Medicare prices should be about right. If megaproviders can keep their costs below the target price, then they will have earned their right to remain intact. If they fail to keep costs down, they will have no choice but to divest and return autonomy to doctors and smaller hospitals.

COMPETITION AMONG INDIVIDUAL PROVIDERS

The Horizontal Merger Guidelines continue to provide the right foundation for preserving competition among individual providers. In tailoring the guidelines to health care providers, the agencies have made sensible choices. For example, the agencies allow independent physicians to get together and jointly offer an accountable care organization, provided they do not have more than a 30 percent share of a relevant market (roughly defined as a specialty in a metropolitan area). This preserves competition among at least three groups of providers in a relevant market.

Uncloaking Mergers

While the agencies have the right rules for governing horizontal combinations, they do not always have the right information. The Hart, Scott, and Rodino Act requires large firms to report their merger activity to the federal agencies. Roughly speaking, if the transaction is valued at less than $50 million, the parties need not notify the agencies. Thus, most hospital mergers require Hart-Scott-Rodino (HSR) filings. Other provider mergers do not. Hiding behind a cloak of HSR invisibility, mergers that may lead to monopolies in physician markets, dialysis treatment, or long-term care escape antitrust scrutiny.

This is not entirely by accident. The HSR filing threshold is large because the process can be very costly. Merging firms often engage lawyers and consultants to prepare brief antitrust and efficiencies analyses, at a cost to the firms of $1 million or more. Agency review of each HSR filing is also costly. By setting the threshold for review at $50 million, the agencies only hear about those mergers whose threat to competition is big enough to justify the filing costs. This makes a lot of sense for most industries, and very little sense for health care, especially physician practices. One problem that applies across health care is that markets tend to be local, so firms can easily monopolize local markets without triggering HSR reporting requirements. A handful of medical groups (e.g, DaVita) have done exactly this, creating a powerful and highly profitable duopoly in dialysis treatment by rolling up individual clinics.

A second problem, which largely applies to physicians, is that they punch way above their weight in the amount of the health spending they generate. While the value of a relatively small medical group of ten physicians would fall well short of the HSR reporting threshold, the value of the health spending attributable to that group would almost certainly exceed the threshold. We know of no other business that has such a big multiplier effect on spending, which is why we feel that there needs to be an HSR exception for physicians.

We do not propose that the agencies investigate every provider merger. But they should know about them, and act when the mergers threaten to diminish competition without generating concomitant efficiencies. The agencies should also have clearly communicated standards for when a merger crosses the line and invites further scrutiny. To this end, the FTC should streamline reporting requirements for all provider mergers. Prior to submitting an HSR filing, merging entities should submit a prenotification, which informs the FTC about the numbers of providers; their locations; and, in the case of physician mergers, their specialties. The merging parties should also report the impact of the merger on local market shares. Any merger that falls short of a market-share threshold—we suggest 40 percent—would be exempt from an HSR filing unless it separately exceeds the traditional $50 million reporting threshold. Any merger that exceeds the threshold would require an HSR filing, regardless of the dollar amounts involved. This would include acquisitions by providers whose shares already exceed the threshold. We expect that for most mergers, prenotification will be sufficient, and no further action will be required.

We cannot expect providers to define antitrust markets every time they merge, and providers should not face unnecessary uncertainty about antitrust risk. It is therefore incumbent on the FTC to provide clear and simple guidance for measuring market shares, starting with information for defining the product and geographic components of the market. Product markets are fairly straightforward. For physicians, the FTC should continue to consider each specialty a distinct market. Defining geographic markets is a bit trickier, as doing so in a way that will stand up in court can be data-intensive and very expensive, which may deter too many defensible mergers. For the purposes of determining whether a merger requires an HSR filing, the geographic market should be something easy to identify, such as the county or the metropolitan statistical area (MSA).

Once merging parties have defined the relevant market, they can compute market shares and compare them against a predetermined threshold. It may be difficult for merging parties to obtain the revenue data from competitors usually required for computing market shares. If so, shares could be based on the number of providers (this would make the most sense for physician mergers), the number of operating suites (which should be available for ambulatory surgery centers), or other commonly available metrics.

This sounds more complicated than it is. The FTC has for decades been engaged in similar reviews of joint physician pricing initiatives, and has ramped up activity since passage of the Affordable Care Act and the creation of Medicare ACOs. Most physicians understand the concepts of market shares and efficiencies. The Advocacy Division of the American Medical Association does a good job informing physicians about these issues, and even provides limited antitrust advice to its members. We are not advocating anything new here; we are merely applying existing practices to a new purpose.

Cross-Market Mergers

On October 1, 2018, the Memorial Hermann Health System, based in Houston, and Baylor, Scott and White Health, based in Dallas, announced their plans to merge. Although the combined system would have boasted sixty-eight hospitals, it likely would have survived a traditional antitrust analysis, because the systems served different geographic markets. Even so, many observers in academia and the business community alike felt uneasy about the sheer size of the combination. With recent research showing how cross-market mergers can lead to substantial price increases, there was good reason to worry. The issue became moot when, in February 2019, the systems ended merger talks. No one is saying whether the two systems determined that they could not get along, or whether pressure from the FTC and the Texas attorney general's office had something to do with the decision.

In August 2017, Charlotte-based Atrium Health, which owned forty-eight hospitals in the Carolinas and Georgia, and Research Triangle–based UNC Health, owner of seven hospitals, announced plans to merge. This cross-market merger fell apart when the two sides could not agree on key governance issues. Atrium has not given up its expansion plans, and in April 2019 it announced that it would merge with Wake Forest Baptist's seven-hospital system. Again, this will be a cross-market merger. The pace of cross-market mergers appears to be accelerating across the United States, and while few if any will be as big as the Texas tandem or the Atrium deals, nearly every deal will affect millions of stakeholders. What should the agencies do?

The merger guidelines seem to give a free pass to cross-market mergers. The guidelines call for a structural analysis of each merger, which requires defining geographic markets and measuring the change in concentration in each market. Normally it is appropriate to narrowly define geographic markets, so as to more realistically capture the effects of a merger on prices. If we narrowly define geographic markets for cross-market mergers, they would all pass muster. It would be hypocritical for the agencies to decide that when it comes to cross-market mergers, it is appropriate to define broad geographic markets. Besides, even with a geographic market being defined as something as broad as a state, most cross-market mergers would survive a structural analysis. Even the Memorial Hermann / Baylor, Scott, White deal would have given the combined hospital system control of only 15 percent of Texas hospitals. Yet there remains this sinking feeling that cross-market mergers are a problem, and that application of antitrust law is the solution.

There is a way to use the merger guidelines to escape this morass. Although most merger analyses focus on the structural analysis and market concentration thresholds in the Horizontal Merger Guidelines, it might be better to rely on a different section of the HMGs that emphasizes predictive modeling. In other words, rather than indirectly inferring merger effects from market concentration statistics, we can use prior research evidence, plus economic models developed to assess the merger in hand, to directly predict the impact on prices. The HMGs recommend rejecting deals that are directly predicted to increase price without any tangible benefit to quality.

The problem with directly modeling cross-market effects, at least for the time being, is that economists have yet to develop convincing predictive models. As we have described in chapter 7, existing models would have us reject all cross-market mergers. That is a nonstarter. There is a lot of ongoing research in this area, and clearer guidelines will surely emerge. This raises the question of what to do in the interim. We recommend letting things run their course. If economic research, including retrospective reviews of consummated cross-market mergers, identifies the most egregious ones, we have few qualms about breaking them up. There is little that binds these systems together except the financial arrangements, and there should be little difficulty undoing them.

Antisteering Restrictions

In chapter 7 we described a number of contractual provisions demanded by megaproviders that exploit and extend their power. Broadly speaking, the industry calls these antisteering restrictions. These include all-or-nothing contracts, mandatory extortionary out-of-network prices, antitiering restrictions, and gag rules. These provisions should be illegal. The fact that powerful systems demand them is reason enough to suspect that they further enhance system power and revenues. As we discussed in chapter 7, there are also good theoretical reasons to be concerned. The first two provisions enable systems with must-have providers to force network inclusion of all of their member providers, thus avoiding the "unseemly" pricing that might attract the attention of even the most forgiving legislators. Antitiering restrictions and gag rules limit the ability and incentives of patients to find and choose the lowest-price in-network providers. It is easy to see why expensive megaproviders love these provisions.

What about Mandatory Price Disclosure?

As we write this, the Trump administration is considering both a ban on gag rules and mandatory price disclosure. While the two seem to go hand-in-hand, we only support the former. Why are we hesitant to force price disclosure? It is one thing for government to forbid a tactic that limits competition. It is quite another for it to mandate a tactic to encourage it. Price disclosure is far from simple; aside from commodities like MRIs and vaccinations, pricing is complex and may vary from patient to patient, depending on the exact mix of services they will require. Mandatory disclosure is sure to come with an extensive set of rules and regulations. We believe that insurers, rather than the government, should decide the best way to provide pricing information. Some insurers may prefer to provide very limited information, especially insurers that have negotiated especially low rates. If those rates became public, other insurers would ask for the same deals. Through backward induction, we may infer that providers would not give such a good deal in the first place.

This is not the only thing to worry about. Mandatory disclosure might inform some providers that they are underpriced. What may be worse is that strategists have long known that public pricing facilitates collusion among small numbers of competitors. Conversely, secret pricing can intensify competition.[10] This is one reason why it is illegal for erstwhile competitors to agree to exchange price information. We know far too little about the implications of mandatory price disclosure among health care providers. The unintended side effects could be worse than the problem that disclosure is intended to cure.

Qualified Risk-Sharing Arrangement Exemptions

When faced with legal challenges to their anticompetitive tactics, megaproviders have argued that the whole of a system is greater than the sum of its parts. They say that after pulling together myriad hospitals, physicians, and other providers into an integrated delivery network, it makes no sense for government to impose restrictions that allow insurers to contract piecemeal. They argue that if they achieve clinical integration, we should leave them be.[11] There are two problems with this conclusion. First, as an operational rule for policymaking, a "clinical integration exemption" from antitrust law is a nonstarter. As we have explained, there is no simple and well-accepted definition of clinical integration. Second, clinical integration is only a means to an end. The ultimate goal is to reduce costs and improve quality, and not everyone believes that clinical integration is either necessary or sufficient to meet these goals (for good reason: the evidence base is pretty weak).

We are willing to make an exception to the ban on antisteering restrictions, provided that megaproviders are willing to put their money where their mouths are. Systems should be partially exempt from antitrust scrutiny if they offer "qualified risk-sharing arrangements," or QRSAs. QRSAs may be full-risk contracts such as provider-sponsored plans. They may also take the form of shared savings contracts with substantial upside and downside risk, similar to the highest-powered Medicare ACOs. If a system offers a QRSA, it can insist that the contracting insurer cover all its member providers at the highest tier. QRSAs would not exempt systems from merger enforcement. Nor would they exempt systems from allowing access to their monopoly high-end services.

QRSAs would allow megaproviders to pursue their goal of becoming "the next Kaiser." The megaproviders would still face a ban on antisteering rules in traditional PPO contracts. The end result is that QRSAs would open up an additional value chain alongside the new and improved PPO value chains that would emerge in the wake of our other proposals. If megaproviders can make integration work, and if the whole really does exceed the sum of its parts, QRSAs will prove to be the superior value chain. The megaproviders and their patients will share in the benefits.

A Few More Suggestions

Thus far, we have offered several key recommendations for competition policy: think in terms of value chains, identify natural monopolies and regulate accordingly, improve reporting requirements, hone a policy toward cross-market mergers, and ban antisteering restrictions with an exception for QRSAs. We believe that these steps will help end the tyranny of megaproviders. In the remainder of this chapter, we offer some additional proposals that will further unlock the potential for competition to move us closer to achieving the triple aim.

UNIFY ELECTRONIC HEALTH RECORDS

The health care community has long understood the importance of interoperability of electronic health records. Advocates point to the benefits that patients will enjoy if all providers could easily access their health records. We can add another benefit of interoperable EHRs— namely, that they will make it easier for providers to remain independent. With a standardized low-cost method for accessing patient records, independent providers could afford to keep their own practices while enjoying what is perhaps the most tangible benefit of integration. We should note that hospitals that join systems do not necessarily standardize on the same EHR.[12] Unifying the EHR thus remains problematic, but perhaps the procompetitive benefits might serve as a further incentive to find a solution.

LIBERATE THE FEDERAL TRADE COMMISSION

The FTC Act prohibits the agency from taking action against anticompetitive conduct by nonprofit firms.[13] This is why the Department of Justice investigated Carolinas Health System's antisteering provisions, and why state attorneys general have had to go it alone in investigating conduct by Partners, Sutter, UPMC, and others. This is a waste of resources, and it may not give the best outcomes. The FTC has enormous experience in investigating provider mergers, and it has learned valuable lessons about how health care providers compete, how to define their markets, and how to assess potential efficiencies—all of which are central to investigations of conduct. Preventing the FTC from also investigating the conduct of providers is like limiting a math teacher to addition and subtraction while leaving multiplication to the biology teacher. This is hardly the best division of labor. An amendment to the FTC Act is long overdue.

END COPA

Certificate of Public Advantage (COPA), which allows states to exempt hospitals from federal antitrust laws, represents government regulation at its worst, a textbook example of the regulated industry capturing the regulators. The best that can be said for it, and this is damning it with very faint praise, is that it represents states thumbing their noses at federal legislators. There may be lots of reasons to be suspicious of federal regulation, but in the case of antitrust oversight of hospitals, states are picking the wrong opponent. Too many states have shirked their responsibility to protect consumers from powerful megaproviders. COPA is the worst possible example, and states with COPA laws should repeal them—immediately.

A New Statement

The Horizontal Merger Guidelines are the bible for merger enforcement policy across all industries. In preparing the HMGs, the Department of Justice and the Federal Trade Commission take guidance from antitrust economists with a range of views, from free-market fanatics to those who see cartels in every closet. As a result, the courts view the HMGs as impartial. In the biggest merger cases, both parties hew to the principles of the HMGs, and courts base their decisions on those principles. Moreover, the agencies update the HMGs every ten years or so, incorporating the latest economics research. For example, the most recent HMGs emphasize predictive modeling as a legitimate and potentially superior alternative to structural computations of market shares and concentration indices. As a result, predictive models have taken center stage in cases as diverse as AT&T/Time Warner and Anthem/Cigna.

In August 1996, the DOJ and the FTC recognized the growing importance and unique features of health care markets by releasing "Statements of Antitrust Enforcement Policy in Health Care."[14] The statements addressed local hospital mergers and a wide array of joint ventures among hospitals and physicians. For a while, they were the bible for enforcement activity in these areas, especially joint ventures. At the time of the statements, the agencies could not have anticipated the emergence of megaproviders, the importance of cross-market mergers, or the myriad of contract provisions that are at issue today. Nor could they have anticipated the rush of academic research on provider integration and market power. As a result, the 1996 "Statements" now seem almost archaic.

It is time for the agencies to prepare a new statement. We offer our suggestions as a starting point, though our colleagues may find that we have gone too far or not far enough, or have entirely missed the boat. The point is that we need a new bible for health-care antitrust enforcement. This will lay out guidelines to benefit consumers, and provide certainty for providers and insurers who watch politicians bemoan the growth of market power and see the writing on the wall.

In the end, the purpose of competition policy is to allow markets to work their magic. That magic begins with individuals finding better ways of creating value for consumers. Our reading of the last thirty years is that health care providers are still struggling to create value. In our final chapter we will offer some thoughts about how providers can turn the vision of Enthoven, Shortell, and others of efficient, high-quality coordinated care into reality.

11
RECOMMENDATIONS FOR MANAGEMENT POLICY

"So much of what we call management consists in making it difficult for people to work."

PETER DRUCKER[1]

We have argued in the preceding chapters that payment solutions, such as pay-for-performance and shared savings, and structural solutions, such as horizontal and vertical integration of providers, have failed to address the three core problems in every health care system: reducing cost, improving quality, and enhancing access. Given that horizontal and vertical integration have been the favorite "go-to" strategies for health care providers for decades, what else needs to be done? Do organizational and management theory offer any solutions for providers? The sections below describe more promising avenues for provider executives to travel. We start with the "big picture."

A Big-Picture View

As a large body of research documents, payment and structural solutions have not yet transformed the US health care industry, no matter how much transformation advocates say they have.[2] The movement to alternative payment models may stall at the stage of bundled payments, since physicians do not want to assume full capitation-based, professional services risk. Most physicians still prefer fee-for-service payments, though they are willing to accept some penalties and rewards. By itself, bundling is unlikely to make a big impact. Bundling is useful for a wide range of surgical procedures, but is far less practical for chronic care, where capitation of a "year in the life" may be the norm. Besides, even if there are bundled or capitated payments to organizations, those organizations must still find a way to push the financial risk onto physicians who, as we previously noted, will not wish to bear it. Even worse news is that several recently published evaluations of a mandatory bundled payment program (comprehensive joint replacement) show the program does not improve quality and does not save much money.

Greater use of alternative payment models may simply lower provider reimbursements without transforming care delivery. The result will be cuts in provider budgets and personnel that make transformation more difficult to staff and execute. Hospitals may be forced to shift attention from transformation to basic "blocking and tackling" cost containment strategies—for example, shortening lengths of stay, or reducing unnecessary admissions by the use of rules and protocols imposed from above—that hark back to the efforts by impolite and unpopular HMOs in the 1990s. This does not mesh well with hospital CEOs' preference to grow revenues rather than cut costs.[3]

So, what are the prospects and options for managing whatever will come from transformation? One possibility is to resign ourselves to a future in which transformation fails to make an impact, spending continues to outpace income, and quality only holds its own. That this result is heartily undesired by all does not make it impossible; we have lived it for the past four decades! Spending can continue to grow at its current pace—with at least the dividend of better new technology—as long as real income grows. The doomsday prophecy that "medical care costs are increasing so fast that no one can afford them" is mildly preposterous. We have heard this prophecy before, again for at least four decades, and there is no reason why we might not hear it four decades from now. Besides, if no one can or will spend more, spending cannot rise. There will, following Stein's law, eventually be a slowdown, even if it happens at a higher share of spending on medical care and a lower share on other things than at present. Neither the health care system nor the overall economy are doomed.

The challenges in this scenario are twofold. One is that the intense desire to quickly change things that cannot easily be changed may lead to regulation, frustration, false promises, associated waste, and the political turmoil that a more realistic evaluation of the prospects could avoid. A policy of keeping an open door for new innovations, whatever the source, may be superior to one of grasping at straws or planning what cannot be planned successfully. A key feature of such a policy would be to permit and even encourage insurers, health systems, independent providers, and even outsiders like Jeff Bezos, Warren Buffett, and Jamie Dimon to develop new methods for allocating resources and organizing physicians without handicapping one form or another. Assuming that monopolies have not taken over our markets, we could then let consumer choice work it out.

Regardless of who is footing the bill, if payers and providers are to effect positive change, they need to shift their focus away from a single-minded effort to reform the payment system to broader efforts to (1) change physician behavior, and (2) use new technologies to reform and reorganize care delivery. Here again, current evidence does not endorse a particular strategy to deal with these problems. Indeed, it may be that no single strategy provides the silver bullet that so many seek. It may therefore be smarter to count on small steps ("bronze buckshot"). This seems to be all that can be expected from current transformation models, but perhaps one percentage point lower cost from accountable care organizations, added to a couple of percentage points from bundled payment (if we are lucky) and another two or three points from stricter merger enforcement, might add up to real money. We explore some examples of this approach below. The challenge here is the limited bite these measures can take out of the "one-third of all spending [that] is waste"—if that adage is indeed true. If these changes could shave percentage points from spending *growth* rates rather than from spending levels—something the HMOs of the 1990s failed to do—that would amount to something significant over time.

We can always hope for the big one. We do not know yet what it might be, but there is always the possibility that someone somewhere will invent a method of payment or management that can slow spending growth appreciably without harming quality. We suspect that it will have to affect physicians and technology. This seems to be the inspiration behind Clay Christensen's theory of "disruptive innovation." The only problem with his theory is that disruptive innovation has failed to show up at health care's doorstep for the past twenty years since he advanced the idea. The last "disruption" that everyone embraced, integrated delivery networks, utterly failed. The one before that, HMOs, was utterly rejected by consumers. We earlier chronicled some of the most recent efforts at disruption and saw some glimmers of hope. Optum Health might prove transformative, given its large revenues ($100 billion) and free cash flows (estimated at $1 billion a month); much of this is concentrated in its pharmacy benefit management and analytics businesses, however. We will have to wait and see whether the provider acquisitions tied to its Medicare Advantage plans disrupt the businesses of incumbent hospitals. Or perhaps Bezos and the others will use their very deep pockets as levers to force change onto a system that seems immovable. Time will tell. Again, it is critical that we maintain competition; established monopolists have little incentive to disrupt the status quo that serves them so well.

(Here is our two-minute take on national health policy. The debate largely boils down to a simple question: Would you rather have competing private organizations try to work things out, or would you prefer a monopoly government payer? Where you stand on this ought to dictate where you stand on "Medicare for All." For what it is worth, we stand on the side of markets, at least for now. We recognize that a commercial insurance industry entails costs that could be avoided by a government monopsonist, though the purported savings are likely overstated for a variety of reasons that would require at least one more chapter to explain. While we are also skeptical about many of the efforts at disruption, we cannot completely dismiss any of them. It will only take one or two successes for the "gale of creative destruction" to positively transform health care in ways that no government could. Yes, this is a leap of faith; but it is one that has well served almost every other sector of the economy. We see no reason why competitive forces cannot do the same for health care, and we fear the toxic combination of stasis and political rent seeking that will surely result if government takes over. Should megaproviders prevail and we fail to restore competition to health care, then the case for markets significantly weakens.)

Are there more concrete ways to change the system? For starters, we may need to stop bashing fee-for-service models and look for other ways to retool this payment method. With the rapid growth of high-deductible health plans that almost all pay fee for service and require patient consent to bearing the cost, fee-for-service may get a new lease on life. At present, the ideal of coordinated care fits poorly with consumers paying something per unit of service. Would consumers be willing to pay out of pocket for coordinating services? The growth of concierge medicine suggests that the answer is yes, at least for wealthy patients, but designing a coordinated care model that offers the right out-of-pocket payment signals to patients to seek out and partake in coordination is a serious and so far untackled challenge.

We must also accept that provider reorganization is not the silver bullet. Thus far, consolidation is associated with higher costs and doubtful improvements in quality, contrary to what transformation advocates envision. When the bargain-basement Mayo Clinic or Geisinger emerges, we will know there is hope. We are not optimistic here: Geisinger, once considered an exemplar of disruption, has recently pivoted to become a more traditional specialist- and procedurally-oriented provider to drive revenue growth.[4]

Getting Physicians to Change Their Behavior

As much as we have criticized many of the past mantras of health care delivery, there is one that bears repeating: physicians directly and indirectly control 85 percent of all spending. It stands to reason that if you want to change the health care system, you have to change how physicians use their pens. More than anything else, this is where megaproviders have failed. While megaproviders seem ready to take on financial risk through shared savings and provider-sponsored plans, they seem unable to get physicians to act as if they bear the same financial responsibility. This problem is hardly exclusive to health systems; all organizations face the same problem. It is a simple fact about human nature that workers will place their own parochial interests above those of their organization. An important challenge for all managers is to create a team-first mentality.

This challenge is magnified in health care systems, where physicians are the most important contributors to organizational success, yet often feel that their "physician team" stands in opposition to management, or is at best indifferent. Among all the stakeholders of large health care systems, physicians are the least satisfied, and they play little part in administration. This is not how things work in other businesses that are dependent on their frontline professional staff. The most obvious comparison is with law firms, which are invariably run by lawyers; or with high-tech engineering firms where the C-suite and the rank and file share the same occupational training, language, and culture. The leadership teams of Boeing and 3M are packed with engineers and scientists. Data scientists and engineers hold most of the top positions at Apple and Google. Our own homes for the last four decades, large research universities, are almost always run by academics. (US universities are admittedly not always bastions of efficiency, but they are the envy of the rest of the world.) We cannot imagine our lives if university administrators were all MBAs with no "in-the-trench" understanding of what it takes to teach and conduct research. Nor can we fathom how we would react if our MBA bosses told us that we were not researching efficiently enough and, by the way, would we mind serving on a committee to find ways to cut teaching costs? Yet that is very much the position many physicians find themselves in on a daily basis: forced to accept direction from administrators whom they neither trust nor respect.

The general principle of involving professional staff in strategic decision making applies to businesses across the economy. Yet, if we look at the biggest health care systems, it is difficult to find physicians or nurses in leadership positions. According to Bloomberg, there are four physicians among the top twenty-five executives at Sutter Health.[5] At UPMC, two of the eleven top executives are doctors.[6] Northshore has four doctors and one nurse among its top twenty executives. New York

Presbyterian does a bit better, with seven physicians and two nurses among its top thirty leadership positions. Partners is an outlier, with physicians and nurses making up half of the leadership team. This is another example of the pendulum swinging too far back. Four decades ago, physicians were at the helm of many poorly run hospitals. Hospital boards replaced them with MHAs and MBAs, hospital finances improved, and today the business ethos remains in place. What choice do hospitals have? Physicians who have the desire and skills to manage a health care enterprise are few and far between. Given the often adversarial relationship that exists between many system C-suites and their medical staffs, it is difficult to imagine that there is much enthusiasm among physicians to enter management. Even so, there is some evidence—albeit not very rigorous—that health care organizations run by physicians are more successful.[7]

It may be difficult for physicians to envision themselves as corporate executives. They certainly must feel that healing and managing require two very different skill sets. Yet many physicians have proven to be excellent CEOs: Glenn Steele at Geisinger, John Noseworthy at Mayo, Toby Cosgrove at the Cleveland Clinic, and Marc Harrison at Intermountain all come to mind. Business schools can help pave the way for more physician leaders. Several schools—including our two homes, Wharton and Kellogg—offer short programs that introduce business fundamentals to physicians. They can do more, for example, by offering "weekend MBA" programs exclusively for physicians. With hundreds of systems encompassing thousands of hospitals, not to mention countless large multispecialty physician practices and other provider groups, there is plenty of room for more physicians to become business leaders.

Regardless of whether MBAs, MDs, or RNs are at the helm, they must grapple with a fundamental problem. Physicians are the dominant medical decision makers, and are willing to address the issue of waste in the health care system. Yet they see waste as someone else's fault and not necessarily under their individual control. This may explain why physicians are (1) averse to contracting for risk they feel they cannot control, and (2) skeptical about new organizational models to improve quality or reduce cost. Beyond these sentiments, physician behaviors may undermine both alternative payment models and new organization models. A recent case study highlighted the high rate of physician turnover in the Partners HealthCare ACO.[8] Only 52 percent of physicians were on contract over the first three years, with many physicians coming and going each year. The downside here is that departing physicians sometimes take their patients, the ACO beneficiaries, with them. This partly explains why ACOs also experience high patient turnover. Both types of turnover likely undermine quality, cost, and population health efforts. After one accounts for the nonrandom exit of physicians from ACOs, the evidence that they improve quality or reduce costs becomes almost nonexistent.[9]

Some ACO advocates now suggest that financial incentives currently offered inside new organizational models may be too weak to motivate physicians to change their behaviors and deliver more cost-effective care. One problem is that the amount of compensation at risk in pay-for-performance programs is too low—an issue we return to below. Another problem is that risk-bearing provider organizations frequently avoid passing the risk down to their rank-and-file practitioners. Still others argue that financial incentives for physicians usually change their behavior—just not always in the desired direction leading to desired outcomes. The health economics literature is rife with studies of how payment reforms that focus on a piece of the health care pie led to harmful unintended consequences. Paying for performance encourages providers to skimp on valuable services that are not included in the performance metrics.[10] Medicare's Hospital Readmissions Reduction Program, introduced with much fanfare a decade ago, may have discouraged readmissions that would have saved lives.[11] These examples are just the tip of the iceberg. Instead of or in addition to financial incentives, according to advocates, ACOs must employ robust nonfinancial motivational strategies to change (in turn) PCPs' behaviors, PCPs' care delivery (e.g., use of teams, physician champions, data sharing, care coordination), and hopefully their costs, quality, and patient outcomes. Below, we offer some suggestions for how to make this happen. Others suggest that only a large-scale shift to capitation can prevent the kind of financial games that providers play. The unanswered question is whether enough physicians will accept such change at a low enough price.

A more fundamental issue with physician engagement in transformation is the downward gradient from the hospital C-suite to clinician leaders to rank-and-file clinicians in their favorable views of transformation. When asked about the impact of value-based care delivery on quality, more executives responded favorably than did clinician leaders or rank-and-file clinicians. A similar gradient was observed when people were asked about the impact of alternative payment models or the value of Medicaid demonstration programs. Executives and physicians also differ in their views about how to reduce costs. The divide separating the C-suite from practicing physicians is based in part on geographic location (hospital system headquarters versus hospital-specific clinical departments), hierarchical level, and professional training (e.g., MHA or MBA versus MD). The multiple fault lines suggest that alignment and engagement are likely to be difficult, and are even deteriorating. Surveys show a decrease in physicians reporting intellectual stimulation, collegial interaction, financial rewards, and the prestige of medicine as being the most satisfying aspects of their practice. These issues may in turn cause downstream problems with quality improvement and cost control: disengaged physicians are reportedly a cause of poor quality and medical errors.

Why is this so? Physicians report being on a "treadmill" in their hospital practice: forced to be more productive to avoid stagnating incomes, but also faced with rising patient complexity that demands more of their time. They also feel that quality metrics from payers are (1) "the bane of their existence" and/or (2) what managers want to extract from electronic health records, rather than what doctors or their patients perceive as quality care (e.g., listening to patients). With the growing size and bureaucracy of hospital systems, physicians feel that the C-suite is increasingly detached from the reality of frontline medicine, and is increasingly focused on data, metrics, and policies (e.g., standardization, in-house referrals). Some medical groups also have reportedly ditched clinical integration mechanisms (i.e., "care management practices") that were originally designed to improve quality of care, due to their perceived ineffectiveness and the disruption they have caused to their practices.

There are also reports of growing physician "burnout" at the front-line of care delivery. This dissatisfaction may increase even further as alternative payment models receive greater impetus and as the shortage of physicians grows worse. Recently, ten health system executives labeled physician burnout as a "public health crisis." Some analysts have called for an extension of Berwick's triple aim to encompass "the quadruple aim" of improving the work lives of providers. Burnout can perhaps be addressed by bolstering five factors of engagement that, according to survey research, are correlated with it: organizational support for the physician's desired work-life balance, the organization's responsiveness to the physician's input, professional autonomy to manage one's individual practice, executive actions that reflect the goals and priorities of clinicians, and the organization's recognition of excellent clinical work.[12]

Moreover, despite payer efforts to promote value-based purchasing, physicians continue to deliver the wrong care in the wrong place at the wrong time. Part of the problem is that of staying current with the growing scientific literature. Medical practices that have diffused are often contradicted by recently published evidence, but physicians lag in altering their practice patterns. Physicians also make low use of quality or cost data in their referrals.

What is needed, then? At a minimum, putting more physicians and nurses in C-suites might engender greater trust between the executive office and clinical staff, thereby improving corporate culture and facilitating the use of informal incentives. We will return to this point below. This is no panacea, as rank-and-file clinicians can be just as distrustful of MD and RN leaders as MBAs. Some call for investing in the "capabilities" of clinical staff (physicians, nurses, social workers, discharge planners, etc.) with additional support from their organizations.[13] What capabilities might be desired? One might be the ability to deal with the stress associated with treating complex, severely ill patients. Another might be more autonomy delegated to the front-line staff in managing such patients, and the ability to tailor the work environment (including the electronic health record and data reporting requirements) to the needs of the professionals doing the work. Surveys mention the importance to physicians of innovative clinical roles, team-based support, and autonomy in the face of externally-imposed performance goals. The overall goal, drawn from decades of research in organizational behavior, is to increase the intrinsic satisfaction and fulfillment of professionals in working on the front line, and to foster more productive professional cultures.[14]

Integration

Everyone criticizes the US health care system for being fragmented. The problem is global, not domestic. There are roughly twenty to twenty-five industries that comprise what we call the health care system: insurers, hospitals, physicians, long-term care providers, dentists, pharmacies, wholesalers, group purchasing organizations, pharmaceutical makers, medical device makers, biotechnology firms, capital equipment makers, and so on. Most of these industries developed independently of one another, as siloes. Thus, we do not have a health care "system," but rather a health care "ecosystem" in which firms in multiple verticals exchange with one another.[15] The same is true in every country. No one has a "system" rationally designed and implemented from the top down.

According to sociologists, the antidote to fragmentation is integration. But how do you achieve this in an ecosystem of siloed sectors that has evolved naturally over time? It is akin to getting all the beasts of the jungle to assemble in peace at the watering hole, much in the manner of Thomas Hicks's painting *The Peaceable Kingdom*.

Advocates like to speak of "integrated health systems" as the solution, but this misses the mark. Our megaproviders fall short because they largely begin and end with financial integration—placing all aspects of the health care value chain under one corporate owner. True integration must occur at multiple levels simultaneously. First, the personnel and resources required for face-to-face patient care must be coordinated, using multidisciplinary teams, patient and family input, continued interactions, care transitions, and so on. Care coordination could also be accomplished by an individual or team with that specific responsibility—sort of a hospitalist for the entire continuum of care. Second, coordination may benefit from having the continuum of care services required by the patient under one corporate roof, or at least with dedicated suppliers under contractual relationship. Third, the lessons of population health and the social determinants of health suggest that such coordinated care should occur in a broader environmental context that includes the efforts of community and social welfare agencies. This is a lot of coordination. We may be in this for the long haul.

While we wait for an ecosystem-level approach to integration to develop, there are many smaller steps to be taken to improve integration. Such steps might include:

- improving the interoperability of electronic health records within and across providers,

- increasing the amount of care delivered in patients' homes (e.g., using community health workers or home health aides),

- improving transitions and referrals of patients to needed services and specialists,

- improving communications among providers and between providers and patients,

- locating providers physically near patients (e.g., doctors and nurses on the same patient floor), and

- increasing the tenures of executives and physicians inside the organization to promote management stability and the prospects for working together constructively.

Our Colleagues Weigh In

We reached out to several of our health care management colleagues around the country to hear their thoughts.[16] Their suggestions mirror many of ours. For executives, they recommended assembling collaborative teams that establish aspirational goals and adopt a learning mindset (rather than a performance-based or metric-based mindset), that engage frontline professionals in figuring out the appropriate workflow to achieve it, and then measure their collaboration with one another and with clinicians as an additional outcome. Similarly, physicians need to embrace a learning mindset and collaborate with other professionals and executives in pursuing it, accepting new members and roles into their care teams and embracing the patient's perspective more deeply.

Regarding hospital-physician integration, studies indicate that physicians will not perform well if they feel they are being too tightly controlled through external policies or managerial supervision. In a recent analysis, researchers found that physicians' perceptions of their clinical autonomy are a very strong moderator of the relationship between their reported satisfaction with their job and their adherence to well established clinical guidelines.[17] Such findings, which can be explained by self-determination theory, are growing stronger and indicate that executives need to be very mindful of how they work with physicians. As a starting point, hospitals that acquire and employ physicians need to respect their clinical autonomy and ensure opportunities for their participation in enterprise-wide governance. These findings are not new; the more things change, the more they stay the same. That said, what will be important is that physicians have "responsible clinical autonomy." In other words, they will remain the "captains of the ship" if they make clinical decisions that advance the mission of the organization rather than just their own parochial goals. This will require some alignment between the goals of physicians and those of organizations. Physicians will not compromise care quality in order to boost profits. Nor should they boost their own profits by heedlessly driving up costs. This cannot be resolved by contracts. Instead, trust must be rebuilt.

Process Rather Than Structure

The answer to the problems in health care may rest not in finding a few big disruptive innovations. but rather in implementing lots of small ones. Such small innovations center around changing organizational processes on the ground, rather than implementing major structural changes from above, such as vertical integration. Years ago, Rosabeth Moss Kanter, then editor of the *Harvard Business Review*, published an essay called "When a Thousand Flowers Bloom."[18] Her essay focused on the lower-level processes (small-scale tasks performed by individuals and groups) that generate innovation. These tasks included idea generation, coalition building, idea realization (prototype production), and diffusion (commercialization of the product). What is important for our purposes is her focus on "process" rather than "structure." The literature on integrating hospitals with physicians demonstrates that structural approaches do not fare well; they cost a lot of money (to employ physicians, for instance) and deliver very little on commitment or perceived alignment. Instead, the research is clearer about the importance of processes in the eyes of physicians: involvement in governance, having a role in decision making, good communications with the C-suite, trust in executives, and so on.[19] Such findings have been replicated in several earlier field and survey investigations.

ILLUSTRATIONS OF "PROCESS"

Success in managing physicians may rest on unobtrusive controls over provider behavior rather than obtrusive structures or overt performance measures—an approach that dates back to Nobel Prize winner Herbert Simon and his work on economics and organization sciences.[20] One illustration is the use of "choice architecture" in the design of electronic health records, which subtly guides physicians using "nudges." Nudges provide and help to frame information, enabling physician choice by increasing options and then guiding the physician's choice through default options which serve as the path of least resistance to behavioral change. For example, the EHR may initially present the physician with a choice of the generic prescription drug and then require more navigation to select a higher-cost branded drug. Such nudges do not involve financial incentives and do not increase the physician's decision-making load or "cognitive burn." Such an approach incorporates the sociotechnical system model noted above, through its integration of technology with the physician's workflow. The overarching aim is "friction management": adding barriers to care paths that are not desired, while removing barriers from care paths that are not desired. The disruption here is not the technology, but rather a new set of circumstances under which new behaviors supplant older ones. Imposing data and technology on physicians may only serve to undermine their sense of mastery and self-purpose.

Use of Informal Metrics

One of the great lessons of the 1990s integrated delivery network debacle was that systems cannot employ physicians without providing performance incentives. Thus, the professional service agreements and medical practice plan contracts of the 2010s are laden with incentives, from relative value unit (RVU) requirements, that are often linked to quality standards, to modest pay for performance bonuses based on cost reductions, care processes, and patient satisfaction. Physicians appreciate the certainty that if they deliver more RVUs, or perform better on patient surveys, they will be tangibly rewarded. MBA executives appreciate the ability to motivate physicians to achieve specific, measurable goals. This is all well and good, but it is not good enough.

Physicians are beginning to resemble the commercial realtors of Glengarry Glen Ross, where you either sell property or lose your job. Hospitals are not real estate pressure cookers in which success can be reduced to simple formulas based on easily observed metrics. Formulas can never capture the complexity of the vertically integrated health system, let alone the commitment and alignment of physicians. Consider the quality bonuses built into many physician contracts. These are based on rudimentary outcome measures, adherence to protocols, and patient satisfaction. In principle, the best physicians should receive the biggest bonuses. Yet if you ask the medical staff to rank the quality of physicians, or to identify the colleagues who have contributed the most to the success of the health system, the results would probably look quite different from the metrics-based rankings. There is a lot of informal knowledge about physician performance that contracts do not capture—a point to which we will return below.

This is not to say that contracts cannot play a role. Evidence from the alternative quality contract in Massachusetts and elsewhere shows that changes in provider contracts can yield desirable cost and quality results. To be fruitful, however, the contracts have to span (1) *time* (five years), in order to provide incentives to invest; (2) *space*, across the full continuum of care to be able to manage the total cost of care; and (3) *performance measures*, to be accountable for both quality and re-source use. The quality measures themselves need to focus on process of care, outcomes of care, the patient's experience, and outcomes that matter to patients (i.e., functional status).[21] Some providers seem to grasp this, with performance metrics now including total costs of care, and not just RVUs. Still, we are a long way from contracts that get providers to take the big picture into account.

Even if contracts are effective ways to motivate providers, we question whether integration is required. In fact, one of the basic tenets of organizational economics is that integration is not automatically nec-essary for contracts to be effective. The reason for this is simple. Con-tracts can only be based on actions and outcomes that are easily ob-servable. That is, you can enforce a contract only if you can measure the things the contract rewards. If so, then it is probable that the same contracts are available to independent firms. For example, consider a megaprovider that pays its physicians for performance incentives based on processes, outcomes, and patient satisfaction. Insurers could give the same incentives in their contracts with independent providers, and this has become commonplace in contracts between insurers and provider-sponsored accountable care organizations. Moreover, the in-dependent providers may have more control over their performance, making such arms-length contracts more effective.

If megaproviders are to prove their worth, they must find ways to motivate and reward physicians that can not be achieved through arms-length contracts. We have repeatedly discussed the frustration of physicians who feel unrewarded for work they perform on behalf of their hospitals and health systems. It is impossible to specify in a con-tract all the ways in which physicians—and nurses, for that matter—contribute. Fifty-page professional service agreements barely scratch the surface. This is not a weakness of health systems. Quite the oppo-site: this is a remarkable opportunity.

Any adult with a pen can sign a contract. True leaders give direction to an organization and convince their stakeholders that anyone who helps steer the organization in that direction will be rewarded, even if the rewards are not spelled out in writing. This means that the rewards should be based on both objective measures, and subjective evaluations may help with the convincing.[22] Bonuses should be big, perhaps double the 5 to 10 percent that we currently observe.[23] The bonuses should also be hard to get. Currently, nearly everyone makes a large percentage of their bonus, compressing the pay gap between the top performers and everyone else so as to almost make the incentives meaningless.

While compensation-based incentives will change provider behavior—there is abundant research support for this claim—there are limits to what health systems can accomplish in this regard. While most businesses have many tools for rewarding and motivating professional staff—salaries, bonuses, promotions, and even stock options—hospitals and health care systems can only rely on salaries and bonuses. Moreover, a system may not want to create too much disparity in compensation among its staff, as resentment may work against what is largely a team-oriented care delivery process. When compensation-based incentives have their limits, systems must find other ways to motivate their medical staff. Offering resources through research, new treatment programs, or other "pet projects" can be a powerful inducement. Even this may not be enough, and it can prove very costly. At some point, systems must rely on the intrinsic motivations of their medical staff. This will require transitioning from the status quo, in which physicians are unhappy and resentful of system leadership, to a situation in which physicians want their systems to succeed. This in turn will require a change in organizational culture.

Culture

As a means to encourage workers to embrace their organizations, culture is an important complement to leadership. One of the major lessons in corporate America, attributed—falsely, it turns out—to Peter Drucker, is that "culture eats strategy for breakfast." Culture is an admittedly squirrely term in academic and management circles. A popular strategy textbook describes culture as a "set of values, beliefs, and norms of behavior shared by its members that influences employee preferences and behaviors."[24] Culture takes a long time to develop, since it rests on deeply embedded norms and values, but it can be destroyed in an instant—for example, through an ill-conceived or ill-implemented integration attempt.

While it is easy to spot an organization with a positive culture, especially when the culture is viewed from within the organization, it is less obvious how to create one. One thing for certain is that culture is not the same as formal, contractual incentives. When a strong culture is in place, workers believe that if they do right by the firm for their employer, the firm will do right by them, even if this is not spelled out in a contract. Given the current level of physician discontent, it is hardly surprising that many hospitals currently do not enjoy strong cultures. Consider these examples. A physician friend of ours recently put in hundreds of hours of unpaid overtime to plan and supervise a major relocation of her hospital department. She received a thank-you note from management. Another physician colleague worked with the hospital's IT department to make the electronic health record far more user-friendly. He received a thank-you from a few of his colleagues. A third colleague, a renowned surgeon, grew reluctant to take referrals of the most challenging cases because his contract penalized him when things went wrong. No one could challenge the contributions that each of these physicians made to their hospitals. Yet in every case the physicians questioned whether management appreciated their efforts. In these and countless other ways, compensation that relies on contracts and is bereft of informal incentives creates a stifling culture that demoralizes physicians, and in which management and medical staff no longer hold the same values and beliefs, and no longer agree on the most appropriate behaviors.

Informal incentives involve much more than thank-you notes and pats on the back. Public recognition matters a lot, and medical professionals will take pride in knowing that the entire organization, their colleagues as well as top management, appreciates their efforts. But we cannot escape the importance of tangible rewards. Management must reward medical staff for contributions that are not spelled out in contracts. This can take the form of discretionary bonuses or funding for new projects. It requires judicial managerial discretion. The key is that the medical staff must trust management to use its discretion wisely, or the informal incentives will seem arbitrary, and will fail to provide the right motivation. This brings us back to the importance of involving physicians in executive decision making.

Another approach to developing a strong culture is to engage in "selective employment"—hiring the right people, who have personal orientations and goals that match what the organization seeks to accomplish. Boost the bonus pay to 20 percent, and see which physicians complain. Maybe they are too selfish to remain. Replacements can be found who are more in sync with the organization's goals and less concerned with their own job security. Kaiser has enjoyed such favorable selection of physicians oriented to HMO-style medicine for decades; Geisinger followed a similar approach in more recent years. The University of Pennsylvania Health System (UPHS) has focused on recruiting top scientists with an entrepreneurial bent and an interest in commercializing their discoveries, many from the West Coast, as part of its effort to develop a "Cellacon Valley" in Philadelphia. Not every physician is cut out for these organizations, and that is OK. To paraphrase Napoleon, the organization that pleases every physician pleases no one.

Independent organizations can achieve something akin to a culture through long-term relationships where each party gives a little so that the other can thrive. Cigna and Aetna's collaborative accountable care (CAC) arrangements with physicians, in which the insurers offer higher reimbursements while physicians implement cost containment strategies, are a powerful example. The insurers do not spell out specific requirements for their CAC physicians, and the physicians do not insist on specific compensation for each of their specific cost-cutting activities. Instead, the contracts are renewed on the basis of bilateral trust that the joint venture makes sense for all parties—insurers, physicians, and patients.

Long-term relationships may never fully substitute for the leadership and culture of the most successful integrated health systems. The other benefits of independence—the powerful incentives associated with entrepreneurship and the freedom from bureaucracy—may be enough to allow virtual organizations to stand side-by-side with the best megaproviders, or even outcompete them.

Focus

One of the chief lessons of integration research, which has been lost on almost everyone, is that integration is not for everyone. Focus is the order of the day. An early illustration of this is research that shows that care coordination is best focused on just a subset of patients: those with several severe chronic conditions. This subset drives most of the spending and demonstrates most of the improvement from care coordination. What care coordination mechanisms are needed? These include improving communications among providers and patients, teaching patients self-care behaviors and other techniques to improve medication adherence, identifying exacerbations early on, and having reliable information about the patient's pharmacy regimen and pharmacist.[25]

Focus is also critical for hospitals in their cost-cutting efforts. At UPHS, two-thirds of patients have primary care physicians outside the system; moreover, most of the care provided is not built around definable patient episodes. As a result, population health is hard to accomplish. Instead, UPHS concentrates on reducing readmissions by risk-stratifying patients at the time of admission, targeting its efforts at those at high risk, and then anticipating their need for care in lower-cost postacute care settings. It also focuses on reducing variations in care for certain conditions treated in the inpatient setting. At Jefferson Health, the telemedicine initiative is focused and customized for patients in the local market, not patients across the nation.

Focus on process over technology may also be key. Stanford University's Clinical Excellence Research Center identified thirteen distinguishing characteristics of consistent, high-performing sites of primary care. They include creation of deeper patient relationships through extended hours, adherence to practice guidelines leveraging decision-making support systems, aggressively closing gaps in care outside patient visits, full use of nonmedical staff that allows physicians to focus on the more chronic patients, work spaces that are shared by physicians and nonphysician staff, use of patient complaints to guide care improvement, and risk-stratified care management.[26] Financial incentives and organizational structures are not mentioned. Indeed, one characteristic of such high-performing systems is low overhead, just the opposite of what one typically finds in horizontally and vertically-integrated systems.

Bottom-Up Change

Finally, any effort to "transform," let alone change, the US health care system should learn the lessons of corporate America. Foremost among these concerns is "top-down" managerial change. Most proposed solutions to organizational problems are formulated by the CEO, by the vice president for strategic planning, or by someone else delegated to provide a vision, and then are pushed down the hierarchy for others to implement—often with minimal input, guidance, or revision by those responsible for carrying out the solution. For years we have known that such an approach usually fails. And yet this approach is pursued widely in health care. We have typically described it in terms of the disconnect between the C-suite, which decides what to do and what to change, and the doctors and nurses who are supposed to carry out the plans. We know that if clinicians are not engaged, the effort is likely to fail. And yet popular efforts to foster capitation and other alternative payment models are part of the transformation top management is supposed to engineer. Plans to engage physicians have stalled as most physicians do not want these payment methods, and their organizations prefer to still pay them by fee-for-service, however the payment to the system is calculated. Links, logical or social, between the new incentives at the top and the needed behavior changes down the chain have not yet been invented, and so the changes are left to befuddled lower-level managers and provider committees to work out as best they can.

What is to be done? One solution is to allow and enable clinicians to develop many of the needed changes. The engineer Ted Hoff developed the microprocessor as a solution to a technical business problem for a customer of Intel, and then spent a year convincing Andy Grove and other Intel executives that they had something of value. Similarly, Brent James and David Burton developed local-level approaches to quality improvement organized around information systems at Intermountain Healthcare starting in the 1970s, and then waited nearly two decades for their collection of small-scale pilot projects to roll up into Intermountain's official corporation-wide strategy that is still ongoing today.[27] Letting a thousand flowers bloom can work, but it surely is not quick. The same strategy of funding lots of development projects for clinical and service improvement is currently underway at UPHS and elsewhere, usually under the banner of an "innovation center" housed in an academic medical center. The structure—the "center"—is not the key ingredient, however; it is the process of identifying, launching, and learning from such projects. These are the same themes we have addressed in this chapter. There is nothing new under the sun.

Such initiatives will have to cover more topics than just quality improvement. To deal with constrained reimbursement and declining hospital margins, hospitals will need to engage their frontline clinical personnel in productivity improvements. These initiatives will necessarily involve "the last ten feet of the supply chain," where clinicians use medical supplies and drugs in their care of patients on hospital floors and in outpatient departments. They will also involve efforts to minimize the documentation burden of providers and find nonphysician personnel to assume some clinical tasks.[28] At a more general level, these initiatives will need to focus on "reducing friction" in the provision of care (e.g., making it faster, with fewer barriers), removing some care tasks from the hospital to the outpatient area and from the outpatient area to the home, and structuring the work environment and electronic health records to make it easier for physicians to practice high-value care.

The Eternal Importance of Technological Change

We close this book by returning to the theme with which we opened chapter 1: the importance of technological change. Unfortunately, new medical technology, embodied in new medicines, diagnostics, or surgical techniques, has almost always meant higher spending. By some accounts, new technologies are responsible for more than half of overall health care inflation.[29] Looking ahead, the most transformative technologies may be not those that add to the physician's arsenal of treatments, but those that alter where and how physicians deliver those treatments. Many are optimistic that these technologies will dramatically lower health care spending. If we look in the rear view mirror, we might temper our optimism.

Many efforts to alter where and how physicians deliver medical care were initially trotted on stage as disruptive, yet ultimately failed to disrupt. These included (1) ambulatory surgery centers, many of which have been assimilated by hospitals; (2) retail clinics, which offered a complement (not a substitute) to primary care services and increased total utilization; and (3) single-specialty hospitals, on which the federal government initially placed a moratorium through the Medicare Modernization Act of 2003, and later outlawed through the Patient Protection and Affordable Care Act of 2010. Now electronic health records are supposed to change everything. As we have chronicled in chapter 6, we are both hopeful and skeptical—hopeful because we are not sure what else is out there to rescue health systems, and skeptical because of the facts on the ground.

Artificial Intelligence and Digital Medicine

There are several "new kids on the block." These include artificial intelligence (AI), data analytics, telemedicine, and mobile health. It is not clear if, how, and when these will disrupt health care. There is some promising recent evidence that algorithms and AI can help physicians diagnose patients by improving detection and reducing false positives.[30] While algorithms can speed up the processing of information that physicians use all the time, they are not designed to replace clinicians. To be successful, AI needs to be focused on specific problems to be solved, such as interpreting specific images for which there is little clinical variation, or identifying subtypes of chronically ill patients. This may prove more difficult than AI proponents believe. AI is terrific at mining data to make predictions about patients' health, but it does not necessarily identify what physicians should do to improve it. Moreover, AI and machine learning are not just about getting the coding right. There needs to be an infrastructure for their use, including more information profiling physicians and their patients. Such data volume, which adds to statistical power in assessing variations, is more important than complex modeling. More data is needed at the point of care, where physicians and patients are more likely to use it. Finally, AI works best when there are rules. It fares worse when there is imperfect information and less structure, and when there are more of the grey areas in decision-making that define medicine.[31]

The benefits of telemedicine are less clear-cut. There is little evidence of cost savings, and insurers are reluctant to pay for it. This chicken-and-egg problem may not be resolved soon. The benefits of mobile health are even more sketchy at the moment, perhaps because such applications may be in greater use by the worried well than by the chronically ill. Beyond that, digital health may promote "social iatrogenesis" (e.g., excessive use of preventive therapies, or "anticipatory therapy"). Indeed, Stanford University researchers who studied all published trials of screening for deadly diseases found that "reductions in all-cause mortality with screening tests were very rare or nonexistent."[32] As one analyst put it, "It is hard to make a person without complaints better and interacting with health care comes with risks."[33] Digital health may also promote a "cultural iatrogenesis" in which the patient relies on technological apps rather than on adaptation to disease. What is the danger here? Just imagine if your son's iPhone and Google maps app don't work, thus forcing him to rely on a road atlas.

Genomics and Personalized Medicine

There is evidence of personalized medicine yielding breakthrough therapies—albeit at a very high cost, for small patient populations. Moreover, sequencing the genomes of the asymptomatic "worried well" can identify up to twelve potentially harmful variations in one's DNA that may lead to further diagnostic testing, even though the therapeutics to attack these variants are limited to small patient populations. Lifestyle diseases are linked to hundreds of gene variations which collectively may explain only a small portion of the variation in health status that is likely more strongly linked to patient behaviors.[34]

Does Capital Ever Substitute for Labor in Health Care?

Health care is labor-intensive. If we cut costs, we almost surely have to reduce labor input. Unfortunately, new technologies often require new personnel to use them. X-ray machines begat X-ray technicians, electronic health records required health scribes, analytics require specialists in information technology, and AI may replace only the more mundane and easily predictable aspects of clinical diagnosis. As MIT researcher Eric Byrnjolfsson explains:

> There are 27 distinct tasks that a radiologist does. One of them is reading medical images. A machine learning algorithm might be 97 percent accurate and a human might be 95 percent accurate, and you might think, OK have the machine do it. Actually, that would be wrong. You're better off having the machine do it and then a human check it afterwards. Then you go from 97 percent to 99 percent accuracy because humans and machines make different kinds of mistakes.[35]

This blunts any effort in health care to substitute capital for labor. This does not mean we should ignore the technology. Rather, we should be prepared to spend more in order to improve outcomes. In this way, AI and other new technologies resemble medical technologies of the past: they drive up quality, but add to our spending burden. Another thing to keep in mind is the lesson from sociotechnical systems theory: new technologies must fit into the daily routines of health care professionals to be useful and used. Finally, one must remember "Amara's Law," credited to Roy Amara, founder of Institute for the Future: "We tend to overestimate the effect of a technology in the short run and underestimate the effect in the long run." We are not sure how "long" the long run is. Given the slow pace of real change in health care, as well as the decades-long unsuccessful effort to control health care costs, we could be in for the long haul.

Coda

We have offered several suggestions for improving vertical linkages between hospitals and physicians, but we have been silent on improving the performance of horizontal linkages between hospitals. That is because there is little left to say. There have never been great opportunities for hospital mergers to save money; certainly consumers have not realized any benefits. To save money, as Alfred Chandler argued long ago, CEOs need to physically combine the merged hospitals, reduce plant capacity, and increase throughput, perhaps by automation of lean management techniques. No one seems to want or be able to do what is necessary. Perhaps someone will eventually figure out how to make system hospitals more efficient than their independent rivals, but this will be challenging. Research shows that systems of any size are no more efficient than freestanding hospitals, and are usually less so. Moreover, the bigger they get, the less efficient they seem to become. The only bright light here is that smaller systems that are geographically concentrated (perhaps in a single market), organizationally centralized, and organized around teaching hospital hubs may slightly outperform the others. The challenge is in centralizing what can be centralized, and in making the systems "more systemic."[36] Until then, vigorous antitrust enforcement of horizontal mergers remains the order of the day.

What then do we make of vertically integrated delivery systems? If they are to help us fulfill the goals first laid out by the Committee on the Cost of Medical Care, and echoed in later years in the iron triangle and the triple aim, it is because they will have figured out how to fix the value chain. First and foremost, this will require a dramatic change in the relationship between managers and physicians. Physicians may hold the pens that dictate health spending, but managers can provide the leadership and establish the culture that guide the physician's hand. Managers can also ease the transition for physicians who want to use electronic health records and machine learning to make better decisions. We have offered a few specific ideas for making all this happen, but we have only scratched the surface. After all, academics are far more suited for commenting on what has and has not worked in the past than in offering innovative solutions for tomorrow. To be fair, no one really knows the future, and most prognostications—particularly the optimistic long-range forecasts of so-called futurists—are likely to disappoint. The best ideas likely will come from those who have spent time in the trenches: perhaps the physicians and nurses who make the toughest and costliest life-and-death decisions. Until then, we need to make sure that markets remain competitive, allowing those with new visions for managing health care delivery to compete against white-elephant megaproviders that have done so much to enlarge and enrich themselves, and so little for the rest of us.

Epilogue

MEGAPROVIDERS AND COVID-19

When we submitted our completed manuscript to our publisher, reining in spending was the number-one health policy priority. While COVID-19 and public health have justifiably taken center stage, we think the pandemic and megaproviders are inextricably linked. When the dust settles, we should expect further consolidation.

When the crisis started, the American Hospital Association estimated that hospitals would lose $200 billion between March 1 and June 30, with losses of $50 billion per month continuing to pile up until COVID-19 was all but wiped out.[1] It is not so much the money hospitals have lost treating COVID patients—many insurers covered the full cost of treatment—as it is the losses the hospitals incur when patients postpone or cancel elective procedures. As the pandemic has stretched on, the financial situation has worsened. We expect many hospitals to see their bottom lines shrink by $10 million or more. Even if the federal government makes up part of this shortfall, many hospitals will teeter on the edge of collapse. Some have already fallen; by June 30, 2020, forty-two hospitals had closed or filed for bankruptcy.[2] More will follow. It is likely that many physician practices, imaging centers, home health agencies, and other medical providers will follow suit. If struggling health care providers wish to stay open, they will need someone to buy them out.

For megaproviders looking to extend their dominance, this will be a buyer's market. Flush with cash and other investible assets totaling in the billions of dollars, Sutter, Partners, UPMC, Northwell, the

Cleveland Clinic, and most of the rest should be able to expand on the cheap.[3] And why wouldn't they? Once the pandemic subsides, the demand for "normal" medical care will surge. There are good times ahead for providers that can survive the current storm. Megaproviders will be the healthiest survivors.

In the meantime, megaproviders have had a chance to prove their "systemness" by finding creative ways to manage the crisis. Locally organized systems with a strong degree of system centralization might be better suited to to allocate personal protective equipment (PPE) across system facilities, to conduct COVID testing at convenient sites, to coordinate COVID response across their continuum of providers, to facilitate clinical trials, and to ensure that best practices in patient and provider safety get replicated across system sites. In the fog of the pandemic, it is difficult to know whether megaproviders have excelled in any of these ways. In the end, it may be wishful thinking that large hospital systems can make a positive dent in dealing with the COVID crisis, whose ultimate outcome seems to be mostly in the hands of medical researchers and those at "ground zero"—everyday citizens and their families.

ACKNOWLEDGMENTS

We have benefited from decades of interactions with countless research colleagues, health care managers, and antitrust attorneys. We are particularly grateful to Henry Allen, Leemore Dafny, Martin Gaynor, Mark Pauly, and Jeff Goldsmith for their thoughtful advice. We also thank Amy Tingle and Tina Horowitz for their research and editorial support. Lastly we thank Chuck Myers, Alicia Sparrow, and Noor Shawaf at the University of Chicago Press for guiding us through the process from initial idea to publication.

NOTES

Introduction

1. Matt Scuffham, "Goldman Tracking Ahead of $5 Billion Revenue Goal by 2020," *Reuters*, November 5, 2018, https://www.cnbc.com/2018/11/05/goldman-tracking -ahead-of-5-billion-revenue-goal.html, accessed March 19, 2019; Lucy Handley, "The Luxury Sector Is Growing Faster Than Many Others and Gucci is in the Lead," CNBC, October 4, 2018, https://www.cnbc.com/2018/10/04/the-luxury -sector-is-growing-faster-than-many-others-and-gucci-leads.html, accessed March 19, 2019. Pew Research Center, *State of the News Media 2016* (Washington: Pew Research Center, 2016).
2. Systems on this list drawn from National Institute for Health Care Management, "Hospital Consolidation: Trends, Impacts and Outlook," https://www.nihcm.org /categories/hospital-consolidation-trends-impacts-outlook, accessed January 23, 2020.
3. While they are not the focus of our book, it is worth noting that vertically inte-grated megaproviders are also emerging across Europe, where providers and gov-ernment payers somewhat surprisingly look to the United States for ways to fix their own health systems. See Anna Charles et al., *A Year of Integrated Care Sys-tems: Reviewing the Journey So Far* (London: The Kings Fund, September 2018); World Health Organization, *Integrated Care Models: An Overview* (Copenhagen: Health Services Delivery Programme, WHO Regional Office for Europe, October 2016).
4. Alex Kacik, "Highest-Paid Not-for-Profit Health System Executives Earn 33% Raise in 2017," *Modern Healthcare*, June 22, 2019, https://www.modernhealthcare.com /executive-compensation/highest-paid-not-profit-health-system-executives-earn -33-raise-2017, accessed September 17, 2019.
5. According to a November 2018 Gallup survey, 73 percent of Americans believe that the US health care system either is in a state of crisis (15 percent) or has major prob-lems (55 percent). These figures are largely unchanged for the past fifteen years. Only 3 percent of respondents feel the system has no problems. "Healthcare Sys-

tem," Gallup.com, accessed March 12 2019, https://news.gallup.com/poll/4708
/healthcare-system.aspx.

6. Jacqueline LaPointe, "Doctors, Employers Disagree on Healthcare Payment Reform
   Strategy," *Revcycle Intelligence*, February 6, 2018, https://revcycleintelligence.com
   /news/doctors-employers-disagree-on-healthcare-payment-reform-strategy,
   accessed June 18, 2018.

7. AP News, "AHF: Rep. Cummings to Haul Greedy Drug Company CEOs before
   House Oversight Committee," AP News, January 28, 2019, https://www.apnews
   .com/0674ba254c6d4b9f91d99e4bd26a0bbb, accessed January 23, 2010; Frank
   David, "Pharma CEOs Should Take a Stand on Egregious Price Increase—But
   They Won't." *Forbes*, September 20, 2015. https://www.forbes.com/sites/frank
   david/2015/09/20/why-pharma-companies-should-take-a-stand-on-turings
   -drug-pricing-and-why-they-probably-wont/#29970ba15f90, accessed January
   23, 2020; "The Rapacious Prescription Drug Industry," *California Free Press*, May
   25, 2008, https://www.californiafreepress.net/will_blog_for_food/2008/05/the
   -rapacious-prescription-drug-industry.html; Pearl Korn, "Those Rapacious Health
   Insurers Raise Premiums 9% This year for Job-Based Health Insurance," Huffpost,
   December 5, 2011, https://www.huffingtonpost.com/pearl-korn/health-insurance
   -premiums_b_995633.html, accessed January 23, 2020; Joe Weisenthal, "Guess
   What: Health Insurers Don't Even Make That Much Money," Business Insider,
   October 25, 2009, https://www.businessinsider.com/fact-check-health-insurer
   -profits-not-so-fat-2009-10, accessed January 23, 2020; Deborah Gordon and Anna
   Ford, "We're Entering the Lawless Age of Health Care," The Hill, October 4, 2018,
   https://thehill.com/opinion/healthcare/409893-were-entering-the-lawless-age-of
   -health-care, accessed January 23, 2020.

8. Gigi A. Cuckler et al., "National Health Expenditure Projections, 2017–26: Despite
   Uncertainty, Fundamentals Primarily Drive Spending Growth," *Health Affairs*
   37, no. 3: 482–92. Many expensive drugs eliminate the need for more even more
   costly hospitalizations, so that the 11 percent figure overstates their impact on total
   health spending; https://www.healthaffairs.org/doi/full/10.1377/hlthaff.2017.1655,
   accessed January 23, 2020.

9. For example, see Francis J. Crosson, "Change the Microenvironment. Delivery
   System Reform Essential to Control Costs," *Modern Healthcare* 39, no. 17: 20–21.
   https://www.commonwealthfund.org/publications/publication/2009/apr/change
   -microenvironment-delivery-system-reform-essential, accessed January 23, 2020.

10. It is difficult to track down the source of this quip. A Google search turns up a
    reference in a 2010 book by Francis Crosson and Laura A. Tollen, though we feel
    certain the quip predates this. See Francis J. Crosson and Laura A. Tollen, eds.,
    Partners in Health: How Physicians and Hospitals Can Be Accountable Together
    (Hoboken, NJ: John Wiley & Sons, 2010).

11. Zack Cooper, Stuart V. Craig, Martin Gaynor, and John Van Reenen, "The Price
    Ain't Right? Hospital Prices and Health Spending on the Privately Insured," *Quar-
    terly Journal of Economics* 134, no. 1 (February 2019): 51–107. This paper received the

prestigious 2019 NIHCM Research Award from the National Institute for Health Care Management.
12. The other half is due to variation in the intensity of services received by patients.
13. Kenneth J. Arrow, "Uncertainty and the Welfare Economics of Medical Care," in *Uncertainty in Economics*, eds. Peter Diamond and Michael Rothschild (Cambridge, MA: Academic Press, 1978), 345–75; George J. Stigler, "The Economies of Scale," *Journal of Law and Economics* 1 (1958): 54–71.
14. This is not to say that big firms cannot eventually abuse their power, and we do not wish to engage here in the ongoing debate as to whether power inevitably corrupts.
15. Lawton R. Burns and Mark V. Pauly, "Transformation of the Healthcare Industry: Curb Your Enthusiasm?" *Milbank Quarterly* 96, no. 1 (March 2018): 57–109.
16. Clayton M. Christensen, Richard M. J. Bohmer, and John Kenagy, "Will Disruptive Innovations Cure Health Care?" *Harvard Business Review* 78, no. 5 (2000): 102–12.

Chapter 1

1. From a 2013 interview in *The Guardian*. Cited in "Eduardo Galeano," newhistorian.com, https://www.newhistorian.com/2015/04/15/eduardo-galeano/3509/, accessed April 18, 2019.
2. Committee on the Costs of Medical Care, *Medical Care for the American People* (Chicago: University of Chicago Press, 1932).
3. Victor R. Fuchs, "Major Trends in the US Health Economy since 1950," *New England Journal of Medicine* 366, no. 11 (2012): 973–77.
4. Consumer Reports, *Blue Cross and Blue Shield: A Historical Compilation* (Yonkers, NY: Consumer Reports, March 2013), https://advocacy.consumerreports.org/wp-content/uploads/2013/03/yourhealthdollar.org_blue-cross-history-compilation.pdf, accessed February 12, 2019.
5. Frech and Ginsburg (1978) describe how Blue Cross Blue Shield chose these parameters to promote the interest of their provider-sponsors. H. E. Frech III and Paul B. Ginsburg, "Competition among Health Insurers," in *Competition in the Health Care Sector*, ed. Warren Greenberg (Germantown, MD: Aspen Systems Corporation, 1978), 210–37.
6. These were called prepaid health plans at the time. Paul Ellwood coined the term "HMO" in 1970.
7. This is detailed in litigation from the 1940s. *American Medical Ass'n. v. United States*, 317 U.S. 519 (1943).
8. Richard McNeil Jr. and Robert E. Schlenker, "HMOs, Competition, and Government," *Milbank Memorial Fund Quarterly. Health and Society* 53, no. 2 (Spring 1975): 195–224.
9. Philip C. Kissam, "Health Maintenance Organizations and the Role of Antitrust Law," *Duke Law Journal* 27, no. 2 (1978): 487–581.
10. For details of this case, see Joseph Rosenheck, "The American Medical Association

and the Antitrust Law," *Fordham Law Review* 8 (1939): 82. http://ir.lawnet.fordham .edu/flr/vol8/iss1/5.

11. Lawrence G. Goldberg and Warren Greenberg, "The Determinants of HMO Enrollment and Growth," *Health Services Research* 16, no. 4 (1981): 421–38.

12. This was the Republican alternative to Senator Edward Kennedy's proposal for a single-payer system.

13. See Federal Trade Commission, *Findings, Opinions, and Orders: July 1, 1976 to December 31, 1976*, vol. 88. (Washington: Federal Trade Commission), https:// www.ftc.gov/enforcement/cases-proceedings/commission-decision-volumes /volume-88, accessed March 6, 2019.

14. See *United States v. American Soc. of Anesthesiologists*, 473 F Supp. 147 (S.D.N.Y, 1979). https://law.justia.com/cases/federal/district-courts/FSupp/473/147/21 48462/, accessed March 6, 2019.

15. See Federal Trade Commission, *Findings, Opinions, and Orders: July 1, 1976 to December 31, 1976*, vol. 94. (Washington: Federal Trade Commission), https:// www.ftc.gov/enforcement/cases-proceedings/commission-decision-volumes /volume-94, accessed March 6, 2019.

16. Michael G. Vita, "Regulatory Restrictions on Selective Contracting: An Empirical Analysis of 'Any-Willing-Provider" Regulations,'" *Journal of Health Economics* 20, no. 6 (2001): 955–66.

17. Close to 60 percent of HMO enrollees live in just twelve coastal states. For more details, see "Kaiser Family Foundation State Health Facts: Total HMO Enrollment," Kaiser Family Foundation, https://www.kff.org/other/state-indicator/total-hmo -enrollment/?currentTimeframe=0&sortModel=%7B%22colId%22:%22Location %22,%22sort%22:%22asc%22%7D, accessed March 21, 2019.

18. For more on Hill-Burton, see "Hill-Burton Free and Reduced-Cost Health Care," Human Resources and Services Administration, https://www.hrsa.gov/get-health -care/affordable/hill-burton/index.html, accessed March 6, 2019.

19. "Truman Library," Truman Library, https://www.pbs.org/newshour/health/novem ber-19-1945-harry-truman-calls-national-health-insurance-program.

20. Julian E. Zelizer, "How Medicare was Made," *New Yorker*, February 15, 2015, https:// www.newyorker.com/news/news-desk/medicare-made.

21. American Hospital Association, *AHA Hospital Statistics* (Chicago: Health Forum LLC, selected years.)

22. Alan L. Hillman and J. Sanford Schwartz, "The Adoption and Diffusion of CT and MRI in the United States: A Comparative Analysis," *Medical Care* 23, no. 11 (1985): 1283–94.

23. Source: AMA and Census Bureau data as reported in AEI. Mark Perry, "American Medical Association: The Strongest Trade Union in the U.S.A," July 5, 2012. http:// www.aei.org/publication/american-medical-association-the-strongest-trade -union-in-the-u-s-a/, accessed March 6, 2019.

24. Source: AMA data cited "Total Number of Doctors of Medicine in the U.S. from 1949 to 2015," Statista, https://www.statista.com/statistics/186260/total-doctors -of-medicine-in-the-us-since-1949/, accessed March 6, 2019.

25. Thomas S. Bodenheimer and Kevin Grumbach, *Understanding Health Policy: A Clinical Approach*, 4th edition (New York: McGraw-Hill, 2004); Marc L. Rivo and David A. Kindig, "A Report Card on the Physician Work Force in the United States," *New England Journal of Medicine* 334, no. 14 (1996): 892–96.

26. An early study found that rate setting lowered inflation by 3 to 4 percentage points. Brian Biles, Carl J. Schramm, and J. Graham Atkinson, "Hospital Cost Inflation under State Rate-Setting Programs," *New England Journal of Medicine* 303, no. 12 (1980): 664–68. After correcting for mean regression, a later study lowered the estimate to 1 to 2 points. David Dranove and Kenneth Cone, "Do State Rate Setting Regulations Really Lower Hospital Expenses?" *Journal of Health Economics* 4, no. 2 (1985): 159–65.

27. Leemore S. Dafny, "How Do Hospitals Respond to Price Changes?" *American Economic Review* 95, no. 5 (2005): 1525–47.

28. Liran Einav, Amy Finkelstein, and Neale Mahoney, "Provider Incentives and Healthcare Costs: Evidence from Long-Term Care Hospitals," *Econometrica* 86, no. 6 (2018): 2161–2219.

29. There is abundant evidence that when regulators reduce the amount they pay for medical services, quality suffers. For a review of this literature, see David Dranove, "Health Care Markets, Regulators, and Certifiers," in *Handbook of Health Economics*, vol. 2 (Amsterdam: Elsevier, 2011), 639–90.

30. Milton I. Roemer, "Bed Supply and Hospital Utilization: A Natural Experiment." *Hospitals* 35 (1961): 36–42.

31. Sallyanne Payton and Rhoda M. Powsner, "Regulation through the Looking Glass: Hospitals, Blue Cross, and Certificate-of-Need," *Michigan Law Review* 79, no. 2 (1980): 203–77.

32. Payton and Powsner. "Regulation through the Looking Glass."

33. This may explain why research at the time failed to find any impact on hospital spending. David S. Salkever and Thomas W. Bice, "The Impact of Certificate-of Need Controls on Hospital Investment." *Milbank Memorial Fund Quarterly: Health and Society* 54 (1976): 185–214; Fred J. Hellinger, "The Effect of Certificate-of-Need Legislation on Hospital Investment." *Inquiry* 13, no. 2 (1976): 187–93; Christopher J. Conover and Frank A. Sloan, "Does Removing Certificate-of-Need Regulations Lead to a Surge in Health Care Spending?" *Journal of Health Politics, Policy and Law* 23, no. 3 (1998): 455–81. More recent studies are not very compelling, with no proper before-and-after analyses to help identify causality. For what it is worth, recent studies produce mixed results. For example, see James Bailey, Tom Hamami, and Daniel McCorry. "Certificate of Need Laws and Health Care Prices," *Journal of Health Care Finance* 43, no. 4 (2016): 1–7; Thomas Stratmann and Matthew Baker, "Barriers to Entry in the Healthcare Markets: Winners and Losers from Certificate-of-Need Laws," Mercatus Research Paper, George Mason University, 2017; and Jomon A. Paul, Huan Ni, and Aniruddha Bagchi, "Does Certificate of Need Law Enhance Competition in Inpatient Care Market? An Empirical Analysis." *Health Economics, Policy and Law* 14, no. 3 (2017): 400–420.

34. Jeff C. Goldsmith, "The Health Care Market: Can Hospitals Survive?" *Harvard Business Review* 58, no. 5 (1980): 100–112.

35. Source: "History," Ambulatory Surgery Center Association, https://www.ascassociation.org/aboutus/whatisanasc/history, accessed March 6, 2019.

36. Source: The Lewin Group analysis of AHA Annual Survey data. Taken from Austin Frakt, "What Caused Outpatient Spending Growth," December 7, 2010, https://theincidentaleconomist.com/wordpress/what-caused-outpatient-spending-growth/, accessed May 9, 2018.

37. Source: American Hospital Association, *AHA Guide to the Healthcare Field* (Chicago: American Hospital Association, various years).

38. Authors' estimates based on enrollment data reported in Health Insurance Association of America, *Sourcebook of Health Insurance Data* (Washington: Health Insurance Association of American, 1980).

39. To this day it is unclear why hospitals did not charge "infinity" or something close to it. They may have been constrained by rules limiting the profits of nonprofit hospitals. Or perhaps they feared bad publicity and the resulting regulatory repercussions.

40. David Dranove, *The Economic Evolution of American Health Care: From Marcus Welby to Managed Care* (Princeton, NJ: Princeton University Press, 2009).

41. Both economic theory and empirical research show that it is, in fact, employees who bear the brunt of rising health spending. As health benefit costs increase, wages fall almost dollar to dollar. For the general theory, see Janet Currie and Brigitte C. Madrian, "Health, Health Insurance and the Labor Market," in *Handbook of Labor Economics* 3, ed. Orley C Ashenfelter and David Card (Amsterdam: Elsevier Science, 1999), 3309–3416. For the most convincing evidence, see Jonathan Gruber, "The Incidence of Mandated Maternity Benefits," *American Economic Review* 84, no. 3 (1994): 622–41; and Katherine Baicker and Amitabh Chandra, "The Labor Market Effects of Rising Health Insurance Premiums," *Journal of Labor Economics* 24, no. 3 (2006): 609–34.

42. Kaiser Family Foundation *Employer Health Benefits Annual Survey* (San Francisco: Kaiser Family Foundation, various years).

43. Source: Health Care Financing Administration, as reported in Kaiser Family Foundation, *Medicaid and Managed Care: Policy Brief* (Washington: Kaiser Family Foundation, May 30, 1995).

44. Gretchen Jacobson, Anthony Damico, Tricia Neuman, and Marsha Gold, *Medicare Advantage 2017 Spotlight: Enrollment Market Update* (Washington: Kaiser Family Foundation, June 6, 2017), https://www.kff.org/medicare/issue-brief/medicare-advantage-2017-spotlight-enrollment-market-update/.

Chapter 2

1. "Acquisitions Quotes," BrainyQuote, https://www.brainyquote.com/topics/acquisitions, accessed June 19, 2019.

2. Alain C. Enthoven, "Consumer-Choice Health Plan: Inflation and Inequity in

Health Care Today: Alternatives for Cost Control and an Analysis of Proposals for National Health Insurance," *New England Journal of Medicine* 298, no. 12 (March 1978): 650–58.

3. Paul M. Ellwood and Alain C. Enthoven, "'Responsible Choices': The Jackson Hole Group Plan for Health Reform," *Health Affairs* 14, no. 2 (Summer 1995): 24–39.

4. Ross Perot. *United We Stand: How We Can Take Back Our Country* (New York: Hyperion, 1992).

5. For the full text of the act, see Health Security Act, S. 1757, 103d Cong. (1993), https://www.govtrack.us/congress/bills/103/s1757/text. For a summary, see Thomas F. A. Plaut and Bernard S. Arons, "President Clinton's Proposal for Health Care Reform: Key Provisions and Issues," *Hospital and Community Psychiatry* 45, no. 9 (September 1994): 871–76, https://www.ncbi.nlm.nih.gov/pubmed/7989016.

6. I Kings 18:22.

7. Keith Korenchuk, *Transforming the Delivery of Health Care: Mergers, Acquisitions and Physician-Hospital Organizations* (Englewood, CO: Medical Group Management Association, 1992).

8. Russell C. Coile, *The Five Stages of Managed Care* (Chicago: Health Administration Press, 1997).

9. Russell C. Coile, "Integrated Delivery Networks," *Health Trends* 7. no. 12 (1995): 1.

10. Walter Zelman, *The Changing Health Care Marketplace* (San Francisco: Jossey-Bass, 1996).

11. Russell C. Coile, *The Five Stages of Managed Care* (Chicago: Health Administration Press, 1997).

12. Robert Town et al., "Revisiting the Relationship between Managed Care and Hospital Consolidation," *Health Services Research* 42, no. 1 (2007): 219–38.

13. APM/University HealthSystem Consortium, "How Markets Evolve," *Hospitals and Health Networks*, March 5, 1995, 60; Voluntary Hospitals of America, *Integration: Market Forces and Critical Success Factors* (Dallas: Voluntary Hospitals of America, 1994).

14. Lawton R. Burns et al., "Managed Care, Market Stages, and Integrated Delivery Systems: Is There a Relationship?" *Health Affairs* 16, no. 6 (1997): 204–18.

15. American College of Healthcare Executives, *Advanced Integrated Delivery Systems: Achieving Peak Performance* (Chicago: American College of Healthcare Executives, 1998); Advisory Board, *The Grand Alliance: Vertical Integration Strategies for Physicians and Health Systems* (Washington: Advisory Board Co., 1998).

16. Voluntary Hospitals of America, *Integration*.

17. Eric G. Campbell, Joel S. Weissman, and David Blumenthal, "Relationship between Market Competition and the Activities and Attitudes of Medical School Faculty," *Journal of the American Medical Association* 278, no. 3 (1997): 222–26; Stephen M. Shortell et al., *Remaking Health Care in America: Building Organized Delivery Systems* (San Francisco: Jossey-Bass, 1996).

18. Dean C. Coddington and Barbara J. Bendrick, *Integrated Health Care: Case Studies* (Englewood, CO: Center for Research in Ambulatory Health Care Administration, 1994); Dean C. Coddington, Keith D. Moore, and Elizabeth Fischer, *Integrated*

Health Care: Reorganizing the Physician, Hospital and Health Plan Relationship (Englewood, CO: Center for Research in Ambulatory Health Care Administration, 1994); Dean C. Coddington, Cary R. Chapman, and Katherine M. Pokoski, *Making Integrated Health Care Work: Case Studies* (Englewood, CO: Center for Research in Ambulatory Health Care Administration, 1996); Dean C. Coddington, Keith D. Moore, and Elizabeth Fischer, *Making Integrated Health Care Work* (Englewood, CO: Center for Research in Ambulatory Health Care Administration, 1996).

19. Schumpeter, "Harvard Business School Risks Going from Great to Good," *Economist*, May 4, 2017.

20. David W. Young and Sheila McCarthy, *Managing Integrated Delivery Systems: A Framework for Action* (Chicago, IL: Health Administration Press, 1999).

21. Robin R. Gillies et al., "Conceptualizing and Measuring Integration: Findings from the Health Systems Integration Study," *Hospital & Health Services Administration* 38, no. 4 (1993): 467–90.

22. One of us (Dranove) had just joined the Kellogg faculty and was a fly on the wall at the meeting.

23. Stephen M. Shortell et al., "Remaking Health Care in America," *Hospitals & Health Networks* 70, no. 6 (1996): 43–44.

24. Based on a Lexis-Nexis search of the term "integrated delivery."

25. David Burda, "Seamless Delivery: Integrated Approach Gets Experts' Vote as an Efficient, Competitive Approach," *Modern Healthcare* 22, no. 42 (October 19, 1992): 38.

26. Stephen M. Shortell et al., *Remaking Health Care in America: Building Organized Delivery Systems* (San Francisco: Jossey-Bass, 1996), 34 (emphasis added).

27. Lawton R. Burns et al., "Managed Care, Market Stages, and Integrated Delivery Systems: Is There a Relationship?" *Health Affairs* 16, no. 6 (1997): 204–18.

28. Jeff Goldsmith, "The Illusive Logic of Integration," *Healthcare Forum Journal* 37, no. 5 (1994): 26–31; Stephen Walston, John Kimberly, and Lawton R. Burns, "Owned Vertical Integration and Health Care: Promise and Performance," *Health Care Management Review* 21, no. 1 (1996): 83–92; Lawton R. Burns and Darrell P. Thorpe, "Physician-Hospital Organizations: Strategy, Structure, and Conduct," in *Integrating the Practice of Medicine*, ed. Ronald Conners (Chicago: American Hospital Publishing, 1997): 351–71.

29. IDNs were such a new concept in 1992 that no data on them were collected. See *Healthcare 2000: A Strategic Assessment of the Health Care Environment in the U.S.* (Irving, TX: Voluntary Hospitals of America and Deloitte and Touche, 2000), which cites SMG Marketing Group, 1999, for these figures.

30. American Hospital Association, *AHA Chartbook* (Chicago: American Hospital Association, 2010).

31. Lawton R. Burns and Darrell P. Thorpe, "Trends and Models in Physician-Hospital Organization," *Health Care Management Review* 18, no. 4 (1993): 7–20.

32. Aventis Pharmaceuticals, *Managed Care Digest 2000* (previously known as HMR Managed Care Digest) (Bridgewater, NJ: Aventis Pharmaceuticals, 2000).

33. American Hospital Association, *AHA Chartbook* (Chicago: American Hospital Association, 2010).

34. Gloria Bazzoli, Linda Dynan, and Lawton R. Burns, "Capitated Contracting of Integrated Health Provider Organizations," *Inquiry* 36, no. 4 (2000): 426–44.

35. Health insurance plans also pursued changes in governance and structure in the 1980s. In contrast to the nonprofit Kaiser and Group Cooperative plans, other health plans rapidly reorganized as for-profit firms. The percentage of for-profit plans rose dramatically from 18 to 67 percent between 1982 and 1988. See Karen Davis, Karen Scott Collins, and Cynthia Morris, "Managed Care: Promise and Concerns," *Health Affairs* 13, no. 4 (1994): 176–85. This transition facilitated the spread of the PPOs and IPA-HMO models, and likely the race to expand enrollment and geographic coverage. The decade also saw the emergence of national chains of insurers such as Aetna, Cigna, and Prudential. Health plans formed chains to gain market share, geographic breadth, covered lives, and revenues. Organized national chains could more easily contract with national employers to cover their workers. Between 1988 and 1994, the percentage of enrollees in national chains rose from 39.5 to 53.5 percent. The insurers also diversified their products to include the HMO and PPO models during the late 1980s and 1990s, along with their traditional indemnity (fee-for-service) offerings.

36. "Your Career as a Healthcare Executive," American College of Healthcare Executives, last modified 2019, https://www.ache.org/career-resource-center/special -groups/resources-for-students-and-early-careerists/your-career-as-a-healthcare -executive.

37. Jeff C. Goldsmith, *Can Hospitals Survive? The New Competitive Health Care Market* (Homewood, IL: Dow-Jones Irwin, 1981).

38. The state of California prohibits hospitals from employing physicians. Instead, many hospitals have exclusive relationships with quasi-independent physician groups. Kaiser's relationship with the Permanente Medical Group is the quintessential example.

39. California prohibits hospitals from directly employing physicians. Instead, hospitals set up medical foundations that employ physicians who, in turn, work exclusively at the sponsoring hospitals. The Kaiser Permanente Foundation is the best-known example.

Chapter 3

1. For a representative argument in favor of the Patient Bill of Rights, see George J. Annas, "A National Bill of Patients' Rights," *Legal Issues in Medicine* 338, no. 10 (1998): 695–99.

2. Harold S. Luft, "How Do Health-Maintenance Organizations Achieve Their Savings? Rhetoric and Evidence," *New England Journal of Medicine* 298, no. 24 (1978): 1336–43.

3. Joseph P. Newhouse, *Free for All?: Lessons from the RAND Health Insurance Experiment* (Boston: Harvard University Press, 1996).

4. Katherine Ho, "Barriers to Entry of a Vertically Integrated Health Insurer: An Analysis of Welfare and Entry Costs," *Journal of Economics & Management Strategy* 18, no. 2 (2009): 487–545.

5. "Hospital Compare Overall Hospital Rating," Centers for Medicare & Medicaid Services, https://www.medicare.gov/hospitalcompare/Data/Hospital-overall-ratings-calculation.html, accessed August 22, 2018.

6. Richard P. Rumelt, "Towards a Strategic Theory of the Firm," in *Resources Firms and Strategies: A Reader in the Resource-Based Perspective*, ed. Nicolai J. Foss (Oxford: Oxford University Press, 1997), 131–45.

7. This section draws on Lawton R. Burns et al., "The Fall of the House of AHERF: The Allegheny Bankruptcy," *Health Affairs* 19, no. 1 (2000): 7–41, as well as our experiences as testifying experts in the lawsuit brought by AHERF's creditors against Price Waterhouse Coopers, AHERF's auditor at the time.

8. Mary Chris Jaklevic, "AHERF-like Symptoms: Struggling Detroit Medical Center Works on Turnaround," *Modern Healthcare* 28, no. 49 (1998): 22–23.

9. Stuart Bunderson, Shawn Lofstrom, and Andrew Van de Ven, "Conceptualizing and Measuring Professional and Administrative Models of Organizing," *Organization Behavior Research* 3, no. 4 (2000): 366–91.

10. Lawton Burns, Jeff Goldsmith, and Aditi Sen, "Horizontal and Vertical Integration of Physicians: A Tale of Two Tails," in *Annual Review of Health Care Management: Revisiting the Evolution of Health Systems Organization, Advances in Health Care Management, Volume 15*, ed. Jim Goes, Grant T. Savage, and Leonard Friedman (Bingley, UK: Emerald Publishing, 2013), 39–117.

11. Glenn Troyer, David Jose, and Andrea Brashear, "Governance Issues for Nonprofit Healthcare Organizations and the Implications of the Sarbanes-Oxley Act," *Indiana Health Law Review* 1, no. 1 (2004): 179–211.

12. Mary Witt and Laura Jacobs, *Physician-Hospital Integration in the Era of Health Reform* (Oakland, CA: California Healthcare Foundation, 2010).

13. Stephen Walston, John Kimberly, and Lawton Burns, "Owned Vertical Integration and Health Care: Promise and Performance," *Health Care Management Review* 21, no. 1 (1996): 83–92; Lawton R. Burns and Darrell P. Thorpe, "Physician-Hospital Organizations: Strategy, Structure, and Conduct," in *Integrating the Practice of Medicine*, ed. Robert Conners, (Chicago: American Hospital Association Publishing, 1997): 351–71; Lawton R. Burns et al., "Physician Commitment to Organized Delivery Systems," *Medical Care* 39, no. 7 (July 2001): I 9–29; Gloria Bazzoli et al., "Is Provider Capitation Working? Effects on Physician-Hospital Integration and Costs of Care," *Medical Care* 38, no. 3 (2000): 311–24; Lawton R. Burns, "Polarity Management: The Key Challenge for Integrated Health Systems," *Journal of Healthcare Management* 44, no. 1 (1999): 14–33.

14. Stephen M. Shortell et al., "Creating Organized Delivery Systems: The Barriers and Facilitators," *Journal of Healthcare Management* 38, no. 4 (1993): 447; Stephen M. Shortell, Robin R. Gillies, and Kelly J. Devers, "Reinventing the American Hospital," *Milbank Quarterly* 73, no. 2 (1995): 131–60; Stephen M. Shortell et al.,

"Remaking Health Care in America," *Hospitals & Health Networks* 70, no. 6 (1996): 43–44.

15. Lawton R. Burns and Darrell P. Thorpe, "Why Provider-Sponsored Health Plans Don't Work," *Healthcare Financial Management: 2001 Resource Guide* (2001): 12–16.

16. Studies include Federico Ciliberto and David Dranove, "The Effect of Physician-Hospital Affiliations on Hospital Prices in California," *Journal of Health Economics* 25, no. 1 (2006): 29–38; Alison Evans Cuellar and Paul J. Gertler, "Strategic Integration of Hospitals and Physicians," *Journal of Health Economics* 25, no. 1 (2006): 1–28; Kristin M. Madison, "Hospital-Physician Affiliations and Patient Treatments, Expenditures, and Outcomes," *Health Services Research* 39, no. 2 (2004): 257–78; and Thomas T. H. Wan, Blossom Yen-Ju Lin, and Allen Ma, "Integration Mechanisms and Hospital Efficiency in Integrated Health Care Delivery Systems," *Journal of Medical Systems* 26, no. 2 (2002): 127–43. All of the studies rely on an excessively coarse survey measure of hospital-physician integration that indicates whether the hospital employs any physicians, but not how many.

17. Lawton R. Burns and Mark V. Pauly, "Integrated Delivery Networks (IDNs): A Detour on the Road to Integrated Healthcare?" *Health Affairs* 21, no. 4 (2002): 128–43.

18. Burns, Goldsmith, and Sen, "Horizontal and Vertical Integration of Physicians."

19. Institute of Medicine, *To Err Is Human: Building a Safer Health System* (Washington: National Academy Press, 2000); Institute of Medicine, *Crossing the Quality Chasm: A New Health System for the 21st Century* (Washington: National Academy Press, 2001).

20. John Eisenberg, "Physician Utilization: The State of Research About Physicians' Practice Patterns," *Medical Care* 40, no. 11 (2002): 1016–35; Alan Sager and Deborah Socolar, "Health Costs Absorb One-Quarter of Economic Growth, 2000–2005," Boston University School of Public Health, data brief no. 8, Boston University, 2005.

21. James C. Robinson and Harold S. Luft, "The Impact of Hospital Market Structure on Patient Volume, Average Length of Stay, and the Cost of Care," *Journal of Health Economics* 4, no. 4 (1985): 333–56.

22. For an excellent description of the winner's curse in real life, see Richard Thaler, *The Winner's Curse: Paradoxes and Anomalies of Economic Life* (New York: Simon and Schuster, 2012).

23. Named after a scenario where two prisoners are tricked into ratting on each other, a prisoner's dilemma arises when individuals pursue their own self-interest at the expense of the greater good.

24. Michael L. Figliuolo, Paul D. Mango, and David H. McCormick, "Hospital, Heal Thyself," *McKinsey Quarterly*, no. 1 (2000): 90–97.

25. Lawton R. Burns et al., "The Fall of the House of AHERF: The Allegheny Bankruptcy," *Health Affairs* 19, no. 1 (2000): 7–41.

26. Aditi Sen, Lawton R. Burns, and Suzanne Sawyer, "Physician Referral Practices

and the Potential for Delivery System Change in Philadelphia," presentation to Academy of Management annual meeting, August 2014.

27. Lawton R. Burns and Douglas Wholey, "The Impact of Physician Characteristics in Conditional Choice Models for Hospital Care," *Journal of Health Economics* 11, no. 1 (1992): 43–62.

28. Ed Murphy, presentation to the Wharton School, spring 2004.

29. Louise Kertesz, "The Game of Risk; Providers are Fighting Back," *Modern Health-care*, February 5, 1996, https://www.modernhealthcare.com/article/19960205/PREMIUM/602050304/cover-story-the-game-of-risk-providers-are-fighting-back-fuming-over-hmos-high-margins-and-lower-payments-they-are.

30. Lawton Burns and Ralph Muller, "Hospital-Physician Collaboration: Landscape of Economic Integration and Impact on Clinical Integration," *Milbank Quarterly* 86, no. 3 (2008): 375–434.

31. This section draws heavily on Lawton R. Burns and Douglas Wholey, "Respond-ing to a Consolidating Healthcare System: Options for Physician Organizations," in *Advances in Health Care Management*, Volume 1, ed. Jim Goes, Grant T. Savage, and Leonard Friedman (Bingley, UK: Emerald Publishing, 2000), 273–335.

32. Lawton R. Burns et al., "Physician Commitment to Organized Delivery Systems," *Medical Care* 39, no. 7 (July 2001): I 9–29; Lawton R. Burns, Jeffrey Alexander, and Ronald Andersen, "How Different Governance Models May Impact Physician-Hospital Alignment," *Health Care Management Review* (August 2018), doi: 10.1097/HMR.0000000000000214.

33. Ernst & Young, *Physician-Hospital Organizations: 1995 Profile* (Washington: Ernst & Young, 1995); InterStudy, *InterStudy Competitive Edge: HMO Industry Report 7.1* (Minneapolis: InterStudy, 1997).

34. Karen Pallarito, "Florida PHO Pulls Plug, Declares Bankruptcy," *Modern Health-care* 29, no. 29 (July 1999): 2–3.

35. Jeffrey Alexander et al., "An Exploratory Analysis of Market-Based Physician-Organization Arrangements," *Hospital and Health Services Administration* 41, no. 3 (1996): 311–29.

36. Several structural charts are presented in Lawton R. Burns and Darrell P. Thorpe, "Trends and Models in Physician-Hospital Organization," *Health Care Manage-ment Review* 18, no. 4 (1993): 7–20.

37. Stephen M. Shortell, *Effective Hospital-Physician Relationships* (Ann Arbor, MI: Health Administration Press, 1991); Prospective Payment Assessment Commission, *Winners and Losers under the Medicare Program* (Washington: ProPAC, 1992).

38. David Dranove and Richard Lindrooth, "Hospital Consolidation and Costs: Another Look at the Evidence," *Journal of Health Economics* 22, no. 6 (2003): 983–97; Matt Schmitt, "Do Hospital Mergers Reduce Costs?" *Journal of Health Eco-nomics* 52 (2017): 74–94. The former paper finds mixed evidence of economies for local systems. The latter paper documents purchasing economies for regional sys-tems, but no economies for local systems.

39. Lawton R. Burns and Darrell P. Thorpe, "Physician-Hospital Organizations:

Strategy, Structure, and Conduct," in *Integrating the Practice of Medicine*, ed. Robert Conners, (Chicago: American Hospital Association Publishing, 1997): 351–71.

40. Lawton R. Burns and Darrell P. Thorpe, "Why Provider-Sponsored Health Plans Don't Work," *Healthcare Financial Management: 2001 Resource Guide* (2001): 12–16.

41. Lawton R. Burns, Gilbert Gimm, and Sean Nicholson, "The Financial Performance of Integrated Health Organizations (IHOs)," *Journal of Healthcare Management* 50, no. 3 (2005): 191–213.

42. This section draws on Salomon Brothers, "Salomon Brothers PPM Perspectives Series: Wharton Professor Interview," Salomon Brothers, 1997.

43. Uwe Reinhardt, "The Rise and Fall of the Physician Practice Management Industry," *Health Affairs* 19, no. 1 (2000): 42–55.

44. After a complex set of transactions spelled the end of MedPartners's PPM business, its pharmacy and US home care businesses reemerged as Caremark. It sold its foreign homecare business to Fresenius, which today is the largest provider of dialysis care in the United States.

45. Peter Elkind, "Vulgarians at the Gate," *Fortune*, June 21, 1999.

Chapter 4

1. Isabel Paterson, *The God of the Machine* (New York: G. P. Putnam's Sons, 1993), 172.

2. For-profit systems are still around, led by HCA, Tenet (a merger of NME and AMI), Community Health Systems, and Vanguard, among others.

3. This is not to say that for-profits did not cut corners when they could. To take an example, for-profit hospitals were more likely to exploit loopholes in Medicare reimbursement formulas so as to maximize revenues. See Leemore S. Dafny, "How Do Hospitals Respond to Price Changes?" *American Economic Review* 95, no. 5 (2005): 1525–47.

4. These counts may not coincide with other published figures, for several reasons. We limit the count to the system's home region. We include children's hospitals and other specialty hospitals, as well as joint venture facilities. Systems may list separate campuses as a single hospital (we count them as two hospitals), and may list affiliated hospitals as part of a system when in fact they remain independent. Systems are constantly expanding and occasionally contracting. For all these reasons, it is difficult to get an exact count at any specific moment.

5. Martin Gaynor, former chief economist at the Federal Trade Commission's Bureau of Competition, summarized the research this way: "The research evidence shows that hospitals and doctors who face less competition charge higher prices to private payers, without accompanying gains in efficiency or quality." Statement of Martin Gaynor, Carnegie Mellon University, in *Examining the Impact of Health Care Consolidation: Statement before the Committee on Energy and Commerce Oversight and Investigations Subcommittee, US House of Representatives*, February 14, 2018.

6. "Health Affairs ahead of Print: National Health Spending In 2017," *Health Affairs Blog*, December 6, 2018, DOI: 10.1377/hblog20181206.671046.

7. Robert Town, Douglas Wholey, Roger Feldman, and Lawton R. Burns, "Hospital Consolidation and Racial/Income Disparities in Health Insurance Coverage," *Health Affairs* 26, no. 4 (2007): 1170–80.

8. There is some ambiguity as to which agency has responsibility for which mergers. Broadly speaking, the Federal Trade Commission handles provider cases and the Department of Justice handles insurer cases, although there are exceptions.

9. James C. Robinson and Harold S. Luft, "The Impact of Hospital Market Structure on Patient Volume, Average Length of Stay, and the Cost of Care," *Journal of Health Economics* 4, no. 4 (1985): 333–56.

10. There are usually alternative providers of outpatient services, so a hospital merger is not as likely to lessen competition in the outpatient services market.

11. *United States v. General Dynamics Corporation*, 341 F. Supp. 534 (N.D. Ill. 1972).

12. Kenneth G. Elzinga and Thomas F. Hogarty, "The Problem of Geographic Market Definition Revisited: The Case of Coal," *Antitrust Bulletin* 23 (1968): 1–18.

13. The year indicates when the enforcement agency challenged the merger. Typically, the merger would have been announced one or two years earlier.

14. *United States v. Long Island Jewish Medical Center and North Shore Health System, Inc.*, 983 F. Supp. 121 (E.D.N.Y. 1997).

15. Despite this commitment, there are frequent reports of Spectrum Health raising prices by well above the rate of inflation. See Sue Thoms, "Spectrum Health Raising Prices Nearly 6 Percent in Grand Rapids, Projects over $4 Billion in Revenue," Michigan Live, June 6, 2013, https://www.mlive.com/business/west-michigan/index.ssf/2013/06/spectrum_health_raising_prices.html; Sue Thoms, "Spectrum Health Plans Another Significant Rate Hike at Grand Rapids Hospital," Michigan Live, June 6, 2011, https://www.mlive.com/business/west-michigan/index.ssf/2011/06/spectrum_health_plans_8_percen.html.

16. This term can be traced to Burton Weisbrod, *The Nonprofit Economy* (Cambridge, MA: Harvard University Press, 1988).

17. *Federal Trade Commission v. Butterworth Health Corporation*, 946 F. Supp. 1285 at 1302 (W.D. Mich. 1996).

18. Gregory J. Werden, "The Use and Misuse of Shipments Data in Defining Geographic Markets," *Antitrust Bulletin* 26, (1981): 719–37; Gregory J. Werden, "The Limited Relevance of Patient Migration Data in Market Delineation for Hospital Merger Cases," *Journal of Health Economics* 8, no. 4 (1990): 363–76.

19. The first paper, published in a law journal, uses specific examples, while the latter, published in an economics journal, adds more equations in order to generalize the findings.

20. H. E. Frech III, James Langenfeld, and R. Forrest McCluer, "Elzinga-Hogarty Tests and Alternative Approaches for Market Share Calculations in Hospital Markets," *Antitrust Law Journal* 71, (2004): 921–49.

21. The key here is "all else equal." If the monopolist got that way by discovering a low-cost way to produce its product, it might underprice competitive firms. If the monopolist got that way by buying up all the competition, then we would normally expect higher prices.

22. For the past several years, several organizations have offered actual transaction price data to academic researchers, but during the 1990s and 2000s, there was little that researchers could do at the time that E-H was under scrutiny.

23. Cory Capps and David Dranove, "Hospital Consolidation and Negotiated PPO Prices," *Health Affairs* 23, no. 2 (2004): 175–81.

24. Steven Tenn, "The Price Effects of Hospital Mergers: A Case Study of the Sutter-Summit Transaction," *International Journal of the Economics of Business* 18, no. 1 (2001): 65–82.

25. Michael G. Vita and Seth Sacher, "The Competitive Effects of Not-For-Profit Hospital Mergers: A Case Study," *Journal of Industrial Economics* 49, no. 1 (2001): 63–84.

26. Aileen Thompson, "The Effect of Hospital Mergers on Inpatient Prices: A Case Study of the New Hanover–Cape Fear Transaction," *International Journal of the Economics of Business* 18, no. 1 (2011): 91–101.

27. Cory Capps et al., "Antitrust Policy and Hospital Mergers: Recommendations for a New Approach," *Antitrust Bulletin* 47, no. 4 (2002): 677–714.

28. Robert Town and Gregory Vistnes, "Hospital Competition in HMO Networks," *Journal of Health Economics* 20, no. 5 (2001): 733–53.

29. ENH economists disagreed about the magnitude of the price increase.

30. Robert Town and Gregory Vistnes, "Hospital Competition in HMO Networks," *Journal of Health Economics* 20, no. 5 (2001): 733–53.

31. Cory Capps, David Dranove, and Mark Satterthwaite, "Competition and Market Power in Option Demand Markets," *RAND Journal of Economics* 34, no. 4 (2003): 737–63.

32. Cory Capps, David Dranove, and Chris Ody, "Physician Practice Consolidation Driven by Small Acquisitions, So Antitrust Agencies Have Few Tools to Intervene," *Health Affairs* 36, no. 9 (2017): 1556–63.

33. Two prominent examples are Kaiser Permanente Medical Group–Washington and Group Health Cooperative; and Hill Physicians Medical Group and Muir Medical Group.

Chapter 5

1. Cory Capps et al., "The Silent Majority Fallacy of the Elzinga-Hogarty Criteria: A Critique and New Approach to Analyzing Hospital Mergers," National Bureau of Economic Research working paper 8216, Cambridge, MA, April 2001. For a rigorous model of hospital/insurer bargaining, see Kate Ho and Robin S. Lee, "Insurer Competition in Health Care Markets," *Econometrica* 85, no. 2 (2017): 379–417.

2. Lawton R. Burns and Mark V. Pauly, "Transformation of the Healthcare Industry: Curb Your Enthusiasm?" *Milbank Quarterly* 96, no. 1 (March 2018): 57–109.

3. The concept of the Triple Aim was introduced in Don Berwick, Thomas Nolan, and John Whittington, "The Triple Aim: Care, Health, and Cost," *Health Affairs* 27, no. 3 (2008): 759–69.

4. John Kenneth Galbraith, *A Short History of Financial Euphoria* (Knoxville, TN: Whittle Books, 1990).

5. The term "hospitalists" was introduced in Robert Wachter and Lee Goldman, "The Emerging Role of 'Hospitalists' in the American Health Care System," *New England Journal of Medicine* 335, no. 7 (1996): 514–17.

6. David Meltzer et al., "Effects of Physician Experience on Costs and Outcomes on an Academic General Medicine Service: Results of a Trial of Hospitalists," *Annals of Internal Medicine* 137, no. 11 (2002): 866–74.

7. Janet Coffman and Thomas Rundall, "The Impact of Hospitalists on the Cost and Quality of Inpatient Care in the United States: A Research Synthesis," *Medical Care Research & Review* 62, no. 4 (2005): 379–406; Bruce Dixon, "Hospitalists' Impact on Outcomes Not So Clear: Large Study Finds No Evidence That Hospitalists Affect Average Length of Stay, Costs, or Patient Outcomes," *Internal Medicine News,* July 1, 2005; Peter Lindenauer et al., "Outcomes of Care by Hospitalists, General Internists, and Family Physicians," *New England Journal of Medicine* 357, no. 25 (2007): 2589–2600; Hoangmai Pham et al., "Hospitalists and Care Transitions: The Divorce of Inpatient and Outpatient Care," *Health Affairs* 27, no. 5 (2008): 1315–27; Heather White and Richard Glazier, "Do Hospitalist Physicians Improve the Quality of Inpatient Care Delivery? A Systematic Review of Process, Efficiency, and Outcome Measures," *BMC Medicine* 9, no. 58 (2011); Jean-Sebastian Rachoin et al., "The Impact of Hospitalists on Length of Stay and Costs: Systematic Review and Meta-Analysis," *American Journal of Managed Care* 18, no. 1 (2012): e23–e30; Daniel Elliott, Robert Young, and Joanne Brice, "Effect of Hospitalist Workload on the Quality and Efficiency of Care," *JAMA Internal Medicine* 174, no. 5 (2014): 786–93; Jennifer Stevens, David Nyweide, and Sha Maresh, "Comparison of Hospital Resource Use and Outcomes among Hospitalists, Primary Care Physicians, and Other Generalists," *JAMA Internal Medicine* 177, no. 12 (2017): 1781–87.

8. Jean-Sebastian Rachoin et al., "The Impact of Hospitalists on Length of Stay and Costs: Systematic Review and Meta-Analysis," *American Journal of Managed Care* 18, no. 1 (2012): e23–e30; Yong-Fang Kuo and James S. Goodwin, "Association of Hospitalist Care with Medical Utilization after Discharge: Evidence of Cost Shift from a Cohort Study," *Annals of Internal Medicine* 155, no. 3 (2011): 152–59.

9. Dave Barkholz, "Hospitals Find Launching Health Plans Remains an Expensive Experiment" *Modern Healthcare,* September 23, 2017, http://www.modernhealth care.com/article/20170923/NEWS/170929947/hospitals-find-launching-health -plans-remains-an-expensive-experiment.

10. Lawton R. Burns and Mark V. Pauly, "Transformation of the Healthcare Industry: Curb Your Enthusiasm?" *Milbank Quarterly* 96, no. 1 (March 2018): 57–109. See also Sandra Tanenbaum, "Pay for Performance in Medicare: Evidentiary Irony and the Politics of Value," *Journal of Health Politics, Policy and Law* 34, no. 5 (2009): 717–46.

11. Bruce Hillman and Jeff Goldsmith, "Imaging: The Self-Referral Boom and the Ongoing Search for Effective Policies to Contain It," *Health Affairs* 29, no. 12 (2010):

2231–36; David Levin, Vijay Rao, Laurence Parker, and Andrea Frangos, "The Disproportionate Effects of the Deficit Reduction Act of 2005 on Radiologists' Private Office MRI and CT Practices Compared with Those of Other Physicians," *Journal of the American College of Radiology* 6, no. 9 (2009): 620–25.

12. John Hargraves and Julie Reiff, "Shifting Care from Office to Outpatient Settings: Services Are Increasingly Performed in Outpatient Settings with Higher Prices," *Health Care Cost Institute (HCCI) Blog: #HealthyBytes*, April 2, 2019, https://health costinstitute.org/in-the-news/shifting-care-office-to-outpatient.

13. David Dranove and Chris Ody, "Employed for Higher Pay? How Medicare Facility Fees Affect Hospital Employment of Physicians," *American Economic Journal: Policy* (forthcoming).

14. "Accountable Care Organization Learning Network Toolkit," Brookings Institution, January 2011, https://xteam.brookings.edu/bdacoln/Documents/ACO%20Toolkit %20January%202011.pdf, accessed October 4, 2012.

15. Valerie A. Lewis, Elliott S. Fisher, and Carrie H. Colla, "Explaining Sluggish Savings under Accountable Care," *New England Journal of Medicine* 377, no. 19 (2017): 1809–11.

16. Harold Demsetz, "Two Systems of Belief about Monopoly," in *Industrial Concentration: The New Learning*, ed. Harvey J. Goldschmid, H. Michael Mann, and J. Fred Weston (Boston: Little, Brown, 1974).

17. See Cathy Schoen, Sabrina K. H. How, Ilana Weinbaum, John E. Craig Jr., and Karen D. Davis, *Public Views on Shaping the Future of the US Health System* (New York: Commonwealth Fund, 2006); Commonwealth Fund, *The Commonwealth Fund Commission on a High Performance Health System: Why Not the Best? Results from a National Scorecard on US Health System Performance, National Scorecard on US Health System Performance* (New York: Commonwealth Fund, 2006); and Stuart Guterman et al., "Using Medicare Payment Policy to Transform the Health System: A Framework for Improving Performance," *Health Affairs* 28, no. 2 (2009): w238–w250.

18. Michael Porter and Thomas Lee, "From Volume to Value in Health Care: The Work Begins," *Journal of the American Medical Association* 310, no. 10 (2016): 1047–48.

19. Brady Post, Thomas Buchmueller, and Andrew Ryan, "Vertical Integration of Hospitals and Physicians: Economic Theory and Empirical Evidence on Spending and Quality," *Medical Care Research & Review* 75, no. 4 (2017): figure 1.

20. Lawton R. Burns and Mark V. Pauly, "Integrated Delivery Networks (IDNs): A Detour on the Road to Integrated Healthcare?" *Health Affairs* 21, no. 4 (2002): 128–43.

21. Pooja Kumar, Anna Sherwood, and Saumya Sutaria, "Engaging Physicians to Transform Operational and Clinical Performance," McKinsey, May 2013, https:// healthcare.mckinsey.com/sites/default/files/MCK_Hosp_MDSurvey.pdf.

22. Lawton R. Burns, Jeffrey A. Alexander, and Ronald Andersen, "Does the Governance Model Used in Physician-Hospital Relationships Impact Physician Alignment?" *Health Care Management Review* (forthcoming).

23. See Lawton R. Burns, Jeffrey A. Alexander, and Ronald M. Andersen, "How Different Governance Models May Impact Physician-Hospital Alignment," *Health Care Management Review* (August 3, 2018), https://www.ncbi.nlm.nih.gov/pubmed/30080711.
24. Lawton R. Burns, Jeffrey A. Alexander, and Ronald Andersen, "Does the Governance Model Used in Physician-Hospital Relationships Impact Physician Alignment?" *Health Care Management Review* (forthcoming).
25. Stephen M. Shortell et al., *Remaking Health Care in America: Building Organized Delivery Systems* (San Francisco: Jossey-Bass, 1996).
26. Lawton R. Burns and Ralph Muller, "Hospital-Physician Collaboration: Landscape of Economic Integration and Impact on Clinical Integration," *Milbank Quarterly* 86, no. 3 (2008): 375–434.
27. Burns and Muller, "Hospital-Physician Collaboration."
28. George Santayana, *The Last Puritan: A Memoir in the Form of a Novel* (Boston: MIT Press, 1995).
29. For an extended discussion of the differences, see Lawton R. Burns and Mark V. Pauly, "Accountable Care Organizations May Have Difficulty Avoiding the Failures of Integrated Delivery Networks of the 1990s," *Health Affairs* 31 (2012): 2407–16.

Chapter 6

1. "Failure Quotes," Goodreads, https://www.goodreads.com/quotes/tag/failure, accessed June 19, 2019.
2. Martin Gaynor and Robert Town, "The Impact of Hospital Consolidation: Update," *Synthesis Project Policy Brief* 9 (June 2012).
3. Zack Cooper, Stuart V. Craig, Martin Gaynor, and John Van Reenen, "The Price Ain't Right? Hospital Prices and Health Spending on the Privately Insured," *Quarterly Journal of Economics* 134, no. 1 (2018): 51–107.
4. Nancy D. Beaulieu et al., "Changes in Quality of Care after Hospital Mergers and Acquisition," *New England Journal of Medicine* 382 (2020): 51–59.
5. Matt Schmitt, "Do Hospital Mergers Reduce Costs?" *Journal of Health Economics* 52 (2017): 74–94.
6. Consulting firms occasionally produce studies favorable to hospital mergers. See, for example, Monica Noether and Sean May, "Hospital Merger Benefits: Views from Hospital Leaders and Econometric Analysis," Charles River Associates, January 2017, https://www.aha.org/system/files/2018-04/Hospital-Merger-Full-Report-FINAL-1.pdf. This study finds that acquired hospitals enjoy 2.5 percent lower costs per admission. These studies are not usually subjected to peer review, and generally lack the depth of analysis required of academic publications. Besides, if hospital costs fall but prices increase (the evidence on the latter is overwhelming), then it is difficult to see how consumers have benefited.
7. Sayaka Nakamura, Cory Capps, and David Dranove, "Patient Admission Patterns and Acquisitions of 'Feeder' Hospitals," *Journal of Economics & Management*

Strategy 16, no. 4 (2007): 995–1030. Sayaka Nakamura, "Hospital Mergers and Referrals in the United States: Patient Steering or Integrated Delivery of Care?" *INQUIRY: The Journal of Health Care Organization, Provision, and Financing* 47, no. 3 (2010): 226–41.

8. Kristin Madison, "Hospital–Physician Affiliations and Patient Treatments, Expenditures, and Outcomes," *Health Services Research* 39, no. 2 (2004): 257–78; John E. Kralewski et al., "Effects of Medical Group Practice and Physician Payment Methods on Costs of Care," *Health Services Research* 35, no. 3 (2000): 591–613; John E. Kralewski, Bryan E. Dowd, Yi "Wendy" Xu, and David Knutson, "The Organizational Characteristics of Best Medical Group Practices," unpublished manuscript, February 2011; Michael Pesko et al., "Spending per Medicare Beneficiary Is Higher in Hospital-Owned Small- and Medium-Sized Physician Practices," *Health Services Research* 53, no. 4 (August 2018); Rachel Mosher Henke et al., "Impact of Health System Affiliation on Hospital Resource Use Intensity and Quality of Care," *Health Services Research* 53, no. 1: 63–86; John E. Kralewski, Terence D. Wingert, David J. Knutson, and Christopher E. Johnson, "The Effects of Medical Group Practice Organizational Factors on Physicians' Use of Resources," *Journal of Healthcare Management* 44, no. 3 (1999): 167–82; John E. Kralewski et al., "Effects of Medical Group Practice and Physician Payment Methods on Costs of Care," *Health Services Research* 35, no. 3 (2000): 591–613.

9. Michael Pesko et al., "Spending per Medicare Beneficiary Is Higher in Hospital-Owned Small- and Medium-Sized Physician Practices," *Health Services Research* 53, no. 4 (August 2018).

10. Tara F. Bishop et al., "Trends in Hospital-Ownership of Physician Practices and the Effect on Processes to Improve Quality," *American Journal of Managed Care* 22, no. 3 (2016): 172–76; John N. Mafi et al., "Association of Primary Care Practice Location and Ownership with the Provision of Low-Value Care in the United States," *JAMA Internal Medicine* 177, no. 6 (2017): 838–45.

11. Vance M. Chunn et al., "Integration of Cardiologists with Hospitals," *Health Care Management Review*, published ahead of print, October 5, 2018, doi: 10.1097/HMR.0000000000000223.

12. Stephen M. Shortell et al., "An Empirical Assessment of High Performing Physician Organizations: Results from a National Study," *Medical Care Research and Review* 62, no. 4 (August 2005): 407–34; Diane R. Rittenhouse et al., "Improving Chronic Illness Care: Findings from a National Study of Care Management Processes in Large Physician Practices," *Medical Care Research and Review*, 67, no. 3 (June 2010): 301–20; James Robinson et al., "Financial Incentives, Quality Improvement Programs, and the Adoption of Clinical Information Technology," *Medical Care* 47, no. 4 (April 2009): 411–17; Stephen M. Shortell et al., "Improving Chronic Illness Care: A Longitudinal Cohort Analysis of Large Physician Organizations," *Medical Care* 4, no. 9 (September 2009): 932–39; Diane R. Rittenhouse et al., "Small and Medium-Size Physician Practices Use Few Patient-Centered Medical Home Processes," *Health Affairs* 30, no. 8 (August 2011): 1575–84.

13. John E. Kralewski, Bryan E. Dowd, Yi "Wendy" Xu, and David Knutson, "The Organizational Characteristics of Best Medical Group Practices," unpublished manuscript, February 2011.

14. Thomas Koch, Brett W. Wendling, and Nathan Wilson, "The Effects of Physician and Hospital Integration on Medicare Beneficiaries' Health Outcomes," Bureau of Economics Federal Trade Commission, WP no. 337, July 2018, https://ssrn.com /abstract=3221282 or http://dx.doi.org/10.2139/ssrn.3221282. See also Ian McCarthy, "Physician Affiliation and Hospital Production," unpublished manuscript, Emory University, 2019.

15. Cory Capps, David Dranove, and Christopher Ody, "The Effect of Hospital Acquisitions of Physician Practices on Prices and Spending," *Journal of Health Economics* 59 (2018): 139–52.

16. Caroline S. Carlin, Roger Feldman, and Bryan Dowd, "The Impact of Provider Consolidation on Physician Prices," *Health Economics* 26, no. 12 (2017): 1789–1806.

17. Caroline S. Carlin, Bryan Dowd, and Roger Feldman, "Changes in Quality of Health Care Delivery after Vertical Integration," *Health Services Research* 50, no. 4 (2015): 1043–68.

18. Cory Capps, David Dranove, and Christopher Ody, "The Effect of Hospital Acquisitions of Physician Practices on Prices and Spending," *Journal of Health Economics* 59 (2018): 139–52. One might wonder why powerful hospitals need to acquire more physicians to raise their prices. This bears on an antitrust concept known as the "law of one monopoly profit." We discuss this at length in the next chapter.

19. Lawton R. Burns and Ralph W. Muller, "Hospital-Physician Collaboration: Landscape of Economic Integration and Impact on Clinical Integration," *Milbank Quarterly* 86, no. 3 (2008): 375–434; Kirsten W. Scott et al., "Changes in Hospital-Physician Affiliations in US Hospitals and Their Effect on Quality of Care," *Annals of Internal Medicine* 166, no. 1 (2017): 1–8.

20. Michaela J. Kerrissey et al., "Medical Group Structural Integration May Not Ensure That Care Is Integrated, from the Patient's Perspective," *Health Affairs (Millwood)* 36, no. 5 (2017): 885–92.

21. Ann Curoe, John Kralewski, and Amer Kaissi, "Assessing the Cultures of Medical Group Practices," *Journal of the American Board of Family Medicine* 16, no. 5 (2003): 394–98; John E. Kralewski et al., "Measuring the Culture of Medical Group Practices," *Health Care Management Review* 30, no. 3 (2005): 184–93.

22. John E. Kralewski et al., "The Influence of the Structure and Culture of Medical Group Practices on Prescription Drug Errors," *Medical Care* 43, no. 8 (2005): 817–25.

23. Stephen M. Shortell et al., "An Empirical Assessment of High Performing Physician Organizations: Results from a National Study," *Medical Care Research and Review* 62, no. 4 (August 2005): 407–34; David N. Gans, "Why Hospital-Owned Medical Groups Lose Money," *MGMA Connexion* 12, no. 4 (2012): 19–20.

24. Advisory Board, *Stopping the Bleed: Executive Briefing* (Washington: Health Care Advisory Board, 1999).

25. David N. Gans, "Why Hospital-Owned Medical Groups Lose Money," *MGMA Connexion* 12, no. 4 (2012): 19–20.

26. Jeff Goldsmith, Alex Hunter, and Amy Strauss, "Do Most Hospitals Benefit from Directly Employing Physicians?" *Harvard Business Review*, May 29, 2018.

27. The authors thank Dave Gans for sharing the survey results.

28. J. E. Kralewski et al., "The Effects of Medical Group Practice Organizational Factors on Physicians' Use of Resources," *Journal of Healthcare Management* 44, no. 3 (1999): 167–82.

29. Gary Baldwin, "The Price of I.T. Progress?" *HealthData Management*, May 1, 2012, http://www.healthdatamanagement.com/issues/20_5/hospital-physician-i.t. -information-technology-ehr-44378-1.html, accessed on May 25, 2013.

30. David N. Gans and Larry Wolper, "Management Makes the Difference: Optimizing Medical Group Performance," *ACMPE Executive View*, Spring 2013.

31. Tara Bannow, "Docs Don't Drain Hospital Finances, Systems Say," *Modern Healthcare*, July 16, 2018, 18–21.

32. David N. Gans, "Why Hospital-Owned Medical Groups Lose Money," *MGMA Connexion* 12, no. 4 (2012): 19–20; David N. Gans, "Perspective Is Everything: Look beyond Reported Losses," *MGMA Connexion* 12, no 10 (2012): 17–19.

33. "2018 Healthcare Marketplace Report," Knowledge Leader, https://knowledge -leader.colliers.com/editor/2018-healthcare-marketplace-report/.

34. Richard M. Scheffler, Daniel R. Arnold, and Christopher M. Whaley, "Consolidation Trends in California's Health Care System: Impacts on ACA Premiums and Outpatient Visit Prices," *Health Affairs* 37, no. 9 (September 2018): 1409–16.

35. Bradley Herring et al., Comparing the Value of Nonprofit Hospitals' Tax Exemption to Their Community Benefits," *Inquiry: The Journal of Health Care Organization, Provision, and Financing* 55 (February 13, 2008), doi: 0046958017751970.

36. Rita Sverdlik, Lisa Goldstein, Kendra M. Smith, *Medians: Operating Pressures Exist as Growth in Expenses Exceeds Revenue* (New York: Moody's Investors Service, August 28, 2018).

37. "Health System Financial Analysis: Data Charts," Navigant Consulting, 2018.

38. Jeff Goldsmith, Rulon Stacey, and Alex Hunter, "Stiffening Headwinds Challenge Health Systems to Grow Smarter," Navigant Consulting, September 2018.

39. Fitch Ratings, *What Investors Want to Know: U.S. Not-for-Profit Hospitals and Health Systems* (London: Fitch Ratings, November 15, 2018).

40. Lawton R. Burns, Stephen M. Shortell, and Ronald M. Andersen, "Does Familiarity Breed Contentment? Attitudes and Behaviors of Integrated Physicians," in *Research in the Sociology of Health Care*, vol. 15, ed. Jennie Kronenfeld (Greenwich, CT: JAI Press, 1998); Lawton R. Burns, Jeffrey Alexander, Stephen Shortell, Howard Zuckerman, Peter Budetti, Robin Gillies, and Teresa Waters, "Physician Commitment to Organized Delivery Systems," *Medical Care* 39, no. 7 (July 2001): Physician System Alignment Supplement I 9–29; Janet M. Dukerich, Brian R. Golden, and Stephen M. Shortell, "Beauty Is in the Eye of the Beholder: The Impact of Organizational Identification, Identity, and Image on the Cooperative Behaviors of Physicians," *Administrative Science Quarterly* 47, no. 3 (2002): 507–33.

41. Tim Van Biesen et al., *Front Line of Healthcare Report 2017: Giving Physicians a Say: Why Involving Doctors Can Help Improve US Healthcare* (Boston: Bain and Company, 2017).

42. Tamara Rosin, "Ten Prominent Health System CEOs: Physician Burnout Is a Public Health Crisis; Here Are Eleven Things We Commit to Do about It," *Becker's Hospital Review*, March 28, 2017, https://www.beckershospitalreview.com/hospital-physician-relationships/ceos-of-mayo-cleveland-clinic-partners-and-other-health-systems-pen-call-to-action-on-physician-burnout.html, accessed November 27, 2017.

43. Kerstin Edwards and David Muhlestein, *Examining Pessimism among Physicians* (Salt Lake City: Leavitt Partners, 2018).

44. Lawton R. Burns, Jeffrey Alexander, Stephen Shortell, Howard Zuckerman, Peter Budetti, Robin Gillies, and Teresa Waters, "Physician Commitment to Organized Delivery Systems," *Medical Care* 39, no. 7 (July 2001): Physician System Alignment Supplement I 9–29.

45. Stuart Bunderson, Shawn Lofstrom, and Andrew Van de Ven, "Conceptualizing and Measuring Professional and Administrative Models of Organizing," *Organization Behavior Research* 3, no. 4 (2000): 366–91.

46. Ann Curoe, John Kralewski, and Amer Kaissi, "Assessing the Cultures of Medical Group Practices," *Journal of the American Board of Family Medicine* 16, no. 5 (2003): 394–98.

47. Tim Van Biesen et al., *Front Line of Healthcare Report 2017: Giving Physicians a Say: Why Involving Doctors Can Help Improve US Healthcare* (Boston: Bain and Company, 2017).

48. Lawton R. Burns, Jeffrey Alexander, and Ronald Andersen, "How Different Governance Models May Impact Physician-Hospital Alignment," *Health Care Management Review* (August 2018), doi: 10.1097/HMR.0000000000000214.

49. Lawton R. Burns, Jeff C. Goldsmith, and Ralph Muller, "History of Hospital/Physician Relationships: Obstacles, Opportunities, and Issues," in *Partners in Health*, ed. Jay Crosson and Laura Tollen (Oakland, CA: Kaiser Permanente Institute for Health Policy, 2010).

50. Stephen M. Shortell, *Effective Hospital-Physician Relationships.* (Ann Arbor, MI: Health Administration Press, 1991).

51. Randolph Gordon, Steve Burrill, and Christine Chang, *Deloitte 2018 Survey of U.S. Physicians* (Washington: Deloitte Center for Health Solutions, 2018).

52. Paul H. Keckley, Sheryl Coughlin, and Elizabeth Stanley, *Deloitte 2013 Survey of U.S. Physicians* (Washington: Deloitte Center for Health Solutions, 2013).

53. Burns, Goldsmith, and Muller, "History of Hospital/Physician Relationships."

54. Paul H. Keckley, Sheryl Coughlin, and Elizabeth Stanley, *Deloitte 2013 Survey of U.S. Physicians* (Washington: Deloitte Center for Health Solutions, 2013).

55. David Muhlestein, Robert S. Saunders, and Mark B. McClellan, "Growth of ACOs and Alternative Payment Models in 2017," Health Affairs Blog, June 28, 2017, https://www.healthaffairs.org/do/ 10.1377/hblog20170628.060719/full, accessed November 27, 2017.

56. John M. Hollingsworth et al., "Medicare Accountable Care Organizations Are Not Associated with Reductions in the Use of Low-Value Coronary Revascularization," *Circulation: Cardiovascular Quality and Outcome* 11, no. 6 (June 14, 2018).

57. Ryan Duggal, Yongkang Zhang, and Mark L. Diana, "The Association between Hospital ACO Participation and Readmission Rates," *Journal of Healthcare Management* 63, no. 5 (September/October 2018): e100–e114.

58. Reed Abelson, "Cornerstone: The Rise and Fall of a Health Care Experiment," *New York Times*, December 23, 2016, https://www.nytimes.com/2016/12/23/business/cornerstone-the-riseand-fall-of-a-health-care-experiment.html, accessed November 27, 2017.

59. Ashish Jha, "ACO Winners and Losers: A Quick Take," An Ounce of Evidence (blog), August 30, 2016, https://blogs.sph.harvard.edu/ashish-jha/2016/08/30/aco-winners-and-losers-a-quick-take, accessed November 27, 2017.

60. J. Michael McWilliams et al., "Medicare Spending after Three Years of the Medicare Shared Savings Program," *New England Journal of Medicine* 379 (September 5, 2018): 1139–49.

61. Leeann N. Comfort et al., "Medicare Accountable Care Organizations of Diverse Structures Achieve Comparable Quality and Cost Performance," *Health Services Research* 53, no. 4 (August 2018): 2302–23.

62. John Schulz, Matthew DeCamp, and Scott A. Berkowitz, "Spending Patterns among Medicare ACOs That Have Reduced Costs," *Journal of Healthcare Management* 63, no. 6 (November/December 2018): 374–81.

63. K. John McConnell et al., "Early Performance in Medicaid Accountable Care Organizations: A Comparison of Oregon and Colorado," *JAMA Internal Medicine* 177, no. 4 (2017): 538–45.

64. Elizabeth Whitman, "Lured by MACRA Bonuses, More Medicare ACOs Venture into Risk," *Modern Healthcare*, March 4, 2017.

65. American Hospital Association, *The Work Ahead: Activities and Costs to Develop an Accountable Care Organization* (Washington: American Hospital Association, 2011).

66. Valerie A Lewis, Eliiott S. Fisher, and Carrie H. Colla, "Explaining Sluggish Savings under Accountable Care," *New England Journal of Medicine* 377, no. 19 (2017): 1809–11.

67. "Value-Based Care: Winning the Shift from Volume to Value," Deloitte, https://www2.deloitte.com/us/en/pages/lifesciences-and-health-care/articles/value-based-care-life-sciencesand-health-care-services.html, accessed November 27, 2017; Tim Van Biesen et al., *Front Line of Healthcare Report 2017: Giving Physicians a Say: Why Involving Doctors Can Help Improve US Healthcare* (Boston: Bain and Company, 2017).

68. Andrew M. Ryan et al., "Salary and Quality Compensation for Physician Practices Participating in Accountable Care Organizations," *Annals of Family Medicine* 14, no. 4 (2015): 321–24.

69. Tim Van Biesen et al., *Front Line of Healthcare Report 2017: Giving Physicians a Say: Why Involving Doctors Can Help Improve US Healthcare* (Boston: Bain and Company, 2017).

70. Claudia L. Schur and Janet P. Sutton, "Physicians in Medicare ACOs Offer Mixed Views of Model for Health Care Cost and Quality," *Health Affairs (Millwood)* 36, no. 4 (2017): 649–54.

71. Mark W. Friedberg et al., "Effects of Health Care Payment Models on Physician Practice in the United States," *Rand Health Quarterly* 5, no. 1 (July 15, 2015); Mark W. Friedberg et al., *Effects of Health Care Payment Models on Physician Practice in the United States: Follow-up Study* (Santa Monica: RAND Corporation, 2018).

72. Mark A. Schuster, Sarah E. Onorato, and David O. Meltzer, "Measuring the Cost of Quality Measurement: A Missing Link in Quality Strategy," *Journal of the American Medical Association* 318, no. 13 (2017): 1219–20.

73. The Medicare Access and CHIP Reauthorization Act of 2015.

74. Virgil Dickson, "MedPAC Votes 14–2 to Junk MIPS, Providers Angered," *Modern Healthcare*, January 11, 2018, https://www.modernhealthcare.com/article/20180111/NEWS/180119963/medpac-votes-14-2-to-junk-mips-providers-angered, accessed December 10, 2018.

75. Pooja Kumar, Anna Sherwood, and Saumya Sutaria, *Engaging Physicians to Transform Operational and Clinical Performance* (Chicago: McKinsey & Company; 2013), http://healthcare.mckinsey.com/sites/default/files/MCK_Hosp_MDSurvey.pdf, accessed November 27, 2017.

76. Physicians Foundation / Merritt Hawkins, *2016 Survey of America's Physicians: Practice Patterns and Perspectives* (Coppell, TX: Physicians Foundation / Merritt Hawkins: 2016), http://www.physiciansfoundation.org/uploads/2017/12/Biennial_Physician_Survey_2016.pdf, accessed November 27, 2017.

77. Leemore Dafny and Thomas H. Lee, "New Marketplace Survey: Physicians and Hospitals Differ on How to Reduce Costs," *NEJM Catalyst*, March 3, 2016. https://catalyst.nejm.org/doi/full/10.1056/CAT.16.0895.

78. Thomas W. Feeley and Namita Seth Mohta, "Transitioning Payment Models: Fee-for-Service to Value-Based Care," *NEJM Catalyst Insights Report*, November 2018.

79. Richard B. Gunderman, "Poor Care Is the Root of Physician Disengagement," *NEJM Catalyst*, January 10, 2017, https://catalyst.nejm.org/poor-care-root-physician-disengagement, accessed November 27, 2017; "We Asked Thirteen Physicians What They Really Think of Their Hospital," *Becker's Hospital Review*, August 2, 2016, https://www.beckershospitalreview.com/hospital-physician-relationships/we-asked-13-physicians-what-they-really-think-of-their-hospital.html, accessed November 27, 2017.

80. "Value-Based Care: Winning the Shift from Volume to Value," Deloitte, https://www2.deloitte.com/us/en/pages/life-sciences-and-health-care/articles/value-based-care-life-sciences-and-health-care-services.html, accessed November 27, 2017.

81. Andrew J. Jager, Michael A. Tutty, Audiey C. Kao, "Association between Physician Burnout and Identification with Medicine as a Calling," *Mayo Clinic Proceedings* 92, no. 3 (2016): 415–22; Tait D. Shanafelt et al., "Burnout and Satisfaction with

Work-Life Balance among US Physicians Relative to the General US Population," *Archives of Internal Medicine* 172, no. 18 (2012): 1377–85.

82. Thomas Bodenheimer and Christine Sinsky, "From Triple to Quadruple Aim: Care of the Patient Requires Care of the Provider," *Annals of Family Medicine* 12, no. 6 (2014): 573–76.

83. Megan Knowles, "Dallas Hospital Co-Founder Admits to Bribing Physicians for High-Volume Surgeries," *Becker's Hospital Review*, July 26, 2018, https://www .beckershospitalreview.com/legal-regulatory-issues/dallas-hospital-co-founder -admits-to-bribing-physicians-for-high-volume-surgeries.html; Ayla Ellison, "Florida Healthcare Exec Convicted in $1.3B Fraud Case," *Becker's Hospital Review*, April 8, 2019, https://www.beckershospitalreview.com/legal-regulatory-issues /florida-healthcare-exec-convicted-in-1-3b-fraud-case.html.

84. Mackenzie Garrity, "Nine More Physicians Charged in $950M Spine Surgery Kick-back Scheme: 7 Things to Know," *Beckers Hospital Review*, June 29, 2018, https:// www.beckersspine.com/spine/item/41661-9-more-physicians-charged-in-950m -spine-surgery-kickback-scheme-7-things-to-know.html; Ayla Ellison, "Texas Hospital Co-Founder Admits Bribing Physicians as Part of $200M Billing Scheme," *Becker's Hospital Review*, October 26, 2018, https://www.beckershospitalreview .com/legal-regulatory-issues/texas-hospital-co-founder-admits-bribing-physi cians-as-part-of-200m-billing-scheme.html; "10 Big Anti-Kickback Cases Involv-ing Hospitals in 2010," *Becker's Hospital Review*, January 26, 2011, https://www .beckershospitalreview.com/hospital-management-administration/10-big-anti -kickback-cases-involving-hospitals-in-2010.html; Frank Gluck, "Lee Health Faced with Federal Whistleblower Lawsuit for Alleged Medicare Fraud," *Fort Myers Press-News*, December 10, 2018.

85. Larry Bye, "Datagraphic: Building a Culture of Health: What Americans Think," *Health Affairs (Millwood)* 35 no. 11 (2016): 1982–90.

86. Judith Hibbard, "The Patient Activation Measure and Care Transitions," presented at Healthy Transitions Colorado, Denver, May 21, 2014.

87. Kenneth Thorpe, *An Unhealthy Truth: Rising Rates of Chronic Disease and the Future of Health in America*, (Washington: Partnership to Fight Chronic Disease, 2007), http://www.prevent.org/data/files/ initiatives/thorpeslides11–30–07.pdf, http://www.caaccess.org/pdf/6_unhealthy_truths.pdf.

88. "Patients Don't Know How to Best Manage Their Cholesterol, Survey Finds," American Heart Association, April 10, 2017, http://news.heart.org/patients-dont -know-how-to-best-manage-their-cholesterol-survey-finds, accessed November 27, 2017.

89. Mark V. Pauly and Lawton R. Burns, "When Is Medical Care Price Transparency a Good Thing (and When Isn't It)?" *Advances in Health Care Management-Price Transparency: Stakeholder and Policy Perspectives on Health Systems* 19 (Bingley, UK: Emerald Press, 2020): 75–97.

90. Congressional Budget Office, *Evidences on the Costs and Benefits of Healthcare Information Technology* (2008), https://www.cbo.gov/sites/default/files/cbofiles /ftpdocs/91xx/doc9168/maintext.3.1.shtml.

91. For example, see David Dranove et al., "The Trillion Dollar Conundrum: Comple-
     mentarities and Health Information Technology," *American Economic Journal:
     Economic Policy* 6, no. 4 (2014): 239–70; Ryan McKenna, Debra Dwyer, and John A.
     Rizzo, "Is HIT a Hit? The Impact of Health Information Technology on Inpatient
     Hospital Outcomes," *Applied Economics* 50, no. 27 (2018): 3016–28; Deepa Wani
     and Manoj Malhotra, "Does the Meaningful Use of Electronic Health Records
     Improve Patient Outcomes?" *Journal of Operations Management* 60 (May 2018):
     1–18.

92. National Physician Poll on Electronic Health Records, http://med.stanford.edu
     /ehr/electronic-health-records-poll-results.html, accessed October 22, 2018.

93. Erika Fry and Fred Schulte, "Death by a Thousand Clicks: Where Electronic Health
     Records Went Wrong," *Fortune*, March 18, 2019.

94. Marcia Frellick, "Almost Half of Physicians Say EHRs Have Hurt Quality of Care,"
     Medscape, May 1, 2019.

95. "25 Quotes That Show Just How Fed Up Physicians Are with EHRs," *Becker's Hospi-
     tal Review*, October 2, 2015, https://www.beckershospitalreview.com/healthcare
     -information-technology/25-quotes-that-show-just-how-fed-up-physicians-are
     -with-ehrs.html.

96. Allan Baumgarten, "Analysis of Integrated Delivery Systems and New Provider-
     Sponsored Health Plans (Princeton, NJ: Robert Wood Johnson Foundation, June
     2017).

97. Northwell claims that the majority of losses were attributable to payments it made
     to the New York state health insurance exchange. These reflected overpayments
     from the state, due to Northwell enjoying favorable risk selection in the state insur-
     ance exchange. Had Northwell been able to control costs, it would have enjoyed a
     net profit from participating in the exchange.

98. Bob Herman, "Wisconsin Systems are Leaders in Offering Their Own Health
     Plans," *Modern Healthcare*, December 14, 2015, 12.

99. Austin Frakt, Steven Pizer, and Roger Feldman, "Plan-Provider Integration, Premi-
     ums, and Quality in the Medicare Advantage Market," *Health Services Research* 48,
     no. 6 (2013): 1996–2013.

100. Natasha Parekh et al., "Relationships between Provider-Led Health Plans and
     Quality, Utilization, and Satisfaction," *American Journal of Managed Care* (Decem-
     ber 2018).

101. Gunjan Khanna, Deepali Narula, and Neil Rao, *The Market Evolution of Provider-
     Led Health Plans* (New York: McKinsey, 2016).

102. Natasha Parekh et al., "Relationships between Provider-Led Health Plans and
     Quality, Utilization, and Satisfaction," *American Journal of Managed Care*, Decem-
     ber 2018; Brett Caplan et al., "The Association between Provider-Sponsored Health
     Plans and Nonprofit Hospital Bond Ratings," *Journal of Health Care Finance* 43
     (Summer 2016).

103. Melanie Evans, "Hospital Health Plans Heighten Tensions with Insurers," *Modern
     Healthcare*, March 23, 2015, 9.

104. Shubham Singhal, "Payors in Care Delivery: When Does Vertical Integration Make Sense?" Health Affairs Blog, February 5, 2014.

105. Economists describe this as avoiding "double marginalization."

106. Jeff Goldsmith et al., *Integrated Delivery Networks: In Search of Benefits and Market Effects* (Washington: National Academy of Social Insurance, 2015).

Chapter 7

1. C. J. Redwine, *The Traitor Prince* (New York: Balzer and Bray, 2018).

2. For example, see Zack Cooper et al., "The Price Ain't Right? Hospital Prices and Health Spending on the Privately Insured," National Bureau of Economic Research working paper w21815, Cambridge, MA, 2015.

3. For a discussion of these cases, see Cory S. Capps, "From Rockford to Joplin and Back Again: The Impact of Economics on Hospital Merger Enforcement, *Antitrust Bulletin* 59 no. 3 (2014): 443–78.

4. Capps, "From Rockford to Joplin and Back Again," 18.

5. *Commonwealth vs. Partners Healthcare System & others.* Memorandum of Decision and Order on Joint Motion for Entry of Amended Final Judgment by Consent. Superior Court SUCV2014-02033-BLS2.

6. For a summary of case documents, Federal Trade Commission, Penn State Hershey Medical Center, FTC and Commonwealth of Pennsylvania v., https://www.ftc.gov /enforcement/cases-proceedings/141-0191-d09368/penn-state-hershey-medical -center-ftc-commonwealth.

7. Matthew S. Lewis and Kevin E. Pflum, "Hospital Systems and Bargaining Power: Evidence from Out-of-Market Acquisitions," *RAND Journal of Economics* 48, no. 3 (2017): 579–610.

8. Leemore Dafny, Kate Ho, and Robin S. Lee, "The Price Effects of Cross-Market Mergers," *RAND Journal of Economics* 50, no. 2 (2019).

9. Einstein was referring to the perturbations that occur in one place when a quantum particle is acted upon somewhere else. Just as collisions are not required for particles to interact, presence in the same geographic market is not required for hospitals to raise prices.

10. Matt Schmitt, "Multimarket Contact in the Hospital Industry, *American Economic Journal: Economic Policy* 10 no. 3 (2018): 361–87.

11. Quoted in Melanie Evans, "Hospital Deal to Create Midwestern Giant," *Wall Street Journal*, June 28, 2019, section B, page 3.

12. The exceptions were radiologists, anesthesiologists, and pathologists, but these hospital-based specialists did not have their "own" patients in the manner of PCPs, internists, or even surgeons.

13. Gregory C. Pope and Russel T. Burge, "Economies of Scale in Physician Practice," *Medical Care Research and Review* 53, no. 4 (1996): 417–40; Larry J. Kimbell and John H. Lorant, "Physician Productivity and Returns to Scale," *Health Services Research* 12, no. 4 (1977): 367; Robert Rosenman and Daniel Friesner, "Scope

and Scale Inefficiencies in Physician Practices," *Health Economics* 13, no. 11 (2004): 1091–1116.

14. Abe Dunn and Adam Hale Shapiro, "Do Physicians Possess Market Power?" *Journal of Law and Economics* 57, no. 1 (2014): 159–93; Laurence Baker et al., "Physician Practice Competition and Prices Paid by Private Insurers for Office Visits, *Journal of the American Medical Association* 312, no. 16 (2014): 1653–62; Daniel R. Austin and Laurence C. Baker, "Less Physician Practice Competition Is Associated with Higher Prices Paid for Common Procedures," *Health Affairs(Millwood)* 34, no. 10 (2015): 1753–60.

15. Thomas Koch and Shawn W. Ulrick, "Price Effects of a Merger: Evidence from a Physicians' Market," Federal Trade Commission working paper 333, Washington, 2017.

16. Cory Capps, David Dranove, and Chris Ody, "Physician Practice Consolidation Driven by Small Acquisitions, so Antitrust Agencies Have Few Tools to Intervene," *Health Affairs* 36, no. 9 (2017): 1556–63.

17. Thomas Koch, Brett Wendling, and Nathan Wilson, "Physician Market Structure, Patient Outcomes, and Spending: An Examination of Medicare Beneficiaries," *Health Services Research* 53 (October 5, 2018): 3549–68.

18. *Federal Trade Commission, Keystone Orthopaedic Specialists, LLC, and Orthopaedic Associates of Reading, Ltd., In the Matter of,* https://www.ftc.gov/enforcement /cases-proceedings/141–0025/keystone-orthopaedic-specialists-llc-orthopaedic -associates, accessed March 5, 2019.

19. Federal Trade Commission, St. Luke's Health System, Ltd., and Saltzer Medical Group, P.A., https://www.ftc.gov/enforcement/cases-proceedings/121–0069/st -lukes-health-system-ltd-saltzer-medical-group-pa, accessed March 5, 2019.

20. Esther Gal-Or, "The Profitability of Vertical Mergers between Hospitals and Physician Practices," *Journal of Health Economics* 18, no. 5 (1999): 623–54.

21. For a timeline and detailed court documents, see *The United States Department of Justice, U.S. v. AT&T Inc., DirectTV Group Holdings LLC, and Time Warner Inc.,* https://www.justice.gov/atr/case/us-v-att-inc-directv-group-holdings-llc-and -time-warner-inc, accessed March 5, 2019.

22. *Federal Trade Commission, Cabell Huntington Hospital / St. Mary Medical Center, in the Matter of,* https://www.ftc.gov/enforcement/cases-proceedings/141–0218 /cabell-huntington-hospitalst-marys-medical-center-matter, accessed March 5, 2019.

23. *Parker v. Brown,* 317 U.S. 341 (1943).

24. Press release dated January 31, 2018.

25. We can think of worse. States might use COPA to permit urban systems to merge, and then use their profits to purchase rural hospitals. This would completely obscure the source of rural hospital funding. Sutter Health is using a similar argument to defend its exercise of market power in urban markets. It seems to want to take the place of government and voters in deciding how much to spend to prop up rural hospitals.

26. *Federal Trade Commission, Phoebe Putney Health System, Inc., Phoebe Putney*

Memorial Hospital, Inc., Phoebe North, Inc., HCA Inc., Palmyra Park Hospital, Inc., and Hospital Authority of Albany-Dougherty County, In the Matter of, https://www .ftc.gov/enforcement/cases-proceedings/111–0067/phoebe-putney-health-system -inc-phoebe-putney-memorial, accessed March 5, 2019.

27. David Dranove, Craig Garthwaite and Christopher Ody, "How Do Nonprofits Respond to Negative Wealth Shocks? The Impact of the 2008 Stock Market Collapse on Hospitals," *RAND Journal of Economics* 48, no. 2 (2017): 485–525.

28. Elena Prager, "Tiered Hospital Networks, Health Care Demand, and Prices," job market paper, Wharton School, University of Pennsylvania, 2016.

29. Catalyst for Payment Reform, "The State of the Art of Price Transparency Tools and Solutions," (Berkeley, CA: Catalyst for Payment Reform, 2013), 6, https://www .catalyze.org/wp-content/uploads/2017/04/2013-The-State-of-the-Art-of-Price -Transparency-Tools-and-Solutions.pdf.

30. Sunita Desai et al., "Association between Availability of a Price Transparency Tool and Outpatient Spending," *Journal of the American Medical Association* 315, no. 17 (2016): 1874–81.

31. Christopher Whaley et al., "Association between Availability of Health Service Prices and Payments for These Services," *Journal of the American Medical Association* 312, no. 16 (2014): 1670–76.

32. Sutter insists that if its "run of the mill" providers (a term Sutter would never use) are out of network, the insurer must pay nearly full charges, which is well above typical out-of-network rates. This is usually enough of an inducement for insurers to include them in network.

33. Partners may argue that all-or-nothing improves coordination of care. If a PPO did limit its contract to Massachusetts General, it is possible that Partners would hold out for an even higher price, attempting to capture all its profits through this one hospital. This might push its price to astonishing heights.

34. Though not technically a tying case, plaintiffs must meet the same bar for demonstrating monopoly power.

35. These are Carolinas's estimated annual revenues in 2018.

36. In a high-profile case, the DOJ challenged the practice of American Express whereby it prevented retailers from informing customers about lower cost (to the retailer) credit card alternatives. American Express prevailed, but mainly on the issue of whether it had monopoly power in a well-defined market. Otherwise, the case likely sets no precedent for disputes about antisteering provisions.

Chapter 8

1. Arianna Huffington, "The Way We're Working Isn't Working," *Vanity Fair*, February 22, 2019, https://www.vanityfair.com/london/2018/12/arianna-huffington -sustainability-wellness-huffington-post-thrive-global, accessed December 11, 2019.

2. Leemore S. Dafny, "Evaluating the Impact of Health Insurance Industry Consolidation: Learning from Experience," Commonwealth Fund, November 20, 2015,

https://www.commonwealthfund.org/publications/issue-briefs/2015/nov/evalu
ating-impact-health-insurance-industry-consolidation.

3. American Medical Association, *Competition in Health Insurance Markets, 2018 Update* (Chicago: American Medical Association, 2018).

4. Market share data from Health Insurance Association of America, *Sourcebook of Health Insurance Data* (Washington: Health Insurance Association of America, 1990).

5. This does not mean that high-value monopolists and duopolists are exempt from antitrust scrutiny. Actions that protect their market dominance while harming consumers may violate antitrust laws.

6. The other author of this book, Burns, served as an expert in the Aetna-Humana merger case.

7. One cannot simply compare premiums across different geographies. Consider Alabama, where the local Blue has a market share of 80 percent or higher in virtually every MSA, but premiums are lower than in New York, where the largest insurer in any given MSA has a share closer to 40 or 50 percent. Are premiums lower in Alabama because of the local Blue's dominance, or is it because pretty much everything is more expensive in New York? It is surprisingly difficult to sort out these multiple explanations.

8. Leemore Dafny, Mark Duggan, and Subramaniam Ramanarayanan, "Paying a Premium on Your Premium? Consolidation in the US Health Insurance Industry," *American Economic Review* 102, no. 2 (2012): 1161–85.

9. Jose R. Guardado, David W. Emmons, and Carol K. Kane, "The Price Effects of a Large Merger of Health Insurers: A Case Study of UnitedHealth-Sierra," *Health Management, Policy and Innovation* 1, no. 3 (2013): 16–35.

10. Leemore Dafny, "Are Health Insurance Markets Competitive?" *American Economic Review* 100, no. 44 (2010): 1399–1431.

11. Quoted in Andrew Harris and David McLaughlin, "Anthem, Cigna Unsealed CEO Testimony Shows Deep Clash over Deal," *Hartford Courant*, November 29, 2016, https://www.courant.com/business/hc-anthem-cigna-unsealed-testimony-2016 1129-story.html, accessed February 20, 2019.

12. There are a few places, including California, where Blue Cross and Blue Shield plans compete against one another. In addition, an employer may ask a local Blue plan to "cede" coverage to another Blue. This may occur when an employer headquartered in one state has many employees in another, and prefers to be covered by the Blue plan in the second state.

13. See Michael E. Porter, *Competitive Strategy: Techniques for Analyzing Industries and Competitors* (New York: Simon and Schuster, 2008).

14. David Dranove, Dov Rothman, and David Toniatti, "Up or Down? The Price Effects of Market Intermediary Mergers" *Antitrust Law Journal*, no. 2 (2019).

15. Federal Trade Commission, "Market Division or Customer Allocation," https://www.ftc.gov/tips-advice/competition-guidance/guide-antitrust-laws/dealings-competitors/market-division-or.

Chapter 9

1. Leemore Dafny and Namita Seth Mohta, "New Marketplace Survey: The Sources of Health Care Innovation," *NEJM Catalyst*, February 16, 2017, https://catalyst .nejm.org/disruptive-innovation-in-healthcare-survey/.

2. Joseph A. Schumpeter, "Creative Destruction.," in Joseph A. Schumpeter, *Capitalism, Socialism and Democracy* (New York: Harper and Row, 1942), 82–85.

3. On a tangential note, we are somewhat appalled that the overwhelming majority of our MBA students are unfamiliar with Schumpeter or the gale of creative destruction. If only Schumpeter were on Twitter.

4. William Kissick, *Medicine's Dilemmas* (New Haven, CT: Yale University Press, 1994).

5. Lawton R. Burns, Guy David, and Lorens Helmchen, "Strategic Responses by Providers to Specialty Hospitals, Ambulatory Surgery Centers, and Retail Clinics," *Population Health Management* 14, no. 2 (2011): 69–77.

6. Mark Pauly, "'We Aren't Quite as Good, but We Sure Are Cheap': Prospects for Disruptive Innovation in Medical Care and Insurance Markets," *Health Affairs* 27, no. 5 (September-October 2008).

7. Atul Gawande, "The Cost Conundrum," *New Yorker*, May 25, 2009, 36–44.

8. Atul Gawande, "Big Med," *New Yorker*, August 6. 2012, 53–63.

9. Jon Kamp and Anna Mathews, "New Details of Amazon, Berkshire Hathaway, JPMorgan Health Venture Emerge in Court Testimony," *Wall Street Journal*, February 20, 2019.

10. Quoted in Chris Isidore, "Buffett Expects Health Care Effort with Amazon, JPMorgan to Open Up to Other Companies," CNN Business, February 26, 2018, https://money.cnn.com/2018/02/26/news/companies/warren-buffett-health-care -amazon-jpmorgan/index.html, accessed February 25, 2019.

11. Https://bestcompany.com/health-insurance/company/oscar, accessed February 6, 2019. To be fair, Oscar's overall rating is on a par with the best health insurers, which generally fair badly. It is just that Oscar is bad in different ways than other insurers.

12. Research2Guidance, "mHealth App Developer Economics 2016: The Current Status and Trends of the Health App Market," October 2016, https://research2guidance .com/product/mhealth-app-developer-economics-2016/.

13. Oyungerai Byambasuren et al., "Prescribable mHealth Apps Identified from an Overview of Systematic Reviews," *Digital Medicine* 1 (2018):12, doi:10.1038/s41746- 018-0021-9.

14. Kyan Safavi et al., "Top-Funded Digital Health Companies and Their Impact on High-Burden, High-Cost Conditions," *Health Affairs* 38, no. 1 (2019): 115–23.

15. National Business Group on Health, "2019 Large Employers' Health Care Strategy and Plan Design Survey," https://www.healthleadersmedia.com/strategy/employer -health-system-networks-become-more-exclusive, accessed February 6, 2019.

16. Willis Towers Watson, "2018 Best Practices in Health Care Employer Survey

Report," https://www.willistowerswatson.com/en-US/Insights/2018/12/best
-practices-in-healthcare-2018-next-steps, accessed February 6, 2019.

17. Some might argue that Walmart is simply better than everyone else at negotiating. This seems unlikely. Insurers have years of experience in negotiating with providers; and besides, negotiation is not a scarce skill.

18. National Business Group on Health, "2019 Large Employers' Health Care Strategy and Plan Design Survey."

19. Amanda Starc and Robert J. Town, "Internalizing Behavioral Externalities: Benefit Integration in Health Insurance," National Bureau of Economic Research working paper 21783, Cambridge, MA, April 2018.

20. CVS Health, "CVS Health to Acquire Aetna" (corporate press statement), December 3, 2017.

21. Mandy Roth, "CVS-Aetna Aims to Complement Health Systems, Says Chief Digital Officer," *HealthLeaders*, November 19, 2018.

22. The following section is taken from the testimony of Lawton R. Burns before the California insurance commissioner in June 2018. Lawton R. Burns, "CVS Health & Aetna: Analysis of the Proposed Merger," California Insurance Commission, June 2018.

23. David Yanofsky, "Eight out of Ten Americans Are within Ten Miles of a CVS," *Yahoo! Finance*, https://finance.yahoo.com/news/eight-10-americans-within
-10-183801924.html, accessed April 1, 2019.

24. Clayton Christensen, Richard Bohmer, and John Kenagy, "Will Disruptive Innovations Cure Health Care?" *Harvard Business Review* 78, no. 5 (September-October 2000); Clayton Christensen, Jerome Grossman, and Jason Hwang, *The Innovator's Prescription: A Disruptive Solution for Health Care* (New York: McGraw-Hill, 2009).

25. Kalorama Information, *Retail Clinics 2017* (New York: Kalorama, 2017).

26. Adam Fein, "As CVS-Aetna Looms, Retail Pharmacy Clinic Growth Stalls," *Drug-Channels*, March 6, 2018, http://www.drugchannels.net/2018/03/as-cvs-aetna
-looms-retail-pharmacy.html.

27. Jordan Stone, "Profit from Convenient Primary Care, 2013–2014," Health Care Advisory Board, https://www.advisory.com/-/media/Advisory-com/Research
/HCAB/Events/Webconference/2014/Profit-from-Convenient-Primary-Care
-052914.pdf.

28. Jason Hwang and Ateev Mehrotra, "Why Retail Clinics Failed to Transform Health Care," *Harvard Business Review*, December 25, 2013.

29. Emarketer.com, https://retail-index.emarketer.com/company/data/5374f24e4d4afd
2bb444662b/5374f2784d4afd824cc158f1/lfy/false/cvs-real-estate.

30. Sharon Terlep and Joseph Walker, "Generic-Drug Trends Squeeze Walgreens Profit," *Wall Street Journal*, April 2, 2019.

31. David Larsen and Matt Dellelo, *HCIT & Distribution* (Boston: Leerink, December 18, 2017).

32. Https://www.digitalcommerce360.com/2019/02/25/cvs-will-pony-up-big-bucks
-to-go-even-more-digital/, February 25, 2019, accessed April 1, 2019.

33. Thomas Sabatino, "Statement, House Judiciary Committee, Subcommittee on Regulatory Reform, Commercial and Antitrust Law," February 27, 2018, https://docs.house.gov/meetings/JU/JU05/20180227/106898/HHRG-115-JU05-Wstate-SabatinoT-20180227.pdf.

34. Adam Cohen and Kyan Safavi, "The Oversell and Undersell of Digital Health," *Health Affairs*, February 27, 2019.

35. Corinne Abrams, "Google's Effort to Prevent Blindness Shows AI Challenges," *Wall Street Journal*, January 26, 2019.

36. John Halamka, "Using Big Data to Make Wiser Medical Decisions," *Harvard Business Review*, December 14, 2015.

37. Guy David, Aaron Smith-McLallen, and Benjamin Ukert, "The Effect of Predictive Analytics-Driven Interventions on Healthcare Utilization," *Journal of Health Economics* 4, no. 3 (April 3, 2019).

38. Leila Agha, "The Effects of Health Information Technology on the Costs and Quality of Medical Care," *Journal of Health Economics* 34 (2014): 19–30.

39. Casey Ross, "IBM Pitched its Watson Supercomputer as a Revolution in Cancer Care. It's Nowhere Close," *Stat*, September 5, 2017.

40. Thomas Maddox, John Rumsfeld, and Philip Payne, "Questions for Artificial Intelligence in Health Care," *Journal of the American Medical Association* 321, no. 1 (December 10, 2018): E1–E2.

41. American Medical Association, "AMA Urges DOJ to Challenge CVS-Aetna Merger," August 8, 2018, https://www.ama-assn.org/press-center/press-releases/ama-urges-doj-challenge-cvs-aetna-merger, accessed April 18, 2019.

42. Uwe E. Reinhardt, "The Disruptive Innovation of Price Transparency in Health Care," *Journal of the American Medical Association* 310, no. 18 (2013): 927–28.

43. Sunita Desai et al., "Association between Availability of a Price Transparency Tool and Outpatient Spending," *Journal of the American Medical Association* 315, no. 17 (2016): 1874–81; Anna D. Sinaiko and Meredith B. Rosenthal, "Examining a Health Care Price Transparency Tool: Who Uses it, and How they Shop for Care," *Health Affairs* 35, no. 4 (2016): 662–70.

44. The answer is likely to come from payment reform. "Reference pricing" caps the amount that insurers pay for a given procedure. Patients who choose more expensive providers must pay the difference. There have been a handful of promising experiments with reference pricing, though for now it has limited take-up and it applies to only a limited set of procedures. See James C. Robinson, Timothy T. Brown, and Christopher Whaley, "Reference Pricing Changes the 'Choice Architecture' of Health Care for Consumers," *Health Affairs* 36, no. 3 (2017): 524–30.

45. Bruce Japsen, "If CVS Bets Big on Urgent Care, Hospitals Should Worry," *HealthLeaders*, November 5, 2018.

46. Bruce Japsen, "Walgreens Partnership Strategy Won't End with Microsoft," *Forbes*, January 17, 2019.

47. Lawton R. Burns and Mark V. Pauly, "Detecting BS in Health Care," *PennLDI*, November 26, 2018, https://ldi.upenn.edu/brief/detecting-bs-health-care; Law-

ton R. Burns and Mark V. Pauly, "Detecting BS in Health Care 2.0," *PennLDI*, February 11, 2019, https://ldi.upenn.edu/brief/detecting-bs-health-care-20.

Chapter 10

1. Brainyquote.com, https://www.brainyquote.com/topics/antitrust, May 28, 2019. Senator Hatch directed this remark to the Internet, but it applies equally well to health care.
2. We wish to thank Leemore Dafny and Marty Gaynor, who generously shared their ideas for improving competition policy, many of which are central to the proposals in this chapter.
3. We do not wish to wade into this complicated debate. We acknowledge that on many metrics, such as life expectancy, the United States is middle of the pack at best. These metrics fail to control for factors largely beyond the control of a health system, such as gun violence, obesity, and overall societal stress levels. On other metrics, such as access to the latest technologies and newest drugs, as well as clinical outcomes for cancer care, the United States is at the forefront.
4. Desmond Sheridan and Desmond Julian, "Achievements and Limitations of Evidence-Based Medicine," *Journal of the American College of Cardiology* 68, no. 2 (2016): 204–13; Carmelo Lafuente-Lafuente et al., "Knowledge and Use of Evidence-Based Medicine in Daily Practice by Health Professionals: A Cross-Sectional Survey," *BMJ Open* 9, no. 3 (2019).
5. Dafny is currently a professor at Harvard. Gaynor is at Carnegie Mellon. In a recent publication, Gaynor and two coauthors offer a complementary set of proposals for competition policy. See Martin Gaynor, Farzad Mostashari, and Paul B. Ginsburg, "Making Health Care Markets Work: Competition Policy for Health Care," *Journal of the American Medical Association* 317, no 13 (2017): 1313–14.
6. Joseph Antos et al., "Bending the Curve," (New York: Engelberg Center for Health-care Reform at Brookings, 2013): 31. Coauthors include former top-level government officials including former US Senate Majority Leader Tom Daschle and former Secretaries of Health and Human Services Michael Leavitt and Donna Shalala, as well as professors from Harvard, Columbia, the University of Pennsylvania, the University of California, and elsewhere.
7. In a recent review of the literature on consolidation, David Cutler and Fiona Scott Morton lump together two forms of innovation: the use of new technologies, such as new surgical techniques, and the development of new information systems and incentives, such as new protocols for postsurgical care. They conclude that consolidation has not systematically retarded innovation as a whole. We think this conclusion is premature, for two reasons. First, Cutler and Morton lump together two forms of innovation when only the latter is likely to have important long-run implications for costs and quality. Academic research has mostly focused on the former, in part because the data are easier to come by. Second, prior research does not pay attention to the level of competition among value chains. In our experience, it is competition at this level that provides the biggest payoff for innovation. See

David M. Cutler and Fiona Scott Morton, "Hospitals, Market Share, and Consolidation," *Journal of the American Medical Association* 310, no. 18 (2013): 1964–70.

8. The seminal paper is Timothy F. Bresnahan and Peter C. Reiss, "Entry and Competition in Concentrated Markets," *Journal of Political Economy* 99, no. 5 (1991): 977–1009. Subsequent studies echo these findings, and the notion that markets require "four or five" competitors is well accepted by economists. There are, of course, differences by industry.

9. Leemore Dafny, "Are Health Insurance Markets Competitive?" *American Economic Review* 100, no. 44 (2010): 1399–1431.

10. David Besanko et al., *Economics of Strategy* (Hoboken, NJ: John Wiley & Sons, 2009); Mark V. Pauly and Lawton R. Burns, "Price Transparency for Medical Devices." *Health Affairs* 27, no. 6 (2008): 1544–53.

11. We are aware of at least one system that explicitly asked for such an exception during settlement talks in an antitrust case.

12. A. Jay Holmgren and Julia Adler-Milstein, "Does Electronic Health Record Consolidation Follow Hospital Consolidation?" Health Affairs Blog, March 7, 2019.

13. FTC Act, section 45(a)(2) and section 44. Section 6b prevents the FTC from studying the insurance industry, which is one reason why DOJ handled the Anthem/ Cigna and Aetna/Humana mergers. Otherwise, the division of federal agency merger enforcement, where the FTC investigates providers and drugs, is largely based on tradition. There are similar divisions of responsibility across other industries. It is unclear how many of these divisions got started. That said, it probably serves the FTC's interests that it does not investigate insurers, as it often needs their support when it challenges provider mergers.

14. US Department of Justice and the Federal Trade Commission, "Statements of Antitrust Enforcement Policy in Health Care" (Washington: US Department of Justice and Federal Trade Commission, 1996).

Chapter 11

1. Cited in Brainyquote.com, https://www.brainyquote.com/topics/management, accessed June 19, 2019.

2. This section is adapted from the following source: Lawton R. Burns and Mark V. Pauly, "Transformation of the Healthcare Industry: Curb Your Enthusiasm?" *Milbank Quarterly* 96, no. 1 (March 2018): 57–109.

3. Jack O'Brien, "Health System CEOs More Concerned with Growth than Costs," *HealthLeaders*, June 12, 2019.

4. Jeff Goldsmith, "Geisinger's Transformation: Balancing Growth and Risk," Health Affairs Blog, March 8, 2017, https://www.healthaffairs.org/do/10.1377/hblog2017 0308.059087/full/.

5. Bloomberg.com, https://www.sutterhealth.org/about/leadership.

6. "UPMC Leadership," UPMC.com, https://www.upmc.com/about/why-upmc /mission/leadership.

7. Amanda Goodall, "Physician-Leaders and Hospital Performance: Is There an

Association?" *Social Science and Medicine* 73, no. 4 (2011): 535–39; James Stoller, Amanda Goodall, and Agnes Baker, "Why the Best Hospitals Are Managed by Doctors," *Harvard Business Review*, December 27, 2016.

8. John Hsu et al., "Substantial Physician Turnover and Beneficiary 'Churn'in a Large Medicare Pioneer ACO," *Health Affairs* 36, no. 4 (2017): 640–48.

9. Adam Markovitz et al., "Performance in the Medicare Shared Savings Program after Accounting for Nonrandom Exit," *Annals of Internal Medicine* 171, no. 1 (2019), doi:10.7326/M18-2539.

10. Kathleen J. Mullen, Richard G. Frank, and Meredith B. Rosenthal, "Can You Get What You Pay For? Pay-for-Performance and the Quality of Healthcare Providers," *Rand Journal of Economics* 41, no. 1 (2010): 64–91.

11. Robert Pearl, "The Deadly Consequences of Financial Incentives in Healthcare," *Forbes*, January 28, 2019, https://www.forbes.com/sites/robertpearl/2019/01/28/financial-incentives/#6b36d9365eb9, accessed June 14, 2019.

12. Jackie Kimmell, "The 5 Biggest Risk Factors for Physician Burnout, According to Our 13,371-Physician Survey," *Advisory Board*, October 30, 2018.

13. Jessica Sweeney-Platt, "The Business Case for Physician Capability," *AthenaInsight*, October 6, 2017, https://www.athenahealth.com/insight/physician-capability-leads-long-term-success, accessed June 14, 2019.

14. Katharina Janus, "The Effect of Professional Culture on Intrinsic Motivation among Physicians in an Academic Medical Center," *Journal of Healthcare Management* 59, no. 4 (2014): 287–303.

15. Lawton Robert Burns, *The US Healthcare Ecosystem* (New York: McGraw-Hill, 2021).

16. We thank Ingrid Nembhard and Gary Young for their suggestions, which are reproduced here.

17. Anthony Waddimba et al., "Job Satisfaction and Guideline Adherence among Physicians: Moderating Effects of Perceived Autonomy Support and Job Control," *Social Science and Medicine* (forthcoming).

18. Rosabeth Moss Kanter, "When a Thousand Flowers Bloom: Structural, Collective, and Social Conditions for Innovation in Organizations," in *Research in Organizational Behavior*, vol. 10 (Greenwich, CT: JAI Press, 1988), 169–211.

19. Lawton R. Burns, Jeffrey Alexander, and Ronald Andersen, "How Different Governance Models May Impact Physician-Hospital Alignment," *Health Care Management Review*, August 2018, doi: 10.1097/HMR.0000000000000214.

20. Herbert Simon, *Administrative Behavior* (New York: Free Press, 1945); James G. March and Herbert Simon, *Organizations* (New York: Wiley, 1958); Lawton R. Burns, Elizabeth Bradley, and Bryan Weiner, *Health Care Management: Organization, Design and Behavior*, 7th edition (Clifton Park, NY: Delmar, 2019).

21. Dana Safran, "The Alternative Quality Contract," presentation to the Wharton School, November 2018.

22. Most organizations rely heavily on promotions to motivate workers. Opportunities for promotion of physicians and nurses are somewhat limited, making it that much more important to get bonus pay right.

23. For example, see Allyson Barnett et al., "Information or Compensation? Under-

standing the Role of Information Technology in Physician Response to Pay-for-Performance," unpublished working paper, 2019.

24. David Besanko et al., *Economics of Strategy* (Hoboken, NJ: John Wiley & Sons, 2009).

25. Randall Brown, "Lessons for ACOs and Medical Homes on Care Coordination for High-Needs Beneficiaries," presentation to AcademyHealth Annual Research Meeting, June 2013.

26. Melora Simon et al., "Exploring Attributes of High-Value Primary Care," *Annals of Family Medicine* 15, no. 6 (2017): 529–34.

27. Brent James and Lucy Savitz, "How Intermountain Trimmed Health Care Costs through Robust Quality Improvement Efforts," *Health Affairs Web First*, June 2011, https://www.healthaffairs.org/doi/full/10.1377/hlthaff.2011.0358, accessed June 14, 2019.

28. Peter Pronovost, Adam Sapirstein, and Alan Ravitz, "Improving Hospital Productivity as a Means to Reducing Costs," Health Affairs Blog, March 26, 2019, https://www.healthaffairs.org/do/10.1377/hblog20190321.822588/full/, accessed June 14, 2019.

29. Congressional Budget Office, *Technological Change and the Growth of Health Care Spending* (Washington: Congressional Budget Office, 2008).

30. Diego Ardila et al., "End-to-end Lung Cancer Screening with Three-Dimensional Deep Learning on Low-Dose Chest Computed Tomography," *Nature Medicine* 25 (May 20, 2019): 954–61.

31. Nirav Shah, "Health Care in 2030: Will Artificial Intelligence Replace Physicians?" *Annals of Internal Medicine* 170, no. 6 (February 26, 2019), doi: 10.7326/M19–0344.

32. Nazmus Saquib, Juliann Saquib, and John P. A. Ioannidis, "Does Screening for Disease Save Lives in Asymptomatic Adults? Systematic Review of Metaanalyses and Randomized Trials," *International Journal of Epidemiology* 44, no. 1 (2015): 264–77.

33. John Mandrola, "A Contrarian View of Digital Health," *Quillette*, May 17, 2019.

34. Christopher Semsarian, "Gene Sequencing for Sale on the NHS," *BMJ* 364 (2019): 1789; Michael J. Joyner and Nigel Paneth, "Promises, Promises, and Precision Medicine," *Journal of Clinical Investigation* 129, no. 3 (2019): 946–48.

35. "The Robots Want to Steal (the Boring Parts of) Your Job," *Wired*, April 22, 2019.

36. Lawton R. Burns et al., "Is the System Really the Solution? Operating Costs in Hospital Systems," *Medical Care Research and Review* 72, no. 3 (2015): 247–72.

Epilogue

1. American Hospital Association report, "Hospitals and Health Systems Face Unprecedented Financial Pressures Due to COVID-19," May 2020.

2. A. Ellison, "42 Hospitals Closed, Filed for Bankruptcy This Year," *Becker's Hospital CFO Report*, June 22, 2020.

3. These deals have a good chance of passing antitrust scrutiny, as the Horizontal Merger Guidelines permit consolidation of competitors when one of the merging parties would have otherwise gone out of business and there are no other willing buyers.

INDEX

ABC (joint venture), 202–5. *See also* Amazon; Berkshire Hathaway; JPMorgan Chase

Abdelhak, Sherif, 57–59

accountable care organizations (ACOs), 9, 107–9, 112, 115–16, 121, 123, 127, 139, 143, 148, 188, 226, 235–36; advocates of, 141–42; failures of, 140; as HMO-lites, 117; savings potential of, 140–42

Adobe System, 2–3

Adventist-Providence St. Joseph, 3

adverse selection, 67, 77–78

Advocate Health System, 2, 93, 102–3, 232, 239; electronic health record (EHR) system, adoption of, 127

Advocate/North Shore, 105; merger, blocking of, 239

Aetna, 157, 181, 183–84, 188–89, 202, 207, 216, 218, 289n35; collaborative accountable care (CAC) initiative, 268; CVS Caremark merger, 112, 212–14, 217, 219–21; Humana merger, 219–20, 315n13; Prudential merger, 185

Affordable Care Act (ACA), 9, 32–33, 108–9, 119, 133, 242; accountable care organizations (ACOs), 115–18, 121, 124; exchanges, 206–7; and integration, 115. *See also* Obamacare; Patient Protection and Affordable Care Act (PPACA)

Alabama, 310n7

Alameda County Medical Center, 92–93

Alamogordo, NM, 104

Albuquerque, NM, 177, 181

Allegheny General Hospital (AGH), 57–59, 126

Allegheny Health Education and Research Foundation (AHERF), 38, 47, 55, 60, 63, 65–67, 73, 78, 110, 122, 148; bankruptcy of, 59, 156; expansion of, 58; origins of, 57; strategic blunders of, 59

Allina Health System, 47–48, 60–61

Alphabet, 208

Alta Bates Hospital, 154

Alta Bates Medical Center, 92, 155; Summit merger, 98

Amara, Roy, 274

Amara's Law, 274

Amazon, 5, 85, 201–3, 219; AmazonGo, 223; PillPack, 204, 216; virtual care, 205

ambulatory care networks, 37, 46

ambulatory surgery centers (ASCs), 25–27, 119, 200, 242, 272

American College of Healthcare Executives, 37

American College of Healthcare Executives Career Resource Center, 46

American Economic Association (AEA), 192–93

American Express, 309n36

American health care, 8, 34; as ailing, 7; bankruptcy, 227; quality of, 226–27. *See also* health care system

American Healthways, 79

American Hospital Association (AHA), 14, 111, 118, 141–42

American Medical Association (AMA), 12, 15–16, 18, 104, 180, 220, 242

American Medical International (AMI), 81

American Society of Anesthesiologists, 17

Amerigroup, 207

Amita Health, acquisition of Presence, 231

Anthem, 179–80, 182, 197; accountable care organization (ACO) contracts, 190; "best of best" integration outcome, 185, 191; Cigna merger, 183–87, 190–94, 219, 233–34, 248; cost containment, 190; as price leader, 190

anticipatory therapy, 273

Anti-Kickback Statutes, 64, 67

antisteering restrictions, 246–47, 309n36; unseemly pricing, 244

antitrust: agencies, 7, 81, 83, 88–90, 92, 103, 110, 152–53, 158, 165, 169–75, 178, 228; big firms, zealotry against, 169, 238; cases, 9, 16, 27, 97, 155, 157–58, 167, 177, 190, 228; clinical integration exemption, 245; competition policy, 227; countervailing power, 192–93; laws, 83–84, 97, 99, 102–3, 105, 151, 155, 157–58, 168, 170, 172, 177–78, 196, 220–21, 228–29, 234, 242, 249; market definition, 85; mergers, 88, 92; monopsony and monopoly, 193

APM (consulting firm), 35

Arrow, Kenneth, 5

artificial intelligence (AI), 217, 219, 272–74; sociotechnical system, 218

Asahi, 196

Ascension Health, 204

Asheville, NC, 172

Association of American Medical Colleges, 57

AT&T, Time Warner merger, 170–71, 221, 248

Athens, GA, 173

Atlanta, GA, 3, 56

Atrium Health, 3, 242–43

Austin, TX, 104

Balanced Budget Act (BBA), 29, 54, 78, 109

Ballad Health COPA, 172

balloon principle, 20–21

Ball Ventures Ahlquist, 236

Baltimore, MD, 56

Baylor, Scott, and White Health, 2, 242–43

Baylor Hospital, 12

Berkeley, CA, 92, 104, 161

Berkshire Hathaway, 202

Berwick, Don, 118; triple aim, 259, 295n3

Beth Israel Deaconess Medical Center, 218

Bezos, Jeff, 7, 202, 252–53

Bhathena, Firdaus, 214

big data, 204, 208, 218–19, 223

BJC Healthcare, 3

Blagojevich, Rod, 24

Blodgett Memorial Hospital, 93–94

Blue Cross and Blue Shield Association, 196–97

Blue Cross Association, 13–14, 197

Blue Cross Blue Shield, 6–7, 16, 27, 50, 184, 186–89, 211, 219–20, 310n7, 310n12; antitrust law, violating of, 196; certificate of need (CON), proponent of, 22; dominance of, 181; health maintenance organizations (HMOs), establishing of, 17; as independent companies, 196–97; local plans, merging of, 182; managed care revolution, as threat to, 182; metropolitan statistical areas (MSAs), market shares in, 180; as national accounts, 181; as non-profits, 182; origin of name, 12–13; as social welfare organizations, 14

BlueCross BlueShield Massachusetts, 202

Blue Cross of California, 62

Blue Cross of Massachusetts, 27

Blues. *See* Blue Cross Blue Shield

Boeing, 255; 737 Max debacle, 6

Boise, ID, 191–92, 231, 234

Borato, Eva, 217

Boston, MA, 153, 160, 216, 231

Brookings Institution, 230–31

Brown and Toland Physicians IPA, 48, 154–55

Buffett, Warren, 7–9, 202–3, 252

bundled payments, 118, 123, 139, 188, 250–52

burnout, 120; as national health crisis, 136, 259; physician, 135–36, 144, 259

Burton, David, 271

Bush, George W., 188

Butterworth Hospital, 93–94

Buyers Health Care Action Group, 34, 47

Byrnjolfsson, Eric, 274

Cabell Huntington Hospital, St. Mary's Medical Center merger, 171

California, 3, 15, 34–35, 44, 49, 56, 92, 98, 107, 155, 162, 171, 182, 189, 205, 289n38, 289n39, 310n12; Affordable Care Act (ACA), 133; integrated delivery network (IDN) models, as seedbed for, 61

CalPERS, 34

Capital G, 208

capitation, 17, 32, 34–35, 45, 51, 54, 59– 60, 62–63, 79, 104; balloon principle, 21; of paid primary care physicians (PCPs), 21; rick-contracting models, morphing into, 108

Capps, Cory, 98–99, 102, 165

Care Connect Insurance, 149

Caremark, 293n44. *See also* MedPartners

Carilion Clinic, 68

Carilion hospitals, 231

Carle Clinic, 49, 63

Carle Foundation Hospital, 49

Carolinas HealthCare, 177

Carolinas Health System, 247

Casper, Gerhard, 74

Catholic Health Initiatives, 149

causal ambiguity, 56–57

Cedar Rapids, IA, 89

Centene, 180, 207

Centers for Medicare & Medicaid Services (CMS), 114–15, 118, 139–42, 188; accountable care organizations (ACOs), promoting of, 116–17; pay for performance (P4P), 113

certificate of need (CON), 22–25, 237

Certificate of Public Advantage (COPA) laws, 171–73, 247, 308n25; repealing of, 248

Chandler, Alfred, 275

Change Healthcare, 191

charity care, 131, 174

Charlotte, NC, 177, 242

Charter Spectrum, 170

Chicago, IL, 1–2, 14, 86, 100–103, 127, 196, 231–32, 239

Children's Hospital of Michigan, 59

Children's Hospital of Pittsburgh, 156

Christensen, Clayton, 7, 199, 200, 214– 15; theory of disruptive innovation, 253

Chrysler, 232

Churchill, Winston, 125

Cigna, 157, 181, 183–88, 192, 202, 207, 289n35; collaborative account-

Cigna (*continued*)
able care (CAC) initiative, 189–91, 268; cost containment, 190; Express Scripts (ESI) merger, 191, 212, 219; innovation of, 189, 190–91, 234; as quantity leader, 190; wellness programs, 189–90
Clayton Act, 84, 86, 90, 101, 193, 234
Cleveland Clinic, 164, 207, 210, 256
clinical integration, 39, 120, 129, 162, 172, 245–46, 258–59
Clinton, Bill, 17, 33; Patient Bill of Rights, proposal of, 54
Clinton, Hillary, 33
Clinton Health Plan, 33–34, 42, 53, 63–64, 108, 228; failure of, 54, 113. *See also* Health Security Act
Coddington, Dean, 37
Coile, Russell, 34–35
collaborative accountable care (CAC) initiative, 189–91, 268
Comcast, 170
Committee on the Cost of Medicare Care (CCMC), 12, 14, 187, 226, 275; hospitals, threat to, 15; and integration, 15
Commonwealth Fund, 118, 228
Community Health Systems, 126
Community Hospital, 98
competition policy, 8–9, 229, 246, 249, 314n5; experimentation, promotion of, 231; among individual providers, 239–40; and mergers, 234, 241–42; secret pricing, 245; value chains, 232–35, 239
continuum of care, 36, 42, 48, 112, 119, 123, 260–61, 265
Cooper, Zack, 4–5
Cordani, David, 186, 188–89
Cornerstone Health Care, 140
COR Solutions, 79
Cosgrove, Toby, 256
cost-effective care, 257; as value-based care, 108

Cottage Health system, 167, 236
countervailing power, 192–93; and innovation, 195
COVID-19 pandemic, 207
Crosson, Francis, 282n10
C-suite, 73, 255–56, 258–59, 263, 270
culture: informal incentives, 267; and leadership, 266, 268; public recognition, 267; selective employment, 268; tangible rewards, 267–68
Cutler, David, 314–15n7
CVS, 204, 215–16, 223; Aetna merger, 171, 212–14, 217, 219–20; analytics, 217; Care Pass, 216; clinical platform, 217
CVS Caremark, 212
CVS Health, 213, 216, 219; Minute-Clinics, 212, 214, 221; Omnicare, 215; Target, in-store pharmacies, 215

Dafny, Leemore, 159, 161, 214, 227, 314n5
Dallas, TX, 2, 208, 242
Danville, PA, 50
Dartmouth-Hitchcock health system, 189
Daschle, Tom, 314n6
data analytics, 108, 123, 125, 183, 204, 207, 223–24, 272
Davis, Pamela, 24
DaVita Medical Group, 164, 220, 223, 240
Deficit Reduction Act, 113, 117
Deloitte, 39, 42
Demsetz, Harold, 117
Department of Justice (DOJ), 16–17, 67, 83–84, 86–88, 91–93, 96, 183–85, 194, 219–20, 221, 234, 248, 294n8, 315n13; antisteering provisions, challenging of, 177, 247, 309n36; dynamic effects, concern over, 187; raising rivals costs theory, 170–71; Stark letters, 67; static effects, 187
Detroit Medical Center (DMC), 59–60

Detroit Receiving Hospital, 59
diagnosis-related groups (DRGs), 20,
43, 112, 173, 226
digital health: cultural iatrogenesis, 273;
social iatrogenesis, 273
Dignity Health, 161
Dimon, Jamie, 7, 202, 252
direct contracting, 210–11
disruption, 211, 222–25, 264, 272; disruptive innovation, 199–200, 214, 253;
disruptor's dilemma, 200
Doctors' Regional Medical Center, 91–
92
Dominican Hospital, Community Hospital merger, 98
Dranove, David, 98–99, 102, 165, 183,
191
Drucker, Peter, 250, 266
Drug Discount Program, 114
drugs, 4, 64, 79, 114, 212, 223–24, 271,
282n8, 314n3, 315n13; generic, 216;
prescription, 79, 216, 221
Dubuque, IA, 89–90
duopoly, 240
Dylan, Bob, 200

East Bay, CA, 92–93, 97, 154–55, 158
economic principles: "make or buy"
problem, 200–201, 212, 215; resource
view of, 200–201
Edward-Elmhurst Health, 232
Edward Hospital, application for certificate of need (CON), 23–24
Einstein, Albert, 307n9
electronic health records (EHRs), 71–72,
74, 77, 104, 107–8, 113–14, 124, 127, 129,
136–37, 143, 208, 219, 223, 226, 247,
261, 274; benefits, mixed evidence of,
146; choice architecture, 263; clinical decision support systems (CDSS),
122–23; computerized physician
order entry (CPOE), 122–23; inaccurate data, 147; and integration, 123;
nudges, use of, 263; physicians, reluc-

tance to integrate, 146–48; problems
of, 147–48; spending, reduction of,
146; unifying of, 247
Ellwood, Paul, 32, 49, 283n6
Elzinga, Kenneth, 87, 95–96, 99, 101
Elzinga and Hogarty (E-H) test, 90,
92–93, 100–101; assault on, 95, 97–99,
102; as flawed, 101; inflow percentage,
87–89, 96; outflow percentage, 87–88,
96; as silver bullet, 123; suspicion
toward, 95
Emory Healthcare, 3
Empire Blue Cross of New York, 27, 91
Employee Retirement and Income
Security Act (ERISA), 28
enterprise resource planning (ERP)
software, 85
Enthoven, Alain, 33, 49, 157, 178, 249;
managed competition, 32
Epic, 148; Care Everywhere EHRs, 146–
47
ESI (pharmacy benefits management),
187
ESPN, 203
Europe, 13, 232, 281n3
Evanston Hospital, 100, 152, 160–61, 163;
Highland Park Hospital merger, 100–
101. See also Evanston Northwestern
Healthcare (ENH)
Evanston Northwestern Healthcare
(ENH), 100–102, 107, 238; Medical
Group, 103–5
Express Scripts (ESI), CSI merger, 191,
212, 219

Facebook, 5, 201, 225
Fairview Health Services, 3
Fargo Clinic, 49
Federal Home Loan Bank, 16
Federal Trade Commission (FTC),
16–17, 83–84, 88–89, 91–93, 98–101,
103, 105, 107, 152, 158, 163–64, 166,
168, 191, 196, 231, 233, 235–36, 239,
247–48, 294n8; Certificate of Pub-

Federal Trade Commission (FTC) (*continued*)
lic Advantage (COPA), opposition to, 173; joint physician pricing initiatives, 242; provider mergers, 241; state action immunity, 171, 173; Statements of Antitrust Enforcement Policy in Healthcare, 104; willingness to pay (WTP), use of, 102
fee-for-service (FFS), 14–15, 34–35, 37, 54, 69, 71–72, 104, 118, 121, 142, 251, 254, 270
Find Care Now (website), 221
Finley Hospital, 89–90
Flexner Report, 12
Florida, 33, 205
FMC, 196
Food and Drug Administration (FDA), 208–9
Forbes Health System, 17
Ford, John, 25
Ford Motor Company, 232
Founders Fund, 208
FPA Medical Management, 51, 76–77
Frech, Ted, 97
Freeman Coal, 86
Freeman Memorial, 89
Fresenius, 293n44
FTC Act, 247, 315n13
futurists, 34, 38, 276

gag rules, 17, 152, 176–77, 244
Galbraith, John Kenneth, 109, 192–93; just price, notion of, 194
Galeano, Eduardo, 11
Gawande, Atul, 202–3, 205
Gaynor, Martin, 95, 227, 293n5, 314n5
Geico, 205
Geisinger Clinic, 50, 63, 254, 256, 268
Geisinger Health System, 50; Health Plan, 148–49
General Dynamics, 86–87
General Motors (GM), 198, 229, 232
genomes, 273

Georgia, 3, 173, 242
Germany, 12
Gerstner, Louis V., Jr., 31
Gillies, Robin, 62
Goldman, Lee, 296n5
Goldsmith, Jeff, 25–26, 80
good network theory, 160
Google, 203, 217, 225; Google Health, 204
Grace Hospital, 59
Grand Rapids, MI, 93
Great Depression, 12, 181
Great Society programs, 18
Greenville-Palmetto, 3
Group Cooperative, 289n35
Group Health, 34
Group Health Association (GHA), 15; antitrust claim against, 16
Group Health Cooperative (GHC) of Puget Sound, 15–17, 55
Grove, Andy, 271

Haas-Wilson, Deborah, 100–101
Hahnemann Medical College, 58
Halamka, John, 218
Harper University Hospital, 59
Harrisburg, PA, 103, 157–58
Harrison, Marc, 256
Hart, Scott, and Rodino Act, 240
Hartenbower, David, 68
Hart-Scott-Rodino (HSR) filings, 240–41
Harvard Business School, 37–38
Harvard Pilgrim, 169, 180–81
Hatch, Mike, 61
Hatch, Orrin, 226
Haven, 202, 205
Health Care Authority, 171
health care providers, 4, 7, 32, 150, 174, 196, 198, 209–10, 226, 228, 230–31, 239, 249–50; and competition, 247; contracts, 264–65; innovation, as threat to, 187; just price, 194–95; mandatory price disclosures, 244–

45; market power of, 238; value chains, 235. *See also* megaproviders

Health Care Services Corporation, 180, 182, 197

health care system, 2, 7, 9, 14, 16, 18, 22, 25–28, 31, 37–38, 40, 46, 55, 59, 72, 76, 80, 87, 93, 96, 106, 108, 148, 154, 174, 187, 195, 198, 202, 205–6, 207–8, 219, 223, 248, 252, 255, 257, 266, 273; alternative payment models, 118; analytics, 217–18; antitrust, 162, 169–70, 177, 228, 249; as broken, 3–4; bundled payments, 118; competition, 85–86, 151, 159, 227, 232, 236, 254; core problems of, 250; cost curve, 78; costs, control of, 274; delivery of, 8, 32, 42, 44, 105, 118, 129, 203, 213, 222, 230–32, 254, 276; delivery solutions, 222; as "different," 83–84, 94, 173; disruption, 199–201, 272; as ecosystem, 260; electronic health records (EHRs), 122, 247; fee-for-service (FFS), move away from, 118; fixing of, 227–28; as fragmented, 39, 78, 229, 260; health planning process, and politics, 23–24; as inaccessible, 12; inflation, 272; information technology, improvement in, 122; innovation, importance of, 231; integrated provider systems, move toward, 118; iron triangle, as cure, 200, 213–14; as labor-intensive, 274; learning mindset, adopting of, 261–62; as local, 5, 23, 214, 240; monopolies, 237; price transparency, 221; as profitable business, 224; and profits, 94–95; quality of, 226; quasi-Darwinian view of, 5–6; reform of, 33–34, 48–49, 139, 208, 225, 228; regional health alliances, 33; risk scores, 218; small innovations, 262–63; spending, 3–5, 8, 11, 13, 19–21, 29, 64, 152, 162, 188–89, 191, 203, 224, 234, 272, 286n41; "stages" of, 78; transforming of, 41, 44, 47, 105, 118–19, 149,

200, 203, 214, 250–51, 253, 270; uneven access to, 32; value chain, 95, 157, 215, 225, 227, 229–30, 232, 260; waste in, 256

health insurance, 4, 8, 27, 44, 74, 148, 157, 169–70, 202, 205–6, 212, 216, 289n35; commercial, 233; as competitive, 179–80, 183; employer-based, 18, 29; exchanges, 32, 220; as highly concentrated, 181, 183, 197; indemnity, 55; as local, 180; mergers, 183–87; national, 12–13, 18; national accounts, 180–81, 183–84; origins of, 12–13; power, accumulation of, 6–7; premiums, 34, 61; private, 9, 45; third-party administrators (TPAs), 183

Health Insurance Plan of Greater New York, 15

health insurers, 4, 6–7, 65, 84, 148, 178, 180, 183, 196, 198, 206, 209, 219, 227; antisteering provisions, 175, 177, 244; direct contracting, 210–11; and exclusivity, 26–27; gag rules, 177; hospitals, symbiotic relationship with, 29–30; just price, 195; megaproviders, 175–77; preferred provider organizations (PPOs), 28; price transparency, promotion of, 175–76; pricing information, providing of, 245; private, 9, 13; and status quo, 187–88; and tiering, 175–76; unique role of, 99

HealthLeaders (consulting firm), 180

health literacy, 145

health maintenance organizations (HMOs), 24, 31–32, 35–36, 43–45, 47–49, 51, 59, 63, 74, 104, 142, 182, 226, 284n17, 289n35; backlash against, 17, 56, 61, 117; boycotts of, 15–17, 163; capitation, turn to, 21; causality, 55; closed-panel, 27, 79; courts, turn to, 15–16; decline in, 17; emergence of, 14–15; employees in large firms, 28–29; enrollment of, 17–18, 28–29; features of, 15; group practice of

health maintenance organizations (HMOs) (*continued*)
   physicians, 15; hospitals, threat to, 15; as innovation, 187–88; as insurer sponsored, 17; integrated, 55; peak of, 17; prepayment, 15; and prevention, 15; regional, 183–84; regulations against, 15; socialism, charge of, 15; swelling of, 54; as term, coining of, 283n6; as threat, to organized medicine, 16

HealthNet, 17

health reimbursement arrangements (HRAs), 208

Health Security Act, 33. *See also* Clinton Health Plan

HealthSouth, 51, 77

HealthSpan Health Systems, 47

Health Systems Integration Study (HSIS), 39, 120

Henry Ford Health System, 60

Herzlinger, Regina, 80

Highland Park Hospital, 100, 103–5

Highmark Blue Cross, 156–57, 180

Hill-Burton Program, 18

HITECH Act, 113–14

HMO Act, 16, 32, 50

Ho, Kate, 56, 159

Hoff, Ted, 270–71

Hogarty, Thomas, 87, 95–96, 99

home health care service, 42, 212

Horizontal Merger Guidelines (HMGs), 84–85, 103, 168, 181, 184–85, 233–34, 239; as bible, for merger enforcement, 167, 248; predictive modeling, 243–44, 248

horizontal mergers, 42, 110, 275; blocking of, 157–58, 219; consumer welfare, 167; cross market, 168–69; with "feeder" institutions, 41. *See also* hospital mergers; mergers; vertical mergers

Hospital Corporation of America (HCA), 81, 126

hospital mergers, 6, 26, 47–48, 81–83, 91, 96, 97–98, 100–101, 103, 126–27, 152, 187, 240, 275; anticompetitive, 84; blocking of, 105, 157–58, 219; community commitment, 94; cross-market mergers, 159–63, 169, 242–44, 246, 248; Elzinga and Hogarty (E-H) test, 87–90, 92–93; limiting principle, 161; market definition, 85–86; monopoly nonprofits, 94; in multiple markets, 161–62; must-have systems, dangers of, 102; presumptively anticompetitive, 85; rebounding of, 110; silent majority fallacy, 99; structural presumption, 85, 88; willingness to pay (WTP), 102. *See also* horizontal mergers; mergers; vertical mergers

hospitals, 4, 11, 24, 39, 41–42, 76, 78, 106, 125, 151, 168, 176, 195, 227, 230, 245, 248, 275; academic medical centers, forming of, 19; adverse selection, 67; ambulatory care market, 46; ambulatory surgery centers (ASCs), 25–27; American medical care, blame on, 142; ancillary revenues, 132; balloon principle, 20; case studies, 37–38; centers of excellence, 119; certificates of need (CON), proponent of, 22; charity care, 174; collaboration, fostering of, 69; and competition, 26, 100; competition, subverting of, 13–14; as complex hierarchies, 80; conflicting objectives, with physicians, 69; construction of, 13; cost-containment effort, 43; cost-cutting efforts, and focus, 209; culture of, 267; diagnostic coding, 20; Drug Discount Program, 114–15; electronic health records (EHRs), 123; employed specialists, 111; and engagement, 120; executives and physicians, disconnect between, 144; fee-for-service payments, 14, 121; four-stage market stages, 35–37, 40; and frameworks,

35; good network theory, 160; gravity model, 68; health maintenance organizations (HMOs), 15; health plan business, entering into, 45; hospitalists, emergence of, 111–12, 260–61, 296n5; hospital systems, breaking apart of, 239; and hypercompetition, 35–36; insurance plans, 12–13; insurers, symbiotic relationship with, 29–30; integrated delivery systems, creating of, 8; and integration, 40, 118–20; kickbacks, 144–45; local market power of, 6, 158; local markets, consolidation of, 8, 23, 25, 107; long-term care facilities, 20–21; managed care, 53; managed care organizations (MCOs), 107; as megaproviders, 25, 228; moral hazard, 67; national health expenditures, 20; outpatient facilities, shift to, 20; pay-for-performance contracts, 143; physician groups, 289n38; physician practice management (PPM) companies, advantages over, 52; physician practices, 110–11; physicians, controlling of, 65; physicians, partnership with, 43–44, 46, 119–22, 127–28, 131–32, 138–39; as physician's sweatshop, 139; post-acute care, return to, 112; prisoner's dilemma, 66–67; private insurers, 13; productivity clauses, 111; and profits, 94–95, 111; provider-sponsored health plans, 107, 112, 149–50; "quicker but sicker" phenomenon, 20; referral defense, 132; risk contracting, 112, 121–22; risk management, 107; rural, 25, 90, 126, 172–73, 308n25; scale economies, 46, 64, 81–82, 162; selective contracting, 28; single specialty, 272; state rate setting, 28; status quo, preserving of, 18; and systemness, 81–82; thriving, of big hospitals, 25; triple aim, 118; unbundling services, 20; unseemliness theory, 160; vertical integration, 31;

willingness to pay (WTP), 102; winner's curse, 65–66
Houston, TX, 242
Huffington, Arianna, 179
Humana, 81, 180, 207, 219, 222
Huntington, WV, 171
Hutzel Women's Hospital, 59
Hyundai, 6

IBM, Watson supercomputer, 219
Idaho, 191–92, 233, 235
Illinois, 86–87, 107, 152, 157–58, 182; corruption in, 24
independent practitioner associations (IPAs), 44, 62, 84, 103, 105
India, 217
Indiana, 182
innovation, 12, 26, 108, 124, 170–71, 188–92, 198, 230–32, 234, 252, 263, 314–15n7; countervailing power, 195; disruptive, 199, 214, 253, 262; "innovation center," 271; innovator's dilemma, 200
Inova, 3, 149
Institute for the Future, 274
Institute of Medicine, 64
insurance mergers, 95
integrated delivery networks (IDNs), 37, 39–40, 45, 47, 49, 53, 57–61, 66–68, 70, 76–78, 91, 108–10, 112, 117–19, 122, 124, 127–28, 136, 226, 245, 264, 288n29; accountable care organizations (ACOs), 116; Affordable Care Act (ACA), 115; aligning incentives, 69; bankruptcy of, 52; bureaucracy, layers of, 73; can't miss strategy, embrace of, 75; case studies of, 55, 62; components of, 41–42; consumers, bad news for, 83; controlling costs, failure of, 150–51; cost and quality, effects of, 63–64; electronic health records (EHRs), as silver bullet for, 123; failure of, 54–55, 79–80, 106; financial losses, 54; health care reform, as response

integrated delivery networks (IDNs) (*continued*)
to, 34; in health insurance business, 44; health maintenance organizations (HMOs), forming of, 74–75; health provider plans, 148–49; hospital-led, 50; hospital systems, as bedrock of, 42; physician-led, 50–51; physicians, alienating of, 106; physicians, controlling of, 65; rise of, and antitrust agencies, 81; risk contracts, 75, 107; structures, focus on, 72; three-letter acronym (TLA), 44; vertical integration, as defining feature of, 64
integrated health care, 37, 39, 43, 45, 52, 218
integrated health care organizations (IHOs), 45, 118. *See also* provider-sponsored plans (PSPs)
integrated salary models (ISMs), 44, 111
integration, 6, 9, 15, 18, 41, 48–49, 53, 55, 74, 78–79, 110–12, 118, 124–25, 128, 131, 137–39, 142, 151, 211–12, 228–30, 265, 268; causal model, 134; as checklist, 121; clinical integration, 39, 120, 129, 162, 172, 245–46, 258–59; continuum of care, 123; coordinated care, 123; drivers of, 113–14; electronic health records (EHRs), 123; as failure, 8, 52; and focus, 269; and fragmentation, 136, 260; as functional, 120; health care, as future of, 40; horizontal, 44, 54, 61, 108, 215, 250; hospital-physician integration, 134, 136, 262; improving of, 261; as innovation, 171, 231; integrated delivery networks (IDNs), 64; justification for, 119; organized delivery systems, 120; patient transitions, 123; physician alignment, 134–35; physician engagement, 135; physician-hospital, types of, 120–21; and physicians, 66–68; as physician-system, 120; prime mover of, 108; resurgence of, 113; trend toward, 109;

types of, 120; vertical, 31–32, 39–40, 44, 54, 61–64, 82, 108, 127, 146, 158, 171, 183, 216, 223–24, 232, 250, 262–63, 275. *See also* megaproviders
Intel, 271
Intermountain Healthcare, 198, 256, 271
Iowa, 162
iron triangle, 124, 200, 202–3, 213–14, 217, 226, 275; triple aim, 108
Israel, Mark, 185

Jackson Hole Group, 32–33
James, Brent, 271
Japan, 196, 232
Jefferson-Einstein, 3
Johns Hopkins Hospital, 198
Johnson, Lyndon B., 18
Joplin, MO, 89–90
JP Morgan Chase, 202–3
JP Morgan Health Care Conference, 214
just price, 194–95

Kaiser, 3, 15, 17–18, 22, 31–32, 34–35, 38, 40, 45, 48–49, 53–54, 60–63, 67–68, 73–74, 77–78, 92, 118, 157, 164, 180–81, 183–84, 196, 200, 214, 224, 230, 246, 268, 289n35, 289n38; boycott of, 163; brand of, 56; culture of, as different, 56–57; expansion of, 55–56; losses of, 149; sterling reputation of, 56; success of, 55–56
Kaiser Permanente Foundation, 289n39
Kaiser Permanente Medical Groups, 18, 164
Kalamazoo, MI, 93
Kanter, Rosabeth Moss, 263
Kavanaugh, Brett, 192
Kennedy, Edward M., 32, 284n12
Kerrey, Bob, 33
Kerr-Mills program, 13
Keystone Orthopaedic Specialists, 166
Kindred, 219

King County Medical Society, 16
Krabbenhoft, Kelby, 162
Kubrick, Stanley, 192

Laboratory Corporation of America, 222
Langenfeld, James, 97
Leavitt, Michael, 314n6
Leavitt Partners, 140
Lee, Robin, 159
Leffler, Keith, 93
Leon, Richard, 170–71, 221
Levine, Stuart, 24
Lewis, Matthew, 159, 161
life expectancy, 118–19, 314n3
Long Island, NY, 2–3, 90–91
Long Island Jewish Medical Center (LIJ), 90–91
long-term care facilities, 20–21, 42, 112, 156
Los Angeles, CA, 15, 231
Loyola Medicine, 2
Lucy Lee Hospital, 91
Luft, Harold, 55
Lurie Children's Hospital, 1
Lynk, Bill, 93–94

Magaziner, Ira, 33
managed care, 32, 34–35, 45, 48, 50, 53, 56, 78, 94, 103–4, 109, 117, 182, 228; backlash against, 188; private-sector managed care, growth in, 29. *See also* health maintenance organizations (HMOs)
managed care organizations (MCOs), 66, 76, 81, 104, 107, 138, 172, 202; growth, response to, 171
mandatory price disclosure, 244–45
Marshfield Clinic, 49, 63; Health Plan, 149
Massachusetts, 107, 153–54, 158–59, 169, 264–65
Massachusetts Eye and Ear Hospital, 154

Massachusetts General Hospital, 11, 27, 153, 198, 309n33
Massachusetts Health Policy Commission (MHPC), 153
Mayo Clinic, 49–50, 149, 164, 198, 210–11, 254, 256
McCluer, Forrest, 97
McKesson Medical, 191, 236
McKinsey, 150
McLaren Health Care, 222
Medica HMO, 47, 60–61
Medicaid, 9, 17, 19–20, 24, 31, 54, 59, 60, 131, 138, 172, 174, 180, 207, 212, 220, 228; cutbacks in, 78, 138; health maintenance organizations (HMOs), 48; in managed care plans, 29; opposition to, 18
Medi-Cal, 62
Medical Group Management Association (MGMA), 130; Cost Survey, 131
medical schools, 57, 59, 68; academic medical centers, forming of, 19; enrollments, swelling of, 19; large hospitals, affiliation with, 14; medical education, reforms in, 12
medical societies, 13; health maintenance organizations (HMOs), boycotting of, 15–16
Medical Society of the District of Columbia, 16
Medicare, 9, 17, 24, 28, 31, 54, 59, 60, 77, 109, 111, 115, 117, 130, 133, 139, 141, 145, 174, 180, 237, 239; accountable care organizations (ACOs), 140, 228, 242, 246; cutbacks in, 78, 138; diagnosis-related groups (DRGs), 20; health care in US, largest purchases of, 19; health maintenance organizations (HMOs), 48; Hospital Readmissions Reduction Program, 257; and innovation, 188; in managed care plans, 29; Medicare Advantage (MA), 45, 149–50, 200, 206–8, 212, 220, 253; opposition to, 18; Part D, 220–21; pay-

Medicare (*continued*)

ments, reduction of, 113; professional fees, 114; prospective payment system (PPS), move to, 20; technical fees, 114

Medicare Access and CHIP Reauthorization Act (MACRA), Merit-Based Incentive Payment System (MIPS), 143

Medicare for All, 227, 253

Medicare Modernization Act, 272

Medicare Payment and Advisory Commission, 143

Medicare Pioneer ACOs, 139–40

MedPAC, 141

MedPartners, 51–52, 76–77, 293n44. *See also* Caremark

megaproviders, 2, 4, 7–8, 25, 105, 158, 160–61, 178–79, 224, 226–28, 238, 248, 260, 265, 268–69, 276; accountable care organizations (ACOs), 9, 116; all-or-nothing contracts, 176; anticompetitive tactics, 245; antisteering restrictions, 244, 246; as biggest employers and political donors, 162–63; breaking up of, 238–39; care coordination, struggle to improve, 215; certificate of need (CON), 22; and competition, 229, 231; competition, avoiding of, 6, 27; executive compensation, 3; expenses, increase of, 134; federal agencies, taking on of, 163; growth of, 117, 133–34; health care markets, concentration of, 6; health care value chain, 230; infrastructure of, 123; and insurers, 175–77; local markets, power of in, 5; lower-quality care, contributing to, 5; as megaemployers, 164; as nonprofits, 133–34; origins of, 11; price transparency, banning of, 176–77; qualified risk-sharing arrangements (QRSAs), 246; resurgence of, 110; revenues, increase of, 134; smart technology, 209; triple aim,

123; and tying, 176. *See also* health care providers; integration

Memorial Hermann Health System, 242–43

Mercy Health Center, 89–90

Mercy Health System, 149

mergers, 194, 228, 238; anticompetitive, 107, 192; and competition, 193, 234, 241–42; Hart-Scott-Rodino (HSR) filings, 240–41; horizontal, 41–42, 157–58, 167–68, 219, 275; and innovation, 232; insurance, 95; nonprofit, 163; physician, 164–65, 242; provider, 95, 163, 230, 240–41, 247; as public benefit, 172; vertical, 167–69. *See also* horizontal mergers; hospital mergers; vertical mergers

MeritCare, 49

Merlo, Larry, 214

Merritt Peralta Medical Center, 94

Mesa County, CO, 104

Mesa County IPA, 104

Metcalf-McCloskey Act, 22

metropolitan statistical areas (MSAs), 180, 183–84, 241

MGMA Cost Survey, 131

Michigan, 3, 93, 222

Microsoft, 5, 203–4; Azure platform, 222

Mid Dakota Clinic, 167

Minneapolis, MN, 60

Minnesota, 12–13, 33–35, 37, 47, 216

MinnesotaCare, 47

minute clinics, 187

Mission Health, 171–72

Missouri, 92

mobile health, 272–73

Modern Healthcare (magazine), 40, 52

modern medicine, 7; innovations in, 12

Molina, 207

monopoly, 172–73, 193–94, 196, 236, 240, 246, 294n21; interventionism theory, 117–18; monopoly hospitals, 126, 175; self-sufficiency theory, 117–18

monopsony, 193–95

moral hazard, 67, 77–78

Morton, Fiona Scott, 238, 314–15n7

Murphy, Ed, 68

Nampa, ID, 191, 233–34

Naperville, IL, 23

national health insurance, 13; opposition to, 12, 18

National Health Planning and Resources Development Act, 22

National Medical Enterprises (NME), 81

NBC Universal, 170

Neighborhood Health Plan, 207

New Hampshire, 154, 158–60

New Jersey, 12, 208

New Mexico, 149, 169, 177, 183

New York, 149, 172, 205, 231, 310n7; Manhattan, 91; New York hospitals, certificate of need (CON), 22–23; prospective payment program, 19–20; Staten Island, 90–91

New York Presbyterian, 11, 27, 41, 93, 198, 255–56

Nixon, Richard M., 16, 32, 50

Nolan, Thomas, 295n3

Non-Horizontal Merger Guidelines, 167

North Carolina, 3, 98–99, 242

North Shore Health System (NSHS), 90–91, 255

North Shore Manhasset, 91

NorthShore University Health, 2, 102–3, 239; Advocate merger, 231. See also Evanston Northwestern Healthcare (ENH)

Northwell Health System, 2–3, 149, 164, 306n97

Northwestern Medicine, 1, 239

Northwestern Memorial HealthCare, 1–2

Northwestern Memorial Hospital, 1–2, 41

Northwestern University, 180; Kellogg School of Management, 39

Noseworthy, John, 256

Oak Hill Hospital, 89

Oakland, CA, 92, 161

Obama, Barack, 118

Obamacare, 108–9, 174. See also Affordable Care Act (ACA); Patient Protection and Affordable Care Act (PPACA)

Ody, Chris, 165

Office Depot, 85

Ohio, 3, 12, 107, 149, 152, 207

Omnicare, 215

Omni Healthcare, 62

Oracle, 85

organizational sociology, 39

Organization of Petroleum Exporting Countries (OPEC), 86

Oscar (insurance company), 205; Cleveland Clinic, partnering with, 207; growth of, 206, 208; Oscar Health, 208; Virtual Primary Care, 207

OSF St. Francis Hospital, 231

PacifiCare, 17

Pacific Business Group on Health, 34

Palo Alto Medical Foundation (PAMF), 48, 154–55, 164

Pareto Principle, 209

Parker v. Brown, 171

Partners Health, 11, 93, 133, 160, 162, 164, 169, 228, 247, 309n33; expansion of, 154, 158–59; Neighborhood Health Plan, 153

Partners HealthCare ACO, 257

Partners in Primary Care, 222

Patient Bill of Rights, 17

Patient Protection and Affordable Care Act (PPACA), 114, 272. See also Affordable Care Act (ACA); Obamacare

Patterson, Isabel, 81

Pauly, Mark, 80, 200

Payton, Sallyanne, 22

Penn State Hershey Medical Center, 105; Pinnacle Health merger, 103, 158

Pennsylvania, 3, 17, 50, 59, 102–3, 107,
148–49, 152, 156–58, 165, 169, 183
PeopleSoft, 85
Peoria, IL, 231
Permanente Medical Groups, 164, 289n38
Perot, Ross, 33
personal health: low importance of, 145;
low value care, 145
personalized medicine, 273
Pessina, Stefano, 222
Pflum, Kevin, 159, 161
pharmacy benefits management (PBM),
79, 212, 216, 219–21
Philadelphia, PA, 3, 58, 59, 65–66, 268
Phoebe Putney Health Systems, 173
Phoenix, AZ, 25
PhyCor, 51, 76, 77
physician-hospital organizations
(PHOs), 44, 62–63, 71, 76; closed-
panel, 70; and collaboration, 69–70;
incentive problems of, 72; open-
panel, 70; "Prune later" philosophy,
70; risk contracting, 70
physician practice management (PPM)
companies, 51, 72, 103, 113, 226; adverse selection, 77; bankruptcy of,
52, 77; collapse of, 76; failure of, 79;
moral hazard, 77; as Ponzi scheme,
77; private insurers, 112; as "vulgarians at the gate," 77
physicians, 4, 52, 65, 71–73, 106, 110,
118, 125, 168, 227, 230, 239, 242, 245,
248, 262, 272; accountable care organizations (ACOs), 141–43; alternate
payment models, aversion to, 142;
American medical care, blame on,
142; burnout, 135–36, 144, 259; cognitive burn, 263; collective negotiation of, 163–64; compensation of, 137;
competition, dislike of, 163; conflicting objectives, with hospitals, 69; and
contracts, 264; economic credentialing of, 46; economies of scale, 164;
electronic health records (EHRs),

adverse reaction to, 146–48; electronic health records (EHRs), incor-
poration of, 113–14; friction management, 263–64; gravity model, 68;
Hart-Scott-Rodino (HSR) filings,
240–41; health care spending, control
of, 64; hospital executives, disconnect
between, 144; hospital management,
distrust of, 137; hospitals, partnership with, 43–44, 46, 119–22, 127–28,
131–32, 138–39; increase in, 19; and
integration, 66–68, 142; managerial
logic, 64; and managers, 275; managers, suspicion of, 136–37; managing
of, 263; mergers of, 103–4, 164–66;
nudges, using of, 263; and nurses, 276,
316n21; organizational culture, 266–
68; outpatient care, 137; performance
incentives, 265; pessimism of, 136,
138; physician alignment, 70, 120, 134,
136, 138, 144; physician engagement,
120, 135–36, 144; physician-hospital
alignment, 134–35; physician-hospital
integration, 127–30, 134; physician
integration, 106–7; physician practice management (PPM) companies,
76–77; productivity-based bonuses,
137; raising of prices, 165; relative
value unit (RVU) requirements, 264;
as self-employed, 164; specialists, 19;
specialty physician practices, 42; unappreciated, feelings of, 138; waste in
system, attitudes toward, 143–44
Piedmont/WellStar, 149
PillPack, 204
PinnacleHealth, 103, 157
Pittsburgh, PA, 3, 57, 156–57, 159–60, 177,
181, 231
Plainfield, IL, 23
point-of-service (POS) plans, 79
Poplar Bluff, MO, 91
population health, 39
Posner, Richard, 88
Powsner, Rhoda, 22

preferred provider organizations (PPOs), 28–29, 31–32, 47–48, 51, 63, 74, 79, 104, 182, 226, 246, 289n35, 309n33; as innovation, 187–88; swelling of, 54

Prentice Women's Hospital, 1

Presbyterian Health Plan, 149

Presbyterian Health System, 169; provider-sponsored plan, 177

Press-Ganey, 120

prevention, 12, 15, 123, 187; as afterthought, 14

primary care physicians (PCPs), 17, 24, 37, 50, 66, 69, 72, 111, 122, 130, 146, 233–34; and capitation, 21, 71; goodwill, 65; merging of, 167

Prime Therapeutics, 219

Progressive, 205

ProMedica, 3

Providence Hospital, 92

provider contracts, 265

provider-sponsored plans (PSPs), 45, 148–50, 171, 177; competition, diminishing of, 170. See also integrated health care organizations (IHOs); megaproviders

Prudential, 181, 185, 289n35

qualified risk-sharing arrangements (QRSAs), 246

RAND National Health Insurance Experiment, 55

Reagan, Ronald, 18

Reed, Wallace, 25

reference pricing, 313n44

Reinhardt, Uwe, 77, 221

relative value unit (RVU) requirements, 264–65

retail clinics, 200, 272; decline in, 215; as disruptive innovation, 214; stalled growth of, 215–16

retail pharmacies, 204, 216

Richmond, VA, 184

risk contracts, 39, 53–54, 61, 70, 75, 77–78, 107–8, 112

Roanoke, VA, 231

Robert Wood Johnson Foundation (RWJF), 126, 228

Rockford, IL, 83, 86–87, 102

Rockford Memorial Hospital, 86, 88; Swedish American Hospital merger, 83

Roemer, Milt, 22

Roemer's Law, 22

Ross-Loos Medical Group, 15

Rumelt, Richard, 56–57

Sabatino, Thomas, 217

Sacramento, CA, 154, 158, 161

Safran, Dana, 202

Saltzer Medical Group, 166–67, 191–92, 233, 235–37

Sanford Health, 167; UnityPoint Health merger, 162

San Francisco, CA, 74, 154–55, 158, 231

Sansum Clinic, 167, 236

Santa Barbara, CA, 167, 236

Santa Cruz, CA, 98

Santayana, George, 121

Satterthwaite, Mark, 102

scale economies, 41, 46, 54, 58–59, 76–77, 81–82

Schmitt, Matt, 161–62

Schumpeter, Joseph, 199, 311n3

Scott and White Health, 63

Scrushy, Richard, 51–52, 77

selective contracting, 28

Shalala, Donna, 314n6

Sherman Act, 16, 104

Shortell, Stephen, 32–33, 39–40, 62, 157, 178, 249

Sierra Health Plan, 185

Simon, Herbert, 263

smart technology, 204; consumer apps, for medical conditions, 208–9; digital health technologies, oversell of, 217; megaproviders, impact on, 209 sociotechnical systems theory, 218, 263, 274

South Carolina, 3, 242

South Dakota, 163

Spectrum Health, 93, 294n15

St. Alphonsus hospital system, 166, 231, 235–37

Stanford, CA, 74

Stanford University, 180, 273; Clinical Excellence Research Center, 269; University of California merger, 73–74

Staples, 85

Stark laws, 64, 67–68

"Statements of Antitrust Enforcement Policy in Health Care," 84, 248–49

State of Minnesota Employees Health Benefit Program, 47

Steele, Glenn, 256

Stein's law, 251–52

Stigler, George, 5

St. John's Regional Medical Center, 89

St. Joseph's Hospital, 49

St. Joseph's Regional Health System, 62

St. Louis, MO, 3

St. Luke's Health System, 49, 166–67, 191, 231, 235–37; Saltzer merger, 191–92, 233

Stocker, Michael, 91

surgery, 12, 19, 46, 71–72, 165, 167, 209–11, 220, 236–37; outpatient, 25–26, 31, 37, 49, 53, 223. See also ambulatory surgery centers (ASCs)

SurgiCenter, 25

Sutter Health, 48–49, 62, 92–93, 97–98, 107, 133, 153–56, 158, 160–62, 164, 177, 189, 198, 228, 247, 255, 308n25, 309n32

Sutter Medical Group (SMG), 62

Swedish American Hospital, 83, 86, 88

Tahoe City, CA, 104

Target, 215

Tax Equity and Fiscal Responsibility Act, 29

technological change, 271–72

telemedicine, 272–73

Tenet system, 91–92

Tennessee, 3, 172

Texas, 205, 242–43

third-party administrators (TPAs), 183–84

3M Company, 255

Time Warner, 170

Toledo, OH, 102

Tollen, Laura A., 282n10

Touche, 42

Town, Robert, 102

Treasure Valley, ID, 166, 233, 235–36

triple aim, 118–19, 123–24, 178, 213, 226, 246, 259, 275, 295n3; cost containment, 108; patient experience, 108; population health, 108

"Triple Aim, The" (Berwick, Nolan, and Whittington), 118

Truman, Harry, 18

Trump, Donald, 24, 152, 176, 203, 227, 244

Tsongas, Paul, 33

Tufts Health Plan, 154

Tulsa, OK, 104

Twin Cities, 3, 47–48, 60, 128

Ukiah Adventist Hospital, 88

Ukiah Valley Medical Center, 88

UNC Health, 242

UnitedHealthcare, 157, 164, 176, 180–81, 184–85, 188, 198, 206–7, 211, 233; DaVita, acquisition of, 223; MedExpress urgent care centers, 216, 220, 222; Optum division, 112, 183, 189, 216, 220, 223–24, 253

United Hospital system, 58

United Regional Healthcare, 172

United States, 12–13, 19, 49, 104, 112, 196, 266; cross-market merger accelera-

tion of, 243; health care spending of, 191; life expectancy in, 314n3
University HealthSystem Consortium (UHC), 35
University of California, San Francisco (UCSF), 73–74
University of Chicago, 2
University of Minnesota, 61
University of Pennsylvania, 180
University of Pennsylvania Health System (UPHS), 268–69, 271
University of Pittsburgh Medical Center (UPMC), 3, 57–58, 75, 107, 126, 133, 153, 159, 162, 164, 169–71, 181, 183, 247, 255; expansion of, 156–58, 160; Presbyterian hospital, 11, 177; Presbyterian Shadyside, 156; provider-sponsored health plan, 156
unseemliness theory, 160, 168
Urbana, IL, 49
US Healthcare, 17
US health care system, 6, 12, 80, 187, 205, 229, 250, 281–82n5; as broken, 3–4; CEOs, salaries of, 133; as ecosystem, 260; as fragmented, 39, 260; private insurers, reliance on, 13; spending, swelling of, 19; top-down managerial change, 270; transforming of, 270

value-based payments, 188
value chains, 236, 246; competition among, 232–35, 239; providers, 235
Verily, 208
Vertical Merger Guidelines (VMG), 168
vertical mergers, 167; double marginalization, 168; good network theory, 168; physician prices, driving up of, 169; theories of, 168; tying and bundling, 168; unseemliness theory, 168. See also horizontal mergers; hospital mergers; mergers
Virginia, 3, 102, 107, 152, 172
Vistnes, Greg, 102

Wachter, Robert, 296n5
Wake Forest Baptist system, 243
Walgreens, 204, 220, 223; bricks and mortar, emphasis on, 222–23; digital marketplace, launching of, 221; Find Care Now website, 221; Humana, partnership with, 222; Laboratory Corporation of America, partnership with, 222; local health systems, partnerships with, 215, 221; McLaren Health Care, collaborating with, 222; Microsoft, pact with, 222; Partners in Primary Care, partnership with, 222; Prime Therapeutics, alliance with, 219; UnitedHealthcare MedExpress, pilot program with, 222
Walmart, 5, 85, 209, 237, 312n17; Centers of Excellence (COE) program, 210; direct contracting, 210–11
Washington, DC, 56, 231
Washington state, 16, 33
Watsonville Community Hospital, 98
Wayne State University, 59
Wellcare, 180
Wellmount-Mountain States, 3
Werden, Greg, 96–97
West Penn Allegheny Health System (WPAHS), 156
West Virginia, 171–72
Whittington, John, 295n3
Whole Foods, 3, 85, 223
Wichita Falls, TX, 172
Wichmann, David, 222
Wild Oats, 85
Wilkes-Barre, PA, 50
willingness to pay (WTP), 102
Wisconsin, 49, 149
Wofford, Harris, 33
World War I, 12
World War II, 13, 18

Yakima, WA, 104